The Voice out of the Whirlwind: The Book of Job

Selected and Edited by

RALPH E. HONE

UNIVERSITY OF REDLANDS

MATERIALS FOR ANALYSIS

Chandler Publishing Company, Inc.

124 SPEAR STREET

SAN FRANCISCO, CALIFORNIA 94105

Science Research Associates, Inc.
259 East Erie Street, Chicago, Illinois 60611
A Subsidiary of IBM

THE VOICE OUT OF
THE WHIRLWIND:
THE BOOK OF JOB

PREFACE

THE FOCUS of this collection of materials on the Book of Job is a literary one. I have been concerned to choose items which point up literary form, style, theme, source and influence, identification and analysis of character, and development of ideas.

I conceive this focus to be not only important to the study of Job but also thoroughly compatible with the aims and interests of the majority of instructors who will wish to use the volumes in this series of Materials for Analysis.

Time needs not now to explain or justify the nature of the controlled-research-materials text. The promised crest of the rapidly increasing college population is forcing teachers to cope with limited library facilities and resources in almost all courses of study. I do not mean to suggest that this volume has been designed as a substitute for research in the library. It does attempt efficiency in providing within one cover readings by means of which the student may be *introduced* to the responsibilities of library research: accuracy and objectivity in report and interpretation. I have in mind also efficiency of the teacher's time: pity the conscientious teacher who during the assignment of the library paper feels constrained to check all of the sources and citations used by thirty students (more or less) in their centrifugal interests! I have added a selective bibliography as a guide for further investigation by the student, to suggest continued individual use of the library.

The teacher will find it pleasant, I believe, to use these selections not only to train his students in recognizing some conception of scale—what grows out of a single verse or chapter of Job; but also to indicate something of the development of the magic of imagination in form and content. Those who place a premium on integration of studies will appreciate the presence of the Book of Job itself in the King James Version, a literary monument and a quasi-primary source for most of the remaining materials.

I have been guided by variety as well as by literary focus. Multiversity of viewpoints and materials is a necessary and inescapable whetstone for the one who seeks to sharpen his conception of truth in thought and experience. Fortunately differing as they do in size and scope, the articles also may be employed so as to help the student to walk before he flies. Short initial assignments of annotated themes may be followed by longer papers in comparison and contrast of interpretations; and there is sufficient material for a full-length research paper. See the list of Suggested Topics for Research Papers.

I have not modernized or standardized the spelling, punctuation, or mechanics of the original texts, other than the Bible texts. I have included a brief headnote to each selection to identify the author and his emphasis.

It is apparent that others have labored and I have entered into their labors. Elsewhere complete acknowledgement is made to publishers who have allowed reprinting by permission or arrangement. I should like to express my gratitude to still others who have aided my efforts: Mr. Howard Chandler, my publisher, first suggested the task and patiently coached it to completion; Dr. William G. Stryker and Dr. William Main, among my colleagues at the University of Redlands, offered steady council; the staffs of the libraries of the University of Redlands, the Honnold at Claremont, and the city of Los Angeles were the most cooperative; my wife was a constant source of encouragement.

CONTENTS

viii *Contents*

THE VOICE OUT OF
THE WHIRLWIND:
THE BOOK OF JOB

To get the final lilt of songs,
To penetrate the inmost lore of poets—to know the mighty ones,
Job, Homer, Eschylus, Dante, Shakspere, Tennyson, Emerson;
To diagnose the shifting-delicate tints of love and pride and doubt
*   —to truly understand,*
To encompass these, the last keen faculty and entrance-price,
Old age, and what it brings from all its past experiences.
                                                    —WALT WHITMAN

PART I

The Book of Job and
Relevant Portions of the Bible

THE AUTHORIZED VERSION

OF

The Book of Job

The translation of the Book of Job which follows is the translation made in 1611, commonly known as the King James or Authorized Version. It was a part of the Old Testament portion assigned to a group of translators which met at Cambridge. (The balance of the work of translation was completed by five other groups, two meeting in Westminster, two in Oxford, and the remaining one also in Cambridge.)

Certain typographical devices are employed in printing this Bible; the mention of two used in the Book of Job may help the student to read with clearer understanding: (1) The name of the deity spelled in capitals, LORD (e.g., Job 1:6), is the Hebrew Tetragrammaton, יהוה (the letters yodh-he-vau-he), often seen in the form Jehovah and transliterated by modern scholars Yahweh. (2) Words printed in the text in italics indicate words supplied by the translators, and not present in the original text, for the purpose of providing smoother reading.

It is perhaps wise at this point to call attention to the major variations in Bible reference which are used in the selections which follow. In general, American publishers denote chapter and verse in the following manner: Job 15:12. British writers generally follow this arrangement: Job xv. 12.

Job's greatness

CHAPTER 1.

1 There was a man in the land of Uz, whose name *was* Job; and that man was perfect and upright, and one that feared God, and eschewed evil.

2 And there were born unto him seven sons and three daughters.

3 His substance also was seven thousand sheep, and three thousand camels, and five hundred yoke of oxen, and five hundred she asses, and a very great household; so that this man was the greatest of all the men of the east.

4 And his sons went and feasted *in their* houses, every one his day; and sent and called for their three sisters to eat and to drink with them.

5 And it was so, when the days of *their* feasting were gone about, that Job sent and sanctified them, and rose up early in the morning, and offered burnt offerings *according* to the number of them all: for Job said, It may be that my sons have sinned, and cursed God in their hearts. Thus did Job continually.

6 ¶ Now there was a day when the sons of God came to present themselves before the LORD, and Satan came also among them.

7 And the LORD said unto Satan, Whence comest thou? Then Satan answered the LORD, and said, From going to and fro in the earth, and from walking up and down in it.

8 And the LORD said unto Satan, Hast thou considered my servant Job, that *there is* none like him in the earth, a perfect and an upright man, one that feareth God, and escheweth evil?

9 Then Satan answered the LORD, and said, Doth Job fear God for nought?

10 Hast not thou made a hedge about him, and about his house, and about all that he hath on every side? thou hast blessed the work of his hands, and his substance is increased in the land.

11 But put forth thine hand now, and touch all that he hath, and he will curse thee to thy face.

12 And the LORD said unto Satan, Behold, all that he hath *is* in thy power; only upon himself put not forth thine hand. So Satan went forth from the presence of the LORD.

13 ¶ And there was a day when his sons and his daughters *were* eating and drinking wine in their eldest brother's house:

14 And there came a messenger unto Job, and said, The oxen were ploughing, and the asses feeding beside them:

15 And the Sabeans fell *upon them,* and took them away; yea, they have slain the servants with the edge of the sword; and I only am escaped alone to tell thee.

16 While he *was* yet speaking, there came also another, and said, The fire of God is fallen from heaven, and hath burned up the sheep, and the servants, and consumed them; and I only am escaped alone to tell thee.

17 While he *was* yet speaking, there came also another, and said, The Chaldeans made out three bands, and fell upon the camels, and have carried them away, yea, and slain the servants with the edge of the sword; and I only am escaped alone to tell thee.

18 While he *was* yet speaking, there came also another, and said, Thy sons and thy daughters *were* eating and drinking wine in their eldest brother's house:

19 And, behold, there came a great wind from the wilderness, and smote the four corners of the house, and it fell upon the young men, and they are dead; and I only am escaped alone to tell thee.

20 Then Job arose, and rent his mantle, and shaved his head, and fell down upon the ground, and worshipped,

21 And said, Naked came I out of my mother's womb, and naked shall I return thither: the LORD gave, and the LORD hath taken away; blessed be the name of the LORD.

22 In all this Job sinned not, nor charged God foolishly.

CHAPTER 2.

1 Again there was a day when the sons of God came to present themselves before the LORD, and Satan came also among them to present himself before the LORD.

2 And the LORD said unto Satan, From whence comest thou? And Satan answered the LORD, and said, From going to and fro in the earth, and from walking up and down in it.

3 And the LORD said unto Satan, Hast thou considered my servant Job, that *there is* none like him in the earth, a perfect and an upright man, one that feareth God, and escheweth evil? and still he holdeth fast his integrity, although thou movedst me against him, to destroy him without cause.

4 And Satan answered the LORD, and said, Skin for skin, yea, all that a man hath will he give for his life.

5 But put forth thine hand now, and touch his bone and his flesh, and he will curse thee to thy face.

6 And the LORD said unto Satan, Behold, he *is* in thine hand; but save his life.

7 ¶ So went Satan forth from the presence of the LORD, and smote Job with sore boils from the sole of his foot unto his crown.

8 And he took him a potsherd to scrape himself withal; and he sat down among the ashes.

9 ¶ Then said his wife unto him, Dost thou still retain thine integrity? curse God, and die.

10 But he said unto her, Thou speakest as one of the foolish women speaketh. What? shall we receive good at the hand of God, and shall we not receive evil? In all this did not Job sin with his lips.

11 ¶ Now when Job's three friends heard of all this evil that was come upon him, they came every one from his own place; Eliphaz the Temanite, and Bildad the Shuhite, and Zophar the Naamathite: for they had made an appointment together to come to mourn with him, and to comfort him.

12 And when they lifted up their eyes afar off, and knew him not, they lifted up their voice, and wept; and they rent every one his mantle, and sprinkled dust upon their heads toward heaven.

13 So they sat down with him upon the ground seven days and seven nights, and none spake a word unto him: for they saw that *his* grief was very great.

CHAPTER 3. *B day curse*

1 After this opened Job his mouth, and cursed his day. - *B. day*

2 And Job spake, and said,

3 Let the day perish wherein I was born, and the night *in which* it was said, There is a man child conceived.

4 Let that day be darkness; let not God regard it from above, neither let the light shine upon it.

5 Let darkness and the shadow of death stain it; let a cloud dwell upon it; let the blackness of the day terrify it.

6 *As for* that night, let darkness seize upon it; let it not be joined unto the days of the year; let it not come into the number of the months.

7 Lo, let that night be solitary; let no joyful voice come therein.

8 Let them curse it that curse the day, who are ready to raise up their mourning.

9 Let the stars of the twilight thereof be dark; let it look for light, but *have* none; neither let it see the dawning of the day:

10 Because it shut not up the doors of my *mother's* womb, nor hid sorrow from mine eyes.

11 Why died I not from the womb? *why* did I *not* give up the ghost when I came out of the belly?

12 Why did the knees prevent me? or why the breasts that I should suck?

13 For now should I have lain still and been quiet, I should have slept: then had I been at rest,

14 With kings and counsellors of the earth, which built desolate places for themselves;

15 Or with princes that had gold, who filled their houses with silver:

16 Or as a hidden untimely birth I had not been; as infants *which* never saw light.

17 There the wicked cease *from* troubling; and there the weary be at rest.

18 *There* the prisoners rest together; they hear not the voice of the oppressor.

19 The small and great are there; and the servant *is* free from his master.

20 Wherefore is light given to him that is in misery, and life unto the bitter *in* soul;

21 Which long for death, but it *cometh* not; and dig for it more than for hid treasures;

22 Which rejoice exceedingly, *and* are glad, when they can find the grave? *intelligence reasoning*

23 *Why is light given* to a man whose way is hid, and whom God hath hedged in?

24 For my sighing cometh before I eat, and my roarings are poured out like the waters.

25 For the thing which I greatly feared is come upon me, and that which I was afraid of is come unto me.

26 I was not in safety, neither had I rest, neither was I quiet; yet trouble came.

1st phase of argument

only whole manner

CHAPTER 4.

1 Then Eliphaz the Temanite answered and said,

2 *If* we assay to commune with thee, wilt thou be grieved? but who can withhold himself from speaking?

3 Behold, thou hast instructed many, and thou hast strengthened the weak hands.

4 Thy words have upholden him that was falling, and thou hast strengthened the feeble knees.

5 But now it is come upon thee, and thou faintest; it toucheth thee, and thou art troubled.

6 *Is* not *this* thy fear, thy confidence, thy hope, and the uprightness of thy ways?

✗7 Remember, I pray thee, who *ever* perished, being innocent? or where were the righteous cut off? *you deserved it* / *"can't be innocent if you're dying*

8 Even as I have seen, they that plough iniquity, and sow wickedness, reap the same.

9 By the blast of God they perish, and by the breath of his nostrils are they consumed.

10 The roaring of the lion, and the voice of the fierce lion, and the teeth of the young lions, are broken.

11 The old lion perisheth for lack of prey, and the stout lion's whelps are scattered abroad.

12 Now a thing was secretly brought to me, and mine ear received a little thereof.

13 In thoughts from the visions of the night, when deep sleep falleth on men,

14 Fear came upon me, and trembling, which made all my bones to shake.

15 Then a spirit passed before my face; the hair of my flesh stood up:

16 It stood still, but I could not discern the form thereof: an image *was* before mine eyes, *there was* silence, and I heard a voice, *saying,*

17 Shall mortal man be more just than God? shall a man be more pure than his Maker?

18 Behold, he put no trust in his servants; and his angels he charged with folly:

19 How much less *in* them that dwell in houses of clay, whose foundation *is* in the dust, *which* are crushed before the moth?

20 They are destroyed from morning to evening: they perish for ever without any regarding *it.*

21 Doth not their excellency *which is* in them go away? they die, even without wisdom.

Eliphaz

CHAPTER 5. *in end* / *you will be rewarded*

1 Call now, if there be any that will answer thee; and to which of the saints wilt thou turn? *maybe you were whatever entitled*

2 For wrath killeth the foolish man, and envy slayeth the silly one. ✗

3 I have seen the foolish taking root: but suddenly I cursed his habitation.

4 His children are far from safety, and they are crushed in the gate, neither *is there* any to deliver *them.*

5 Whose harvest the hungry eateth up, and taketh it even out of the thorns, and the robber swalloweth up their substance.

6 Although affliction cometh not forth of the dust, neither doth trouble spring out of the ground;

7 Yet man is born unto trouble, as the sparks fly upward.

8 I would seek unto God, and unto God would I commit my cause:

9 Which doeth great things and unsearchable; marvellous things without number:

10 Who giveth rain upon the earth, and sendeth waters upon the fields:

11 To set up on high those that be low; that those which mourn may be exalted to safety.

12 He disappointeth the devices of the crafty, so that their hands cannot perform *their* enterprise.

13 He taketh the wise in their own craftiness: and the counsel of the froward is carried headlong.

14 They meet with darkness in the daytime, and grope in the noonday as in the night.

15 But he saveth the poor from the sword, from their mouth, and from the hand of the mighty.

16 So the poor hath hope, and iniquity stoppeth her mouth.

17 Behold, happy *is* the man whom God correcteth: therefore despise not thou the chastening of the Almighty:

18 For he maketh sore, and bindeth up: he woundeth, and his hands make whole.

19 He shall deliver thee in six troubles: yea, in seven there shall no evil touch thee.

20 In famine he shall redeem thee from death: and in war from the power of the sword.

21 Thou shalt be hid from the scourge of the tongue: neither shalt thou be afraid of destruction when it cometh.

22 At destruction and famine thou shalt laugh: neither shalt thou be afraid of the beasts of the earth.

23 For thou shalt be in league with the stones of the field: and the beasts of the field shall be at peace with thee.

24 And thou shalt know that thy tabernacle *shall be* in peace; and thou shalt visit thy habitation, and shalt not sin.

25 Thou shalt know also that thy seed *shall be* great, and thine offspring as the grass of the earth.

26 Thou shalt come to *thy* grave in a full age, like as a shock of corn cometh in in his season.

27 Lo this, we have searched it, so it *is;* hear it, and know thou *it* for thy good.

CHAPTER 6. *Job answers argument* /8

1 But Job answered and said,

2 Oh that my grief were throughly weighed, and my calamity laid in the balances together!

3 For now it would be heavier than the sand of the sea: therefore my words are swallowed up.

4 For the arrows of the Almighty *are* within me, the poison whereof drinketh up my spirit: the terrors of God do set themselves in array against me.

5 Doth the wild ass bray when he hath grass? or loweth the ox over his fodder?

6 Can that which is unsavoury be eaten without salt? or is there *any* taste in the white of an egg?

7 The things *that* my soul refused to touch *are* as my sorrowful meat.

8 Oh that I might have my request; and that God would grant *me* the thing that I long for!

9 Even that it would please God to destroy me; that he would let loose his hand, and cut me off!

10 Then should I yet have comfort; yea, I would harden myself in sorrow: let him not spare; for I have not concealed the words of the Holy One.

11 What *is* my strength, that I should hope? and what *is* mine end, that I should prolong my life?

12 *Is* my strength the strength of stones? or *is* my flesh of brass?

13 *Is* not my help in me? and is wisdom driven quite from me?

14 To him that is afflicted pity *should be shewed* from his friend; but he forsaketh the fear of the Almighty.

15 My brethren have dealt deceitfully as a brook, *and* as the stream of brooks they pass away; _ *He will guilty*

16 Which are blackish by reason of the ice, *and* wherein the snow is hid:

17 What time they wax warm, they vanish: when it is hot, they are consumed out of their place.

18 The paths of their way are turned aside; they go to nothing, and perish.

19 The troops of Tema looked, the companies of Sheba waited for them.

20 They were confounded because they had hoped; they came thither, and were ashamed.

21 For now ye are nothing; ye see *my* casting down, and are afraid.

22 Did I say, Bring unto me? or, Give a reward for me of your substance?

23 Or, Deliver me from the enemy's hand? or, Redeem me from the hand of the mighty?

24 Teach me, and I will hold my tongue: and cause me to understand wherein I have erred.

✱ 25 How forcible are right words! but what doth your arguing reprove?

26 Do ye imagine to reprove words, and the speeches of one that is desperate, *which are* as wind?

27 Yea, ye overwhelm the fatherless, and ye dig *a pit* for your friend.

28 Now therefore be content, look upon me; for *it is* evident unto you if I lie.

29 Return, I pray you, let it not be iniquity; yea, return again, my righteousness *is* in it.

30 Is there iniquity in my tongue? cannot my taste discern perverse things?

CHAPTER 7.

1 *Is there* not an appointed time to man upon earth? *are not* his days also like the days of a hireling?

✱ 2 As a servant earnestly desireth the shadow, and as a hireling looketh for *the reward of* his work;

3 So am I made to possess months of vanity, and wearisome nights are appointed to me.

4 When I lie down, I say, When shall I arise, and the night be gone? and I am full of tossings to and fro unto the dawning of the day.

5 My flesh is clothed with worms and clods of dust; my skin is broken, and become loathsome.

6 My days are swifter than a weaver's shuttle, and are spent without hope.

7 O remember that my life *is* wind: mine eye shall no more see good.

8 The eye of him that hath seen me shall see me no *more:* thine eyes *are* upon me, and I *am* not.

9 *As* the cloud is consumed and vanisheth away; so he that goeth down to the grave shall come up no *more.*

10 He shall return no more to his house, neither shall his place know him any more.

11 Therefore I will not refrain my mouth; I will speak in the anguish of my spirit; I will complain in the bitterness of my soul. *what art to?*

12 *Am* I a sea, or a whale, that thou settest a watch over me?

13 When I say, My bed shall comfort me, my couch shall ease my complaint;

14 Then thou scarest me with dreams, and terrifiest me through visions:

15 So that my soul chooseth strangling, *and* death rather than my life.

16 I loathe *it;* I would not live alway: let me alone; for my days *are* vanity. *What is man?*

17 What *is* man, that thou shouldest magnify him? and that thou *do you* shouldest set thine heart upon him? *directly to god — what expect of man?*

18 And *that* thou shouldest visit him every morning, *and* try him every moment?

19 How long wilt thou not depart from me, nor let me alone till I swallow down my spittle? *I've sinned*

20 I have sinned; what shall I do unto thee, O thou preserver of men? why hast thou set me as a mark against thee, so that I am a burden to myself? *what is sin?*

21 And why dost thou not pardon my transgression, and take away mine iniquity? for now shall I sleep in the dust; and thou shalt seek me in the morning, but I *shall* not *be.* *close to death passionate?*

CHAPTER 8.

Bildad: only wicked suffer. Past determines future

1 Then answered Bildad the Shuhite, and said,

2 How long wilt thou speak these *things?* and *how long shall* the words of thy mouth *be like* a strong wind?

3 Doth God pervert judgment? or doth the Almighty pervert justice?

4 If thy children have sinned against him, and he have cast them away for their transgression;

5 If thou wouldest seek unto God betimes, and make thy supplication to the Almighty;

6 If thou *wert* pure and upright; surely now he would awake for thee, and make the habitation of thy righteousness prosperous.

7 Though thy beginning was small, yet thy latter end should greatly increase.

8 For inquire, I pray thee, of the former age, and prepare thyself to the search of their fathers:

9 (For we *are but of* yesterday, and know nothing, because our days upon earth *are* a shadow:)

10 Shall not they teach thee, *and* tell thee, and utter words out of their heart?

11 Can the rush grow up without mire? can the flag grow without water?

12 Whilst it *is* yet in his greenness, *and* not cut down, it withereth before any *other* herb.

13 So *are* the paths of all that forget God; and the hypocrite's hope shall perish:

14 Whose hope shall be cut off, and whose trust *shall be* a spider's web.

15 He shall lean upon his house, but it shall not stand: he shall hold it fast, but it shall not endure.

16 He *is* green before the sun, and his branch shooteth forth in his garden.

17 His roots are wrapped about the heap, *and* seeth the place of stones.

18 If he destroy him from his place, then *it* shall deny him, *saying,* I have not seen thee.

19 Behold, this *is* the joy of his way, and out of the earth shall others grow.

20 Behold, God will not cast away a perfect *man,* neither will he help the evil doers:

21 Till he fill thy mouth with laughing, and thy lips with rejoicing.

22 They that hate thee shall be clothed with shame; and the dwelling-place of the wicked shall come to nought.

CHAPTER 9.

1 Then Job answered and said,

2 I know *it is* so of a truth: but how should man be just with God?

3 If he will contend with him, he cannot answer him one of a thousand.

4 He *is* wise in heart, and mighty in strength: who hath hardened *himself* against him, and hath prospered?

5 Which removeth the mountains, and they know not; which over-turneth them in his anger;

6 Which shaketh the earth out of her place, and the pillars thereof tremble;

7 Which commandeth the sun, and it riseth not; and sealeth up the stars;

8 Which alone spreadeth out the heavens, and treadeth upon the waves of the sea;

9 Which maketh Arcturus, Orion, and Pleiades, and the chambers of the south;

10 Which doeth great things past finding out; yea, and wonders without number.

11 Lo, he goeth by me, and I see *him* not: he passeth on also, but I perceive him not.

12 Behold, he taketh away, who can hinder him? who will say unto him, What doest thou?

13 *If* God will not withdraw his anger, the proud helpers do stoop under him.

14 How much less shall I answer him, *and* choose out my words *to reason* with him?

15 Whom, though I were righteous, *yet* would I not answer, *but* I would make supplication to my judge. — *needs to hear + see God*

16 If I had called, and he had answered me; *yet* would I not believe that he had hearkened unto my voice. *then will believe*

17 For he breaketh me with a tempest, and multiplieth my wounds without cause.

18 He will not suffer me to take my breath, but filleth me with bitterness.

19 If *I speak* of strength, lo, *he is* strong: and if of judgment, who shall set me a time *to plead?*

20 If I justify myself, mine own mouth shall condemn me: *if I say,* I *am* perfect, it shall also prove me perverse.

21 *Though* I *were* perfect, *yet* would I not know my soul: I would despise my life.

22 This *is* one *thing,* therefore I said *it,* He destroyeth the perfect and the wicked. *laugh at trial of innocent*

23 If the scourge slay suddenly, he will laugh at the trial of the innocent.

24 The earth is given into the hand of the wicked: he covereth the faces of the judges thereof; if not, where, *and* who *is* he?

25 Now my days are swifter than a post: they flee away, they see no good.

26 They are passed away as the swift ships: as the eagle *that* hasteth to the prey.

27 If I say, I will forget my complaint, I will leave off my heaviness, and comfort *myself;*

28 I am afraid of all my sorrows, I know that thou wilt not hold me innocent.

29 *If* I be wicked, why then labour I in vain?

30 If I wash myself with snow water, and make my hands never so clean;

31 Yet shalt thou plunge me in the ditch, and mine own clothes shall abhor me.

32 For *he is* not a man, as I *am,* *that* I should answer him, *and* we should come together in judgment.

33 Neither is there any daysman betwixt us, *that* might lay his hand upon us both.

34 Let him take his rod away from me, and let not his fear terrify me:

35 *Then* would I speak, and not fear him; but *it is* not so with me.

CHAPTER 10.

1 My soul is weary of my life; I will leave my complaint upon myself; I will speak in the bitterness of my soul.

2 I will say unto God, Do not condemn me; shew me wherefore thou contendest with me.

3 *Is it* good unto thee that thou shouldest oppress, that thou shouldest despise the work of thine hands, and shine upon the counsel of the wicked?

4 Hast thou eyes of flesh? or seest thou as man seeth?

5 *Are* thy days as the days of man? *are* thy years as man's days,

6 That thou inquirest after mine iniquity, and searchest after my sin?

7 Thou knowest that I am not wicked; and *there is* none that can deliver out of thine hand.

8 Thine hands have made me and fashioned me together round about; yet thou dost destroy me.

9 Remember, I beseech thee, that thou hast made me as the clay; and wilt thou bring me into dust again?

10 Hast thou not poured me out as milk, and curdled me like cheese?

11 Thou hast clothed me with skin and flesh, and hast fenced me with bones and sinews.

12 Thou hast granted me life and favour, and thy visitation hath preserved my spirit.

13 And these *things* hast thou hid in thine heart: I know that this *is* with thee.

14 If I sin, then thou markest me, and thou wilt not acquit me from mine iniquity. *only God can clear confusion of Job. need for?*

15 If I be wicked, woe unto me; and *if* I be righteous, *yet* will I not lift up my head. I *am* full of confusion; therefore see thou mine affliction;

16 For it increaseth. Thou huntest me as a fierce lion: and again thou shewest thyself marvellous upon me.

17 Thou renewest thy witnesses against me, and increasest thine indignation upon me; changes and war *are* against me.

18 Wherefore then hast thou brought me forth out of the womb? Oh that I had given up the ghost, and no eye had seen me!

19 I should have been as though I had not been; I should have been carried from the womb to the grave.

20 *Are* not my days few? cease *then, and* let me alone, that I may take comfort a little,

21 Before I go *whence* I shall not return, *even* to the land of darkness and the shadow of death;

22 A land of darkness, as darkness *itself; and* of the shadow of death, without any order, and *where* the light *is* as darkness.

CHAPTER 11. *Zophar good will rewarded be rewarded w-punished*

1 Then answered Zophar the Naamathite, and said,

2 Should not the multitude of words be answered? and should a man full of talk be justified?

3 Should thy lies make men hold their peace? and when thou mockest, shall no man make thee ashamed?

4 For thou hast said, My doctrine *is* pure, and I am clean in thine eyes.

5 But oh that God would speak, and open his lips against thee;

6 And that he would shew thee the secrets of wisdom, that *they are* double to that which is! Know therefore that God exacteth of thee *less* than thine iniquity *deserveth*

7 Canst thou by searching find out God? canst thou find out the Almighty unto perfection?

8 *It is* as high as heaven; what canst thou do? deeper than hell; what canst thou know?

9 The measure thereof *is* longer than the earth, and broader than the sea.

10 If he cut off, and shut up, or gather together, then who can hinder him?

11 For he knoweth vain men: he seeth wickedness also; will he not then consider *it*?

12 For vain man would be wise, though man be born *like* a wild ass's colt.

13 If thou prepare thine heart, and stretch out thine hands toward him;

14 If iniquity *be* in thine hand, put it far away, and let not wickedness dwell in thy tabernacles.

15 For then shalt thou lift up thy face without spot; yea, thou shalt be steadfast, and shalt not fear:

16 Because thou shalt forget *thy* misery, *and* remember *it* as waters *that* pass away:

17 And *thine* age shall be clearer than the noonday; thou shalt shine forth, thou shalt be as the morning.

18 And thou shalt be secure, because there is hope; yea, thou shalt dig *about thee, and* thou shalt take thy rest in safety.

19 Also thou shalt lie down, and none shall make *thee* afraid; yea, many shall make suit unto thee.

20 But the eyes of the wicked shall fail, and they shall not escape, and their hope *shall be as* the giving up of the ghost.

CHAPTER 12.

1 And Job answered and said,

2 No doubt but ye *are* the people, and wisdom shall die with you.

3 But I have understanding as well as you; I *am* not inferior to you: yea, who knoweth not such things as these?

4 I am *as* one mocked of his neighbour, who calleth upon God, and he answereth him: the just upright *man is* laughed to scorn.

5 He that is ready to slip with *his* feet *is as* a lamp despised in the thought of him that is at ease.

6 The tabernacles of robbers prosper, and they that provoke God are secure; into whose hand God bringeth *abundantly.*

7 But ask now the beasts, and they shall teach thee; and the fowls of the air, and they shall tell thee:

8 Or speak to the earth, and it shall teach thee; and the fishes of the sea shall declare unto thee.

9 Who knoweth not in all these that the hand of the LORD hath wrought this?

10 In whose hand *is* the soul of every living thing, and the breath of all mankind.

11 Doth not the ear try words? and the mouth taste his meat?

12 With the ancient *is* wisdom; and in length of days understanding.

13 With him *is* wisdom and strength, he hath counsel and understanding.

14 Behold, he breaketh down, and it cannot be built again: he shutteth up a man, and there can be no opening.

15 Behold, he withholdeth the waters, and they dry up: also he sendeth them out, and they overturn the earth.

16 With him *is* strength and wisdom: the deceived and the deceiver *are* his. *unhale state*

17 He leadeth counsellors away spoiled, and maketh the judges fools.

18 He looseth the bond of kings, and girdeth their loins with a girdle.

19 He leadeth princes away spoiled, and overthroweth the mighty.

20 He removeth away the speech of the trusty, and taketh away the understanding of the aged.

21 He poureth contempt upon princes, and weakeneth the strength of the mighty.

22 He discovereth deep things out of darkness, and bringeth out to light the shadow of death. *or what good is punishment*

23 He increaseth the nations, and destroyeth them: he enlargeth the nations, and straiteneth them *again.*

24 He taketh away the heart of the chief of the people of the earth, and causeth them to wander in a wilderness *where there is* no way.

25 They grope in the dark without light, and he maketh them to stagger like *a* drunken *man.*

CHAPTER 13. *Job*

1 Lo, mine eye hath seen all *this,* mine ear hath heard and understood it.

2 What ye know, *the same* do I know also: I *am* not inferior unto you.

3 Surely I would speak to the Almighty, and I desire to reason with God. *desire to know reason*

4 But ye *are* forgers of lies, ye *are* all physicians of no value.

5 Oh that ye would altogether hold your peace! and it should be your wisdom. *be careful what you say*

6 Hear now my reasoning, and hearken to the pleadings of my lips.

7 Will ye speak wickedly for God? and talk deceitfully for him?

8 Will ye accept his person? will ye contend for God?

9 Is it good that he should search you out? or as one man mocketh another, do ye *so* mock him?

10 He will surely reprove you, if ye do secretly accept persons.

11 Shall not his excellency make you afraid? and his dread fall upon you?

12 Your remembrances *are* like unto ashes, your bodies to bodies of clay.

13 Hold your peace, let me alone, that I may speak, and let come on me what *will*.

14 Wherefore do I take my flesh in my teeth, and put my life in mine hand?

15 Though he slay me, yet will I trust in him: but I will maintain mine own ways before him.

16 He also *shall be* my salvation: for a hypocrite shall not come before him.

17 Hear diligently my speech, and my declaration with your ears.

18 Behold now, I have ordered *my* cause; I know that I shall be justified.

19 Who *is* he *that* will plead with me? for now, if I hold my tongue, I shall give up the ghost.

20 Only do not two *things* unto me; then will I not hide myself from thee.

21 Withdraw thine hand far from me: and let not thy dread make me afraid.

22 Then call thou, and I will answer: or let me speak, and answer thou me.

23 How many *are* mine iniquities and sins? make me to know my transgression and my sin.

24 Wherefore hidest thou thy face, and holdest me for thine enemy?

25 Wilt thou break a leaf driven to and fro? and wilt thou pursue the dry stubble?

26 For thou writest bitter things against me, and makest me to possess the iniquities of my youth.

27 Thou puttest my feet also in the stocks, and lookest narrowly unto all my paths; thou settest a print upon the heels of my feet.

28 And he, as a rotten thing, consumeth, as a garment that is moth-eaten.

CHAPTER 14.

1 Man *that is* born of a woman *is* of few days, and full of trouble.

2 He cometh forth like a flower, and is cut down: he fleeth also as a shadow, and continueth not.

3 And dost thou open thine eyes upon such a one, and bringest me into judgment with thee?

4 Who can bring a clean *thing* out of an unclean? not one.

5 Seeing his days *are* determined, the number of his months *are* with thee, thou hast appointed his bounds that he cannot pass;

6 Turn from him, that he may rest, till he shall accomplish, as a hireling, his day.

7 For there is hope of a tree, if it be cut down, that it will sprout again, and that the tender branch thereof will not cease.

8 Though the root thereof wax old in the earth, and the stock thereof die in the ground;

9 *Yet* through the scent of water it will bud, and bring forth boughs like a plant.

10 But man dieth, and wasteth away: yea, man giveth up the ghost, and where *is* he? *what's been accomplished?*

11 *As* the waters fail from the sea, and the flood decayeth and drieth up;

12 So man lieth down, and riseth not: till the heavens *be* no more, they shall not awake, nor be raised out of their sleep.

13 Oh that thou wouldest hide me in the grave, that thou wouldest keep me secret, until thy wrath be past, that thou wouldest appoint me a set time, and remember me!

14 If a man die, shall he live *again?* all the days of my appointed time will I wait, till my change come. *eternal life*

15 Thou shalt call, and I will answer thee: thou wilt have a desire to the work of thine hands.

16 For now thou numberest my steps: dost thou not watch over my sin?

17 My transgression *is* sealed up in a bag, and thou sewest up mine iniquity.

18 And surely the mountain falling cometh to nought, and the rock is removed out of his place.

19 The waters wear the stones: thou washest away the things which grow *out* of the dust of the earth; and thou destroyest the hope of man.

20 Thou prevailest for ever against him, and he passeth: thou changest his countenance, and sendest him away.

21 His sons come to honour, and he knoweth *it* not; and they are brought low, but he perceiveth *it* not of them.

22 But his flesh upon him shall have pain, and his soul within him shall mourn.

CHAPTER 15.

1 Then answered Eliphaz the Temanite, and said,

2 Should a wise man utter vain knowledge, and fill his belly with the east wind?

3 Should he reason with unprofitable talk? or with speeches wherewith he can do no good?

4 Yea, thou castest off fear, and restrainest prayer before God.

5 For thy mouth uttereth thine iniquity, and thou choosest the tongue of the crafty.

6 Thine own mouth condemneth thee, and not I: yea, thine own lips testify against thee.

7 *Art* thou the first man *that* was born? or wast thou made before the hills?

8 Hast thou heard the secret of God? and dost thou restrain wisdom to thyself?

9 What knowest thou, that we know not? *what* understandest thou, which *is* not in us?

10 With us *are* both the grayheaded and very aged men, much elder than thy father.

11 *Are* the consolations of God small with thee? is there any secret thing with thee?

12 Why doth thine heart carry thee away? and what do thy eyes wink at,

13 That thou turnest thy spirit against God, and lettest *such* words go out of thy mouth?

14 What *is* man, that he should be clean? and *he which is* born of a woman, that he should be righteous?

15 Behold, he putteth no trust in his saints; yea, the heavens are not clean in his sight.

16 How much more abominable and filthy *is* man, which drinketh iniquity like water?

17 I will shew thee, hear me; and that *which* I have seen I will declare;

18 Which wise men have told from their fathers, and have not hid *it:*

19 Unto whom alone the earth was given, and no stranger passed among them.

20 The wicked man travaileth with pain all *his* days, and the number of years is hidden to the oppressor.

21 A dreadful sound *is* in his ears: in prosperity the destroyer shall come upon him.

22 He believeth not that he shall return out of darkness, and he is
waited for of the sword.   *wicked alway suffer*

23 He wandereth abroad for bread, *saying,* Where *is it?* he knoweth ✱
that the day of darkness is ready at his hand.

24 Trouble and anguish shall make him afraid; they shall prevail ✱
against him, as a king ready to the battle.

25 For he stretcheth out his hand against God, and strengtheneth
himself against the Almighty.

26 He runneth upon him, *even* on *his* neck, upon the thick bosses
of his bucklers:

27 Because he covereth his face with his fatness, and maketh collops
of fat on *his* flanks.

28 And he dwelleth in desolate cities, *and* in houses which no man
inhabiteth, which are ready to become heaps.

29 He shall not be rich, neither shall his substance continue, neither ✕
shall he prolong the perfection thereof upon the earth.

30 He shall not depart out of darkness; the flame shall dry up his
branches, and by the breath of his mouth shall he go away.

31 Let not him that is deceived trust in vanity: for vanity shall be his
recompense.

32 It shall be accomplished before his time, and his branch shall not
be green.

33 He shall shake off his unripe grape as the vine, and shall cast off
his flower as the olive.

34 For the congregation of hypocrites *shall be* desolate, and fire shall ✱
consume the tabernacles of bribery.

35 They conceive mischief, and bring forth vanity, and their belly
prepareth deceit.

CHAPTER 16. *Job*

1 Then Job answered and said,

2 I have heard many such things: miserable comforters *are* ye all.

3 Shall vain words have an end? or what emboldeneth thee that thou
answerest?

4 I also could speak as ye *do:* if your soul were in my soul's stead, I
could heap up words against you, and shake mine head at you.

5 *But* I would strengthen you with my mouth, and the moving of my
lips should assuage *your grief.*

6 Though I speak, my grief is not assuaged: and *though* I forbear,
what am I eased?

7 But now he hath made me weary: thou hast made desolate all my company.

8 And thou hast filled me with wrinkles, *which* is a witness *against me:* and my leanness rising up in me beareth witness to my face.

9 He teareth *me* in his wrath, who hateth me: he gnasheth upon me with his teeth; mine enemy sharpeneth his eyes upon me.

10 They have gaped upon me with their mouth; they have smitten me upon the cheek reproachfully; they have gathered themselves together against me.

11 God hath delivered me to the ungodly, and turned me over into the hands of the wicked.

12 I was at ease, but he hath broken me asunder: he hath also taken *me* by my neck, and shaken me to pieces, and set me up for his mark.

13 His archers compass me round about, he cleaveth my reins asunder, and doth not spare; he poureth out my gall upon the ground.

14 He breaketh me with breach upon breach; he runneth upon me like a giant.

15 I have sewed sackcloth upon my skin, and defiled my horn in the dust.

16 My face is foul with weeping, and on my eyelids *is* the shadow of death;

17 Not for *any* injustice in mine hands: also my prayer *is* pure.

18 O earth, cover not thou my blood, and let my cry have no place.

19 Also now, behold, my witness *is* in heaven, and my record *is* on high.

20 My friends scorn me: *but* mine eye poureth out *tears* unto God.

21 Oh that one might plead for a man with God, as a man *pleadeth* for his neighbour!

22 When a few years are come, then I shall go the way *whence* I shall not return.

CHAPTER 17.

1 My breath is corrupt, my days are extinct, the graves *are ready* for me.

2 *Are there* not mockers with me? and doth not mine eye continue in their provocation?

3 Lay down now, put me in a surety with thee; who *is* he *that* will strike hands with me?

4 For thou hast hid their heart from understanding: therefore shalt thou not exalt *them*.

5 He that speaketh flattery to *his* friends, even the eyes of his children shall fail.

6 He hath made me also a byword of the people; and aforetime I was as a tabret.

7 Mine eye also is dim by reason of sorrow, and all my members *are* as a shadow.

8 Upright *men* shall be astonied at this, and the innocent shall stir up himself against the hypocrite.

9 The righteous also shall hold on his way, and he that hath clean hands shall be stronger and stronger.

10 But as for you all, do ye return, and come now: for I cannot find *one* wise *man* among you.

11 My days are past, my purposes are broken off, *even* the thoughts of my heart.

12 They change the night into day: the light *is* short because of darkness.

13 If I wait, the grave *is* mine house: I have made my bed in the darkness.

14 I have said to corruption, Thou *art* my father: to the worm, *Thou art* my mother, and my sister.

15 And where *is* now my hope? as for my hope, who shall see it?

16 They shall go down to the bars of the pit, when *our* rest together *is* in the dust.

CHAPTER 18. *Bildad*

1 Then answered Bildad the Shuhite, and said,

2 How long *will it be ere* ye make an end of words? mark, and afterwards we will speak.

3 Wherefore are we counted as beasts, *and* reputed vile in your sight?

4 He teareth himself in his anger: shall the earth be forsaken for thee? and shall the rock be removed out of his place?

5 Yea, the light of the wicked shall be put out, and the spark of his fire shall not shine.

6 The light shall be dark in his tabernacle, and his candle shall be put out with him.

7 The steps of his strength shall be straitened, and his own counsel shall cast him down.

8 For he is cast into a net by his own feet, and he walketh upon a snare.

9 The gin shall take *him* by the heel, *and* the robber shall prevail against him.

10 The snare *is* laid for him in the ground, and a trap for him in the way.

11 Terrors shall make him afraid on every side, and shall drive him to his feet.

12 His strength shall be hungerbitten, and destruction *shall be* ready at his side.

13 It shall devour the strength of his skin: *even* the firstborn of death shall devour his strength.

14 His confidence shall be rooted out of his tabernacle, and it shall bring him to the king of terrors.

15 It shall dwell in his tabernacle, because *it is* none of his: brimstone shall be scattered upon his habitation.

16 His roots shall be dried up beneath, and above shall his branch be cut off.

17 His remembrance shall perish from the earth, and he shall have no name in the street.

18 He shall be driven from light into darkness, and chased out of the world.

19 He shall neither have son nor nephew among his people, nor any remaining in his dwellings.

20 They that come after *him* shall be astonied at his day, as they that went before were affrighted.

21 Surely such *are* the dwellings of the wicked, and this *is* the place of *him that* knoweth not God.

CHAPTER 19.

1 Then Job answered and said,

2 How long will ye vex my soul, and break me in pieces with words?

3 These ten times have ye reproached me: ye are not ashamed *that* ye make yourselves strange to me.

4 And be it indeed *that* I have erred, mine error remaineth with myself.

5 If indeed ye will magnify *yourselves* against me, and plead against me my reproach;

6 Know now that God hath overthrown me, and hath compassed me with his net.

7 Behold, I cry out of wrong, but I am not heard: I cry aloud, but *there is* no judgment.

8 He hath fenced up my way that I cannot pass, and he hath set darkness in my paths.

9 He hath stripped me of my glory, and taken the crown *from* my head.

10 He hath destroyed me on every side, and I am gone: and mine hope hath he removed like a tree.

11 He hath also kindled his wrath against me, and he counteth me unto him as *one of* his enemies.

12 His troops come together, and raise up their way against me, and encamp round about my tabernacle.

13 He hath put my brethren far from me, and mine acquaintance are verily estranged from me. *impatience momentary doubt*

14 My kinsfolk have failed, and my familiar friends have forgotten me.

15 They that dwell in mine house, and my maids, count me for a stranger: I am an alien in their sight.

16 I called my servant, and he gave *me* no answer; I entreated him with my mouth.

17 My breath is strange to my wife, though I entreated for the children's *sake* of mine own body.

18 Yea, young children despised me; I arose, and they spake against me.

19 All my inward friends abhorred me: and they whom I loved are turned against me.

20 My bone cleaveth to my skin and to my flesh, and I am escaped with the skin of my teeth.

21 Have pity upon me, have pity upon me, O ye my friends; for the hand of God hath touched me.

22 Why do ye persecute me as God, and are not satisfied with my flesh?

23 Oh that my words were now written! oh that they were printed in a book!

24 That they were graven with an iron pen and lead in the rock for ever! *confidence & sincerity*

25 For I know *that* my Redeemer liveth, and *that* he shall stand at the latter *day* upon the earth:

26 And *though* after my skin *worms* destroy this *body,* yet in my flesh shall I see God:

27 Whom I shall see for myself, and mine eyes shall behold, and not another; *though* my reins be consumed within me.

28 But ye should say, Why persecute we him, seeing the root of the matter is found in me?

29 Be ye afraid of the sword: for wrath *bringeth* the punishments of the sword, that ye may know *there is* a judgment.

Zophar

CHAPTER 20.

1 Then answered Zophar the Naamathite, and said,

2 Therefore do my thoughts cause me to answer, and for *this* I make haste.

3 I have heard the check of my reproach, and the spirit of my understanding causeth me to answer.

4 Knowest thou *not* this of old, since man was placed upon earth,

5 That the triumphing of the wicked *is* short, and the joy of the hypocrite *but* for a moment?

6 Though his excellency mount up to the heavens, and his head reach unto the clouds;

7 *Yet* he shall perish for ever like his own dung: they which have seen him shall say, Where *is* he?

8 He shall fly away as a dream, and shall not be found: yea, he shall be chased away as a vision of the night.

9 The eye also *which* saw him shall *see him* no more; neither shall his place any more behold him.

10 His children shall seek to please the poor, and his hands shall restore their goods.

11 His bones are full *of the sin* of his youth, which shall lie down with him in the dust.

12 Though wickedness be sweet in his mouth, *though* he hide it under his tongue;

13 *Though* he spare it, and forsake it not, but keep it still within his mouth;

14 *Yet* his meat in his bowels is turned, *it is* the gall of asps within him.

15 He hath swallowed down riches, and he shall vomit them up again: God shall cast them out of his belly.

16 He shall suck the poison of asps: the viper's tongue shall slay him.

17 He shall not see the rivers, the floods, the brooks of honey and butter.

18 That which he laboured for shall he restore, and shall not swallow *it* down: according to *his* substance *shall* the restitution *be,* and he shall not rejoice *therein.*

19 Because he hath oppressed *and* hath forsaken the poor; *because* he hath violently taken away a house which he builded not;

20 Surely he shall not feel quietness in his belly, he shall not save of that which he desired.

21 There shall none of his meat be left; therefore shall no man look for his goods.

22 In the fulness of his sufficiency he shall be in straits: every hand of the wicked shall come upon him.

23 *When* he is about to fill his belly, *God* shall cast the fury of his wrath upon him, and shall rain *it* upon him while he is eating.

24 He shall flee from the iron weapon, *and* the bow of steel shall strike him through.

25 It is drawn, and cometh out of the body; yea, the glittering sword cometh out of his gall: terrors *are* upon him.

26 All darkness *shall be* hid in his secret places: a fire not blown shall consume him; it shall go ill with him that is left in his tabernacle.

27 The heaven shall reveal his iniquity; and the earth shall rise up against him.

28 The increase of his house shall depart, *and his goods* shall flow away in the day of his wrath.

29 This *is* the portion of a wicked man from God, and the heritage appointed unto him by God.

CHAPTER 21.

1 But Job answered and said,

2 Hear diligently my speech, and let this be your consolations.

3 Suffer me that I may speak; and after that I have spoken, mock on.

4 As for me, *is* my complaint to man? and if *it were so,* why should not my spirit be troubled?

5 Mark me, and be astonished, and lay *your* hand upon *your* mouth.

6 Even when I remember I am afraid, and trembling taketh hold on my flesh.

7 Wherefore do the wicked live, become old, yea, are mighty in power?

8 Their seed is established in their sight with them, and their offspring before their eyes.

9 Their houses *are* safe from fear, neither *is* the rod of God upon them.

10 Their bull gendereth, and faileth not; their cow calveth, and casteth not her calf.

11 They send forth their little ones like a flock, and their children dance.

12 They take the timbrel and harp, and rejoice at the sound of the organ.

13 They spend their days in wealth, and in a moment go down to the grave.

14 Therefore they say unto God, Depart from us; for we desire not the knowledge of thy ways.

15 What *is* the Almighty, that we should serve him? and what profit should we have, if we pray unto him?

16 Lo, their good *is* not in their hand: the counsel of the wicked is far from me.

17 How oft is the candle of the wicked put out! and *how oft* cometh their destruction upon them! *God* distributeth sorrows in his anger.

18 They are as stubble before the wind, and as chaff that the storm carrieth away.

19 God layeth up his iniquity for his children: he rewardeth him, and he shall know *it*.

20 His eyes shall see his destruction, and he shall drink of the wrath of the Almighty.

21 For what pleasure *hath* he in his house after him, when the number of his months is cut off in the midst?

22 Shall *any* teach God knowledge? seeing he judgeth those that are high.

23 One dieth in his full strength, being wholly at ease and quiet.

24 His breasts are full of milk, and his bones are moistened with marrow.

25 And another dieth in the bitterness of his soul, and never eateth with pleasure.

26 They shall lie down alike in the dust, and the worms shall cover them.

27 Behold, I know your thoughts, and the devices *which* ye wrongfully imagine against me.

28 For ye say, Where *is* the house of the prince? and where *are* the dwellingplaces of the wicked?

29 Have ye not asked them that go by the way? and do ye not know their tokens,

30 That the wicked is reserved to the day of destruction? they shall be brought forth to the day of wrath.

31 Who shall declare his way to his face? and who shall repay him *what* he hath done?

32 Yet shall he be brought to the grave, and shall remain in the tomb.

33 The clods of the valley shall be sweet unto him, and every man shall draw after him, as *there are* innumerable before him.

34 How then comfort ye me in vain, seeing in your answers there remaineth falsehood?

CHAPTER 22.

1 Then Eliphaz the Temanite answered and said,

2 Can a man be profitable unto God, as he that is wise may be profitable unto himself?

3 *Is it* any pleasure to the Almighty, that thou art righteous? or *is it* gain *to him,* that thou makest thy ways perfect?

4 Will he reprove thee for fear of thee? will he enter with thee into judgment?

5 *Is* not thy wickedness great? and thine iniquities infinite?

6 For thou hast taken a pledge from thy brother for nought, and stripped the naked of their clothing.

7 Thou hast not given water to the weary to drink, and thou hast withholden bread from the hungry.

8 But *as for* the mighty man, he had the earth; and the honourable man dwelt in it.

9 Thou hast sent widows away empty, and the arms of the fatherless have been broken.

10 Therefore snares *are* round about thee, and sudden fear troubleth thee;

11 Or darkness, *that* thou canst not see; and abundance of waters cover thee.

12 *Is* not God in the height of heaven? and behold the height of the stars, how high they are!

13 And thou sayest, How doth God know? can he judge through the dark cloud?

14 Thick clouds *are* a covering to him, that he seeth not; and he walketh in the circuit of heaven.

15 Hast thou marked the old way which wicked men have trodden?

16 Which were cut down out of time, whose foundation was overflown with a flood:

17 Which said unto God, Depart from us: and what can the Almighty do for them?

18 Yet he filled their houses with good *things:* but the counsel of the wicked is far from me.

19 The righteous see *it,* and are glad: and the innocent laugh them to scorn.

20 Whereas our substance is not cut down, but the remnant of them the fire consumeth.

21 Acquaint now thyself with him, and be at peace: thereby good shall come unto thee.

22 Receive, I pray thee, the law from his mouth, and lay up his words in thine heart.

23 If thou return to the Almighty, thou shalt be built up, thou shalt put away iniquity far from thy tabernacles.

24 Then shalt thou lay up gold as dust, and the *gold* of Ophir as the stones of the brooks.

25 Yea, the Almighty shall be thy defence, and thou shalt have plenty of silver.

26 For then shalt thou have thy delight in the Almighty, and shalt lift up thy face unto God.

27 Thou shalt make thy prayer unto him, and he shall hear thee, and thou shalt pay thy vows.

28 Thou shalt also decree a thing, and it shall be established unto thee: and the light shall shine upon thy ways.

29 When *men* are cast down, then thou shalt say, *There is* lifting up; and he shall save the humble person.

30 He shall deliver the island of the innocent: and it is delivered by the pureness of thine hands.

CHAPTER 23.

1 Then Job answered and said,

2 Even to day *is* my complaint bitter: my stroke is heavier than my groaning.

3 Oh that I knew where I might find him! *that* I might come *even* to his seat!

4 I would order *my* cause before him, and fill my mouth with arguments.

5 I would know the words *which* he would answer me, and understand what he would say unto me.

6 Will he plead against me with *his* great power? No; but he would put *strength* in me.

7 There the righteous might dispute with him; so should I be delivered for ever from my judge.

8 Behold, I go forward, but he *is* not *there;* and backward, but I cannot perceive him:

9 On the left hand, where he doth work, but I cannot behold *him:* he hideth himself on the right hand, that I cannot see *him:*

10 But he knoweth the way that I take: *when* he hath tried me, I shall come forth as gold.

11 My foot hath held his steps, his way have I kept, and not declined.

12 Neither have I gone back from the commandment of his lips; I have esteemed the words of his mouth more than my necessary *food.*

13 But he *is* in one *mind,* and who can turn him? and *what* his soul desireth, even *that* he doeth.

14 For he performeth *the thing that is* appointed for me: and many such *things are* with him.

15 Therefore am I troubled at his presence: when I consider, I am afraid of him.

16 For God maketh my heart soft, and the Almighty troubleth me:

17 Because I was not cut off before the darkness, *neither* hath he covered the darkness from my face.

CHAPTER 24.

1 Why, seeing times are not hidden from the Almighty, do they that know him not see his days?

2 *Some* remove the landmarks; they violently take away flocks, and feed *thereof.*

3 They drive away the ass of the fatherless, they take the widow's ox for a pledge.

4 They turn the needy out of the way: the poor of the earth hide themselves together.

5 Behold, *as* wild asses in the desert, go they forth to their work; rising betimes for a prey: the wilderness *yieldeth* food for them *and* for *their* children.

6 They reap *every one* his corn in the field: and they gather the vintage of the wicked.

7 They cause the naked to lodge without clothing, that *they have* no covering in the cold.

8 They are wet with the showers of the mountains, and embrace the rock for want of a shelter.

9 They pluck the fatherless from the breast, and take a pledge of the poor.

10 They cause *him* to go naked without clothing, and they take away the sheaf *from* the hungry;

11 *Which* make oil within their walls, *and* tread *their* winepresses, and suffer thirst.

12 Men groan from out of the city, and the soul of the wounded crieth out: yet God layeth not folly *to them*.

13 They are of those that rebel against the light; they know not the ways thereof, nor abide in the paths thereof.

14 The murderer rising with the light killeth the poor and needy, and in the night is as a thief.

15 The eye also of the adulterer waiteth for the twilight, saying, No eye shall see me: and disguiseth *his* face.

16 In the dark they dig through houses, *which* they had marked for themselves in the daytime: they know not the light.

17 For the morning *is* to them even as the shadow of death: if *one* know *them, they are in* the terrors of the shadow of death.

18 He *is* swift as the waters; their portion is cursed in the earth: he beholdeth not the way of the vineyards.

19 Drought and heat consume the snow waters: *so doth* the grave *those which* have sinned.

20 The womb shall forget him; the worm shall feed sweetly on him; he shall be no more remembered; and wickedness shall be broken as a tree.

21 He evil entreateth the barren *that* beareth not: and doeth not good to the widow.

22 He draweth also the mighty with his power: he riseth up, and no *man* is sure of life.

23 *Though* it be given him *to be* in safety, whereon he resteth; yet his eyes *are* upon their ways.

24 They are exalted for a little while, but are gone and brought low; they are taken out of the way as all *other,* and cut off as the tops of the ears of corn.

25 And if *it be* not *so* now, who will make me a liar, and make my speech nothing worth?

CHAPTER 25.

1 Then answered Bildad the Shuhite, and said,

2 Dominion and fear *are* with him; he maketh peace in his high places.

3 Is there any number of his armies? and upon whom doth not his light arise?

4 How then can man be justified with God? or how can he be clean *that is* born of a woman?

5 Behold even to the moon, and it shineth not; yea, the stars are not pure in his sight.

6 How much less man, *that is* a worm? and the son of man, *which is* a worm?

CHAPTER 26.

1 But Job answered and said,

2 How hast thou helped *him that is* without power? *how* savest thou the arm *that hath* no strength?

3 How hast thou counselled *him that hath* no wisdom? and *how* hast thou plentifully declared the thing as it is?

4 To whom hast thou uttered words? and whose spirit came from thee?

5 Dead *things* are formed from under the waters, and the inhabitants thereof.

6 Hell *is* naked before him, and destruction hath no covering.

7 He stretcheth out the north over the empty place, *and* hangeth the earth upon nothing.

8 He bindeth up the waters in his thick clouds; and the cloud is not rent under them.

9 He holdeth back the face of his throne, *and* spreadeth his cloud upon it.

10 He hath compassed the waters with bounds, until the day and night come to an end.

11 The pillars of heaven tremble, and are astonished at his reproof.

12 He divideth the sea with his power, and by his understanding he smiteth through the proud.

13 By his Spirit he hath garnished the heavens; his hand hath formed the crooked serpent.

14 Lo, these *are* parts of his ways; but how little a portion is heard of him? but the thunder of his power who can understand?

CHAPTER 27.

1 Moreover Job continued his parable, and said,

2 *As* God liveth, *who* hath taken away my judgment; and the Almighty, *who* hath vexed my soul;

3 All the while my breath *is* in me, and the spirit of God *is* in my nostrils;

4 My lips shall not speak wickedness, nor my tongue utter deceit.

5 God forbid that I should justify you: till I die I will not remove mine integrity from me.

6 My righteousness I hold fast, and will not let it go: my heart shall not reproach *me* so long as I live.

7 Let mine enemy be as the wicked, and he that riseth up against me as the unrighteous.

8 For what *is* the hope of the hypocrite, though he hath gained, when God taketh away his soul?

9 Will God hear his cry when trouble cometh upon him?

10 Will he delight himself in the Almighty? will he always call upon God?

11 I will teach you by the hand of God: *that* which *is* with the Almighty will I not conceal.

12 Behold, all ye yourselves have seen *it;* why then are ye thus altogether vain?

13 This *is* the portion of a wicked man with God, and the heritage of oppressors, *which* they shall receive of the Almighty.

14 If his children be multiplied, *it is* for the sword: and his offspring shall not be satisfied with bread.

15 Those that remain of him shall be buried in death: and his widows shall not weep.

16 Though he heap up silver as the dust, and prepare raiment as the clay;

17 He may prepare *it,* but the just shall put *it* on, and the innocent shall divide the silver.

18 He buildeth his house as a moth, and as a booth *that* the keeper maketh.

19 The rich man shall lie down, but he shall not be gathered: he openeth his eyes, and he *is* not.

20 Terrors take hold on him as waters, a tempest stealeth him away in the night.

21 The east wind carrieth him away, and he departeth: and as a storm hurleth him out of his place.

22 For *God* shall cast upon him, and not spare: he would fain flee out of his hand.

23 *Men* shall clap their hands at him, and shall hiss him out of his place.

CHAPTER 28

1 Surely there is a vein for the silver, and a place for gold *where* they fine *it*.

2 Iron is taken out of the earth, and brass *is* molten *out of* the stone.

3 He setteth an end to darkness, and searcheth out all perfection: the stones of darkness, and the shadow of death.

4 The flood breaketh out from the inhabitant; *even the waters* forgotten of the foot: they are dried up, they are gone away from men.

5 *As for* the earth, out of it cometh bread: and under it is turned up as it were fire.

6 The stones of it *are* the place of sapphires: and it hath dust of gold.

7 *There is* a path which no fowl knoweth, and which the vulture's eye hath not seen:

8 The lion's whelps have not trodden it, nor the fierce lion passed by it.

9 He putteth forth his hand upon the rock; he overturneth the mountains by the roots.

10 He cutteth out rivers among the rocks; and his eye seeth every precious thing.

11 He bindeth the floods from overflowing; and *the thing that is* hid bringeth he forth to light.

12 But where shall wisdom be found? and where *is* the place of understanding?

13 Man knoweth not the price thereof; neither is it found in the land of the living.

14 The depth saith, It *is* not in me: and the sea saith, *It is* not with me.

15 It cannot be gotten for gold, neither shall silver be weighed *for* the price thereof.

16 It cannot be valued with the gold of Ophir, with the precious onyx, or the sapphire.

17 The gold and the crystal cannot equal it: and the exchange of it *shall not be for* jewels of fine gold.

18 No mention shall be made of coral, or of pearls: for the price of wisdom *is* above rubies.

19 The topaz of Ethiopia shall not equal it, neither shall it be valued with pure gold.

20 Whence then cometh wisdom? and where *is* the place of under- ✷ standing?

21 Seeing it is hid from the eyes of all living, and kept close from the fowls of the air.

22 Destruction and death say, We have heard the fame thereof with our ears.

23 God understandeth the way thereof, and he knoweth the place thereof.

24 For he looketh to the ends of the earth, *and* seeth under the whole heaven;

25 To make the weight for the winds; and he weigheth the waters by measure.

26 When he made a decree for the rain, and a way for the lightning of the thunder;

27 Then did he see it, and declare it; he prepared it, yea, and searched it out.

28 And unto man he said, Behold, the fear of the Lord, that *is* wisdom; and to depart from evil *is* understanding.

CHAPTER 29.

1 Moreover Job continued his parable, and said,

2 Oh that I were as *in* months past, as *in* the days *when* God preserved me;

3 When his candle shined upon my head, *and when* by his light I walked *through* darkness;

4 As I was in the days of my youth, when the secret of God *was* upon my tabernacle;

5 When the Almighty *was* yet with me, *when* my children *were* about me;

6 When I washed my steps with butter, and the rock poured me out rivers of oil;

7 When I went out to the gate through the city, *when* I prepared my seat in the street!

8 The young men saw me, and hid themselves: and the aged arose, *and* stood up.

9 The princes refrained talking, and laid *their* hand on their mouth.

10 The nobles held their peace, and their tongue cleaved to the roof of their mouth.

11 When the ear heard *me,* then it blessed me; and when the eye saw *me,* it gave witness to me:

12 Because I delivered the poor that cried, and the fatherless, and *him that had* none to help him.

13 The blessing of him that was ready to perish came upon me: and I caused the widow's heart to sing for joy.

14 I put on righteousness, and it clothed me: my judgment *was* as a robe and a diadem.

15 I was eyes to the blind, and feet *was* I to the lame.

16 I *was* a father to the poor: and the cause *which* I knew not I searched out.

17 And I brake the jaws of the wicked, and plucked the spoil out of his teeth.

18 Then I said, I shall die in my nest, and I shall multiply *my* days as the sand.

19 My root *was* spread out by the waters, and the dew lay all night upon my branch.

20 My glory *was* fresh in me, and my bow was renewed in my hand.

21 Unto me *men* gave ear, and waited, and kept silence at my counsel.

22 After my words they spake not again; and my speech dropped upon them.

23 And they waited for me as for the rain; and they opened their mouth wide *as* for the latter rain.

24 *If* I laughed on them, they believed *it* not; and the light of my countenance they cast not down.

25 I chose out their way, and sat chief, and dwelt as a king in the army, as one *that* comforteth the mourners.

CHAPTER 30.

1 But now *they that are* younger than I have me in derision, whose fathers I would have disdained to have set with the dogs of my flock.

2 Yea, whereto *might* the strength of their hands *profit* me, in whom old age was perished?

3 For want and famine *they were* solitary; fleeing into the wilderness in former time desolate and waste:

4 Who cut up mallows by the bushes, and juniper roots *for* their meat.

5 They were driven forth from among *men*, (they cried after them as *after* a thief,)

6 To dwell in the cliffs of the valleys, *in* caves of the earth, and *in* the rocks.

7 Among the bushes they brayed; under the nettles they were gathered together.

8 *They were* children of fools, yea, children of base men: they were viler than the earth.

9 And now am I their song, yea, I am their byword.

10 They abhor me, they flee far from me, and spare not to spit in my face.

11 Because he hath loosed my cord, and afflicted me, they have also let loose the bridle before me.

12 Upon *my* right *hand* rise the youth; they push away my feet, and they raise up against me the ways of their destruction.

13 They mar my path, they set forward my calamity, they have no helper.

14 They came *upon me* as a wide breaking in *of waters:* in the desolation they rolled themselves *upon me.*

15 Terrors are turned upon me: they pursue my soul as the wind: and my welfare passeth away as a cloud.

16 And now my soul is poured out upon me; the days of affliction have taken hold upon me.

17 My bones are pierced in me in the night season: and my sinews take no rest.

18 By the great force *of my disease* is my garment changed: it bindeth me about as the collar of my coat.

19 He hath cast me into the mire, and I am become like dust and ashes.

20 I cry unto thee, and thou dost not hear me: I stand up, and thou regardest me *not.*

21 Thou art become cruel to me: with thy strong hand thou opposest thyself against me.

22 Thou liftest me up to the wind; thou causest me to ride *upon it,* and dissolvest my substance.

23 For I know *that* thou wilt bring me *to* death, and *to* the house appointed for all living.

24 Howbeit he will not stretch out *his* hand to the grave, though they cry in his destruction.

25 Did not I weep for him that was in trouble? was *not* my soul grieved for the poor?

26 When I looked for good, then evil came *unto me:* and when I waited for light, there came darkness.

27 My bowels boiled, and rested not: the days of affliction prevented me.

28 I went mourning without the sun: I stood up, *and* I cried in the congregation.

29 I am a brother to dragons, and a companion to owls.

30 My skin is black upon me, and my bones are burned with heat.

31 My harp also is *turned* to mourning, and my organ into the voice of them that weep.

CHAPTER 31.

1 I made a covenant with mine eyes; why then should I think upon a maid?

2 For what portion of God is *there* from above? and *what* inheritance of the Almighty from on high?

3 *Is* not destruction to the wicked? and a strange *punishment* to the workers of iniquity?

4 Doth not he see my ways, and count all my steps? ✗

5 If I have walked with vanity, or if my foot hath hasted to deceit;

6 Let me be weighed in an even balance, that God may know mine integrity.

7 If my step hath turned out of the way, and mine heart walked after mine eyes, and if any blot hath cleaved to mine hands;

8 *Then* let me sow, and let another eat; yea, let my offspring be rooted out.

9 If mine heart have been deceived by a woman, or *if* I have laid wait at my neighbour's door;

10 *Then* let my wife grind unto another, and let others bow down upon her.

11 For this *is* a heinous crime; yea, it *is* an iniquity *to be punished by* the judges.

12 For it *is* a fire *that* consumeth to destruction, and would root out all mine increase.

13 If I did despise the cause of my manservant or of my maidservant, when they contended with me;

14 What then shall I do when God riseth up? and when he visiteth, what shall I answer him?

15 Did not he that made me in the womb make him? and did not one fashion us in the womb?

16 If I have withheld the poor from *their* desire, or have caused the eyes of the widow to fail;

17 Or have eaten my morsel myself alone, and the fatherless hath not eaten thereof;

18 (For from my youth he was brought up with me, as *with* a father, and I have guided her from my mother's womb;)

19 If I have seen any perish for want of clothing, or any poor without covering;

20 If his loins have not blessed me, and *if* he were *not* warmed with the fleece of my sheep;

21 If I have lifted up my hand against the fatherless, when I saw my help in the gate:

22 *Then* let mine arm fall from my shoulder blade, and mine arm be broken from the bone.

23 For destruction *from* God *was* a terror to me, and by reason of his highness I could not endure.

24 If I have made gold my hope, or have said to the fine gold, *Thou art* my confidence;

25 If I rejoiced because my wealth *was* great, and because mine hand had gotten much;

26 If I beheld the sun when it shined, or the moon walking *in* brightness;

27 And my heart hath been secretly enticed, or my mouth hath kissed my hand:

28 This also *were* an iniquity *to be punished by* the judge: for I should have denied the God *that is* above.

29 If I rejoiced at the destruction of him that hated me, or lifted up myself when evil found him;

30 (Neither have I suffered my mouth to sin by wishing a curse to his soul.)

31 If the men of my tabernacle said not, Oh that we had of his flesh! we cannot be satisfied.

32 The stranger did not lodge in the street: *but* I opened my doors to the traveller.

33 If I covered my transgressions as Adam, by hiding mine iniquity in my bosom:

34 Did I fear a great multitude, or did the contempt of families terrify me, that I kept silence, *and* went not out of the door?

35 Oh that one would hear me! behold, my desire *is, that* the Almighty would answer me, and *that* mine adversary had written a book.

36 Surely I would take it upon my shoulder, *and* bind it *as* a crown to me.

37 I would declare unto him the number of my steps; as a prince would I go near unto him.

38 If my land cry against me, or that the furrows likewise thereof complain;

39 If I have eaten the fruits thereof without money, or have caused the owners thereof to lose their life:

40 Let thistles grow instead of wheat, and cockle instead of barley. The words of Job are ended.

CHAPTER 32. *probably added later*

1 So these three men ceased to answer Job, because he *was* righteous in his own eyes.

2 Then was kindled the wrath of Elihu the son of Barachel the Buzite, of the kindred of Ram: against Job was his wrath kindled, because he justified himself rather than God.

3 Also against his three friends was his wrath kindled, because they had found no answer, and *yet* had condemned Job.

4 Now Elihu had waited till Job had spoken, because they *were* elder than he.

5 When Elihu saw that *there was* no answer in the mouth of *these* three men, then his wrath was kindled.

6 And Elihu the son of Barachel the Buzite answered and said, I *am* young, and ye *are* very old; wherefore I was afraid, and durst not shew you mine opinion.

7 I said, Days should speak, and multitude of years should teach wisdom.

8 But *there is* a spirit in man: and the inspiration of the Almighty giveth them understanding.

9 Great men are not *always* wise: neither do the aged understand judgment.

10 Therefore I said, Hearken to me; I also will shew mine opinion.

11 Behold, I waited for your words; I gave ear to your reasons, whilst ye searched out what to say.

12 Yea, I attended unto you, and, behold, *there was* none of you that convinced Job, *or* that answered his words:

13 Lest ye should say, We have found out wisdom: God thrusteth him down, not man.

14 Now he hath not directed *his* words against me: neither will I answer him with your speeches.

15 They were amazed, they answered no more: they left off speaking.

16 When I had waited, (for they spake not, but stood still, *and* answered no more,)

17 *I said,* I will answer also my part; I also will shew mine opinion.

18 For I am full of matter; the spirit within me constraineth me.

19 Behold, my belly *is* as wine *which* hath no vent; it is ready to burst like new bottles.

20 I will speak, that I may be refreshed: I will open my lips and answer.

21 Let me not, I pray you, accept any man's person; neither let me give flattering titles unto man.

22 For I know not to give flattering titles; *in so doing* my Maker would soon take me away.

CHAPTER 33.

1 Wherefore, Job, I pray thee, hear my speeches, and hearken to all my words.

2 Behold, now I have opened my mouth, my tongue hath spoken in my mouth.

3 My words *shall be of* the uprightness of my heart: and my lips shall utter knowledge clearly.

4 The Spirit of God hath made me, and the breath of the Almighty hath given me life.

5 If thou canst answer me, set *thy words* in order before me, stand up.

6 Behold, I *am* according to thy wish in God's stead: I also am formed out of the clay.

7 Behold, my terror shall not make thee afraid, neither shall my hand be heavy upon thee.

8 Surely thou hast spoken in mine hearing, and I have heard the voice of *thy* words, *saying,*

9 I am clean without transgression, I *am* innocent; neither *is there* iniquity in me.

10 Behold, he findeth occasions against me, he counteth me for his enemy;

11 He putteth my feet in the stocks, he marketh all my paths.

12 Behold, *in* this thou art not just: I will answer thee, that God is greater than man.

13 Why dost thou strive against him? for he giveth not account of any of his matters.

14 For God speaketh once, yea twice, *yet man* perceiveth it not.

15 In a dream, in a vision of the night, when deep sleep falleth upon men, in slumberings upon the bed;

16 Then he openeth the ears of men, and sealeth their instruction,

17 That he may withdraw man *from his* purpose, and hide pride from man.

18 He keepeth back his soul from the pit, and his life from perishing by the sword.

19 He is chastened also with pain upon his bed, and the multitude of his bones with strong *pain:*

20 So that his life abhorreth bread, and his soul dainty meat.

21 His flesh is consumed away, that it cannot be seen; and his bones *that* were not seen stick out.

22 Yea, his soul draweth near unto the grave, and his life to the destroyers.

23 If there be a messenger with him, an interpreter, one among a thousand, to shew unto man his uprightness;

24 Then he is gracious unto him, and saith, Deliver him from going down to the pit: I have found a ransom.

25 His flesh shall be fresher than a child's: he shall return to the days of his youth:

26 He shall pray unto God, and he will be favourable unto him: and he shall see his face with joy: for he will render unto man his righteousness.

27 He looketh upon men, and *if any* say, I have sinned, and perverted *that which was* right, and it profited me not;

28 He will deliver his soul from going into the pit, and his life shall see the light.

29 Lo, all these *things* worketh God oftentimes with man, ✗

30 To bring back his soul from the pit, to be enlightened with the light of the living. *learned* *anguish* · *darkness* *desean*

31 Mark well, O Job, hearken unto me: hold thy peace, and I will speak.

32 If thou hast any thing to say, answer me: speak, for I desire to justify thee.

33 If not, hearken unto me: hold thy peace, and I shall teach thee wisdom.

CHAPTER 34.

1 Furthermore Elihu answered and said,

2 Hear my words, O ye wise *men;* and give ear unto me, ye that have knowledge.

3 For the ear trieth words, as the mouth tasteth meat.

4 Let us choose to us judgment: let us know among ourselves what *is* good.

5 For Job hath said, I am righteous: and God hath taken away my judgment.

6 Should I lie against my right? my wound *is* incurable without transgression.

7 What man *is* like Job, *who* drinketh up scorning like water?

8 Which goeth in company with the workers of iniquity, and walketh with wicked men.

9 For he hath said, It profiteth a man nothing that he should delight himself with God.

10 Therefore hearken unto me, ye men of understanding: far be it from God, *that he should do* wickedness; and *from* the Almighty, *that he should commit* iniquity.

11 For the work of a man shall he render unto him, and cause every man to find according to *his* ways.

12 Yea, surely God will not do wickedly, neither will the Almighty pervert judgment.

13 Who hath given him a charge over the earth? or who hath disposed the whole world?

14 If he set his heart upon man, *if* he gather unto himself his spirit and his breath;

15 All flesh shall perish together, and man shall turn again unto dust.

16 If now *thou hast* understanding, hear this: hearken to the voice of my words.

17 Shall even he that hateth right govern? and wilt thou condemn him that is most just?

18 *Is it fit* to say to a king, *Thou art* wicked? *and* to princes, *Ye are* ungodly?

19 *How much less to him* that accepteth not the persons of princes, nor regardeth the rich more than the poor? for they all *are* the work of his hands.

20 In a moment shall they die, and the people shall be troubled at midnight, and pass away: and the mighty shall be taken away without hand.

21 For his eyes *are* upon the ways of man, and he seeth all his goings.

22 *There is* no darkness, nor shadow of death, where the workers of iniquity may hide themselves.

23 For he will not lay upon man more *than right;* that he should enter into judgment with God.

24 He shall break in pieces mighty men without number, and set others in their stead.

25 Therefore he knoweth their works, and he overturneth *them* in the night, so that they are destroyed.

26 He striketh them as wicked men in the open sight of others;

27 Because they turned back from him, and would not consider any of his ways:

28 So that they cause the cry of the poor to come unto him, and he heareth the cry of the afflicted.

29 When he giveth quietness, who then can make trouble? and when he hideth *his* face, who then can behold him? whether *it be done* against a nation, or against a man only:

30 That the hypocrite reign not, lest the people be ensnared.

31 Surely it is meet to be said unto God, I have borne *chastisement*, I will not offend *any more:*

32 *That which* I see not teach thou me: if I have done iniquity, I will do no more.

33 *Should it be* according to thy mind? he will recompense it, whether thou refuse, or whether thou choose; and not I: therefore speak what thou knowest. *God knows so much more than man's humble*

34 Let men of understanding tell me, and let a wise man hearken unto me.

35 Job hath spoken without knowledge, and his words *were* without wisdom.

36 My desire *is that* Job may be tried unto the end, because of *his* answers for wicked men.

37 For he addeth rebellion unto his sin, he clappeth *his hands* among us, and multiplieth his words against God. *he showed he p unchecked terribly as result*

CHAPTER 35.

1 Elihu spake moreover, and said,

2 Thinkest thou this to be right, *that* thou saidst, My righteousness *is* more than God's?

3 For thou saidst, What advantage will it be unto thee? *and,* What profit shall I have, *if I be cleansed* from my sin?

4 I will answer thee, and thy companions with thee.

5 Look unto the heavens, and see; and behold the clouds *which* are higher than thou.

6 If thou sinnest, what doest thou against him? or *if* thy transgressions be multiplied, what doest thou unto him?

7 If thou be righteous, what givest thou him? or what receiveth he of thine hand? *what good right? God ?! / what give him*

8 Thy wickedness *may hurt* a man as thou *art;* and thy righteousness *may profit* the son of man.

9 By reason of the multitude of oppressions they make *the oppressed* to cry: they cry out by reason of the arm of the mighty.

10 But none saith, Where *is* God my maker, who giveth songs in the night;

11 Who teacheth us more than the beasts of the earth, and maketh us wiser than the fowls of heaven?

12 There they cry, but none giveth answer, because of the pride of evil men.

13 Surely God will not hear vanity, neither will the Almighty regard it.

14 Although thou sayest thou shalt not see him, *yet* judgment *is* before him; therefore trust thou in him.

15 But now, because *it is* not *so,* he hath visited in his anger; yet he knoweth *it* not in great extremity:

16 Therefore doth Job open his mouth in vain; he multiplieth words without knowledge.

CHAPTER 36.

1 Elihu also proceeded, and said,

2 Suffer me a little, and I will shew thee that *I have* yet to speak on God's behalf.

3 I will fetch my knowledge from afar, and will ascribe righteousness to my Maker.

4 For truly my words *shall* not *be* false: he that is perfect in knowledge *is* with thee.

5 Behold, God *is* mighty, and despiseth not *any: he is* mighty in strength *and* wisdom.

6 He preserveth not the life of the wicked: but giveth right to the poor.

7 He withdraweth not his eyes from the righteous: but with kings *are they* on the throne; yea, he doth establish them for ever, and they are exalted.

8 And if *they be* bound in fetters, *and* be holden in cords of affliction;

9 Then he sheweth them their work, and their transgressions that they have exceeded.

10 He openeth also their ear to discipline, and commandeth that they return from iniquity.

11 If they obey and serve *him,* they shall spend their days in prosperity, and their years in pleasures.

12 But if they obey not, they shall perish by the sword, and they shall die without knowledge.

13 But the hypocrites in heart heap up wrath: they cry not when he bindeth them.

14 They die in youth, and their life *is* among the unclean.

15 He delivereth the poor in his affliction, and openeth their ears in oppression.

16 Even so would he have removed thee out of the strait *into* a broad place, where *there is* no straitness; and that which should be set on thy table *should be* full of fatness.

17 But thou hast fulfilled the judgment of the wicked: judgment and justice take hold *on thee*.

18 Because *there is* wrath, *beware* lest he take thee away with *his* stroke: then a great ransom cannot deliver thee.

19 Will he esteem thy riches? *no,* not gold, nor all the forces of strength.

20 Desire not the night, when people are cut off in their place.

21 Take heed, regard not iniquity: for this hast thou chosen rather than affliction.

22 Behold, God exalteth by his power: who teacheth like him?

23 Who hath enjoined him his way? or who can say, Thou hast wrought iniquity?

24 Remember that thou magnify his work, which men behold.

25 Every man may see it; man may behold *it* afar off.

26 Behold, God *is* great, and we know *him* not, neither can the number of his years be searched out.

27 For he maketh small the drops of water: they pour down rain according to the vapour thereof;

28 Which the clouds do drop *and* distil upon man abundantly.

29 Also can *any* understand the spreadings of the clouds, *or* the noise of his tabernacle?

30 Behold, he spreadeth his light upon it, and covereth the bottom of the sea.

31 For by them judgeth he the people; he giveth meat in abundance.

32 With clouds he covereth the light; and commandeth it *not to shine* by *the cloud* that cometh betwixt.

33 The noise thereof sheweth concerning it, the cattle also concerning the vapour.

CHAPTER 37.

1 At this also my heart trembleth, and is moved out of his place.

2 Hear attentively the noise of his voice, and the sound *that* goeth out of his mouth.

3 He directeth it under the whole heaven, and his lightning unto the ends of the earth.

4 After it a voice roareth: he thundereth with the voice of his excellency; and he will not stay them when his voice is heard.

5 God thundereth marvellously with his voice; great things doeth he, which we cannot comprehend.

6 For he saith to the snow, Be thou *on* the earth; likewise to the small rain, and to the great rain of his strength.

7 He sealeth up the hand of every man; that all men may know his work.

8 Then the beasts go into dens, and remain in their places.

9 Out of the south cometh the whirlwind: and cold out of the north.

10 By the breath of God frost is given: and the breadth of the waters is straitened.

11 Also by watering he wearieth the thick cloud: he scattereth his bright cloud:

12 And it is turned round about by his counsels: that they may do whatsoever he commandeth them upon the face of the world in the earth.

13 He causeth it to come, whether for correction, or for his land, or for mercy.

14 Hearken unto this, O Job: stand still, and consider the wondrous works of God.

15 Dost thou know when God disposed them, and caused the light of his cloud to shine?

16 Dost thou know the balancings of the clouds, the wondrous works of him which is perfect in knowledge?

17 How thy garments *are* warm, when he quieteth the earth by the south *wind?*

18 Hast thou with him spread out the sky, *which is* strong, *and* as a molten looking-glass?

19 Teach us what we shall say unto him; *for* we cannot order *our speech* by reason of darkness.

20 Shall it be told him that I speak? if a man speak, surely he shall be swallowed up.

21 And now *men* see not the bright light which *is* in the clouds: but the wind passeth, and cleanseth them.

22 Fair weather cometh out of the north: with God *is* terrible majesty.

23 *Touching* the Almighty, we cannot find him out: *he is* excellent in power, and in judgment, and in plenty of justice: he will not afflict.

24 Men do therefore fear him: he respecteth not any *that are* wise of heart.

CHAPTER 38. ⚹

1 Then the LORD answered Job out of the whirlwind, and said,

2 Who *is* this that darkeneth counsel by words without knowledge?

3 Gird up now thy loins like a man; for I will demand of thee, and answer thou me.

4 Where wast thou when I laid the foundations of the earth? declare, ⚹ if thou hast understanding.

5 Who hath laid the measures thereof, if thou knowest? or who hath stretched the line upon it?

6 Whereupon are the foundations thereof fastened? or who laid the corner stone thereof;

7 When the morning stars sang together, and all the sons of God shouted for joy?

8 Or *who* shut up the sea with doors, when it brake forth, *as if* it had issued out of the womb?

9 When I made the cloud the garment thereof, and thick darkness a swaddling band for it,

10 And brake up for it my decreed *place,* and set bars and doors,

11 And said, Hitherto shalt thou come, but no further: and here shall thy proud waves be stayed?

12 Hast thou commanded the morning since thy days; *and* caused the dayspring to know his place;

13 That it might take hold of the ends of the earth, that the wicked might be shaken out of it?

14 It is turned as clay *to* the seal; and they stand as a garment.

15 And from the wicked their light is withholden, and the high arm shall be broken.

16 Hast thou entered into the springs of the sea? or hast thou walked in the search of the depth?

17 Have the gates of death been opened unto thee? or hast thou seen the doors of the shadow of death?

18 Hast thou perceived the breadth of the earth? declare if thou knowest it all.

19 Where *is* the way *where* light dwelleth? and *as for* darkness, where *is* the place thereof,

20 That thou shouldest take it to the bound thereof, and that thou shouldest know the paths *to* the house thereof?

21 Knowest thou *it,* because thou wast then born? or *because* the number of thy days *is* great?

22 Hast thou entered into the treasures of the snow? or hast thou seen the treasures of the hail,

23 Which I have reserved against the time of trouble, against the day of battle and war?

24 By what way is the light parted, *which* scattereth the east wind upon the earth?

25 Who hath divided a watercourse for the overflowing of waters, or a way for the lightning of thunder;

26 To cause it to rain on the earth, *where* no man *is; on* the wilderness, wherein *there is* no man;

27 To satisfy the desolate and waste *ground;* and to cause the bud of the tender herb to spring forth?

28 Hath the rain a father? or who hath begotten the drops of dew?

29 Out of whose womb came the ice? and the hoary frost of heaven, who hath gendered it?

30 The waters are hid as *with* a stone, and the face of the deep is frozen.

31 Canst thou bind the sweet influences of Pleiades, or loose the bands of Orion?

32 Canst thou bring forth Mazzaroth in his season? or canst thou guide Arcturus with his sons?

33 Knowest thou the ordinances of heaven? canst thou set the dominion thereof in the earth?

34 Canst thou lift up thy voice to the clouds, that abundance of waters may cover thee?

35 Canst thou send lightnings, that they may go, and say unto thee, Here we *are?*

36 Who hath put wisdom in the inward parts? or who hath given understanding to the heart?

37 Who can number the clouds in wisdom? or who can stay the bottles of heaven,

38 When the dust groweth into hardness, and the clods cleave fast together?

39 Wilt thou hunt the prey for the lion? or fill the appetite of the young lions,

40 When they couch in *their* dens, *and* abide in the covert to lie in wait?

41 Who provideth for the raven his food? when his young ones cry unto God, they wander for lack of meat.

CHAPTER 39.

1 Knowest thou the time when the wild goats of the rock bring forth? *or* canst thou mark when the hinds do calve?

2 Canst thou number the months *that* they fulfil? or knowest thou the time when they bring forth?

3 They bow themselves, they bring forth their young ones, they cast out their sorrows.

4 Their young ones are in good liking, they grow up with corn; they go forth, and return not unto them.

5 Who hath sent out the wild ass free? or who hath loosed the bands of the wild ass?

6 Whose house I have made the wilderness, and the barren land his dwellings.

7 He scorneth the multitude of the city, neither regardeth he the crying of the driver.

8 The range of the mountains *is* his pasture, and he searcheth after every green thing.

9 Will the unicorn be willing to serve thee, or abide by thy crib?

10 Canst thou bind the unicorn with his band in the furrow? or will he harrow the valleys after thee?

11 Wilt thou trust him, because his strength *is* great? or wilt thou leave thy labour to him?

12 Wilt thou believe him, that he will bring home thy seed, and gather *it into* thy barn?

13 *Gavest thou* the goodly wings unto the peacocks? or wings and feathers unto the ostrich?

14 Which leaveth her eggs in the earth, and warmeth them in the dust,

15 And forgetteth that the foot may crush them, or that the wild beast may break them.

16 She is hardened against her young ones, as though *they were* not hers: her labour is in vain without fear;

17 Because God hath deprived her of wisdom, neither hath he imparted to her understanding.

18 What time she lifteth up herself on high, she scorneth the horse and his rider.

19 Hast thou given the horse strength? hast thou clothed his neck with thunder?

20 Canst thou make him afraid as a grasshopper? the glory of his nostrils *is* terrible.

21 He paweth in the valley, and rejoiceth in *his* strength: he goeth on to meet the armed men.

22 He mocketh at fear, and is not affrighted; neither turneth he back from the sword.

23 The quiver rattleth against him, the glittering spear and the shield.

24 He swalloweth the ground with fierceness and rage: neither believeth he that *it is* the sound of the trumpet.

25 He saith among the trumpets, Ha, ha! and he smelleth the battle afar off, the thunder of the captains, and the shouting.

26 Doth the hawk fly by thy wisdom, *and* stretch her wings toward the south?

27 Doth the eagle mount up at thy command, and make her nest on high?

28 She dwelleth and abideth on the rock, upon the crag of the rock, and the strong place.

29 From thence she seeketh the prey, *and* her eyes behold afar off.

30 Her young ones also suck up blood: and where the slain *are,* there *is* she.

CHAPTER 40.

1 Moreover the LORD answered Job, and said,

2 Shall he that contendeth with the Almighty instruct *him?* he that reproveth God, let him answer it.

3 ¶ Then Job answered the LORD, and said,

4 Behold, I am vile; what shall I answer thee? I will lay mine hand upon my mouth.

5 Once have I spoken; but I will not answer: yea, twice; but I will proceed no further.

6 ¶ Then answered the LORD unto Job out of the whirlwind, and said,

7 Gird up thy loins now like a man: I will demand of thee, and declare thou unto me.

8 Wilt thou also disannul my judgment? wilt thou condemn me, that thou mayest be righteous?

9 Hast thou an arm like God? or canst thou thunder with a voice like him?

10 Deck thyself now *with* majesty and excellency; and array thyself with glory and beauty.

11 Cast abroad the rage of thy wrath: and behold every one *that is* proud, and abase him.

12 Look on every one *that is* proud, *and* bring him low; and tread down the wicked in their place.

13 Hide them in the dust together; *and* bind their faces in secret.

14 Then will I also confess unto thee that thine own right hand can save thee.

15 ¶ Behold now behemoth, which I made with thee; he eateth grass as an ox.

16 Lo now, his strength *is* in his loins, and his force *is* in the navel of his belly.

17 He moveth his tail like a cedar: the sinews of his stones are wrapped together.

18 His bones *are as* strong pieces of brass; his bones *are* like bars of iron.

19 He *is* the chief of the ways of God: he that made him can make his sword to approach *unto him.*

20 Surely the mountains bring him forth food, where all the beasts of the field play.

21 He lieth under the shady trees, in the covert of the reed, and fens.

22 The shady trees cover him *with* their shadow; the willows of the brook compass him about.

23 Behold, he drinketh up a river, *and* hasteth not: he trusteth that he can draw up Jordan into his mouth.

24 He taketh it with his eyes: *his* nose pierceth through snares.

CHAPTER 41.

1 Canst thou draw out leviathan with a hook? or his tongue with a cord *which* thou lettest down?

2 Canst thou put a hook into his nose? or bore his jaw through with a thorn?

3 Will he make many supplications unto thee? will he speak soft *words* unto thee?

4 Will he make a covenant with thee? wilt thou take him for a servant for ever?

5 Wilt thou play with him as *with* a bird? or wilt thou bind him for thy maidens?

6 Shall the companions make a banquet of him? shall they part him among the merchants?

7 Canst thou fill his skin with barbed irons? or his head with fish spears?

8 Lay thine hand upon him, remember the battle, do no more.

9 Behold, the hope of him is in vain: shall not *one* be cast down even at the sight of him?

10 None *is so* fierce that dare stir him up: who then is able to stand before me?

11 Who hath prevented me, that I should repay *him? whatsoever is* under the whole heaven is mine.

12 I will not conceal his parts, nor his power, nor his comely proportion.

13 Who can discover the face of his garment? *or* who can come *to him* with his double bridle?

14 Who can open the doors of his face? his teeth *are* terrible round about.

15 *His* scales *are his* pride, shut up together *as with* a close seal.

16 One is so near to another, that no air can come between them.

17 They are joined one to another, they stick together, that they cannot be sundered.

18 By his neesings a light doth shine, and his eyes *are* like the eyelids of the morning.

19 Out of his mouth go burning lamps, *and* sparks of fire leap out.

20 Out of his nostrils goeth smoke, as *out* of a seething pot or caldron.

21 His breath kindleth coals, and a flame goeth out of his mouth.

22 In his neck remaineth strength, and sorrow is turned into joy before him.

23 The flakes of his flesh are joined together: they are firm in themselves; they cannot be moved.

24 His heart is as firm as a stone; yea, as hard as a piece of the nether *millstone.*

25 When he raiseth up himself, the mighty are afraid: by reason of breakings they purify themselves.

26 The sword of him that layeth at him cannot hold: the spear, the dart, nor the habergeon.

27 He esteemeth iron as straw, *and* brass as rotten wood.

28 The arrow cannot make him flee: sling stones are turned with him into stubble.

29 Darts are counted as stubble: he laugheth at the shaking of a spear.

30 Sharp stones *are* under him: he spreadeth sharp pointed things upon the mire.

31 He maketh the deep to boil like a pot: he maketh the sea like a pot of ointment.

32 He maketh a path to shine after him; *one* would think the deep *to be* hoary.

33 Upon earth there is not his like, who is made without fear.

34 He beholdeth all high *things:* he *is* a king over all the children of pride.

1 Then Job answered the LORD, and said,

2 I know that thou canst do every *thing,* and *that* no thought can be withholden from thee.

3 Who *is* he that hideth counsel without knowledge? therefore have I uttered that I understood not; things too wonderful for me, which I knew not.

4 Hear, I beseech thee, and I will speak: I will demand of thee, and declare thou unto me.

5 I have heard of thee by the hearing of the ear; but now mine eye seeth thee:

6 Wherefore I abhor *myself,* and repent in dust and ashes.

7 ¶ And it was *so,* that after the LORD had spoken these words unto Job, the LORD said to Eliphaz the Temanite, My wrath is kindled against thee, and against thy two friends: for ye have not spoken of me *the thing that is* right, as my servant Job *hath.*

8 Therefore take unto you now seven bullocks and seven rams, and go to my servant Job, and offer up for yourselves a burnt offering; and my servant Job shall pray for you: for him will I accept: lest I deal with you *after your* folly, in that ye have not spoken of me *the thing which is* right, like my servant Job.

9 So Eliphaz the Temanite and Bildad the Shuhite *and* Zophar the Naamathite went, and did according as the LORD commanded them: the LORD also accepted Job.

10 And the LORD turned the captivity of Job, when he prayed for his friends: also the LORD gave Job twice as much as he had before.

11 Then came there unto him all his brethren, and all his sisters, and all they that had been of his acquaintance before, and did eat bread with him in his house: and they bemoaned him, and comforted him over all the evil that the LORD had brought upon him: every man also gave him a piece of money, and every one an earring of gold.

12 So the LORD blessed the latter end of Job more than his beginning: for he had fourteen thousand sheep, and six thousand camels, and a thousand yoke of oxen, and a thousand she asses.

13 He had also seven sons and three daughters.

14 And he called the name of the first, Jemima; and the name of the second, Kezia; and the name of the third, Keren-happuch.

15 And in all the land were no women found *so* fair as the daughters of Job: and their father gave them inheritance among their brethren.

16 After this lived Job a hundred and forty years, and saw his sons, and his sons' sons, *even* four generations.

17 So Job died, *being* old and full of days.

BIBLIOGRAPHY ENTRY FOR RESEARCH PAPERS:

The Book of Job. King James version.

FOOTNOTES:

    * Job 1:6.
    * Job 1:6-12.

The first of these footnote examples cites a single verse (the sixth verse in the first chapter): the second cites a series of verses (the sixth to the twelfth in the first chapter). The same wording is used for all footnotes to books of the Bible, whether first or subsequent; such devices as *op. cit.* and *ibid.* are unnecessary.

BIBLICAL TEXT RELEVANT

TO

the Book of Job

||||||||||||||||||||||||||||||||||||||||||||||||||||||||||||||||||||||||||||||||||||||||||||||||||||||||||||||||||||||||||||||||||||||||||||||||||||||||||||||||||

The character of Job has not been interpreted through the use of the Old Testament Book of Job alone. Some of the following passages are referred to in the Introductions included in Part II of this collection. Similarly, the character of Satan has not been interpreted through the use of the Book of Job alone. For this reason, the account of the temptation of Jesus has been included, in the language of the Gospel according to Saint Matthew. A parallel passage is Luke 4:1-13.

The verses from Tobias are in the Douay version.

FROM THE BOOK OF TOBIAS, CHAPTER 2

10 Now it happened one day, that being wearied with burying, he came to his house, and cast himself down by the wall and slept,

11 And as he was sleeping, hot dung out of a swallow's nest fell upon his eyes, and he was made blind.

12 Now this trial the Lord therefore permitted to happen to him, that an example might be given to posterity of his patience, as also of holy Job.

13 For whereas he had always feared God from his infancy, and kept his commandments, he repined not against God because the evil of blindness had befallen him,

14 But continued immoveable in the fear of God, giving thanks to God all the days of his life.

15 For as the kings insulted over holy Job: so his relations and kinsmen mocked at his life, saying:

16 Where is thy hope, for which thou gavest alms, and buriedst the
dead?

FROM THE BOOK OF EZEKIEL, CHAPTER 14

12 The word of the LORD[1] came again to me, saying,

13 Son of man, when the land sinneth against me by trespassing grievously, then will I stretch out mine hand upon it, and will break the staff
of the bread thereof, and will send famine upon it, and will cut off man
and beast from it:

14 Though these three men, Noah, Daniel, and Job, were in it, they
should deliver *but* their own souls by their righteousness, saith the Lord
GOD.

FROM THE GOSPEL ACCORDING TO SAINT MATTHEW, CHAPTER 4

1 Then was Jesus led up of the spirit into the wilderness to be
tempted of the devil.

2 And when he had fasted forty days and forty nights, he was after-
ward an hungred.

3 And when the tempter came to him, he said, If thou be the Son of
God, command that these stones be made bread.

4 But he answered and said, It is written, Man shall not live by bread
alone, but by every word that proceedeth out of the mouth of God.

5 Then the devil taketh him up into the holy city, and setteth him on
a pinnacle of the temple,

6 And saith unto him, If thou be the Son of God, cast thyself down:
for it is written, He shall give his angels charge concerning thee: and in
their hands they shall bear thee up, lest at any time thou dash thy foot
against a stone.

---

[1] The name of the deity spelled in capitals is the Hebrew Tetragrammaton.

7 Jesus said unto him, It is written again, Thou shalt not tempt the Lord thy God.

8 Again, the devil taketh him up into an exceedingly high mountain, and sheweth him all the kingdoms of the world, and the glory of them;

9 And saith unto him, All these things will I give thee, if thou wilt fall down and worship me.

10 Then saith Jesus unto him, Get thee hence, Satan: for it is written, Thou shalt worship the Lord thy God, and him only shalt thou serve.

11 Then the devil leaveth him, and, behold, angels came and ministered unto him.

FROM THE GENERAL EPISTLE OF JAMES, CHAPTERS 1 AND 5

1:2 My brethren, count it all joy when ye fall into divers temptations;

3 Knowing *this,* that the trying of your faith worketh patience.

4 But let patience have *her* perfect work, that ye may be perfect and entire, wanting nothing.

1:12 Blessed *is* the man that endureth temptation: for when he is tried, he shall receive the crown of life, which the Lord hath promised to them that love him.

13 Let no man say when he is tempted, I am tempted of God: for God cannot be tempted with evil, neither tempteth he any man:

14 But every man is tempted, when he is drawn away of his own lust, and enticed.

5:7 Be patient therefore, brethren, unto the coming of the Lord. Behold, the husbandman waiteth for the precious fruit of the earth, and hath long patience for it, until he receive the early and latter rain.

8 Be ye also patient; stablish your hearts: for the coming of the Lord draweth nigh.

9 Grudge not one against another, brethren, lest ye be condemned: behold, the judge standeth before the door.

10 Take, my brethren, the prophets, who have spoken in the name of the Lord, for an example of suffering affliction, and of patience.

11 Behold, we count them happy which endure. Ye have heard of the patience of Job, and have seen the end of the Lord; that the Lord is very pitiful, and of tender mercy.

BIBLIOGRAPHY ENTRIES FOR RESEARCH PAPERS:

The Book of Tobias. Douay version.
The Book of Ezekiel. King James version.
The Gospel according to Saint Matthew. King James version.
The General Epistle of James. King James version.

FOOTNOTES:

    * Tobias 2:10-14.
    * Ezekiel 14:12-14.
    * Matthew 4:1-11.
    * James 1:2-4.
    * James 1:12-14.
    * James 5:7-11.

PART II

Introductions to the Study of the Book of Job

A. B. DAVIDSON

ON

the Book of Job

*Andrew Bruce Davidson (1831-1902) was one of the most emi-
nent Hebraists teaching in England during the last century. The
selection that follows is reprinted from pages xiii-xxix and lvi-
lxviii of* The Book of Job, with Notes, Introduction and Appendix
[*The Cambridge Bible for Schools and Colleges*] *(Cambridge:
University Press, 1889). The footnotes have been renumbered to
run in series in each chapter.*

CHAPTER II. THE NATURE

OF THE COMPOSITION.

UNDER the enquiry as to the nature of the composition two questions may
be embraced: (1) the question, Is the Book historical, or is it a pure creation of the mind of the writer? and (2) the question, To what class of
literature does the Poem belong? may we call it a drama, or assign it to any
understood class of writing?

On the former question various opinions have prevailed and are still
entertained. (1) The Book has been considered by some to be strictly historical, both in the narrative and poetical portions. (2) Others have maintained a view directly opposed, regarding the work as wholly unhistorical
and in all its parts a creation of the Poet's mind, and written with a didactic
purpose. (3) And a third class assumes a middle position between these
two extremes, considering that, though mainly a creation of the author's
own mind, the Poem reposes on a historical tradition, which the writer

adopted as suitable for his moral purpose, and the outline of which he has preserved.

Among the Jews in early times the Book appears to have been considered strictly historical. This was probably the opinion of Josephus, who, though he does not quote Job in any of his works[1], appears to embrace it among the thirteen prophetical books forming one division of his Canon[2]. The same was the generally received opinion among the Rabbinical writers. There were exceptions, however, even anterior to the age of the Talmud. A certain Rabbi Resh Lakish sitting in the school before Samuel bar Nachmani gave expression to the opinion that "a Job existed not, and was not created; he is a parable." To this Bar Nachmani replied, "Saith not the scripture, There was a man in the land of Uz, whose name was Job?" Resh Lakish answered, "But how is it then with that place 2 Sam. xii. 3, The poor man had nothing, save one little ewe-lamb which he had bought, &c.? What is that but a common similitude? and so Job is a simple parable." Bar Nachmani could but reply that not only the name of Job but that of his country was mentioned, an answer that probably did not go far to convince his opponent[3]. Resh Lakish was most likely not alone in his opinion, though his view appears to have given scandal to others. A later scholar, Rabbi Hai, the last who bore the title of Gaon (died 1037), maintains that the Talmudic passage reads, "Job existed not and was not created except in order to be a parable (or type, i.e. a model to the children of men), for that he actually existed the passage of scripture proves" (Ezek. xiv. 14)[4]. With this view Rashi agrees, and Ibn Ezra in the beginning of his commentary refers to the passage in Ezekiel as evidence that Job was a real person. Maimonides (died 1204) refers to the difference of opinion existing on the question whether Job was "created," that is, was a real person, and advances the opinion that "he is a parable meant to exhibit the views of mankind in regard to providence[5]." The historical existence of Job appears thus to have been to some extent an open question among the Jewish scholars, though probably up to recent times the belief that the Book was strictly historical continued to be the prevailing one.

The same appears to have been the general view of Christian writers up till the time of the Reformation, when Luther with his usual freedom and sound instincts expressed another opinion. The Reformer was far from denying the existence of Job himself, nor did he doubt that there was his-

[1] Bleek, Introduction, ii. p. 309. [2] *Contra Apion.* i. 18.
[3] Talmud, Baba Bathra, fol. 15, in Magnus, *Comm. on Job*, p. 298.
[4] Ewald and Dukes, *Beiträge*, ii. p. 166.
[5] *Moreh Nevochim*, part iii. ch. 22.

tory in the Book; it was history, however, poetically idealised. In his Table-
talk he expresses himself to that effect: "I hold the Book of Job to be real
history; but that everything so happened and was so done I do not believe,
but think that some ingenious, pious and learned man composed it as it is[6]."
Even during the preceding centuries some dissentient voices had let themselves be heard. More than a thousand years before Luther's day a much
freer judgment than his had been passed upon the Book by Theodore
bishop of Mopsuestia in Cilicia (died 428), a great name in the Antiochean
school of Exegesis, and a man who resembled Luther in some points, especially his free handling of the Canon, though he was without the Reformer's geniality and sound hermeneutical instincts. Theodore, equally
with Luther, believed in the existence of Job himself, but he regarded the
Book as a fiction, written in imitation of the dramas of the heathen by an
author familiar with the Greek wisdom, and nothing short of a slander
upon the godly Patriarch. The dialogue between the Almighty and Satan in
the Prologue gave offence to Theodore; but much worse was what he found
in the Epilogue, where according to the [Septuagint], from which alone the
bishop derived his knowledge of the Book, Job names his third daughter
"Horn of Amalthea". . . . Such a name must have been invented by the
author of the Book from love to the heathen mythology, for what could
an Idumean like Job know of Jupiter and Juno and the heathen gods? And
if he had known would he have bestowed upon a child given him in such
circumstances by God a name borrowed from the history of the deities of
Greece, or thought it any distinction to her? The whole cast of the Book,
however, gave offence to Theodore, as injurious to Job, a godly man whose
history was in every mouth and known far beyond the borders of Israel, and
whose fame the Prophet (Ezekiel) had further enhanced. Hence he condemned alike the irreverent language put into Job's mouth, the unjust
attacks made on him by his friends, and the injurious and insulting speeches
of Elihu. The whole, in his opinion, gave a distorted view of Job's character, detracted from the moral value of his history, and gave occasion to
blame not only the pious sufferer but also the Book[7]. Theodore, though not
without insight, as his rejection of the headings to the Psalms indicates,
was apt to be hasty and narrow in his judgments. His views naturally com-
pelled him to remove the Book of Job from the Canon. Though condemned
as a heretic after his death, the censure does not seem to have fallen upon
him for his critical opinions; he fell under suspicion from his exegetical

[6] *Works*, Walch, xxii. p. 2093. The passage appears to exist under various
forms.
[7] Kihn, *Theodor von Mopsuestia*, p. 68 *seq.*

writings, in which the seeds of the Nestorian heresy were detected, as some of the chief adherents of that error were his pupils and friends.

The comparatively free judgment of Luther regarding the Book naturally gave a handle to the Catholics which they were not slow to seize, and was not appreciated by Protestant writers in the succeeding ages. In his Commentary concerning the Antiquity, &c. of the History of Job (1670) Fred. Spanheim maintains that if Job be not history it is a fraud of the writer, *ni historia sit, fraus scriptoris.* Such a judgment would condemn as wilful frauds not only the majority of modern compositions but the dramas and parabolic writings of all ages. It is hard to see even how an exception could be made in favour of the parables of our Lord. Happily a juster conception of the nature of scripture now prevails, and we are prepared to find in it any form of literary composition which it is natural for men to employ. The view of Spanheim was shared by Albert Schultens, and defended by him in various writings, particularly in his great Commentary on Job (1736). Schultens was prepared to accept even the speeches of Job and his friends as literal transcriptions of what was said, appealing to the remarkable skill in improvising at all times exhibited by the Arabs and other Eastern peoples. The same opinion was maintained by J. H. Michaelis, professor at Halle (died 1738). According to him Job was descended from Nahor, and everything narrated in the Book is literal history, as taught in James v. 11—notwithstanding the Talmud, the Rabbins and Luther. The Patriarch lived between the death of Joseph and the Exodus; and the Book was written by Moses in Midian[8].

Yet even those times were not left without a witness in favour of different views. Grotius (died 1645) reproduced the opinion of Luther that the history in Job was poetically handled, *res vere gesta, sed poetice tractata.* And another Michaelis, John David, grand nephew of John Henry and the most distinguished of his name, professor of Oriental Languages at Goettingen (1750), expressed a judgment regarding Job very different from that of his older relative, and one which shews that critical opinions are scarcely subject to the law of heredity. According to him Job is a pure poetical creation: "I feel very little doubt that the subject of the poem is altogether fabulous, and designed to teach us that 'the rewards of virtue being in another state, it is very possible for the good to suffer afflictions in this life; but that, when it so happens, it is permitted by Providence for the wisest reasons, though they may not be obvious to

---

[8] *Adnotationes in Hagiog. Vet. Test. Libros,* vol. ii. p. 5 *seq.;* comp. Diestel, *Hist. of the O. T. in the Christian Church,* p. 417.

human eyes[9].' " The rise in this age of the critical spirit, which indeed had been partially awakened to life in the preceding century by the publication of Richard Simon's *Critical History of the Old Testament* (1678), naturally led to free discussion of the Book and prepared the way for the comparatively unanimous verdict regarding it of modern times. The history of this discussion need not be pursued here. There are perhaps few scholars now who consider the Book strictly historical in all its parts. The prevailing view, which is no doubt just, is that it reposes on a historical tradition, which the author has used and embellished, and made the vehicle for conveying the moral instruction which it was his object to teach. There are still some, however, who regard the Poem as wholly the creation of the author's invention; and this view is not confined to any critical school, for it numbers among its adherents men so widely apart from one another in their critical positions as Hengstenberg and Reuss.

That the Book is not literal history appears, (1) from the scenes in heaven exhibited in the Prologue (ch. i., ii.), and from the lengthy speeches put into the mouth of the Almighty (ch. xxxviii. *seq.*). (2) From the symbolical numbers three and seven used to describe Job's flocks and his children; and from the fact that his possessions are exactly doubled to him on his restoration, while he receives again seven sons and three daughters precisely as before. (3) From dramatic and ideal nature of the account of the incidence of Job's calamities (ch. i. 13 *seq.*), where the forces of nature and the violence of men alternate in bringing ruin upon him, and in each case only one escapes to tell the tidings. (4) From the nature of the debate between Job and his friends. Both the thought and the highly-wrought imagery of the speeches shew that, so far from possibly being the extemporaneous utterances of three or four persons casually brought together, they could only be the leisurely production of a writer of the highest genius.

On the other hand, it is probable that the Book is not wholly poetical invention, but that it reposes upon a historical tradition, some of the elements of which it has preserved. (1) The allusion of the prophet Ezekiel to Job, where he mentions Noah, Daniel and Job (ch. xiv. 14), appears to be to a tradition regarding him rather than to the present Book. The prophet's knowledge of Daniel must have been derived from hearsay, for the present book of that name cannot have been known to him. And the manner of his allusion suggests that the fame for piety of the three men whom he names was traditional and widely celebrated. (2) Pure liter-

---

[9] See his note in Gregory's *Trans. of Lowth on the Sacred Poetry of the Hebrews*, Lect. 32. Lowth himself (1753) adhered to the view of Luther and Grotius.

ary invention on so large a scale is scarcely to be looked for so early in Israel. Even considerably later the author of Ecclesiastes attaches his work to the name of Solomon; and later still the author of the book of Wisdom does the same. (3) The author of Job has a practical object in view. He does not occupy himself with discussing theories of providence that have only philosophic interest. He desires to influence the thought and the conduct of his generation. And this object would certainly have been better gained by making use of some history that lay slumbering in the popular mind, the lesson of which, when the story was awakened and set living before men, would commend itself more to the mind from not being altogether unfamiliar.

When we enquire, however, what elements of the Book really belong to the tradition, a definite answer can hardly be given. A tradition could scarcely exist which did not contain the name of the hero, and the name "Job" is no doubt historical. A mere name, however, could not be handed down without some circumstances connected with it; and we may assume that the outline of the tradition included Job's great prosperity, the unparalleled afflictions that befell him, and possibly also his restoration. Whether more was embraced may be uncertain. A vague report may have floated down that the mystery of Job's sufferings engaged the attention of the Wise of his country and formed the subject of discussion. It may also be argued that no reason can be suggested for making Uz the country of Job unless there was a tradition to that effect; and that the names of his friends, having nothing symbolical in them, must also belong to the story. This is doubtful. Eliphaz is an old Idumean name, and Teman was famed for wisdom; and "Eliphaz of Teman" might suggest literary combination. The other two names, not occurring again, do not awaken the same suspicions. They might be part of the tradition; but it is equally possible that they are names which the author had heard among the tribes outside of Israel. Even more liable to doubt is the episode of Job's wife, and the malady under which the Patriarch suffered. We can observe three threads running through the Book. One is that of the original tradition; another is the poetical embellishment of this tradition in the Prologue and Epilogue, Job being still treated as an individual. To this belong, for example, the names of Job's daughters, a touch of singular geniality from the hand of a writer who employs such sombre colours in the rest of the Book, and shewing that though crushed under the sorrows of his time he was not incapable on occasions of rising above them. In many places, however, Job appears to outgrow the limits of individual life; his mind and language reflect the situation and feelings of a class, or even of a people. He is the type either of the class of suffering righteous men, or of that afflicted, godly kernel of the people (Is. vi. 13), to which the nationality of Israel was felt still to adhere, and which is known in the Exile under the name of the Servant of the Lord. The history of this suffering remnant under the trials of the Exile has not been written; but that it had a history, marked by great trials and great faith, commanding the attention and kindling the enthusiasm of prophetic men, appears abundantly from the latter part of the Book of Isaiah. It is not easy to say with any certainty to which of these three elements any particular episode or point in the Book ought to be referred. The story of Job's wife may be thought to be just the kind of trait which the popular imagination would retain, or what is the same thing, which it would invent; the inference being that it should be considered part of the tradition. On the other hand, it is possible that her falling away under her sorrows may be but the reflection of the apostasy of many of the people under their trials, the sight of which put so severe a strain upon the faith of those still remaining true. And when we read in Deuteronomy, "The Lord will smite thee with the botch of Egypt . . . the Lord shall smite thee in the knees and in the legs, with a sore botch that cannot be healed, from the sole of thy foot unto the top of thy head" (ch. xxviii. 27, 35), and then in Job that Satan "went forth and smote Job with sore boils, from the sole of his foot unto his crown" (ch. ii. 7); and when further we find in Isaiah (ch. lii.—liii.) the Servant of the Lord represented as afflicted with leprous defilement, the impression can hardly be resisted that the three representations are connected together. Even in Deuteronomy the threat has ideal elements in it; in the Prophet the representation becomes wholly ideal; and the same is probably the case also in the Poet. In Deuteronomy the subject threatened is the people of Israel; in Isaiah the subject is the same, though with the modifications which history since the Exile had introduced, being the godly kernel of the people in captivity, to which the nationality and name and idea of Israel still belonged. And though we may not go so far as to say that Job is Israel or the Servant of the Lord under another name, it can scarcely be doubted that the sufferings of Israel are reflected in those of Job, and that the author designed that the people should see their own features in his, and from his history forecast the issue of their own. These are considerations that make us hesitate to regard Job's malady as part of the tradition regarding him, even though that view be supported by names so distinguished as that of Ewald.

The Book of Job has been called an Epic by some, by others a Drama, or more specifically a Tragedy, and by others still a Didactic Poem. That the Poem has a didactic purpose is unquestionable. It is equally evident that it contains many elements of the drama, such as dialogue, and a plot with an entanglement, development and solution. The action, however, is internal and mental, and the successive scenes are representations of the varying moods of a great soul struggling with the mysteries of its fate, rather than trying external situations. Much in the action may rightly be called tragic, but the happy conclusion is at variance with the conception of a proper tragedy. Any idea of representing his work on a stage never crossed the author's mind; his object was to instruct his countrymen and inspire them with hope in the future, and it is nothing to him that he detracts from the artistic effect of his work by revealing beforehand in the Prologue the real cause of Job's afflictions, the problem which is the subject of the dialogue, and the cause of the successive tragic phases of Job's feeling, in which the action chiefly consists. A more skilful artist according to western ideas might have concealed the explanation of Job's afflictions till the end, allowing it to transpire perhaps in the speeches of the Almighty. If he had allowed God to explain to Job the meaning of the sufferings with which He afflicted him, whatever addition to his literary renown he might have won, the author would have shewn himself much less wise and true as a religious teacher, for the experience of men tells them that they do not reach religious peace through the theoretical solution of the problems of providence; the theoretical solution comes later, if it comes at all, through their own reflection upon their history and the way in which God has led them. And if Job ever knew the meaning of his afflictions he learned it in this way, or he learned it through the teaching of some other man wiser than himself, as we have learned it from the author of this Book.

The Book of Job can hardly be named a drama, though it may justly be called dramatic. The dramatic movement is seen in the varying moods of Job's mind, and in his attitude towards Heaven. The dialogue with his friends partly occasions these moods and partly exhibits them. The progressive advance of the debate, however, is not to be considered as constituting the dramatic action. The commencement, culmination, and exhaustion of the debate do not run parallel with the rise, the increase and climax, and the composure of Job's perplexity of mind and war with Heaven. It is in the latter that the dramatic movement lies, in which the debate is a mere episode, for the state of Job's mind, twice signalised in the Prologue, lies before it, and the perfect composure to which he is brought by the divine speeches lies far behind it. Such a representation therefore as that of Delitzsch can hardly be accepted, who says "the Book of Job is substantially a drama, and one consisting of seven divisions: (1) ch. i.—iii., the opening; (2) ch. iv.—xiv., the first course of the controversy, or the beginning of entanglement; (3) ch. xv—xxi., the second course of the controversy, or the increasing entanglement; (4) ch. xxii.— xxvi., the third course of the controversy, or the increasing entanglement at its highest; (5) ch. xxvii.—xxxi., the transition from the entanglement to the unravelling; (6) ch. xxxviii.—xlii. 6, the consciousness of the unravelling; (7) ch. xlii. 7 *seq.,* the unravelling in outward reality".[10] This representation confuses two things quite distinct, and which do not move parallel to one another, namely the gradual thickening of the conflict between Job and his friends, ending at last in their directly imputing heinous offences to him, and the religious tension of Job's mind under his trials. It is not till the last round that the climax of the debate is reached (ch. xxii.), but the perplexity and violence of Job attain their height in the first round (ch. ix.—x.). Already in ch. xiv. the strain is considerably relieved, and it decreases still more in the speeches culminating in ch. xix., being wholly removed by the interposition of the Almighty.

CHAPTER III. THE IDEA AND PURPOSE OF THE BOOK.

THE Book of Job, as we possess it, conveys the impression that it is a finished and well-rounded composition. Its form, Prologue, Poem and Epilogue, suggests that the writer had a clear idea before his mind, which he started, developed and brought to an issue in a way satisfactory to himself. The Book has not the appearance of a mere fragment, or what might be called a contribution to the ventilation of a great problem, on which the author feels that he has something that may be useful to say, though nothing very definite or final; although this is a view of the Book that some have taken. The author being assumed, however, to have a distinct idea, this idea still remains so obscure, and the question, What is the purpose of the Book? has been answered in so many ways, that a judgment regarding it must be put forth with the greatest diffidence. Almost every theory that has been adopted has found itself in collision with one or more of the parts of which the Book now consists, and has been able

---

[10] *Trans.* i. p. 15.

to maintain itself only by sacrificing these parts upon its altar. With the exception of the speeches of Elihu there is no great division of the Book to which valid objections can be made, except on the ground that it does not harmonise with the idea of the Poem. The Elihu speeches occupy their right place between the discourses of the friends and the answer of Jehovah. They maintain the ground of the former, though they perhaps advance and refine upon it; and they prepare for the speeches of the Almighty, being the expression from the reverent religious consciousness of man of that which the Almighty expresses, if such language may be used, from His own consciousness of Himself. Whether, therefore, these speeches be held original or considered a later insertion they import no new principle into the Book, and may be neglected when the general conception of the Poem is being sought for. It seems fair, however, to take into account all the remaining divisions of the Book.

1. Though the author of the Book does not identify himself with Job, whom, on the contrary, he allows to assume positions which are extreme, and to utter language which is unbecoming, Job is undoubtedly the hero of the piece, and in the sentiments which he expresses and the history which he passes through combined, we may assume that we find the author himself speaking and teaching. Even the exaggerated sentiments which he allows Job to utter are not to be considered mere extravagances; they are not incoherencies which Job flings out in one line, and retracts in the next; they are excesses, which men under trials such as he suffered are driven to commit, and with which the author, amidst the questionings in regard to providence which the terrible sufferings of the time forced on men, was no doubt too familiar, if he had not himself perhaps fallen into them; and as we observe Job's mind gradually and naturally approaching the state in which he commits them, so we see it naturally recovering its balance and effecting a retreat. The discussion of the question of suffering between Job and his friends runs through a large part of the Book (ch. iv.—xxxi.), and in the direction which the author causes the discussion to take we may see revealed one of the chief didactic purposes of the Poem. When the three friends, the representatives of former theories of providence, are reduced to silence and driven off the ground by Job (ch. xxi., xxiii., xxiv.), we may assume that it was the author's purpose to discredit the ideas which they support. The theory that sin and suffering are in all cases connected, and that suffering cannot be where there has not been previous sin to account for the measure of it, is a theory of providence which cannot be harmonised with the facts observed in the world. Job traverses this theory on both its sides. He himself is an instance of suffering

apart from previous sin; and the world is full of examples of notoriously wicked men prospering and being free from trouble till the day of their death. Job offers no positive contribution to the doctrine of evil; his position is negative, and merely antagonistic to that of his friends. Now without doubt in all this he is the mouthpiece of the author of the Book.

Is it natural now to suppose that the author contemplated only this negative result? Would he have thought his task sufficiently fulfilled by pulling down the old fabric under which men had found friendly shelter and comfort for ages, and strewing its ruins on the ground, without supplying anything in its place, beyond perhaps the good advice which he is supposed to give in ch. xxxviii. *seq.?* So far as the rest of the Poem is concerned no further light is cast on the question. Job is left in darkness, and the divine speeches do not touch the point. The author exhibits Job reaching the conclusion that the righteousness of God, as he in common with his friends had always understood it, cannot be detected in the world as God actually rules it. And he exhibits the terrible perplexity into which the discovery threw him. To miss God's righteousness in the world was equivalent to missing it in God Himself, and Job's idea of God threatened to become wholly transformed. He is filled with terror and despair, and in his wrestling with the question he forces his way across the confines of this world, and first demands (ch. xiv., xvi.—xvii.) and then assures himself (ch. xix.) that, if not in his life here, beyond his life here, God's righteousness shall be manifested. By allowing Job to rise to such a thought the author probably meant to signalise it as one of the solutions to which men or himself had been forced. But the time was not yet come, and the darkness that overhung all beyond this life was too thick for men to find repose in this great thought. Hence Job is made to renew his demand for a solution in this life of the riddle of his sufferings (ch. xxxi. 35—37). Does then the author offer no solution? He does not, and no solution is offered to us, unless the Prologue supplies it. This passage, however, when naturally read, teaches that Job's sufferings were the trial of his righteousness. If then we bring the Prologue and the debate into combination we perceive that it was the author's purpose to widen men's views of God's providence, and to set before them a new view of suffering. With great skill he employs Job as his instrument to clear the ground of the old theories, and he himself brings forward in their place his new truth, that sufferings may befall the innocent, and be not a chastisement for their sins but a trial of their righteousness.

This may be considered one great purpose of the Book. This purpose, however, was in all probability no mere theoretical one, but subordinate to some wider practical design. No Hebrew writer is merely a poet or thinker. He is always a teacher. He has men before him in their relations to God. And it is not usually men in their individual relations, but as members of the family of Israel, the people of God. It is consequently scarcely to be doubted that the Book has a national scope. The author considered his new truth regarding the meaning of affliction as of national interest, and to be the truth needful to comfort and uphold the heart of his people in the circumstances in which they were.

2. But the direct teaching of the Book is only half its contents. It presents also a history—deep and inexplicable affliction, a great moral struggle, and a victory. Must not this history also be designed to teach? Is it not a kind of apologue the purpose of which is to inspire new conduct, new faith, and new hopes? In Job's sufferings undeserved and inexplicable to him, yet capable of an explanation most consistent with the goodness and faithfulness of God, and casting honour upon His faithful servants; in his despair bordering upon apostasy, at last overcome; in the higher knowledge of God and deeper humility to which he attained, and in the happy issue of his afflictions—in all these Israel may see itself, and from the sight take courage, and forecast its own history. What the author sets before his people is a new reading of their history, just as another new reading is set before them by the Prophet in the latter part of Isaiah. The two readings are different, but both speak to the heart of the people. Job, however, is scarcely to be considered Israel, under a feigned name. He is not Israel, though Israel may see itself and its history reflected in him. It is the elements of reality in his history common to him with Israel in affliction, common even to him with humanity as a whole, confined within the straitened limits set by its own ignorance; wounded to death by the mysterious sorrows of life; tortured by the uncertainty whether its cry finds an entrance into God's ear; alarmed and paralysed by the irreconcileable discrepancies which it discovers between its necessary thoughts of Him and its experience of Him in his providence; and faint with longing that it might come unto His place, and behold Him not girt with His majesty but in human form, as one looketh upon his fellow—it is these elements of truth that make the history of Job instructive to the people of Israel in the times of affliction when it was set before them, and to men in all ages[1].

The manifold theories of the purpose of the Book that have been put forth cannot be mentioned here. The construction of Ewald, brilliant and

---

[1] *Encyclop. Britann.* Art. "Job."

powerful though it be, has not been accepted by any other writer. Bleek, unable to find any single idea giving unity to the Book, contents himself with stating three truths which the Book appears to teach. (1) That even a pious man may be visited by God with heavy and manifold afflictions without it being necessary to consider these as punishment on account of special sinfulness and as a sign of special divine displeasure; that it is wrong to reproach such a one with his sufferings as if they had their origin in the divine displeasure, seeing they may rather be inflicted or permitted by God in order that his piety may be tried and find suitable opportunity of approving itself (Prologue). (2) That it is foolish presumption on the part of men to strive with God on account of the sufferings befalling them, and to seek to call Him to a reckoning, seeing no man is in a position to fathom the wisdom and counsel of God, man's true wisdom being rather to fear the Lord and eschew evil (Poem). (3) That Jehovah will at last surely have compassion on the pious sufferer and bless and glorify him, if he perseveres in his piety and cleaves to God, or if, having transgressed in his impatience, he repents (Epilogue)[2].

An attractive theory, in some degree a modification of that of Hupfeld and others, has more recently been put forth by some acute writers in Holland. It is to the effect that the author's design is merely to cast some light upon an acknowledged *problem*. The problem is the sufferings of the innocent—how they are to be reconciled with the righteousness of God. This problem is presented in the Prologue, which exhibits a righteous man subjected to great calamities. The Prologue gives no explanation of these calamities; Job's demeanour under his successive troubles merely shews his rectitude: here is undoubtedly a righteous man. In Job's person the problem is embodied and presented. Even the debate between him and his friends has no further effect or purpose than to set the problem in a strong light. The friends attempt an explanation of Job's afflictions, and if they had succeeded the problem would have been at an end. By their failure it is only seen more clearly to be a problem. Job contributes no solution, but his perplexity and despair and danger of apostasy shew how terrible the problem is. The whole point of the Book, therefore, lies in the divine speeches. All the rest is mere fact, or brilliant exhibition of a fact, that there is a terrible problem. The divine speeches do not solve the problem, for the problem is insoluble, but they give some satisfaction: they teach why it is insoluble, namely, because God and His ways are inscrutable. They say in effect two things: man cannot do what God does;

---

[2] Introduction, 4 Ed. p. 534, Trans. ii. p. 277.

and he cannot understand why He does what He does. And the conclusion is that nothing remains for him but acquiescence in the unsearchable providence of God. This is the great lesson which the author designed to teach his generation and mankind[3].

There are difficulties in the way of this theory. 1. Besides that the line of thought found in the Book is rather modern, the reader has difficulty in believing that the author's purpose went no further than to present a problem, pronounce it insoluble, and recommend resignation. 2. The reading of the Prologue which finds in its language no *explanation* of Job's afflictions is unnatural; and this reading of it leaves the function of the Satan entirely unexplained, who becomes a mere "evil spirit", in no connexion with the providence of God. 3. According to this theory Job's afflictions narrated in the Prologue, and these are all his afflictions, have merely the purpose of shewing his righteousness, which only comes to light by them. But in this way the author becomes guilty of a strange inconsequence. He meant to put forward the terrible problem of the sufferings of a righteous man; but these sufferings were necessary to shew that the man was righteous, and thus they are explained, and there is no problem. 4. The reading of the divine speeches is narrow and not natural. 5. The epilogue is an irrelevancy, or hangs in the loosest way to the Poem. It is added merely because "poetic justice" demanded it, or because the author "could not" let his hero die in misery, or for some similar sentimental reason.

[Chapter IV is not included here.]

CHAPTER V. THE AGE AND AUTHORSHIP OF JOB.

As there is nothing in the Book which fixes its date at once with certainty, a great variety of opinion has prevailed upon the question. There is almost no age of the world, from the patriarchal times down to the period after the Captivity, to which the Book has not been assigned. The juster conceptions, however, which now prevail regarding the history of Israel and the advancement in the ideas of the people, occasioned in part by the progress of this history and accompanying it, have considerably narrowed the limits

---

[3] Kuenen, *Onderzoek*, III. 125. More fully and genially Matthes in his excellent commentary, *Het Boek Job*, Deel I.

within which such a work can reasonably be supposed to have appeared. And a more careful examination of the allusions which, in spite of the antique and patriarchal colour thrown over the Book, may be detected in it to the circumstances and events of later times, has still further reduced the range of plausible conjecture. The Book can hardly have been written before the decline and fall of the northern kingdom, nor later than the return of the exiles of Judah from Babylon.

The question of the age of the Book must not be confounded with that of the age of Job himself. Job is represented as living in the patriarchal times. The author has skilfully thrown the colours of this age over his composition and preserved its general features. Thus, though employing the Israelitish name Jehovah himself, he allows the speakers in the Book to use the divine names peculiar to patriarchal times, as *El, Elóah* (Arab. *iláh,* God), *Almighty.* No doubt he betrays his own nationality, which he has no desire to conceal, by letting the name Jehovah escape two or three times from the mouth of Job, in current formulas into which the name entered (ch. i. 21, xii. 9; cf. xxviii. 28). Again, like the great forefathers of Israel, Job is represented as rich in cattle and flocks (ch. i. 3, xlii. 12, comp. Gen. xii. 16, xxiv. 35, xxvi. 13, xxx. 43). In like manner Job, the head of the family, is also its priest and offers sacrifice (ch. i. 5, xlii. 8; comp. Gen. xxii. 13, xxxi. 54), although in another place he is made to say of God that "He leadeth priests away stripped" (ch. xii. 19). Further, the sacrifice in use is the "burnt-offering", as in ancient times, before the more developed ritual in Israel came into operation. The great age, too, to which Job attains is patriarchal (ch. xlii. 16; comp. Gen. xxv. 7, xxxv. 28), though Bildad speaks as if the age of men of his day was greatly reduced in comparison with former standards (ch. viii. 8). The money referred to is the ancient *kesitah* (ch. xlii. 11; comp. Gen. xxxiii. 19, Josh. xxiv. 32); and the musical instruments named are the simple ones of primitive times (ch. xxi. 12, xxx. 31; comp. Gen. iv. 21, xxxi. 27). And, to mention no more, historical allusions of any directness are usually to the great events of the patriarchal world (ch. xviii. 15, xxii. 15 *seq.*).

Nevertheless, the features of the author's own time may often be perceived beneath this patriarchal disguise. Job betrays familiarity with the Law, or at least with social customs and moral ideas of Israel. When he refers in his speeches to pledges (ch. xxiv. 9, see on xxii. 6), and to landmarks (ch. xxiv. 2; comp. Deut. xix. 14, xxvii. 17, Hos. v. 10, Prov. xxii. 28, xxiii. 10); or when he alludes to judicial procedure against those guilty of special forms of idolatry, such as adoration of the sun and moon (ch. xxxi. 26, comp. Deut. iv. 19, xvii. 3—7, Ezek. viii. 16), or against

those guilty of adultery (ch. xxxi. 9, comp. Deut. xxii. 22), the voice is
the voice of a godly child of Israel although the hands may be those of a
son of Edom. The allusions to judicial practices found only as legal enactments in Deuteronomy are remarkable. There is even verbal coincidence in
the two passages, ch. xxxi. 26 and Deut. iv. 19; and those who consider
Deuteronomy a late book might feel justified in fixing the eighteenth year
of Josiah (620) as the point above which the composition of Job cannot
be carried[1]. At all events there is abundant evidence to shew that the age
assigned to Job and the age of the author of the Book lie widely apart. The
statements of Renan that "not one allusion is made to Mosaic customs,
nor to beliefs peculiar to the Jews," that "the atmosphere of the Book is
not more specially Hebrew than Idumean or Ishmaelite," and that "in a
very real sense these precious pages have transmitted to us an echo of the
ancient wisdom of Teman[2]", are exaggerations and part of the romance
with which this brilliant writer delights to invest the sacred subjects which
he treats. The author of Job is a true Israelite, and betrays himself to be so
at every turn, however wide his sympathies be with the life of other peoples,
and however great his power of reanimating the past. The idea that the
Poem is a production of the Desert, written in another tongue and translated into Hebrew, is more than destitute of a shadow of probability, it is
absurd. The Book is the genuine outcome of the religious life and thought
of Israel, the product of a religious knowledge and experience possible
among no other people.

The date of such a Book as Job, which deals only with religious ideas
and general questions of providence, and contains no direct allusions to
the events of history, can be fixed only approximately. Any conclusion on
the subject can be reached only by an induction founded on matters that
do not afford perfect certainty, such as the comparative development of
certain moral ideas in different ages; the pressing claims of certain problems
for solution at particular epochs of the history of the people; points of
contact which the Book may offer with other writings the age of which
may with more certainty be determined; and indirect allusions which may
betray a condition of the national life known to be that of a particular period of its history. These are all lines of reasoning more or less precarious.
Only when several of them unite in pointing to the same result can we feel
much confidence in its justness. The comparison of passages in different
books is apt to be rather barren of fruit. There is such a general unity of

[1] Comp. Job ii. 7 with Deut. xxviii. 35; v. 14 with xxviii. 29; v. 18 with xxxii.
39; vii. 4 with xxviii. 67; viii. 8 with iv. 32; xx. 4 with iv. 32.
[2] *Le Livre de Job, Étude*, p. 16, 27.

thought and language pervading the books of Scripture that similar expressions or even identical phraseology in two writers cannot in all cases be held evidence of literary dependence. The writers of Scripture are for the most part men of the people and speak the popular language, and the same phrase in several books may be original in them all. And even when we cannot escape the conviction that there is dependence, it is usually very difficult to decide which is the original and which the imitator. The argument, on the other hand, founded on the connexion of the thought and literature of Israel with the successive developments of its history, though still a delicate one, is more solid. The mind of the people was intensely national, and the spirit of its literature is for the most part national rather than individual. This is no doubt less true of the poetry and the wisdom. But the truth holds even of a very great part of the poetry, it reflects the consciousness of the nation; and it holds of the wisdom to this extent, that the vicissitudes of the people's history suggested the successive aspects under which the questions reflected on by the Wise presented themselves to their minds.

The opinion expressed in the Talmud, and followed by some writers, that Moses was the author of Job is unworthy of any attention. The thin antique colour of the Book suggested to uncritical minds that it was an ancient composition, and such minds, impatient of uncertainty, everywhere seek to satisfy themselves by ascribing any great anonymous work to some well-known name. But the conjecture is more than improbable. It is the part of the founder of a constitution like Moses to project principles and ideas which are of general truth, and to sketch an outline which succeeding ages may be left to fill up; it is scarcely his part to subject the general principles upon which his constitution is founded to questionings which would undermine them, or to introduce alongside of them the modifications which future generations or society in altered conditions may find needful to make on them. Neither the author of the Law which describes God as "visiting the iniquity of the fathers upon the children unto the third and fourth generation" (Ex. xx. 5), nor any of his contemporaries was likely to have written the words of Job (ch. xxi. 19),

> God (say ye) layeth up his iniquity for his children. —
> Let Him recompense it unto himself that he may know it;
> Let his own eyes see his destruction.

The principle enunciated in the Law may have raised difficulties in some minds at an early time, but the first expression of dissatisfaction with it in any composition to which we can assign a date appears in the prophecies of Jeremiah (ch. xxxi. 29; comp. Ezek. xviii. 2).

The centuries after the Exodus down to the end of the reign of David, times of stirring enterprize and warfare and conquest, were not favourable for the production of a work of deep reflection like Job. Nor, in spite of the repeated humiliations to which the nation was subjected in those ages, can the spirit of the people ever have sunk to that state of exhaustion and despair which appears in this Book. There is evidence too in the Poem that the author was familiar with some of the writings usually ascribed to the Davidic age. There is a distorted reflection of the ideas of Ps. viii. in the passage ch. vii. 17, which is scarcely due to coincidence.

The earliest period to which the Book can be assigned with any propriety is the age of Solomon. A good many general considerations suggest this period. Unless history and tradition are to be alike discredited (1 Kings iv. 29 *seq.*) a strong current of thought sprang up in this age in the direction of reflexion upon human life and the laws of man's well-being, upon God and the ways in which His providence rules the destinies of men. These are the questions which, in a particular form, are discussed in Job. Again, it was at this period that Israel became to some extent a commercial people, and entered into relations with distant lands, with Egypt, the farther East and even the West; and these relations might seem reflected in many allusions in the Book, the author of which is familiar with foreign countries and their products, with the arts and customs of many strange peoples, and draws his illustrations from many distant sources. These considerations have led a number of writers of distinction, such as Delitzsch, to conclude that the Book is a production of this age; and such appears to have been the view of Luther.

If, however, we examine the Book of Proverbs, much in which may be referred to the age of Solomon, particularly the sayings in ch. x.—xxii., though much even in this division may be later, we find scarcely a trace of the problems and questionings that fill the Book of Job. The same general subjects are treated in both books, but in Job they have entered upon a new phase. In Proverbs the teaching on God's providence is still entirely positive. The law stated with such beauty and simplicity in Ps. i., that it is well with the righteous and ill with the wicked, is insisted on in a thousand forms, but not once subjected to doubt. In the settled, well-ordered life of Israel in this peaceful time the general principles of man's well-being were receiving their brightest illustration, and it was the delight of the wise to recognise them and give them expression in compressed and polished aphorisms. Such problems as burn in the pages of Job, the miseries of the just, the prosperity and peaceful end of the ungodly, appear unknown. They were not likely to attract men's attention at such a time. Only later, when the state began to stagger under the blows which it received from without, and when through revolution and civil discord at home great and unmerited sufferings befell the best citizens in the state, would such problems arise, or at least present themselves with an urgency which demanded some solution. It is only in those parts of Proverbs which are later than the great central division that we find allusion to disquietude occasioned to the righteous by the prosperity of the ungodly, and even these references are slight; the difficulty hardly engages a moment's attention (Prov. iii. 11, 31, xxiii. 17 *seq.;* xxiv. 19).

The relation of Job to most parts of the Book of Proverbs is close[3]. The elements of that Book probably belong to different ages. Part of it at least was not published earlier than the days of Hezekiah (ch. xxv. *seq.*) ; and the first division, ch. i.—ix., though its date may be difficult to determine with exactness, can hardly be earlier than this age, if so early. But even this division as well as the central portion, ch. x.—xxii., appears to be anterior to the Book of Job. A pair of instances may suffice as examples. In Prov. xiii. 9 we read, "the lamp of the wicked shall be put out"; and the same formula appears again in another division, ch. xxiv. 20. The principle is stated in all its generality, and nowhere modified in the Book. In this form it continues to be upheld by Bildad, the representative in Job of theories of Providence which the author considers cannot any longer be maintained (ch. xviii. 6). Job, therefore, comes clean athwart it with his demand (ch. xxi. 17),

> How often is the lamp of the wicked put out?
> And how often cometh their destruction upon them?

Again in Prov. i.—ix. Wisdom earnestly presses herself upon men: she loves them that love her. Even when she rises to the highest conception of herself as architect of the world she still offers herself to men and may be embraced by them (ch. viii. 32). But the speaker in Job xxviii. despairs of wisdom: it can nowhere be found, neither in the land of the living nor in the place of the dead, neither by man nor by any creature. The divine thought in creation, the world-plan, effectuating itself in nature and human life, lies beyond the intellectual reach of man. Two such opposing representations can hardly be contemporaneous; that in Job shews an approach

---

[3] Comp. Job v. 17 with Prov. iii. 11; xi. 8 with ix. 18; xv. 7 with viii. 25; xviii. 6 and xxi. 17 with xiii. 9 and xxiv. 20; xxii. 28 with iv. 18; xxviii. 18 with iii. 14 and viii. 11; xxviii. 28 with i. 7; xxxviii. 10 with viii. 29. . . .

towards the position taken by the Preacher (Eccles. iii. 11), and is no doubt the later of the two. Great difficulty, it is true, has been felt in fitting ch. xxviii. into the Book, and it may belong to a time somewhat further down. But even in Job xv. 8 *seq.* the personification of Wisdom in Prov. viii. seems alluded to, or at least there is allusion to personifications similar. Such personifications mark the highest point to which Hebrew thought on the world rose, and cannot belong to an early age. Wisdom, pausing in the work of expounding providence and the laws of human happiness, which she had long instinctively pursued with self-forgetful fascination in her task, becomes self-conscious, and, turning her eyes upon herself, displays her own graces and beauty before the eyes of men. They who attain to her and live as she directs attain to the thought of God Himself and fulfil His purpose; human thought and life coincides with or even coalesces in the divine thought and will. In Proverbs the fear of the Lord is the beginning of wisdom, in Job xxviii. it is all the wisdom possible to man.

The conclusion to which the remarks just made would lead is that the Book of Job cannot be assigned to an earlier date than the 7th century. The coincidences between the Book and the earlier prophets are not very conclusive, though perhaps they confirm the inference just drawn. The phraseology in several passages is so similar to that in Amos that some have concluded that the author like this prophet was a native of the south of Judah[4]; but the similarities hardly justify any inference as to the priority of either book. The same may be said of most of the coincidences between Job and the prophets Hosea and Isaiah. The passage Is. xix. 5, however, compared with Job xiv. 11, perhaps affords some evidence of the priority of Isaiah. In Job the verse reads,

The waters fail from the sea,
And the stream decayeth and drieth up;

and in Isaiah, "and the waters shall fail from the sea, and the stream shall decay and dry up." In the prophet the "sea" is the Nile, and the "stream" the same or its larger branches, and the verse is closely connected with the context, which contains a threat against Egypt. In Job the term "sea" is used of any inland water, and the words are made to express a general fact of experience, which finds a parallel in the complete extinction of the life of man. In Isaiah the term rendered "fail" is somewhat unusual, while in Job there stands for "fail" a word which, though not greatly more in use in

---

[4] Stickel, *Hiob,* p. 263. Comp. Job ix. 8 with Am. iv. 13; ix. 9 with v. 8; xii. 15 with ix. 6; xviii. 16 with ii. 9; xxx. 31 with viii. 10.

the Bible, would certainly be much more common in the mouths of the people in the later period of their history[5].

The most weighty arguments, however, for assigning the Book to an age not earlier than the 7th century are the two facts, closely related together, first, that questions of providence have entered upon a new phase: its laws are no longer calmly expounded but subjected to doubt; from being principles securely acquiesced in they have become problems painfully agitated; and secondly, that a condition of great disorder and misery forms the background of the Poem. These two circumstances naturally go together, and they both point to the same comparatively late period. Even in some of the Psalms which treat of these questions the "ungodly" oppressor, whose felicity occasions disquietude to the religious mind (comp. Job xii. 6), is probably the heathen conqueror. But these shorter pieces in all likelihood preceded in time the more elaborate treatment to which such problems are subjected in Job. But the situation reflected in these pieces and in Job alike is one of suffering and despondency. When we read such words as, "Wherefore giveth He life to the bitter in soul, who long for death and it cometh not, and search for it more than for hid treasures?" (ch. iii. 20); "Is there not a time of hard service to man upon the earth? are not his days also like the days of an hireling?" (ch. vii. 1); "The earth is given into the hand of the wicked; he covereth the faces of the judges thereof" (ch. ix. 24); "The tabernacles of robbers prosper, and they that provoke God are secure, they who carry their god in their hand" (ch. xii. 6; cf. Hab. i. 11, 16); "Out of the city the dying groan, and the soul of the wounded crieth out, yet God regardeth not the wrong" (ch. xxiv. 12)—we feel that the points in the picture are too distinct and in too full relief to be the mere reflection of the gloom that hangs over the mind of the sufferer even in an ordinary condition of society. The passage ch. xii. 17 *seq.* is remarkable,

> He leadeth counsellers away stripped,
> And maketh the judges fools.
> He looseth the bond of kings,
> And girdeth their loins with a girdle.
> He leadeth priests away stripped,
> And overthroweth the long-established caste, &c.

Such a passage might have been written by an eyewitness of the captivity, or as Job says that he learned such details from "ancient" men (ch. xii. 12), it might have been written by one who had heard the harrowing

---

[5] Other similarities are Job xii. 24 with Is. xix. 13; xvii. 12 with v. 20.

events of that time described by one who had himself seen them. Behind
the author's time there probably lay some great public calamity, which reduced multitudes of men to a wretchedness more unendurable than death,
and forced the questions of evil and the righteousness of God upon men's
minds with an urgency that could not be resisted. Such a calamity could
be nothing short of deportation or exile. The question remains whether
it was the exile of the northern nation or of Judah.

Some writers, as Hitzig, think that the author of Job, from his bold
handling of questions of providence, must have belonged to the northern
kingdom, where the attitude of men's minds towards religion was freer.
There is not, perhaps, much in this; but some of the ablest writers on the
Book, such as Ewald, connect it more or less closely with the fall of the
northern state. This judgment might be acquiesced in at once were there
not several things which suggest the question whether the Book may not
rather reflect the circumstances of the Babylonian Captivity. These points
briefly are: (1) the extremely developed form both of the morality and the
doctrine of God in the Book; (2) the points of contact which it presents
with Jeremiah and the ideas of his age; and (3) the strange parallel existing between Job and the "Servant of the Lord" in the second part of
Isaiah.

The first point can hardly be drawn out in detail, but the teaching of
Eliphaz regarding human nature (ch. iv. 17 *seq.*) and the inwardness
of the moral conceptions of Job (ch. xxxi.) are very surprising. The doctrine of God is much the same in principle throughout the whole Old
Testament, the later writers differing from the earlier more in the breadth
with which they express the common conceptions. In Job these conceptions
are expressed with a breadth and loftiness without parallel, except in the
second part of Isaiah and some of the later psalms (e.g. Ps. cxxxix.). It
is true it is chiefly what might be called the natural attributes of God that
are dwelt upon, and this has created in some minds the feeling that the
God of the Book of Job is not the God of the Old Testament[6]. He is certainly without some of the attributes ascribed to Him in such prophets as
Hosea and the later chapters of Isaiah. He is God and not man—so entirely not man that He seems not altogether God. The author's conception
of God is austere and lofty, and we readily understand how its features
in a particular light cast that spectral shadow before Job's eye which he
calls God and which he is in danger of renouncing.

Apart from the Psalms, the date of which is uncertain, the problems

---

[6] Luzzatto, quoted in Del.

discussed in Job first shew themselves in the prophets of the Chaldean age. Jeremiah says, "Let me talk with thee of thy judgments: wherefore doth the way of the wicked prosper? wherefore are all they happy that deal very treacherously?" (ch. xii. 1; cf. Hab. i. 13 *seq.*). Similarly, the other question of visiting the sins of the fathers upon the children occupies the minds of the people (Jer. xxxi. 29; Ezek. xviii.). The history of the nation and its sufferings forced these questions on the attention, and there is a certain probability that a Book like Job devoted to their discussion is the creation of this time. The parallels in thought and language between Job and Jeremiah are numerous, but they strike different minds very differently. Most writers have felt that Job iii. and Jer. xx. 14 *seq.* are not altogether independent of one another, but the question of priority is difficult to settle. The argument that the passage in Job is fresher, more vivid and powerful, and therefore the original has little force. The author of Job was certainly a greater literary artist than Jeremiah, as Shakespeare was superior to the earlier dramatists whose materials he used, but the possible analogy neutralizes the argument for priority. If the author of Job used Is. xix. 5, as is probable, he has recast some of the expressions into the more strict poetical form, and he may have dealt with the language of the other prophet in the same way. Job iii. is highly elaborate and finished, while the impression which the passage in Jeremiah makes on the reader, just on account of its disjointed character and defect in literary grace, is that it is independent. The strong positive statements in Ezekiel that "the soul that sinneth shall die", and that the children shall no more be visited for their fathers' iniquity, might seem to imply that the question had advanced a stage beyond that of debate in which it appears in Job. This is less certain, because it is the peculiarity of the Book of Job that all its new truths are presented through the medium of controversial dialogue[7].

The affinity of the Book of Job to Is. ch. xl. *seq.* is remarkable, and appears in two points, coincidences of expression and thought, and the parallel between the figure of Job and that of the Servant of the Lord. Thus the same lofty conception of God is expressed in both in identical words, *who spreadeth out the heavens alone* (ch. ix. 8, Is. xliv. 24; cf. xlv. 12). Again comp. ch. xxvi. 12—13, "He quelleth the sea with His power, and by His understanding He smiteth through Rahab," with Is. li. 9, "Art thou not it which hath cut Rahab and pierced the dragon?" Compare also Job xiii. 28 with Is. l.9; xv. 35 with lix. 4; xxx. 21 with lxiii. 10. These similar-

---

[7] Comp. Job iii. with Jer. xx. 14; vi. 15 with xv. 18; ix. 19 with xlix. 19 (Is. l. 8); xii. 4 with xx. 7; xix. 23 with xvii. 1; Job xix. 18 with Lam. iii. 15; xvi. 9 with iii. 46; xvi. 13 with iii. 12; xix. 8 with iii. 7; xxx. 9 with iii. 14.

ities of phraseology might be due to dependence of the one writer upon the other. There are, however, many conceptions common to the two writers not expressed in the same phraseology, and the more probable explanation is that they lived surrounded by the same atmosphere of thought.

The similarities between the figure of Job and that of the Servant are numerous and striking. Both are innocent sufferers—"my servant Job, a perfect and upright man" (Job i. 8), "my righteous servant" (Is. liii. 11); both are afflicted in a way that strikes horror into the beholders, and causes them to deem them smitten of God (Is. lii. 14, liii. 4, Job *passim*); both are forsaken of men and subjected to mockery and spitting (Job xix. 4 *seq.*, xvi. 10, xxx. 9 *seq.*; Is. l. 6, liii. 3); both are restored and glorified and receive "double", as they both continued faithful, assured that He was near that should justify them (Job xiii. 18, xvi. 19, xix. 25; Is. l. 8). The points of agreement might be greatly multiplied[8], and, notwithstanding the important differences in the two representations, they suggest some relation between the two figures. The difficulty is to ascertain whether the relation be one of similarity merely or of identity. If Job were the type of the righteous individual sufferer or of the class of individuals, and the servant the suffering righteous Israel, that is, the godly remnant to which the nationality and name belonged, seeing these two subjects are virtually the same under different conceptions, the author of the one picture might have transferred some features from the canvas of his predecessor to his own[9]. The probability is as great that the two authors worked up common conceptions into independent creations; and there are many parts of Job that appear to reflect national feeling and conditions, though of course the author could not allow the formal conception of the nation to appear.

The question enters a region here which is not that of argument but of impressions; but upon the whole probabilities point to the age of the captivity of Judah as that to which the Book belongs.

As to the Author of the Book we are in complete ignorance. He has been supposed to be Job himself, Elihu, Moses, Solomon, Heman the Ezrahite, author of Ps. lxxxviii., Isaiah, Hezekiah, author of the hymn Is. xxxviii., Baruch the friend of Jeremiah, and who not? There are some minds that cannot put up with uncertainty, and are under the necessity of

---

[8] See Dr. Cheyne's interesting Essay, *Isaiah*, II. p. 244. Kuenen has an exhaustive paper on the subject in the *Theolog. Tijds.*, 1873.

[9] This is the later opinion of Kuenen, who considers that the collective or national representation in Isaiah has served in some respects as the model of the individual portrait in Job. In this case Job would be later than the Restoration. It is difficult, however, to believe that the solution of the problem of suffering innocence given in Job could be posterior to the more profound solution found in the prophet.

deluding themselves into quietude by fixing on some known name. There are others to whom it is a comfort to think that in this omniscient age a few things still remain mysterious. Uncertainty is to them more suggestive than exact knowledge. No literature has so many great anonymous works as that of Israel. The religious life of this people was at certain periods very intense, and at these periods the spiritual energy of the nation expressed itself almost impersonally, through men who forgot themselves and were speedily forgotten in name by others.

BIBLIOGRAPHY ENTRY FOR RESEARCH PAPERS:

Davidson, Andrew Bruce. Introduction to *The Book of Job, with Notes, Introduction and Appendix* (The Cambridge Bible for Schools and Colleges). Cambridge: University Press, 1889. Chapters II, III, V reprinted in *The Voice out of the Whirlwind: The Book of Job,* ed. Ralph E. Hone. San Francisco, 1960.

FIRST FOOTNOTE:

* Andrew Bruce Davidson, Introduction to *The Book of Job, with Notes, Introduction and Appendix* [The Cambridge Bible for Schools and Colleges] (Cambridge: University Press, 1889), Chapters II, III, V reprinted in *The Voice out of the Whirlwind: The Book of Job,* ed. Ralph E. Hone (San Francisco, 1960), pages 62-86.

SUBSEQUENT FOOTNOTES:

* Davidson, *op. cit., The Voice,* p. ■.
* Davidson, Introduction, *The Voice,* p. ■.
* Davidson, *The Voice,* p. ■.

In place of *"The Voice,"* "ed. Hone" may be used in these subsequent-footnote forms.

A. B. DAVIDSON AND C. H. TOY

ON

the Book of Job

Andrew Bruce Davidson (1831-1902), co-author of this selection, was also the editor of the Book of Job in the Cambridge Bible for Schools and Colleges. Crawford Howell Toy (1836-1919) was a distinguished American scholar of Hebrew. This selection is their article "Job," from the Encyclopaedia Britannica, *Eleventh Edition (1911).*

JOB

THE Book of Job (Heb. אִיּוֹב *'Iyyob*, Gr. 'Ιώβ), in the Bible, the most splendid creation of Hebrew poetry, is so called from the name of the man whose history and afflictions and sayings form the theme of it.

CONTENTS

As it now lies before us it consists of five parts. 1. The prologue, in prose, chr. i.—ii., describes in rapid and dramatic steps the history of this man, his prosperity and greatness corresponding to his godliness; then how his life is drawn in under the operation of the sifting providence of God, through the suspicion suggested by the Satan, the minister of this aspect of God's providence, that his godliness is selfish and only the natural return for unexampled prosperity, and the insinuation that if stripped of his prosperity he will curse God to His face. These suspicions bring down two severe calamities on Job, one depriving him of children and possessions alike, and the other throwing the man himself under a painful malady. In spite of these afflictions Job retains his integrity and ascribes no wrong to God. Then is described the advent of Job's three friends—Eliphaz the Temanite, Bildad the Shuhite, and Zophar the Naamathite—who, having heard of Job's calamities, come to condole with him. 2. The body of the book, in poetry, ch. iii.—xxxi., contains a series of speeches in which the problem of Job's afflictions and the relation of external evil to the righteousness of God and the conduct of men are brilliantly discussed. This part, after Job's passionate outburst in ch. iii., is divided into three cycles, each containing six speeches, one by each of the friends, and three by Job, one in reply to each of theirs (ch. iv.—xiv.; xv.—xxi.; xxii.—xxxi.), although in the last cycle the third speaker Zophar fails to answer (unless his answer is to be found in ch. xxvii.). Job, having driven his opponents from the field, carries his reply through a series of discourses in which he dwells in pathetic words upon his early prosperity, contrasting with it his present humiliation, and ends with a solemn repudiation of all the offences that might be suggested against him, and a challenge to God to appear and put His hand to the charge which He had against him and for which He afflicted him. 3. Elihu, the representative of a younger generation, who has been a silent observer of the debate, intervenes to express his dissatisfaction with the manner in which both Job and his friends conducted the cause, and offers what is in some respects a new solution of the question (xxxii.—xxxvii.). 4. In answer to Job's repeated demands that God would appear and solve the riddle of his life, the Lord answers Job out of the whirlwind. The divine speaker does not condescend to refer to Job's individual problem, but in a series of ironical interrogations asks him, as he thinks himself capable of fathoming all things, to expound the mysteries of the origin and subsistence of the world, the phenomena of the atmosphere, the instincts of the creatures that inhabit the desert, and, as he judges God's conduct of the world amiss, invites him to seize the reins, gird himself with the thunder and quell the rebellious forces of evil in the universe (xxxviii.—xlii. 6). Job is humbled and abashed, lays his hand upon his mouth, and repents his hasty words in dust and ashes. No solution of his problem is vouchsafed; but God Himself effects that which neither the man's own thoughts of God nor the representations of the friends could accomplish: he had heard of him with the hearing of the ear without effect; but now his eye sees Him. This is the profoundest religious deep in the book. 5. The epilogue, in prose, xlii. 7—17, describes Job's restoration to a prosperity double that of his former estate, his family felicity and long life.

DESIGN.

With the exception of the episode of Elihu, the connexion of which with the original form of the poem may be doubtful, all five parts of the book are esssential elements of the work as it came from the hand of the first author, although some parts of the second and fourth divisions may have been expanded by later writers. The idea of the composition is to be derived not from any single element of the book, but from the teaching and movement of the whole piece. Job is unquestionably the hero of the work, and in his ideas and his history combined we may assume that we find the author himself speaking and teaching. The discussion between Job and his friends of the problem of suffering occupies two-thirds of the book, or, if the space occupied by Elihu be not considered, nearly three-fourths, and in the direction which the author causes this discussion to take we may see revealed the main didactic purpose of the book. When the three friends, the representatives of former theories of providence, are reduced to silence, we may be certain that it was the author's purpose to discredit the ideas which they represent. Job himself offers no positive contribution to the doctrine of evil; his position is negative, merely antagonistic to that of the friends. But this negative position victoriously maintained by him has the effect of clearing the ground, and the author himself supplies in the prologue the positive truth, when he communicates the real explanation of his hero's calamities, and teaches that they were a trial of his righteousness. It was therefore the author's main purpose in his work to widen men's views of the providence of God and set before them a new view of suffering. This purpose, however, was in all probability subordinate to some wider practical design. No Hebrew writer is merely a poet or a thinker. He is always a teacher. He has men before him in their relations to God,[1] and usually not men in their individual relations, but members of the family of Israel, the people of God. It is consequently scarcely to be doubted that the book has a national scope. The author considered his new truth regarding the meaning of affliction as of national interest, and as the truth then needful for the heart of his people. But the teaching of the book is only half its contents. It contains also a history—deep and inexplicable affliction, a great moral struggle, and a victory. The author meant his new truth to inspire new conduct, new faith, and new hopes. In Job's sufferings, undeserved and inexplicable to him, yet capable of an explanation most consistent with the goodness and faithfulness of God, and casting honour upon his faithful servants; in his despair bordering on un-

---

[1] Exceptions must be made in the cases of Esther and the Song of Songs, which do not mention God, and the original writer in Ecclesiastes who is a philosopher.

belief, at last overcome; and in the happy issue of his afflictions—in all this Israel may see itself, and from the sight take courage, and forecast its own history. Job, however, is not to be considered Israel, the righteous servant of the Lord, under a feigned name; he is no mere parable (though such a view is found as early as the Talmud); he and his history have both elements of reality in them. It is these elements of reality common to him with Israel in affliction, common even to him with humanity as a whole, confined within the straitened limits set by its own ignorance, wounded to death by the mysterious sorrows of life, tortured by the uncertainty whether its cry finds an entrance into God's ear, alarmed and paralysed by the irreconcilable discrepancies which it seems to discover between its necessary thoughts of Him and its experience of Him in His providence, and faint with longing that it might come into His place, and behold him, not girt with His majesty, but in human form, as one looketh upon his fellow—it is these elements of truth that make the history of Job instructive to Israel in the times of affliction when it was set before them, and to men of all races in all ages. It would probably be a mistake, however, to imagine that the author consciously stepped outside the limits of his nation and assumed a human position antagonistic to it. The chords he touches vibrate through all humanity—but this is because Israel is the religious kernel of humanity, and because from Israel's heart the deepest religious music of mankind is heard, whether of pathos or of joy.

Two threads requiring to be followed, therefore, run through the book —one the discussion of the problem of evil between Job and his friends, and the other the varying attitude of Job's mind towards God, the first being subordinate to the second. Both Job and his friends advance to the discussion of his sufferings and of the problem of evil, ignorant of the true cause of his calamities—Job strong in his sense of innocence, and the friends armed with their theory of the righteousness of God, who giveth to every man according to his works. With fine psychological instinct the poet lets Job altogether lose his self-control first when his three friends came to visit him. His bereavements and his malady he bore with a steady courage, and his wife's direct instigations to godlessness he repelled with severity and resignation. But when his equals and the old associates of his happiness came to see him, and when he read in their looks and in their seven days' silence the depth of his own misery, his self-command deserted him, and he broke out into a cry of despair, cursing his day and crying for death (iii.). Job had somewhat misinterpreted the demeanour of his friends. It was not all pity that it expressed. Along with their pity they had also brought their theology, and they trusted to heal Job's malady with this. Till a few days before, Job would have agreed with them on the sovereign virtues of this remedy. But he had learned through a higher teaching, the events of God's providence, that it was no longer a specific in his case. His violent impatience, however, under his afflictions and his covert attacks upon the divine rectitude only served to confirm the view of his sufferings which their theory of evil had already suggested to his friends. And thus commences the high debate which continues through twenty-nine chapters.

The three friends of Job came to the consideration of his history with the principle that calamity is the result of evil-doing, as prosperity is the reward of righteousness. Suffering is not an accident or a spontaneous growth of the soil; man is born unto trouble as the sparks fly upwards; there is in human life a tendency to do evil which draws down upon men the chastisement of God (v. 6). The principle is thus enunciated by Eliphaz, from whom the other speakers take their cue: where there is suffering there has been sin in the sufferer. Not suffering in itself, but the effect of it on the sufferer is what gives insight into his true character. Suffering is not always punitive; it is sometimes disciplinary, designed to wean the good man from his sin. If he sees in his suffering the monition of God and turns from his evil, his future shall be rich in peace and happiness, and his latter estate more prosperous than his first. If he murmurs or resists, he can only perish under the multiplying chastisements which his impenitence will provoke. Now this principle is far from being a peculiar crotchet of the friends; its truth is undeniable, though they erred in supposing that it would cover the wide providence of God. The principle is the fundamental idea of moral government, the expression of the natural conscience, a principle common more or less to all peoples, though perhaps more prominent in the Semitic mind, because all religious ideas are more prominent and simple there—not suggested to Israel first by the law, but found and adopted by the law, though it may be sharpened by it. It is the fundamental principle of prophecy no less than of the law, and, if possible, of the wisdom of philosophy of the Hebrews more than of either. Speculation among the Hebrews had a simpler task before it than it had in the West or in the farther East. The Greek philosopher began his operations upon the sum of things; he threw the universe into his crucible at once. His object was to effect some analysis of it, so that he could call one element cause and another effect. Or, to vary the figure, his endeavour was to pursue the streams of tendency which he could observe till he reached at last the central spring which sent them all forth. God, a single cause and explanation, was the object of his search. But to the Hebrew of the later time this was already found. The analysis resulting in the distinction of God and the world had been effected for him so long ago that the history and circumstances of the process had been forgotten, and only the unchallengeable result remained. His philosophy was not a quest of God whom he did not know, but a recognition on all hands of God whom he knew. The great primary idea to his mind was that of God, a Being wholly just, doing all. And the world was little more than the phenomena that revealed the mind and the presence and the operations of God. Consequently the nature of God as known to him and the course of events formed a perfect equation. The idea of what God was in Himself was in complete harmony with His manifestation of Himself in providence, in the events of individual human lives, and in the history of nations. The philosophy of the wise did not go behind the origin of sin, or referred it to the freedom of man; but, sin existing, and God being in immediate personal contact with the world, every event was a direct expression of His moral will and energy; calamity fell on wickedness, and success attended right-doing. This view of the moral harmony between the nature of God and the events of providence in the fortunes of men and nations is the view of the Hebrew wisdom in its oldest form, during what might be called the period of principles, to which belong Prov. x. seq.; and this is the position maintained by Job's three friends. And the significance of the book of Job in the history of Hebrew thought arises in that it marks the point when such a view was definitely overcome, closing the long period when this principle was merely subjected to questionings, and makes a new positive addition to the doctrine of evil.

Job agreed that afflictions came directly from the hand of God, and also that God afflicted those whom He held guilty of sins. But his conscience denied the imputation of guilt, whether insinuated by his friends or implied in God's chastisement of him. Hence he was driven to conclude that God was unjust. The position of Job appeared to his friends nothing else but impiety; while theirs was to him mere falsehood and the special pleading of sycophants on behalf of God because He was the stronger. Within these iron walls the debate moves, making little progress, but with much brilliancy, if not of argument, of illustration. A certain advance indeed is perceptible. In the first series of speeches (iv.—xiv.), the key-note of which is struck by Eliphaz, the oldest and most considerate of the three, the position is that affliction is caused by sin, and is chastisement designed for the sinner's good; and the moral is that Job should recognize it and use it for the purpose for which it was sent. In the second (xv.—xxi.) the terrible fate of the sinner is emphasized, and those brilliant pictures of a restored future, thrown in by all the speakers in the first series, are absent. Job's demeanour under the consolations offered him afforded little hope of his repentance. In the third series (xxii. seq.) the friends cast off all disguise, and openly charge Job with a course of evil life. That their armoury was now exhausted is shown by the brevity of the second speaker, and the failure of the third (at least in the present text) to answer in any form. In reply Job disdains for a time to touch what he well knew lay under all their exhortations; he laments with touching pathos the defection of his friends, who were like the winter torrents looked for in vain by the perishing caravan in the summer heat; he meets with bitter scorn their constant cry that God will not cast off the righteous man, by asking: How can one be righteous with God? what can human weakness, however innocent, do against infinite might and subtlety? they are righteous whom an omnipotent and perverse will thinks fit to consider so; he falls into a hopeless wail over the universal misery of man, who has a weary campaign of life appointed him; then, rising up in the strength of his conscience, he upbraids the Almighty with His misuse of His power and His indiscriminate tyranny—righteous and innocent He destroys alike—and challenges Him to lay aside His majesty and meet His creature as a man, and then he would not fear Him. Even in the second series Job can hardly bring himself to face the personal issue raised by the friends. His relations to God absorb him almost wholly—his pitiable isolation, the indignities showered on his once honoured head, the loathsome spectacle of his body; abandoned by all, he turns for pity from God to men and from men to God. Only in the third series of debates does he put out his hand and grasp firmly the theory of his friends, and their "defences of mud" fall to dust in his hands. Instead of that roseate moral order on which they are never weary of insisting, he finds only disorder and moral confusion. When he thinks of it, trembling takes hold of him. It is not the righteous but the wicked that live, grow old, yea, wax mighty in strength, that send forth their children like a flock and establish them in their sight. Before the logic of facts the theory of the friends goes down; and with this negative result, which the author skilfully reaches through the debate, has to be combined his own positive doctrine of the uses of adversity advanced in the prologue.

To a modern reader it appears strange that both parties were so entangled in the meshes of their preconceptions regarding God as to be unable to break through the broader views. The friends, while maintaining that injustice on the part of God is inconceivable, might have given due weight to the persistent testimony of Job's conscience as that behind which it is impossible to go, and found refuge in the reflection that there might be something inexplicable in the ways of God, and that affliction might have some other meaning than to punish the sinner or even to wean him from his sin. And Job, while maintaining his innocence from overt sins, might have confessed that there was such sinfulness in every human life as was sufficient to account for the severest chastisement from heaven, or at least he might have stopped short of charging God foolishly. Such a position would certainly be taken up by an afflicted saint now, and such an explanation of his sufferings would suggest itself to the sufferer, even though it might be in truth a false explanation. Perhaps here, where an artistic fault might seem to be committed, the art of the writer, or his truth to nature, and the extraordinary freedom with which he moves among his materials, as well as the power and individuality of his dramatic creations, are most remarkable. The rôle which the author reserved for himself was to teach the truth on the question in dispute, and he accomplishes this by allowing his performers to push their false principles to their proper extreme. There is nothing about which men are usually so sure as the character of God. They are ever ready to take Him in their own hand, to interpret His providence in their own sense, to say what things are consistent or not with His character and word, and beat down the opposing consciences of other men by His so-called authority, which is nothing but their own. The friends of Job were religious Orientals, men to whom God was a being in immediate contact with the world and life, to whom the idea of second causes was unknown, on whom science had not yet begun to dawn, nor the conception of a divine scheme pursuing a distant end by complicated means, in which the individual's interest may suffer for the larger good. The broad sympathies of the author and his sense of the truth lying in the theory of the friends are seen in the scope which he allows them, in the richness of the thought and the splendid luxuriance of the imagery—drawn from the immemorial moral consent of mankind, the testimony of the living conscience, and the observation of life—with which he makes them clothe their views. He remembered the elements of truth in the theory from which he was departing, that it was a national heritage, which he himself perhaps had been constrained not without a struggle to abandon; and, while showing its insufficiency, he sets it forth in its most brilliant form.

The extravagance of Job's assertions was occasioned greatly by the extreme position of his friends, which left no room for his conscious innocence along with the rectitude of God. Again, the poet's purpose, as the prologue shows, was to teach that afflictions may fall on a man out of all connexion with any offence of his own, and merely as the trial of his righteousness; and hence he allows Job, as by a true instinct of the nature of his sufferings, to repudiate all connexion between them and sin in himself. And further, the terrible conflict into which the suspicions of the Satan brought Job could not be exhibited without pushing him to the verge of ungodliness. These are all elements of the poet's art; but art and nature are one. In ancient Hebrew life the sense of sin was less deep than it is now. In the desert, too, men speak boldly of God. Nothing is more false than to judge the poet's creation from our later point of view, and construct a theory of the book according to a more developed sense of sin and a deeper reverence for God than belonged to antiquity. In complete contradiction to the testimony of the book itself, some critics, as Hengstenberg and Budde, have assumed that Job's spiritual pride was the cause of his afflictions, that this was the root of bitterness in him which must be killed down ere he could become a true saint. The fundamental position of the book is that Job was already a true saint; this is testified by God Himself, is the radical idea of the author in the prologue, and the very hypothesis of the drama. We might be ready to think that Job's afflictions did not befall him out of all connexion with his own condition of mind, and we might be disposed to find a vindication of God's ways in this. There is no evidence that such an idea was shared by the author of the book. It is remarkable that the attitude which we imagine it would have been so easy for Job to assume, namely, while holding fast his integrity, to fall back upon the inexplicableness of providence, of which there are such imposing descriptions in his speeches, is just the attitude which is taken up in ch. xxviii. It is far from certain, however, that this chapter is an integral part of the original book.

The other line running through the book, the varying attitude of Job's mind towards God, exhibits dramatic action and tragic interest of the highest kind, though the movement is internal. That the exhibition of this struggle in Job's mind was a main point in the author's purpose is seen from the fact that at the end of each of his great trials he notes that Job sinned not, nor ascribed wrong to God (i. 22; ii. 10), and from the effect which the divine voice from the whirlwind is made to produce upon him (xl. 3). In the first cycle of debate (ix.—xiv.) Job's mind reaches the deepest limit of estrangement. There he not merely charges God with injustice, but, unable to reconcile His former goodness with His present enmity, he regards the latter as the true expression of God's attitude towards His creatures, and the former, comprising all his infinite creative skill in weaving the delicate organism of human nature and the rich endowments of His providence, only as the means of exercising His mad and immoral cruelty in the time to come. When the Semitic skin of Job is scratched, we find a modern pessimist beneath. Others in later days have brought the keen sensibility of the human frame and the torture which it endures together, and asked with Job to whom at last all this has to be referred. Towards the end of the cycle a star of heavenly light seems to rise on the horizon; the thought seizes the sufferer's mind that man might have another life, that God's anger pursuing him to the grave might be sated, and that He might call him out of it to Himself again (xiv. 13). This idea of a resurrection, unfamiliar to Job at first, is one which he is allowed to reach out of the necessities of the moral complications around him, but from the author's manner of using the idea we may judge that it was familiar to himself. In the second cycle the thought of a future reconciliation with God is more firmly grasped. That satisfaction or at least composure which, when we observe calamities that we cannot morally account for, we reach by considering that providence is a great scheme moving according to general laws, and that it does not always truly reflect the relation of God to the individual, Job reached in the only way possible to a Semitic mind. He drew a distinction between an outer God whom events obey, pursuing him in His anger, and an inner God whose heart was with him, who was aware of his innocence; and he appeals from God to God, and beseeches God to pledge Himself that he shall receive justice from God (xvi. 19; xvii. 3). And so high at last does this consciousness that God is at one with him rise that he avows his assurance that He will yet appear to do him justice before men, and that he shall see Him with his own eyes, no more estranged but on his side, and for this moment he faints with longing (xix. 25 seq.).[2]

---

[2] This remarkable passage reads thus: *"But I know that my redeemer liveth, and afterwards he shall arise upon the dust, and after my skin, even this body, is destroyed, without my flesh shall I see God; whom I shall see for myself, and mine eyes shall behold, and not as a stranger; my reins within me are consumed* with longing." The redeemer who liveth and shall arise or stand upon the earth is God whom he shall see with his own eyes, on his side. The course of exegesis was greatly influenced by the translation of Jerome, who, departing from the Itala, rendered: "In novissimo die de terra surrecturus sum . . . et rursum circumdabor pella mea et in carne mea videbo deum meum." The only point now in question is whether: (*a*) Job looks for this manifestation of God to him while he is still alive, or (*b*) after death, and therefore in the sense of a spiritual vision and union with God in another life; that is, whether the words "destroyed" and "without my flesh" are to be taken relatively only, of the extremest effects of his disease upon him, or literally, of the separation of the body in death. A third view which assumes that the words rendered "without my flesh," which run literally, "out of my flesh," mean *looking* out from my flesh, that is, clothed with a new body, and finds the idea of resurrection repeated,

After this expression of faith Job's mind remains calm, though he ends by firmly charging God with perverting his right, and demanding to know the cause of his afflictions (xxvii. 2 seq.; xxxi. 35, where render: "Oh, that I had the indictment which mine adversary has written!"). In answer to this demand the Divine voice answers Job out of the tempest: "Who is this that darkeneth counsel by words without knowledge?" The word "counsel" intimates to Job that God does not act without a design, large and beyond the comprehension of man; and to impress this is the purpose of the Divine speeches. The speaker does not enter into Job's particular cause; there is not a word tending to unravel his riddle; his mind is drawn away to the wisdom and majesty of God Himself. His own words and those of his friends are but re-echoed, but it is God Himself who now utters them. Job is in immediate nearness to the majesty of heaven, wise, unfathomable, ironical over the littleness of man, and he is abased; God Himself effects what neither the man's own thoughts of God nor the representations of his friends could accomplish, though by the same means. The religious insight of the writer sounds here the profoundest deeps of truth.

INTEGRITY.

Doubts whether particular portions of the present book belonged to the original form of it have been raised by many. M. L. De Wette expressed himself as follows: "It appears to us that the present book of Job has not all flowed from one pen. As many books of the Old Testament have been several times written over, so has this also" (Ersch and Gruber, *Ency.*, sect. ii. vol. viii.). The judgment formed by De Wette has been adhered

---

perhaps imports more into the language than it will fairly bear. In favour of (*b*) may be adduced the persistent refusal of Job throughout to entertain the idea of a restoration in this life; the word "afterwards"; and perhaps the analogy of other passages where the same situation appears, as Ps. xlix. and lxxiii., although the actual dénouement of the tragedy supports (*a*). The difference between the two senses is not important, when the Old Testament view of immortality is considered. To the Hebrew the life beyond was not what it is to us, a freedom from sin and sorrow and admission to an immediate divine fellowship not attainable here. To him the life beyond was at best a prolongation of the life here; all he desired was that his fellowship with God here should not be interrupted in death, and that Sheol, the place into which deceased persons descended and where they remained, cut off from all life with God, might be overleapt. On this account the theory of Ewald, which throws the centre of gravity of the book into this passage in ch. xix., considering its purpose to be to teach that the riddles of this life shall be solved and its inequalities corrected in a future life, appears one-sided. The point of the passage does not lie in any distinction which it draws between this life and a future life; it lies in the assurance which Job expresses that God, who even now knows his innocence, will vindicate it in the future, and that, though estranged now, He will at last take him to His heart.

to more or less by most of those who have studied the book. Questions regarding the unity of such books as this are difficult to settle; there is not unanimity among scholars regarding the idea of the book, and consequently they differ as to what parts are in harmony or conflict with unity; and it is dangerous to apply modern ideas of literary composition and artistic unity to the works of antiquity and of the East. The problem raised in the book of Job has certainly received frequent treatment in the Old Testament; and there is no likelihood that all efforts in this direction have been preserved to us. It is probable that the book of Job was but a great effort amidst or after many smaller. It is scarcely to be supposed that one with such poetic and literary power as the author of chap. iii.—xxxi., xxxviii.—xli. would embody the work of any other writer in his own. If there be elements in the book which must be pronounced foreign, they have been inserted in the work of the author by a later hand. It is not unlikely that our present book may, in addition to the great work of the original author, contain some fragments of the thoughts of other religious minds upon the same question, and that these, instead of being loosely appended, have been fitted into the mechanism of the first work. Some of these fragments may have originated at first quite independently of our book, while others may be expansions and insertions that never existed separately. At the same time it is scarcely safe to throw out any portion of the book merely because it seems to us out of harmony with the unity of the main part of the poem, or unless several distinct lines of consideration conspire to point it out as an extraneous element.

The arguments against the originality of the prologue—as, that it is written in prose, that the name Yahweh appears in it, that sacrifice is referred to, and that there are inconsistencies between it and the body of the book—are of little weight. There must have been some introduction to the poem explaining the circumstances of Job, otherwise the poetical dispute would have been unintelligible, for it is improbable that the story of Job was so familiar that a poem in which he and his friends figured as they do here would have been understood. And there is no trace of any other prologue or introduction having ever existed. The prologue, too, is an essential element of the work, containing the author's positive contribution to the doctrine of suffering, for which the discussion in the poem prepares the way. The intermixture of prose and poetry is common in Oriental works containing similar discussions; the reference to sacrifice is to primitive not to Mosaic sacrifice; and the author, while using the name Yahweh freely himself, puts the patriarchal Divine names into the mouth of Job and his friends because he regards them as belonging to the patriarchal age and to a country outside of Israel. That the observance of this rule had a certain awkwardness for the writer appears perhaps from his allowing the name Yahweh to slip in once or twice (xii. 9, cf. xxviii. 28) in familiar phrases in the body of the poem. The discrepancies, such as Job's references to his children as still alive (xix. 17, the interpretation is doubtful), and to his servants, are trivial, and even if real imply nothing in a book admittedly poetical and not historical. The objections to the epilogue are equally unimportant—as that the Satan is not mentioned in it, and that Job's restoration is in conflict with the main idea of the poem—that earthly felicity does not follow righteousness. The epilogue confirms the teaching of the poem when it gives the divine sanction to Job's doctrine regarding God in opposition to that of the friends (xlii. 7). And it is certainly not the intention of the poem to teach that earthly felicity does not follow righteousness; its purpose is to correct the exclusiveness with which the friends of Job maintained that principle. The Satan is introduced in the prologue, exercising his function as minister of God in heaven; but it is to misinterpret wholly the doctrine of evil in the Old Testament to assign to the Satan any such personal importance or independence of power as that he should be called before the curtain to receive the hisses that accompany his own discomfiture. The Satan, though he here appears with the beginnings of a malevolent will of his own, is but the instrument of the sifting providence of God. His work was to try; that done he disappears, his personality being too slight to have any place in the result.

Much graver are the suspicions that attach to the speeches of Elihu. Most of those who have studied the book carefully hold that this part does not belong to the original cast, but has been introduced at a considerably later time. The piece is one of the most interesting parts of the book; both the person and the thoughts of Elihu are marked by a strong individuality. This individuality has indeed been very diversely estimated. The ancients for the most part passed a very severe judgment on Elihu: he is a buffoon, a boastful youth whose shallow intermeddling is only to be explained by the fewness of his years, the incarnation of folly, or even the Satan himself gone a-mumming. Some moderns on the other hand have regarded him as the incarnation of the voice of God or even of God himself. The main objections to the connexion of the episode of Elihu with the original book are: that the prologue and epilogue know nothing of him; that on the cause of Job's afflictions he occupies virtually the same position as the friends; that his speeches destroy the dramatic effect of the divine manifestation by introducing a lengthened break between Job's challenge and the answer of

God; that the language and style of the piece are marked by an excessive mannerism, too great to have been created by the author of the rest of the poem; that the allusions to the rest of the book are so minute as to betray a reader rather than a hearer; and that the views regarding sin, and especially the scandal given to the author by the irreverence of Job, indicate a religious advance which marks a later age. The position taken by Elihu is almost that of a critic of the book. Regarding the origin of afflictions he is at one with the friends, although he dwells more on the general sinfulness of man than on actual sins, and his reprobation of Job's position is even greater than theirs. His anger was kindled against Job because he made himself righteous before God, and against his friends because they found no answer to Job. His whole object is to refute Job's charge of injustice against God. What is novel in Elihu, therefore, is not his position but his arguments. These do not lack cogency, but betray a kind of thought different from that of the friends. Injustice in God, he argues, can only arise from selfishness in Him; but the very existence of creation implies unselfish love on God's part, for if He thought only of Himself, He would cease actively to uphold creation, and it would fall into death. Again, without justice mere earthly rule is impossible; how then is injustice conceivable in Him who rules over all? It is probable that the original author found his three interlocutors a sufficient medium for expression, and that this new speaker is the creation of another. To a devout and thoughtful reader of the original book, belonging perhaps to a more reverential age, it appeared that the language and bearing of Job had scarcely been sufficiently reprobated by the original speakers, and that the religious reason, apart from any theophany, could suggest arguments sufficient to condemn such demeanour on the part of any man. (For an able though hardly convincing argument for the originality of the discourses of Elihu see Budde's *Commentary*.)

It is more difficult to come to a decision in regard to some other portions of the book, particularly ch. xxvii. 7—xxviii. In the latter part of ch. xxvii. Job seems to go over to the camp of his opponents, and expresses sentiments in complete contradiction to his former views. Hence some have thought the passage to be the missing speech of Zophar. Others, as Hitzig, believe that Job is parodying the ideas of the friends; while others, like Ewald, consider that he is recanting his former excesses, and making such a modification as to express correctly his views on evil. None of these opinions is quite satisfactory, though the last probably expresses the view with which the passage was introduced, whether it be original or not. The meaning of ch. xxviii. can only be that "Wisdom," that is, a theoretical comprehension of providence, is unattainable by man, whose only wisdom is the fear of the Lord or practical piety. But to bring Job to the feeling of this truth was just the purpose of the theophany and the divine speeches; and, if Job had reached it already through his own reflection, the theophany becomes an irrelevancy. It is difficult, therefore, to find a place for these two chapters in the original work. The hymn on Wisdom is a most exquisite poem, which probably originated separately, and was brought into our book with a purpose similar to that which suggested the speeches of Elihu. Objections have also been raised to the descriptions of leviathan and behemoth (ch. xl. 15—xli.). Regarding these it may be enough to say that in meaning these passages are in perfect harmony with other parts of the Divine words, although there is a breadth and detail in the style unlike the sharp, short, ironical touches otherwise characteristic of this part of the poem. (Other longer passages, the originality of which has been called into question, are: xvii. 8 seq.; xxi. 16-18; xxii. 17 seq.; xxiii. 8 seq.; xxiv. 9, 18-24; xxvi. 5-14. On these see the commentaries.)

DATE.

The age of such a book as Job, dealing only with principles and having no direct references to historical events can be fixed only approximately. Any conclusion can be reached only by an induction founded on matters which do not afford perfect certainty, such as the comparative development of certain moral ideas in different ages, the pressing claims of certain problems for solution at particular epochs of the history of Israel, and points of contact with other writings of which the age may with some certainty be determined. The Jewish tradition that the book is Mosaic, and the idea that it is a production of the desert, written in another tongue and translated into Hebrew, want even a shadow of probability. The book is a genuine outcome of the religious life and thought of Israel, the product of a religious knowledge and experience that were possible among no other people. That the author lays the scene of the poem outside his own nation and in the patriarchal age is a proceeding common to him with other dramatic writers, who find freer play for their principles in a region removed from the present, where they are not hampered by the obtrusive forms of actual life, but are free to mould occurrences into the moral form that their ideas require.

It is the opinion of some scholars, *e.g.* Delitzsch, that the book belongs to the age of Solomon. It cannot be earlier than this age, for Job (vii. 17) travesties the ideas of Ps. viii. in a manner which shows that this hymn was well known. To infer the date from a comparison of literary coincidences and allusions is however a very delicate operation. For, first, owing to the unity of thought and language which pervades the Old Testament, in which, regarded merely as a national literature, it differs from all other national literatures, we are apt to be deceived, and to take mere similarities for literary allusions and quotations; and, secondly, even when we are sure that there is dependence, it is often uncommonly difficult to decide which is the original source. The reference to Job in Ezek. xiv. 14 is not to our book, but to the man (a legendary figure) who was afterwards made the hero of it. The affinities on the other hand between Job and Isa. xl.—lv. are very close. The date, however, of this part of Isaiah is uncertain, though it cannot have received its final form, if it be composite, long before the return. Between Job iii. and Jer. xx. 14 seq. there is, again, certainly literary connexion. But the judgment of different minds differs on the question which passage is dependent on the other. The language of Jeremiah, however, has a natural pathos and genuineness of feeling in it, somewhat in contrast with the elaborate poetical finish of Job's words, which might suggest the originality of the former.

The tendency among recent scholars is to put the book of Job not earlier than the 5th century B.C. There are good reasons for putting it in the 4th century. It stands at the beginning of the era of Jewish philosophical inquiry—its affinities are with Proverbs, Ecclesiasticus, Ecclesiastes, and the Wisdom of Solomon, a body of writings that belongs to the latest period of pre-Christian Jewish literary development. . . . Its points of connexion with Isa. xl.—lv. relate only to the problem of the suffering of the righteous, and that it is later than the Isaiah passage appears from the fact that this latter is national and ritual in scope, while Job is universal and ethical.

The book of Job is not literal history, though it reposes on historical tradition. To this tradition belong probably the name of Job and his country, and the names of his three friends, and perhaps also many other details impossible to specify particularly. The view that the book is entirely a literary creation with no basis in historical tradition is as old as the Talmud (*Baba Bathra*, xv. 1), in which a rabbi is cited who says: Job was not, and was not created, but is an allegory. This view is supported by Hengstenberg and others. But pure poetical creations on so extensive a scale are not probable in the East and at so early an age.

AUTHOR.

The author of the book is wholly unknown. The religious life of Israel was at certain periods very intense, and at those times the spiritual energy of the nation expressed itself almost impersonally, through men who forgot themselves and were speedily forgotten in name by others. Hitzig conjectures that the author was a native of the north on account of the free criticism of providence which he allows himself. Others, on account of some affinities with the prophet Amos, infer that he belonged to the south of Judah, and this is supposed to account for his intimate acquaintance with the desert. Ewald considers that he belonged to the exile in Egypt, on account of his minute acquaintance with that country. But all these conjectures localize an author whose knowledge was not confined to any locality, who was a true child of the East and familiar with life and nature in every country there, who was at the same time a true Israelite and felt that the earth was the Lord's and the fullness thereof, and whose sympathies and thought took in all God's works.

LITERATURE.

Commentaries by Ewald (1854); Renan (1859); Delitzsch (1864); Zöckler in Lange's *Bibelwerk* (1872); F. C. Cook in *Speaker's Comm.* (1880); A. B. Davidson in *Cambridge Bible* (1884); Dillmann (1891); K. Budde (1896); Duhm (1897). See also Hoekstra, "Job de Knecht van Jehovah" in *Theol. Tijdschr.* (1871), and, in reply, A. Kuenen, "Job en de leidende Knecht van Jahveh," ibid. (1873); C. H. H. Wright in *Bib. Essays* (1886); G. G. Bradley, *Lects. on Job* (2nd ed., 1888); Cheyne, *Job and Solomon* (1887); Dawson, *Wisd. Lit.* (1893); D. B. Macdonald, "The Original Form of the Legend of Job" in *Journ. Bib. Lit.* (1895); E. Hatch, *Essays in Bib. Gk.* (1889); A. Dillmann, in *Trans. of Roy. Pruss. Acad.* (1890).

<hr>

BIBLIOGRAPHY ENTRY FOR RESEARCH PAPERS:

Davidson, Andrew Bruce, and Crawford Howell Toy. "Job." *Encyclopaedia Britannica,* 11th ed. (1911). Reprinted in *The Voice out of the Whirlwind: The Book of Job,* ed. Ralph E. Hone. San Francisco, 1960.

FIRST FOOTNOTE:

    * Andrew Bruce Davidson and Crawford Howell Toy in *Encyclopaedia Britannica,* 11th ed. (1911), *s.v.* "Job," reprinted in *The Voice out of the Whirlwind: The Book of Job,* ed. Ralph E. Hone (San Francisco, 1960), pp. 87-103.

SUBSEQUENT FOOTNOTES:

    * Davidson and Toy, *op. cit., The Voice,* p. ■.
    * Davidson and Toy, "Job," *The Voice,* p. ■.
    * Davidson and Toy, *The Voice,* p. ■.

In place of *"The Voice,"* "ed. Hone" may be used in these subsequent-footnote forms.

MORRIS JASTROW

ON

the Literary Form of Job

Morris Jastrow (1861-1921) was an outstanding American Orientalist who was born in Warsaw, Poland, and at five years of age taken to Philadelphia, where his father, a rabbi, had been called. He was educated at the University of Pennsylvania and in French and German universities. Returning to teach in the University, he became professor of Semitic languages and literature. He authored many books on Assyrian and Babylonian studies and on Old Testament literature. The selection is from his The Book of Job, Its Origin, Growth and Interpretation, Together with a New Translation Based on a Revised Text *(Philadelphia: J. B. Lippincott Company, 1920), pp. 174-181.*

THE LITERARY FORM OF JOB— A SYMPOSIUM NOT A DRAMA

WITH the Book of Job thus consisting of three distinct strata [the original book and its supplements; the speeches of Elihu; the speeches of Jahweh], each representing a composite growth, the unity given to the book by the final group of editors is purely on the surface. These editors welded the three strata together and embodied the hundreds of comments, glosses, additional lines, popular maxims, and reflections of pious commentators into the text as though forming genuine ingredients; but even by accepting the many intentional changes to tone down the sharpness of Job's utterances and the confusing arrangement of speeches in order to put orthodox sentiments into the mouth of Job, no genuine unity could be obtained. There is no inherent unity in the completed Book of Job if we accept the results of a critical analysis, any more than there is such a unity in the Pentateuch, composed of several documents enclosed in a framework of laws of gradual growth with all kinds of comments, additions and illustrative instances.

The question, therefore, that is often raised whether Job is a drama is almost irrelevant, since a drama implies an inherent unity in its composition. The situation in the folktale of Job is, to be sure, dramatic, but the same applies to the romantic story of Joseph in Genesis and to many incidents in the historical books of the Bible, as *e.g.,* Saul's visit to the Witch of Endor, to David's encounters with Saul or Nathan's appearance before Solomon. The story of Ruth is dramatic as is the tale of Esther, but neither is for that reason a drama; they belong in the category of the romantic novel written as political and religious propaganda, not unlike the modern novel "with a purpose." The story of Job has dramatic possibilities, as have dozens of tales woven into Biblical narratives. Job can be made into a drama but the circumstances that the story, as we have seen, is to be separated from the original Symposium, and this again from the two appendices precludes [*sic*] the possibility of interpreting even the apparent unity given to the book in its final form as a dramatic composition. The drama is foreign to the ancient Hebrew spirit. Nor is it encountered in the old civilizations of the East. The drama is the outcome of individual authorship, whereas, as we have seen, the methods of literary composition in the ancient Orient tend to place the author in the background. Where we find the drama in the Orient as among the Hindus, it is late and may be due to outside influences.[128] At all events, it is not accidental that the Greeks among whom we first encounter individual authorship are also the ones who gave to the world the drama in the real sense of the term, as a distinct subdivision of literature.

The unity of the Book of Job even in its final form does not go further than the attempt to connect the three strata by editorial headings attached to the chapters, and by occasional editorial comments and by additions to gloss over discrepancies in the various strata of which the book consists. The main concern of the final editors, indeed their *only* concern, was to present the book as a support for the current orthodoxy.

---

[128] Some Indologists like Weber and Windisch were inclined to ascribe the Sanskrit drama, which does not make its appearance till the first century of our era, to contact with the Greeks, but this view has now been abandoned. See Macdonnell, *Sanskrit Literature,* p. 416.

The thought of regarding the completed book as a progressive and systematically constructed dramatic composition could not have entered the mind of the final editors, for the sufficient reason that as Orientals they were under the sway of the oriental method of composition as a gradual growth. If we wish to specify the literary character of the book more precisely than by designating it as a composite philosophical poem, we may call it a composite Symposium, but never a drama.

All efforts to present the Book of Job as a drama rest on the assumption now shown to be erroneous that the book is a literary unit. This applies to the two recent attempts by Prof. R. G. Moulton[129] and by Dr. H. M. Kallen, [130] as it does to all earlier ones. Prof. Moulton does not go so far as to divide the book into acts and scenes as did Theodor Beza as far back as 1587, but he does assume *dramatis personae* and introduces "asides" and other stage directions in his division of the book into fifty continuous sections instead of into chapters. Now all this is as foreign to the whole character of the book as possible. Quite apart from the total lack of evidence that the Jews of post-exilic days, even after they had come under Greek influence, ever developed the drama as a species of literary composition, we fail to penetrate into the spirit of Job by regarding it as a composition logically and progressively unfolding a theme as is demanded by the canons of dramatic composition. The point is that the Book of Job consists of a foundation on which a number of independent superstructures have been erected. There is no logical development of a theme, but merely a series of discussions of one and the same theme from various angles. All attempts, therefore, to distinguish in the book a progressive series of solutions for the mystery of suffering,[131] corresponding in a measure to the successive acts of a drama, are doomed to failure. Even in the original Book of Job there is no such progressive evolution to be noted as a dramatic composition assumes. The speeches are not in the nature of logical replies, answering point for point and opposing argument by counter argument. There are only four distinct points brought forward by the three friends[132] and these are emphasized by all, irrespective of Job's replies. Nor is there any progress in the setting forth of the problem as we proceed from one series of speeches to the next. In fact, it would be nearer to the truth to

---

[129] *The Book of Job* in the "Modern Reader's Bible (New York, 1896).

[130] *The Book of Job as a Greek Tragedy* (New York, 1918).

[131] Prof. Moulton in his Introduction assumes five solutions successively brought forward.

[132] Above, p. 72. [Jastrow's page; not included in this selection.]

call one series of speeches an imitation of the other, the three series representing so many endeavors to present the same thoughts and the same arguments in different fashion. This applies also to the ten speeches of Job. In all of them he complains of his sufferings, in all he protests his innocence and in all he hurls back the rebukes which the three friends introduce in their speeches with counter accusations of lack of sympathy and with ironical or bitter retorts. Job in his replies does not specifically take into account what Eliphaz, Bildad or Zophar has said. One could take any of his speeches and transfer it to another place in the Symposium without affecting the argument. Similarly, the reply to Eliphaz's first speech would fit in just as well as a reply to a speech of Bildad or Zophar; and so with the other replies.

In view of all this, it is needless to enlarge upon Dr. Kallen's theory that the Book of Job as we have it, is actually based on the model of a Greek tragedy, and that the thought of writing a Jewish drama was suggested to a Jewish writer by having witnessed a production of a play of Euripides in some Greek city. Prof. Moulton does not go quite so far and contents himself with describing Job as "Wisdom Literature Dramatized," whereas Dr. Kallen regards the book as it stands written as a drama, not only with acts and scenes of action—although there is no action in any proper sense—but with a chorus and semi-chorus and a *Deus ex Machina* introduced towards the close, just as in a drama of Euripides. But in order to get a "drama" out of Job, Kallen takes portions of speeches of Job and arbitrarily assigns them to a purely hypothetical chorus and semi-chorus. Yahweh speaking out of the whirlwind corresponds, according to Dr. Kallen, to the appearance of the Deity in a Greek play[133] to pronounce a final verdict or to unravel the problem of the play. All this is ingenious but entirely beside the mark. The theory misconceives the entire spirit of the book both in its original and in its enlarged form. Job as a drama is devoid of meaning. Job as a series of discussions of a vital religious problem gradually taking shape under many hands with the problem viewed from various angles—unorthodox and orthodox—is full of significance. Such a composite production is precisely what we should expect to find issuing out of the intellectual and religious atmosphere prevailing in

---

[133] In order to carry out his theory, Dr. Kallen is obliged to offer a translation for a verb in the epilogue 42,6 for which there is no warrant; and other liberties are taken by Dr. Kallen in a reconstruction which is not based on a *critical* study of the text. Dr. Kallen follows the conventional Authorized Version without apparently realizing that hundreds of passages are now differently rendered by modern scholars on the basis of critical researches.

Palestine from the close of the fifth century B.C. and continuing to the threshold of the Christian era.

If there is any influence of Greek literary models to be sought in Job it lies in the Greek Symposium as a medium for the discussion of philosophic theories—always involving religious beliefs—which becomes through Plato such a characteristic division of Greek literature. But even this hypothesis is entirely unnecessary, since we can account for the book without it. At the same time, if we could bring down the date of the original Book of Job to as late a period as the close of the fourth century B.C. when Greek influence even of a literary character could be assumed to have penetrated into Palestine, there would be nothing inherently improbable in the conjecture that the Symposium in Job was suggested by the Greek dialogue.[134] We have seen, however, that we need not go further down than the end of the fifth century to account for the rise of an independent group of thinkers among the Jews, free enough from conventional views to seek an answer for the mystery of innocent suffering in a world created by a Power conceived of as just and merciful.

If we could discover traces of Greek philosophic thought and speculation in any part of Job, one could more readily admit Greek influence, but though some scholars incline to see in the skeptical trend of the original book the reaction of the freedom of the Greek mind in boldly investigating in a rationalistic spirit the phenomena of nature and of human experiences, it must be confessed that the evidence is not satisfactory. It is certainly not decisive, just as the endeavor to see in the philosophy of Koheleth the influence of the Stoic attitude or of Epicurean thought is futile.[135] Perhaps in a very general way one may conjecture that a wave of rationalism spread over the ancient Orient in the fifth and succeeding centuries which would account for the rise of such a remarkable religious system as Zoroastrianism.[136] Intellectual currents having their rise in Greece may possibly have flowed eastwards even before the Greek armies of Alexander brought about a free interchange between Orient and Occident that was destined to be fraught with such significant results. In this way we may help to account for the strength which free thought, untrammelled by piety or tradition, must have acquired in Palestine before circles could have arisen bold enough to challenge generally accepted beliefs.

---

[134] It should be remembered, however, that we have the dialogue in ancient Babylonian Literature. See a specimen in a German translation by Ebbeling (*Mitteilungen der Deutsch Orientgesellschaft*, No. 58, pp. 35-38).

[135] See *A Gentle Cynic*, p. 147 *seq.*

[136] Or more correctly Zarathushtrianism, since the founder's name is Zarathushtra, of which Zoroaster is a corrupt form.

BIBLIOGRAPHY ENTRY FOR RESEARCH PAPERS:

Jastrow, Morris. *The Book of Job, Its Origin, Growth and Interpretation, Together with a New Translation Based on a Revised Text.* Philadelphia: J. B. Lippincott Company, 1920. Excerpt reprinted in *The Voice out of the Whirlwind: The Book of Job,* ed. Ralph E. Hone. San Francisco, 1960.

FIRST FOOTNOTE:

* Morris Jastrow, *The Book of Job, Its Origin, Growth and Interpretation, Together with a New Translation Based on a Revised Text* (Philadelphia: J. B. Lippincott Company, 1920), excerpt reprinted in *The Voice out of the Whirlwind: The Book of Job,* ed. Ralph E. Hone (San Francisco, 1960), pp. 104-108.

SUBSEQUENT FOOTNOTES:

* Jastrow, *op. cit., The Voice,* p. ■.
* Jastrow, *Job, The Voice,* p. ■.
* Jastrow, *The Voice,* p. ■.

In place of *"The Voice,"* "ed. Hone" may be used in these subsequent-footnote forms.

PASCAL P. PARENTE

ON

the Meaning of Job

The Reverend Dr. Pascal P. Parente, author of The Ascetical
Life, The Mystical Life, Roma Inoccidua, *and of monographs
and articles pertaining to asceticism and mysticism, was at the
time of the publication of the following selection Associate Professor of Dogmatic, Ascetic, and Mystic Theology in the School of
Sacred Theology at the Catholic University of America in Washington, D.C. It appeared in* The Catholic Biblical Quarterly,
VIII (1946), pp. 213-219.

NOTE: *Scriptural citations employed in Father Parente's
article follow the reading of the Confraternity Edition.*

THE BOOK OF JOB: REFLECTIONS ON THE MYSTIC VALUE OF HUMAN SUFFERING

IN BOTH the prose and the brilliant poetry of the Book of Job we find the
most comprehensive answer to the ever recurring problem of human suffering. Specifically, the book sheds light on the mysterious motives behind all
the trials and afflictions of the just and the innocent in this life. Job's
friends, especially the first three of them, are in perfect agreement with
regard to the nature of human afflictions: they are a punishment for sin.
They argue that Job must have sinned very grievously for being subjected
to such extreme punishments. But because his life has been outwardly
blameless, they become suspicious and very exasperating, even for Job,
when they press him for confession or admission of guilt.

We have here the oldest and most common answer to the problem of human suffering. This philosophy of suffering is evidently in accordance with Genesis, 3:16 ff. The first man and the first woman were perfectly happy in the garden of Eden as long as they retained their innocence. The day they committed sin, their happiness came to an end. Sorrow, toil, sweat, agony, and death became their portion, and forthwith were they ejected from paradise. Sometime later, a terrible crime shook Adam's family: Cain committed murder: he killed his own brother. The voice of the Lord was heard on the wide plains, and that voice was a curse of the sinner: "Now, therefore, cursed shalt thou be upon the earth . . . When thou shalt till it, it shall not yield to thee its fruit: a fugitive and a vagabond shalt thou be upon the earth."[1] When the wickedness of men increased and became almost universal, punishment in the form of a destructive deluge was inflicted upon the children of Adam: "I will destroy man, whom I have created, from the face of the earth, from man even to the beasts."[2] More recent in the mind of Job's friends was the case of Sodom and Gomorrha.[3] With these and similar facts for their guidance, those four old amateurs of ethical science stood firmly by their theory, because, so they thought, it was based on indisputable principles. "Remember, I pray thee," says Eliphaz the Themanite, "who ever perished being innocent? or when were they destroyed? On the contrary, I have seen those who work iniquity, and sow sorrows, and reap them, perishing by the blast of God, and consumed by the spirit of his wrath."[4] Baldad the Suhite appeals to the wisdom of the fathers and the experience of past generations in order to convince Job that he is deceiving himself by not admitting that the present affliction is well deserved: "Inquire of the former generation, and search diligently into the memory of the fathers . . . and they shall teach thee. . . . Can the rush be green without moisture? or a sedge-brush grow without water? . . . Even so are the ways of all that forget God, and the hope of the hypocrite shall perish."[5] Thus, according to Baldad, Job was feigning innocence and justice when his terrible afflictions proved him guilty before God. He was, therefore, a hypocrite, one who had forgotten the just judgments of the Lord. The other friend, Sophar the Naamathite, thinks that he has discovered the reason of such a blameworthy attitude in Job's own vanity and pride: "A vain man is lifted up into pride, and thinketh himself born free like a wild ass's colt. But thou has [*sic*] hardened thy heart, and hast spread thy hands to him."[6] Eliu, the fourth of his friends, observes that Job has been adding blasphemy to his other sins by maintaining his in-

---

[1] Gen. 4:11ff. [2] Gen. 6:7. [3] Gen. 19:1ff.
[4] Job, 4:7ff. [5] Job, 8:8ff. [6] Job, 11:12ff.

nocence, for in this case he would have been more just than God who presumably was afflicting and punishing him without cause: "Job hath spoken foolishly, and his words sound not discipline. . . . Because he addeth blasphemy upon his sins."[7]

This, then, was the theory on the cause of man's sufferings in this life according to men who pretended to know the ways of God. Their false premises and foolish conclusion kindled the Lord's wrath and indignation. The Fathers of the Church have rightly regarded these theorizers of old as the forerunners of heretics, because as the heretics argued from isolated or mutilated texts, ignored tradition and the analogy of faith, thus obtaining false conclusions or half-truths, so Job's friends drew their conclusion from premises which were both particular in nature and from which nothing could be inferred: *Nihil sequitur geminis ex particularibus unquam!* For it is true only in some particular cases that he who suffers trials and afflictions in this life is being punished for his own sins. The problem still remains unsolved: Why do the just and innocent suffer?

Eliu, the fourth of those friends, is not included in God's condemnation of them, because he seems to have offered the key to the solution of the problem: "Who can search out his [God's] ways? or who can say to him: Thou has [*sic*] wrought iniquity? . . . Behold, God is great, exceeding our knowledge."[8] The same idea expressed here seems to underlie God's answer which is implied in everything that is said from chapter 38 to 41 of the book of Job: God's transcendent wisdom, power, and providence as manifested in the wonders of His creation prove the insufficiency of man's mind in knowing the exalted reasons of God's dealing with His saints. Even though conscious of his innocence, Job humbly acknowledges this truth: "I have spoken unwisely, and things that above measure exceed my knowledge"[9] and, being a saint, he immediately resolves to do penance for his imperfection: "Therefore I reprehend myself and do penance in dust and ashes" (*Ibidem*). "For there is no just man upon earth, that doth good, and sinneth not."[10] Yet, his many and great trials were by no means a punishment for faults such as are found even in the life of the just. The idea of retribution is ruled out by both the introductory chapter of the book of Job and by what is said in Ezechiel (14:1ff.) "Hast thou considered my servant Job," says the Lord bearing testimony to Job's innocence and sanctity, "that there is none like him in the earth, a man simple and upright, and fearing God, and avoiding evil, and still keeping his innocence? But thou hast moved me against him, that

7 Job, 34:37ff.   8 Job, 36:23ff.
9 Job, 42:3ff.   10 Eccles. 7:21.

I should afflict him without cause."[11] Job's justice was an extraordinary one; had he been living in the midst of a sinful people whom the Lord had singled out for destruction, he would have been spared on account of his virtue: "Son of man, when a land shall sin against me, so as to transgress grievously, I will stretch forth my hand upon it, and I will break the staff of the bread thereof: and I will send famine upon it, and will destroy man and beast out of it. And if these three men, Noe, Daniel, and Job, shall be in it: they shall deliver their own souls by their justice, saith the Lord of hosts."[12]

Little had been revealed to the saints of that period in the Old Testament about the glory that shall be revealed in us in the world to come, a glory that far surpasses and outweighs the sufferings of this life: "I reckon that the sufferings of this time are not worthy to be compared with the glory to come that shall be revealed in us."[13] Temporal death with its retinue of sorrows and pains, inflicted upon Adam and his children as retribution for sin, was staring men of those generations too boldly in the face to allow them to view the sufferings of the present life as anything but a punishment. With the spirit of love characteristic of the New Testament, in opposition to the spirit of fear of the Old Law, temporal suffering has taken on a new meaning. When suffering is accompanied by the love of God, it seems to lose the meaning of punishment. Like all other things, then, it works unto good: "To them that love God, all things work together unto good."[14] Sorrow that had become the sad inheritance of Adam's children, under the purging and satisfying effect of divine love, was turned into gold of supernatural merit, into a just claim to a crown of glory and to never-ending joy. After the Son of God had become "the man of sorrows" and had preferred to suffer the agony of death and the ignominy of the cross and thus enter into his glory,[15] suffering acquired a redeeming value for sinful mankind. The great lesson of love contained in the work of creation had been wasted on man. The good Lord undertook to give man another lesson of divine love, one that he might understand better than the former after so many centuries of toil, sweat, agony, and death. This second lesson was preached for nearly thirty-three years by the Savior of mankind and received its most eloquent peroration on the cross on Calvary. It was the lesson of human redemption, a redemption wrought by the love of God by means of the suffering and death of the Word Incarnate: "In this we know the charity of God, because he hath laid down his life for us."[16] The Passion and Death of Jesus Christ were the most

---

11 Job, 2:3.   12 Ezech. 14:13ff.   13 Rom. 8:18.
14 Rom. 8:28.   15 Luke, 24:26.   16 I Jn., 3:16.

convincing argument of the love of God for man. And when man had seen God proving His love for man by suffering for him, he began to love suffering for the love of God. Thus, the Christian Religion became the religion of love or charity and was represented by a cross, the symbol of suffering. Love and suffering are the elements of Christian heroism. The Christian carries his cross daily, following Christ and tending to perfection. Christian perfection without love and suffering is inconceivable. Even the ordinary sorrow for sin becomes perfect only when transformed into love of God. The common trials and afflictions that cast gloom and darkness on the life of the unbeliever are turned into golden light of eternal glory when touched by the love of God. This, then, is the secret why God chastises and afflicts his good servants in this life, whereas the wicked are seemingly spared altogether. Temporal suffering would ordinarily be wasted on the obdurate sinner. By way of contrast, we may say with St. Augustine that to them that do not love God all things seem to work together unto evil.

It is, therefore, in the light of the New Law that we obtain a most satisfying and gratifying solution to the ancient problem of the sufferings of the innocent and the just. Job could only assert his innocence and proclaim that his trials were not deserved. If he in his heart saw the real reason for his afflictions, he was certainly at a loss in expressing it in words to his friends, in spite of his great imagination and eloquence. Trials are for the man who loves God an opportunity for practicing patience, and Job was to become a champion of this virtue for all future generations: "Now this trial the Lord therefore permitted to happen to him [Tobias], that an example might be given to posterity of his patience, as also of holy Job."[17] Patient suffering renders a Christian more conformable to the image of the Son of God, the crucified Savior of mankind.[18] It purges, illumines, and sanctifies the soul by detaching it from all created things and prepares it for an eternal life of glory.

This last mentioned effect is attained in various ways and in different degrees according to the generosity of the individual and his co-operation with grace. We have, in this respect, the ordinary common trials and annoyances of the daily life. These are the daily cross we are requested to bear. The cross is made up of both active and passive mortification which demand patience, self-denial, humble submission to the will of God. St. James offers to all Christians two splendid examples of patience and endurance: "We account them blessed who have endured. You have heard of the patience of Job, and you have seen the end of the Lord."[19] No better

---

[17] Tob. 2:12.   [18] Rom. 8:29.   [19] Jam. 5:11.

words could express the Christian attitude in time of trials and afflictions than the words used by Job: "The Lord gave, and the Lord hath taken away: as it hath pleased the Lord so is it done: blessed be the name of the Lord."[20] "Think of Job," wrote St. Jerome to Paula, who was mourning the death of her daughter Blessilla, "think of all he had to endure and you will see how sensitive you are in comparison."[21] "The virtue of patience," says St. Gregory the Great, "is tried in three ways, for there are things we must bear from the side of God, others from the old enemy, the devil, and still others from our neighbor. We must tolerate persecutions, losses, and insults from our neighbor, temptations from the devil, punishment from God."[22] Job's patience was tried in all these different ways most extensively.

Patience is a most necessary virtue. No virtue, not even charity the queen of all virtues, will endure without patience according to St. Cyprian: *"Tolle ille patientiam, et desolata non durat."*[23] It is patience that bears persecutions, overcomes temptations, consummates suffering and martyrdom. After the grace of God, it is patience that contributes most to our final perseverance.

Passive trials assume sometimes an extraordinary form and are intended for an extraordinary purpose. Mystic writers have called them *dark night,* for as darkness means absence of light, so such trials are an absolute privation of all human and divine comforts. Purpose of the dark night is a thorough purgation of the soul. "We must know," writes St. John of the Cross, "that a soul, in order to attain to the state of perfection, has ordinarily to pass first through two principal kinds of nights, which spiritual persons call purgations or purifications of the soul, and here we call them nights for in the one as well as in the other the soul journeys, as it were, in darkness."[24] The two nights mentioned by St. John of the Cross are the night of the senses and the night of the spirit. Each may be active or passive. The entire Book of Job offers a typical example of a mystical or passive dark night of both the senses and the spirit. Passive purgations occur ordinarily in the life of saintly persons, of men and women of stout virtue and of great purity of conscience, whom the Lord has called to the higher mystical ways. Job was such a soul. The Lord himself said that there was no other like him on the earth, "simple, and upright, and fearing

---

20 Job, 1:21.   21 St. Jerome, *Epist.* 39,5.
22 St. Gregory the Great, *Homiliae in Evang.* 35,9.
23 St. Cyprian, *De Bono Patientiae,* 15.
24 St. John of the Cross, *Subida del Monte Carmelo,* Prologo.

God, and avoiding evil."[25] Deprived, within a short time, of all his children and of all his substance, he was finally struck with ulcers from head to foot and seemingly abandoned by God and men: "My kinsmen have forsaken me, and they that knew me, have forgotten me. . . . I called my servant, and he gave me no answer . . . Even fools despised me. . . . Have pity on me, at least you my friends, because the hand of the Lord hath touched me."[26] One could hardly picture to himself a darker night of the spirit and of the senses than that into which Job's body and soul were plunged. His plight fully resembles that of the mystic soul as described by St. John of the Cross in the two books of his *Noche Oscura*. This is manifest in his many utterances and lamentations: "Behold I shall cry suffering violence, and no one will hear: I shall cry aloud and there is none to judge. He hath hedged in my path round about, and I cannot pass, and in my way he hath set darkness."[27] "I waited for light, and darkness broke out."[28] The dark night is, therefore, the painful privation of all human and divine comforts to which the spiritual person was accustomed in his communion with God. In the darkness of this mystic night the soul feels that everything has been lost irretrievably. Sooner or later, however, the same soul will discover what a sublimely happy loss it has been. So it was with Job: "And the Lord gave Job twice as much as he had before."[29] We have no doubt that this great reward refers not only to his material possessions but also to spiritual blessings and graces. In this respect holy Job remains a model and a patron saint for all mystic souls.

Our present generation has been plunged into a long dark night of trials and afflictions without parallel. To a great extent these afflictions are a just retribution for the apostasy of the modern age, a divine visitation upon the unbelief of so many once devout children of the Church. Yet, so many are the innocent and God-fearing persons groping in this dark night and taking such a large share of agony, suffering, and death that we cannot abide by the sole idea of punishment as Job's friends did. We must recall the many redeeming values of human suffering mentioned before and not exclude them in this case. The redeeming value of trials and afflictions consists in this that they open the eyes of the mind and disentangle the heart from the vanities of this world. Prosperity and worldly success becloud the soul, afflictions and adversities illumine it: *"Sicut enim cordis oculos flagella aperiunt, sic mentis aciem aliquoties successus prosperi retundunt."*[30] Will humanity rise again from this abyss and emerge out of

---

[25] Job, 2:3.   [26] Job, 19:14ff.   [27] Job, 19:7ff.
[28] Job, 30:26.   [29] Job, 42:10.
[30] St. Gregory the Great, *In Septem Psalmos Poen.*, V.

the present dark night into the light of a new day? It will, but on condition that in the present hour men follow closely for their guidance the light of faith and of charity which will lead them to the blessings of justice and to the beauty of peace. Hope of redemption and resurrection never fails during the mystic night of the soul. Holy Job had clung almost desperately to this hope in his afflictions and was amply rewarded: "I know that my Redeemer liveth . . . this my hope is laid up in my bosom."[31]

BIBLIOGRAPHY ENTRY FOR RESEARCH PAPERS:

Parente, Pascal P. "The Book of Job: Reflections on the Mystic Value of Human Suffering." *The Catholic Biblical Quarterly*, 8 (1946), pp. 213-219. Reprinted in *The Voice out of the Whirlwind: The Book of Job*, ed. Ralph E. Hone. San Francisco, 1960.

FIRST FOOTNOTE:

* Pascal P. Parente, "The Book of Job: Reflections on the Mystic Value of Human Suffering," *The Catholic Biblical Quarterly*, 8 (1946), pp. 213-219, reprinted in *The Voice out of the Whirlwind: The Book of Job*, ed. Ralph E. Hone (San Francisco, 1960), pp. 110-117.

SUBSEQUENT FOOTNOTES:

* Parente, *op. cit.*, *The Voice*, p. ■.
* Parente, "Job," *The Voice*, p. ■.
* Parente, *The Voice*, p. ■.

In place of the *"The Voice,"* "ed. Hone" may be used in these subsequent-footnote forms.

---

31 Job, 19:25ff.

HILLEL A. FINE

ON

the Meaning of Job

Hillel A. Fine is an instructor in the Hebrew Union College-Jewish Institute of Religion. The selection that follows appeared in the Journal of Biblical Literature, LXXIV (1955), pp. 28-32.

THE TRADITION OF A PATIENT JOB

HONESTY, NOT PATIENCE is the real virtue of Job. There is a patient Job, and we meet him for a couple of chapters. "Shall we receive good at the hand of God, and shall we not receive evil?" he asks; or "The Lord it is who gave, and the Lord who hath taken away. Blessed be the name of the Lord." But this is not the Job who curses his day; who cries that God has wounded him heavily without cause (9:17); whose vexation is heavier than the sand of the seas (6:3). This is not the Job who is summoned by God from the whirlwind as one who darkeneth understanding through words without knowledge (38:2).[1]

The first two chapters and also the brief epilogue of the Book of Job tell of the patient hero. Job does not here question God's righteousness nor

---

[1] On the theory that the prologue and epilogue constitute a *Volksbuch*, written in a different spirit from the dialogues, cf. K. Budde, *Beiträge zur Kritik des Buches Hiob* (1876), pp. xiii f.; D. B. Duhm, *Das Buch Hiob*, "KHC," pp. vii f., etc. Perhaps the term *Volksbuch* is misleading. The simplicity of these chapters seems to be contrived. The perfect piety of Job, and the absolute disaster which overtakes him are symbolic rather than realistic. For these, as well as for the imaginative heavenly scenes, a more sophisticated style would have been out of place.

dispute his justice. Instead, he is the example of piety, always ready to accept his portion, and rewarded, at last, because he spoke straightforwardly of God (42:7). But even in the divine sentence which promises his reward, the friends of Job are angrily rebuked. And we wonder: What role did the friends play in this history of the patient Job? Were they an additional temptation, like his impious wife? Did they too urge him to "curse God and die"?

Perhaps, in addition to the prologue and epilogue, two additional chapters preserve the tradition of a patient Job, and preach the virtue of submission to the will of God. Hitherto, there have been no satisfactory explanations of chaps. 27 and 28 in their present context in the Book. At least the first six verses of chap. 27 are addressed to a plural audience. If the words are spoken by Job, as the superscription says, he is clearly addressing his three friends. But if one of the friends is the speaker, there is no indication of who could be his audience. When we come to vss. 11 and 12, we are in the same situation:

> I will teach you (pl.) about the hand of God;
> That which is with the Almighty I will not hide.
> As for you, all of you, you have seen,
> So why have you become entirely vain?

But if these verses seem to be spoken by Job, little in the rest of the chapter can be reconciled with his views.

> This is the portion of a wicked man with God,
> And the possession which oppressors receive
> from the Almighty . . . .
> Terrors overtake him like water;
> In the night, a whirlwind has stolen him away.

This is the argument which Job's friends have been expounding with persistent monotony. It would hardly be possible that they should now be uttered by a repentant Job, in order to teach these very friends the lesson which they have understood better than he.[2]

The most satisfactory explanations of this chapter hitherto have divided it into fragments, some spoken by Job, others addressed to him by

---

2 Of those who regard the whole of chap. 27 as a unit spoken by Job, cf. Budde, *op. cit.*, pp. 4-11; G. H. Ewald, *The Book of Job* (translated by J. F. Smith, 1882), pp. 252-256; A. Dillmann, *Hiob* (Leipzig, 1891), pp. 228 ff.; A. Weiser, *Das Buch Hiob* (Göttingen, 1951), pp. 191-195.

a friend.[3] Little sequence of thought could be discovered to connect these fragments. But it was assumed that considerable dislocation was to be found throughout the final section of the dialogues. Chap. 27 was only an outstanding example of such confusion.

Nevertheless, chap. 27 can be understood as a cohesive unit if it is read in the spirit of the prologue and epilogue. We may suppose that Job, having been tempted by his wife to abandon God, was next approached by his three friends. His wife has used practical arguments: Since life has no further advantage to offer you, but only pain, it would be most expedient if you were to curse God and die. Job's answer to her proves his integrity and provides the final refutation of the Satan's charge. The Satan had accused Job of having ulterior motives for his righteousness. The words of Job's wife make it clear that Job has nothing more to gain by flattering God. Job withstood the temptation to curse God, when such wickedness could not have increased his agony, but would have brought only the relief of death. He thereby proved that his righteousness was only for the sake of God.

The friends turned from the practical argument—"You can only gain now by the sin of blasphemy"—to a theological argument. You refuse to blaspheme and deny God's justice. Look about you at the prosperity of the wicked and the misfortune of the righteous. Consider whether God deserves your loyalty, and whether you are honest in justifying his ways to you.

In his answer, Job reaffirms the very qualities for which the prologue already has praised him.

עודנו מחזיק בתמתו

God says of Job in the prologue, "He still holds on to his uprightness" (2:3). And with a different emphasis,

עודך מחזיק בתמתך

---

[3] Thus T. K. Cheyne, *Job and Solomon* (London, 1887), pp. 38, 114; G. Bickel, *Das Buch Job* (Vienna, 1894), pp. 43 f.; Duhm, *op. cit.,* pp. 131-134; H. Torczyner, *Das Buch Hiob* (Vienna, 1920), pp. 189 ff.; S. R. Driver and G. B. Gray, *The Book of Job,* "ICC," pp. xxxviii ff., 225 ff.; P. Dhorme, *Le Livre de Job* (Paris, 1926), pp. xxxviii ff.; R. H. Pfeiffer, *Introduction to the Old Testament* (New York, 1941), pp. 663 f.; etc.

For the most part these critics divide the verses of chap. 27 between Job and Zophar, and take chap. 28 as an independent poem. Pfeiffer assigns the verses which are not Job's to Bildad. Bickel considers that part of chap. 28 is spoken by Job (*loc. cit.*).

"Do you still hold on to your uprightness?" his wife ironically asks (2:9).
Now, to confirm his determination, Job uses almost their very words.

עד אנוע לא אסיר תמתי ממני
בצדקתי החזקתי לא ארפה

Until I perish I shall not remove my uprightness from me;
I have held on to my righteousness, I shall not let it go (27:5b,
6a).

Only here, in all the central chapters of the dialogues, do we find the echo
of this key phrase of the prologue. Job holds fast to his righteousness.
He refuses to be tempted by misfortune or by arguments to abandon the
right way.

As in the prologue, the most feared of sins is here the sin of blasphemy (cf. 1:5), and Job, who had been meticulous even about an unspoken curse, is still careful to keep his mouth from sin.

My lips shall not speak iniquity;
My tongue shall not utter guile . . . .
I have held on to my righteousness and shall not let it go;
My mind shall not have[4] blasphemed[5] from the beginning of
my days (27:4, 6).

Job's refusal to curse God is the vital issue involved in the legend of the
pious Job. It is hardly relevant in the discussions of theodicy in the main
body of the dialogues.

Nor are vss. 8–10 explicable as the orthodox reproaches of wickedness
made by Job's friends.[6] If Eliphaz and his companions have had one con-

---

[4] On the use of the imperfect to denote future perfect time, cf. the similar
construction in I Sam 25:28.

[5] The root חרף is used both in the *qal* and *piel* to refer either to the reviling of
God or to the taunting of men. In the Psalms especially this root is used to describe
the wickedness of those who revile God (e.g. Ps 79:10; cf. Prov 14:31; see Ps 69:
10 for the use of the *qal* participle in this sense). To be sure the verb is always transi-
tive in the Bible. But in rabbinic Hebrew, the root is used intransitively in the sense of
"blaspheme." (Thus, in Sanh. 94a, b: בעצמו נפרע הקדוש ברוך הוא ממנו בעצמו. סנחריב
שחירף על ידי שליח נפרע הקב'ה ממנו על ידי שליח פרעה שחירף. See II Kings 19:23).
There is no reason to suppose, since the *qal* and *piel* are synonymous in the Bible,
that in late biblical Hebrew the *qal* might not have been used intransitively in this
sense of blaspheming God.
  It seems forced, therefore, to take ימי as the object of the verb, as is done by
many interpreters. The natural sense of ימי is "from the beginning of my days"; cf.
I Kings 1:6; Job 38:12; I Sam 25:28.

[6] Most of the interpreters who maintain the composite nature of chap. 27
(see note 3, above) assign these verses to Bildad or Zophar. But contrast Dhorme,
loc. cit., who recognizes that the verses must be spoken by Job.

sistent theme in their arguments, it is this: However wicked Job may have been, repentance is always possible (5:17 ff.; 8:5 ff.; 11:13 ff.). Even in the most violent condemnation of Job to which Eliphaz is finally forced, he still holds out the same hope (22:22 ff.). But the thought expressed in chap. 27 is the exact opposite of what the friends have been maintaining in these chapters. When disaster comes at last to the wicked man, no flattery could induce God to change the sentence. Conceivably the Job of the dialogues might have spoken in this way to his friends: "If I have been so wicked, would hypocritical words now save me; does God just want me to snivel before him?" But in the context of the surrounding verses, with their emphasis on the punishment of the wicked, these words also can be understood much more readily in the mouth of the uncomplaining Job.

Having refused to blaspheme or to join the ranks of the wicked, the pious Job comes next to the specific arguments of his friends. You say that the wicked prosper. I assure you that their prosperity is temporary. A terrible fate awaits them—What greater disaster could Job then describe than that which already had befallen him?—

> If his sons increase, it is for the sword,
> And his offspring shall not have enough bread (27:14).[7]

With irony, perhaps, but still without bitterness, Job derides this belief in the prosperity of the wicked.

At last, however, the most difficult question must be faced. The prosperity of the wicked may, we admit, be temporary. But what of the unspeakable suffering of the righteous? To this problem Job proposes an answer (chap. 28) similar in spirit to that of the "Voice from the Whirlwind" (chaps. 38 and 39). Real wisdom is beyond human reach; though man can uncover the precious stones which no eye has seen before, he can never come to the place of wisdom. He cannot understand God's ways, therefore; the problem of theodicy is beyond him. But God has given him a kind of wisdom:

יראת אדני היא חכמה
וסור מרע בינה

---

[7] Since no one in this legend has questioned for a moment the piety of Job, there can be no danger that his words will be twisted, and that his friends (or the reader) will assert the contrary of his proposition: Your prosperity also came to a sudden end; therefore your wickedness also must have been great. But contrast, e.g., Driver and Gray, *op. cit.,* pp. 229 f.

The fear of the Lord, that is wisdom
And to turn from evil is understanding (28:28).

This was the practice as well as the precept of Job. In almost the same words, the prologue tells us that Job was

ירא אלהים וסר מרע

"one who feared God, and turned from evil." It can scarcely be doubted that the final verse of chap. 28 had this Job of the prologue in mind.

Chaps. 27 and 28, therefore, constitute a unit separate from the main context of the dialogues. Moreover, the editors of the Book must have had some knowledge of their separate origin and function. Although Job has just been speaking in chap. 26, chap. 27 begins anew:

ויסף איוב שאת משלו ויאמר

("And Job again took up his parable and said"). In the same way, when chap. 28 is concluded and the other Job is speaking again, the same formula introduces his words (29:1). Instead of supposing that these superscriptions were the work of editors who completely misunderstood the argument of the poem, it can now be maintained that even the editors may have had some idea of what they were doing.

Of course, all the questions about these chapters have not been answered. Are chaps. 27 and 28 earlier or later than the main body of the dialogues?[8] Were they written by the same author as the prologue and epilogue, or should we assume otherwise, because of their greater affinity in style and vocabulary to the dialogues as a whole?[9] Was the poem on wisdom (chap. 28) especially written with Job in mind, or was the last verse, with its specific reference to the pious Job, a means of adapting a previous composition to its present context? These and similar questions remain.

But the chapters, at least in their present form, constitute a unit. They are the pious words spoken by Job in his readiness to accept whatever

---

[8] Evidently there is some interdependence in style. Cf. 27:10a and 22:26a. Cf. also 27:13 and 20:29.

[9] E. g. the parallelism between the divine names אל and אלוה on the one hand, and שדי on the other (27:2, 10, 13), occurring so frequently in the dialogues. The prologue commonly uses either the Tetragrammaton or else אלהים as the divine name. But note the use of אדני in 28:28.

Cf. also note 8, above.

portion God sends to him; rebuking the impious advice of his friends. He is not, here, the hero who defies God. He is not the giant wrestling with new problems beyond the scope of man. But his also is a worthy message for men who, wrestle though they may, must often encounter failure:

Behold, the fear of God, that is wisdom,
And to turn from evil is understanding.

BIBLIOGRAPHY ENTRY FOR RESEARCH PAPERS:

Fine, Hillel A. "The Tradition of a Patient Job." *Journal of Biblical Literature,* 74 (1955), pp. 28-32. Reprinted in *The Voice out of the Whirlwind: The Book of Job,* ed. Ralph E. Hone. San Francisco, 1960.

FIRST FOOTNOTE:

* Hillel A. Fine, "The Tradition of a Patient Job," *Journal of Biblical Literature,* 74 (1955), pp. 28-32, reprinted in *The Voice out of the Whirlwind: The Book of Job,* ed. Ralph E. Hone (San Francisco, 1960), pp. 118-124.

SUBSEQUENT FOOTNOTES:

* Fine, *op. cit., The Voice,* p. ■.
* Fine, "The Tradition," *The Voice,* p. ■.
* Fine, *The Voice,* p. ■.

In place of *"The Voice,"* "ed. Hone" may be used in these subsequent-footnote forms.

PART III

Sermons Interpreting
the Book of Job

JOHN CALVIN

ON

the Example of Job

‖‖

This selection is reprinted from Sermons from Job, *by John Calvin [1509-1564], ed. Leroy Nixon (Grand Rapids: Wm. B. Eerdmans Publishing Co., 1952), in which it is Sermon 2, pp. 18-30 (in turn from* Calvini Opera, Corpus Reformatorum, *volume 33, pp. 91-103). The editor writes in his preface (p. v): "Of all the sermons by Calvin, the 159 on the book of Job have probably been the most famous. They express clearly his sense of the majesty of God." There is a close relationship between the sermons on Job and Calvin's most important work,* The Institutes of the Christian Religion. *The text of the following sermon, treated three times in the* Institutes, *expresses Calvin's piety very well.*

THE LORD GAVE; THE LORD HAS TAKEN AWAY

Then Job arose, and tore his robe, and sheared his head, and threw himself upon the ground, and worshipped, and said, "Naked came I out of my mother's womb, naked I shall return there; the Lord has given it, and the Lord has taken it away; blessed be the name of the Lord." In all this Job sinned not at all, nor attributed anything unreasonable to God.—JOB 1:20-22

WE MAY well say that patience is a great virtue, as indeed it is; since there are very few who know what the word "patience" means; from which fact it might be concluded that we slightly value being patient and having this virtue at which we grab so long. Now God, seeing such indifference on the part of men, wishes to put before their eyes that which is so needful for us. For if we are not patient, our faith must have vanished; for it cannot be maintained apart from this means. This being so, God wills that amidst the miseries of this world we may always have a peaceable heart, and that we may be so assured of His goodness that we may rejoice and content ourselves therein, and that we may be able to glory against Satan and against all our enemies. And how is it possible, unless we regard ourselves as higher than this world, and we consider that, although our condition is miserable with respect to the opinion of the flesh, yet, since our God loves us, we surely must suffer? Now this passage is also the most excellent there is in Holy Scripture to show us what the word "patience" implies. We must be taught by it if we wish that God should acknowledge us as patient in our afflictions. We commonly say that a man is patient, although he may not have any true patience; for whoever suffers evil is called patient; but however much we may hold back being patient, we must abate our sadness. If there is some evil, may it be sweetened by recognizing that God never ceases to procure our salvation, that we must be subject to Him, and that it is entirely right that He should govern us according to His will. That is how patience is shown. But there is nothing better nor more useful than to behold the mirror which is here held up to us. We have seen that Job could have been overwhelmed,[1] having heard so much bad news. Now it is said that he has arisen, and has torn his robe, has sheared himself, and has thrown himself to the ground to humble himself before God. Here we see in the first place that those who are patient bear well an affliction, that they feel displeased and anguished in their heart; for if we were as a tree trunk or a stone, there would be no virtue in us. Is a man who is not aware of his illness worthy of being praised? We shall surely see a feeble-minded person who laughs, who mocks all the world, and yet he is at the edge of the grave, but he is not aware of his illness. This, then, does not deserve to be held or accounted as virtue, for it is stupidity; brute beasts sometimes feel nothing, but they are not virtuous on that account. So then, let us note that the word "patience" does not mean that men should be drugged,[2] that they should have no sadness, that they should not be at all offended when they experience some affliction; but the virtue is when they are able to restrain themselves and so hold themselves in bounds that they do not cease to glorify God in the midst of all their affliction, that they are not troubled by anguish and so swallowed up as to

---

[1] Fr. *abysme,* cast down to the depths.
[2] Fr. *eslourdis,* weighed down (mentally).

quit everything; but that they fight against their passions until they are able to conform to the good pleasure of God, and to conclude as Job here does, and to say that He is entirely just.

This is what we have to note when it is said, "Job has torn his robe, and has shorn his head." For such fashions were customary in oriental countries, as we know that there were more ceremonies in those regions which do not exist at all in the cold countries where we live. For when something happened which could move men to great anger, as a sign of grief they tore their clothes. So much for one item. Then, in that country, where they were accustomed to letting hair grow, they sheared themselves to display grief; on the other hand, where they sheared themselves, when they displayed grief they let the hair grow. They are, then, signs of the grief which here overtakes Job when he tears his robe and shears himself. Now it is certain that his act was not in any sense feigned, as quite often those who wish to disguise themselves assume masks in order that no one may guess that they are in great sadness and that they may not cease to laugh in their heart. Job has not used such hypocrisy. Let us know, then, when he has torn his robe and he has shorn his hair, that it was anguish and unlimited displeasure, and when he threw himself to the ground, it was yet another testimony. But it seems that Job here releases the bridle to his sadness, which would be a vice to condemn. For we know that men are only too excessive and overflowing in their passions. For although they restrain themselves and correct themselves as much as they can, yet they do not cease to go out of bounds, and there is nothing more difficult than to so restrain ourselves that we keep rule and compass on ourselves. We see that men cannot rejoice without being too gay. Grief or sadness is a much more violent passion which carries men further away than does joy. So then, we have to be on our guard always and whenever God sends us some adversity, for this is where we are accustomed to overflowing the most. Now it is here said that Job tore his robe; it seems that he wishes to spur himself to be more sad than he was (for a man who sees himself so disfigured is astonished at himself) and then when it comes to his hair it could be said that he sought aids to needle himself and add to his grief, and that he was as it were driving himself to despair. And this (as I have said) would surely be condemnable; but in the first place let us note that the Scripture here wished to express to us that the sadness of this holy person was so great and so vehement that he was not able to satisfy himself, that he went beyond ordinary custom by tearing his robe, to show that he experienced such anguish that it had grieved him to the bottom of his heart. This is what the Scripture wishes to express to us. Now although men ought to be on their guard lest they be swallowed up by sadness when they are afflicted, yet whenever God sends us some evil we must think about it. For the common manner of repulsing every trial is very bad; and yet this is the way men have been in this respect; when they wished to be patient they extinguished all thoughts of their maladies, they pushed them far away, and they withdrew from them; briefly, they wished to be so stupefied that they might know or discern nothing. Now entirely on the contrary, when God afflicts us it is not to give us blows of the mallet upon the head in order that we may be dazed and drowsy, but He wills to induce us to think of our miseries. How? Beyond the necessity for keeping in memory our sins in order to ask pardon for them and to be all the more careful to walk in the proper way, we are also instructed it is part of our life, in order not to please ourselves, in order not to be inflated by vanity, nor by presumption as we are, and then to acknowledge the obligation that we have to our God in that He treats us so tenderly, in that He carries us, as it were, in His bosom; and then when we see that He cares for our life, let us look further, that is to say, let us reach toward the eternal kingdom, wherein is our true joy and rest. This, then, is how God does not cease to be pitiful toward us when He sends us some affliction; for it is in order that, examining what is in us, we may also acknowledge our condition. Also it is good and useful that believers, when God afflicts them, are incited to think to themselves, "Who am I? What of me? Why am I thus afflicted?" Let them think (I say) of all these things. Now this is how Job was able to tear his clothes and then to shear his head without offending God; not that he wished to be precipitated in too great anger, but it tended to humility; as also it was to the ancients a sign of repentance; for if God sent pestilence or war, they wore sackcloth and threw ashes on their heads. Why that? It was not to nourish an evil sadness, of which Saint Paul speaks (2 Cor. 7:10), which he says is according to the world (we must flee from that), but that was of another sadness which he says is according to God, when men, after having known that they are poor sinners, come before their Judge; that they are there condemned, and they show that they deserve to be confounded. For he who wears sackcloth, who has ashes on his head, protests that he no longer has any basis to glorify himself, that he must keep his mouth closed, that he is as if he were already buried, as if to say, "I am not worthy that earth should sustain me, but it ought to be on top of me; and God should cast me down so low that I should be as it were trodden under foot."

This is what Job meant by it; seeing that God invited him to humility, he surely wished to conform; and for this cause he tore his robe and sheared his hair. Now though we see (as I have already mentioned) that patience is not without affliction, that it is very necessary that children of God should be sad, experiencing their pains; nevertheless they do not cease to have the virtue of patience when they resist their passions in such a way that they do not fret against God, that they do not go out of bounds, that they do not kick against hope, but rather that they give glory to God; as immediately follows in the text, *"Job threw himself to the ground, he did it to worship."* Now it is true that this word means "to recline" or "to lie down," but the purpose of humbling oneself before God and doing him homage is implied. We see some who throw themselves on the ground, but they continue to be so angry that, if it were possible, they would ascend above the clouds to wage war against God. We see those who are so carried away by spite, but it is because they cannot rush against God as they wish. Now Job, entirely to the contrary, throws himself on the ground, in order to worship, indeed looking to God to humble himself before His high majesty. For when we experience the hand of God, it is then that we ought to do Him more homage than ever. It is true that if God treats us kindly we ought to be moved thereby to come to Him, as in fact He does invite us. The great goodness He uses—what is it except that He wishes to draw us to Himself? But since we are so lazy about coming, He has to summon us and show what right He has over us; as when a prince sees his vassal who is slow to do his duty, he sends him his officer to summon him. So God, seeing that we do not take into account coming to Him, or perhaps that we do not come with such ardent affection as would be properly required, invites us and calls us. Job then, knowing the purpose and true use of afflictions, threw himself on the ground, in order to do homage to God, as if to say, "Lord, it is true that until now I have served and honored Thee, while I prospered, and I was in my great triumphs, I delighted in doing Thee service. But what of it? I did not fully know myself; and now I see my weakness, that we are miserable creatures. So then, Lord, I come now to do Thee a new homage, when it pleases Thee to afflict me in the world; Lord, I voluntarily yield myself to Thee, and ask not unless it be to render myself subject to Thy hand, whatever may come of it." So much for the saying "Job threw himself to the ground, having the aim of worshipping God."

We come now to the saying, namely, that Job recognized man's condition. "Naked came I out of my mother's womb," he says, "and naked I shall return there." When he says "there," he implies that he is from elsewhere, namely, from the womb of earth which is the mother of all; or perhaps, like a man who has a heart ailment,[3] he does not express all the words, but he speaks half, as we see that those who are extremely sad do not express all their words. Yet this protestation is clear enough, namely, that Job wishes to say, "Well, I must return to the earth, just as I came out of the womb of my mother." It is true that this passage could be taken in a double sense: namely, firstly, that it was as a general statement. Behold men who came naked into the world, and when they return it is likewise; they do not take their riches, nor their honors, nor their pomp, nor their delights; they must go away in decay; the earth must receive them. But the other exposition is more suitable, that Job applies this to himself, as if he said, "Naked I came out of the womb of my mother; for a time God willed to enrich me, that I had a great quantity of livestock, I had a large family, I had a multitude of children; in brief, I was well-adorned with gifts and blessings with which God had enlarged me. Now He wills that I go away entirely naked; He had enriched me with all these things, and He has taken them from me, in order that I may return to my first estate, and that I may now get ready to go to the grave." Now this sentence is good to note. For Job could not better prove his patience than by resolving to be entirely naked, inasmuch as the good pleasure of God was such. Surely men resist in vain; they may grit their teeth, but they must return entirely naked to the grave. Even the pagans have said that death alone shows the littleness of men. Why? For we have a gulf of covetousness, that we would wish to gobble up all the earth; if a man has many riches, vines, meadows, and possessions, it is not enough; God would have to create new worlds, if He wished to satisfy us. But what if we die? Six feet under we decay and are reduced to nothing. So then, death shows what our nature is; nevertheless, we see many who fight against such a necessity; they build worthy sepulchers, they have triumphant funerals; it seems that such people wish to resist God, but they do not succeed at all. Now such is the general condition of men; but as for us, we must suffer patiently to be despoiled when we have been clothed with goods and riches; we must allow (I say) that God should deprive us of everything, and that we should live entirely undressed and naked, and that we should be prepared to return to the grave in such condition. This (I say) is how we shall prove that we are patient. And it is what Job wished to indicate in this passage. Thus however and whenever we shall

---

[3] Fr. *qui a le coeur serré.*

lack the goods of this world, we shall be hungry and thirsty, we shall be pressed by some afflictions, and we shall not have any help, let us think of our origin, let us look at ourselves and who we are and where we are going. For men abuse the fatherly care of God toward them when He proves to them what must happen to them. Surely we ought to have this very well imprinted on our hearts: namely, that God does not will that we lack anything, that He would not have put us in the world unless He was willing to feed us; yet we must always acknowledge that this comes from outside ourselves, and we should not suppose that we have by our own right what we possess by the gratuitous goodness of our God. If a man should feed me out of his pure liberality and should say to me, "Come every day; you shall have so much wine, so much bread; I wish to entertain you; and it is not that I would oblige myself to you, but I would give you this;" if thereupon I wished to bring suit to collect what I ought to beg for each day, receiving substance from his hand, if I wished to gain an income by what he gives me out of his pure liberality, would it not be too villainous an ingratitude? I would deserve that someone should spit in my face. All the more are we bound to receive the goods which God gives us with all modesty, knowing that He owes us nothing and, because we are poor, we must come to Him to beg every day from His infinite liberality. So then, when we have some need, let us run to Him (as I have said) and acknowledge, "Whence came I out? From the womb of my mother, entirely naked, a poor, miserable creature; I needed help and to be cleansed from the poverty in which I was; I would have utterly perished unless I had been helped from elsewhere. It pleased God, then, to feed and preserve me until now and to do me an infinite number of favors. And howsoever now He may will to afflict me, it is very right that I should bear everything patiently, since it comes from His hand." This is what we have to note from what is shown us by Job, "Naked I came out of my mother's womb, and also naked I shall return to the grave." In summary, we think, when God shall have placed in our hands some goods, that the ownership of them ought to remain ours, that we shall be so accompanied by our riches that they will come with us to the grave, that we ought never to be deprived of them. Now let us not reckon that way; for we deceive ourselves; but on the contrary let us know that if the good pleasure of God is to take away from us the goods with which He may have enlarged us, the next day we must be ready to be deprived of them, that it would do us no harm to be despoiled in a minute of everything that we may have been able to acquire in our whole lifetime.

Besides Job leads us still further, saying, *"God had given it, and He has taken it away; yet blessed be the Name of the Lord."* When he says that God had given it, he shows that it is reasonable that God should dispose of what He has put in our hands, since it is His own; for when God sends us riches, it is not that He gives up His title, that He may no longer have lordship (as He ought to have), since He is Creator of the world. For the word "Creator" implies that He has done everything in such a way that all power and sovereign dominion must remain His. And although men possess each one their portion according as God has enlarged them by the goods of this world, yet He must always remain Lord and master of them. Job, then, acknowledged this, entirely subjected himself to the good pleasure of God; and all of us confess this thing to be more than equitable; however, no one is willing to conform to it. Though this may be, as soon as God shall have let us enjoy for three days some blessing, it seems to us, if He takes it away from us, that He greatly injures us; we shall murmur against Him. And what is to be said of this? Recently I discussed ingratitude, that it seems to us when God has shown Himself one time liberal toward us through His gratuitous goodness that He ought never to fail us, no matter what we do. This then is a statement which is common enough but so poorly practiced that it is clearly seen that it is understood by a very small number. So much more must we think over the meaning of "The Lord had given it, and the Lord has taken it away;" that we may acknowledge what liberty our Lord has to give us enjoyment of His goods and also, when it may please Him, to deprive us of them in a minute. And this is why Saint Paul exhorts us (1 Cor. 7:30) that, inasmuch as the face of this world passes away and all things wear out and vanish, we should possess as though we possessed not, that is to say, we should not bind our courage;[4] as is said in another place (1 Tim. 6:17), "We must not trust in the uncertainty of riches;" we must always be ready to say with Job, "When God will have despoiled us of what He has given us," or perhaps, "Lord, Thou hast exercised Thy right, Thou hadst given it, and Thou hast taken it away when it pleased Thee." Here, then, is the summary of this passage, namely, whenever we think of the goods of this world we should remember that we hold everything from God. And on what condition? It is not by property right, that He should not longer wish any claim over it, and that He should no longer have any mastery over it; but if it pleased him to put it in our hands, it is on the

---

[4] Fr. *que nous n'y ayons point nostre courage attaché.* Perhaps he means we should not set our hearts on things.

condition that He may take it back when it seems good to Him. Let us acknowledge then, that we are so much more obligated to Him when He shall have caused us to enjoy some benefit, a day, a month, or some space of time, and afterwards, if He despoils us of it, that we should not find it too strange; but that we should run back to that acknowledgment which I have said, "May God always retain such superiority over us that He can dispose of His own as seems good to Him." If it is lawful for mortal men to control their wealth as they wish, ought not much more control to be attributed to the living God? Seeing then how God ought to have mastery not only over what we possess but also over our persons and over our children, we ought to humble ourselves before Him by subjecting ourselves entirely to His holy will, without any contradiction. But what do we see? There are very few who do this homage to God. It is true that everyone will surely say that it is God Who has given them all that they possess; but what do they do about it? They claim Him, and raise themselves as it were in defiance of Him. And what is this? I pray you, is it not a mockery? Indeed it is unbearable hypocrisy, when, after having protested that we hold everything from God, we nevertheless are never willing that He should dispose of it, we are not willing that He should change anything, but wish that He would leave us in peace and go away from us, as if we were separated from Him and exempt from His jurisdiction. It is just as if someone said, "Oh, I am content to acknowledge that such a one is my Prince, I shall do Him enough homage and obedience; but He should not enter my house, He should not come to ask for anything, He should not cause me any trouble." The world could not suffer such villainy. Nevertheless this is how they frolic with God. And what is the meaning of the confession "Let us hold everything to be from Him" while we are not willing that He should touch anything? We see, then, how the world openly mocks God; but we must always follow what is here shown, namely, since God has given us what is in our hands, He may claim it back and take it back when He wills.

Furthermore the final implication is added. "Blessed be *the name of the Lord.*" For by this Job so submits himself to God that He confesses Him to be good and just, although he is harshly afflicted from His hand. I have said that this implies more, inasmuch as one might still be able to attribute to God entirely sovereign power by saying, "Very well, since He has given it, He can surely take it away," but nevertheless he would not confess that God did it justly and reasonably, as there are many who when they are afflicted accuse God of cruelty, or of too great a severity, so that they cannot reserve for Him the right to take back what He has given to them; and they do not consider (as I have said) that they should possess wealth in such a way that they could be stripped of it the next day. There are very few who hold this consideration in such a way that remain peaceable in it and confess that there is nothing better than to be entirely subject to the majesty of God and to recognize that if He let us do according to our desires there would be only confusion; but when He governs us according to His will, it is for our profit and salvation. This is the point of view to which we must come. So, we see now that the sentence implies more when it is said, "Blessed be the name of the Lord." For we must not only split hairs over words,[5] we must consider from what affection this proceeds, and that it is said in truth and without pretense. For how is it possible that we should bless the name of God, except by first of all confessing that He is just. Now he who murmurs against God as if He were cruel and inhuman thereby curses God and as much as is in him rises against Him; he who does not recognize that God is his father and that he is His child, who does not render testimony of His goodness, does not bless God at all. And why not? For those who do not taste the mercy and the grace which God performs toward men when He afflicts them must gnash their teeth, throw and disgorge some venom against Him. To bless, then, the name of God implies that we are well persuaded that He is just and equitable in His nature; and not only this, but that he is good and merciful. This is how we shall be able to bless (according to the example of Job) the name of God: it will be by acknowledging His justice and His equity, and then by acknowledging also His grace and His fatherly goodness toward us.

And this is why the text also adds in conclusion: *In all these things Job sinned not, nor attributed to God anything unreasonable.* Or literally: Job put forward nor imposed upon God nothing which was without reason; and it is a manner of speaking which is very worthy to be observed. Why is it that men fret so when God sends them things entirely contrary to their desire, except that they do not acknowledge that God does everything by reason and that He has just cause? For if we had well-imprinted on our hearts "All that God does is founded in good reason" it is certain that we would be ashamed to chafe so against Him when, I say, we know that He has just occasion to dispose thus of things, as we see. Now, therefore, it is especially said that Job attributed to God nothing without reason, that is to say, that he did not imagine that God did anything which

---

[5] Fr. *esplucher les mots,* pick words.

was not just and equitable. So much for one item. But we must note above all the word "in God"[6] or "to God." This implies much, for we do not think that the works of God should be spoken of so abominably as we speak of them. As soon as God does not send what we have desired, we dispute against Him, we bring suit, not that we appear to do this, but our manner shows that this is nevertheless our intent. We consider every blow, "And why has this happened?" But from what spirit[7] is this pronounced? From a poisoned heart; as if we said, "The thing should have been otherwise, I see no reason for this." Meanwhile God will be condemned among us. This is how men exasperate themselves.[8] And in this what do they do? It is as if they accused God of being a tyrant or a hairbrain who asked only to put everything in confusion. Such horrible blasphemy blows out of the mouths of men. Yet very few think about it. However, the Holy Spirit wished to tell us that, if we wish to render glory to God and to bless His name properly, we must be persuaded that God does nothing without reason. So then, let us not attribute to Him either cruelty or ignorance, as if He did things in spite and unadvisedly, but let us acknowledge that He proceeds in everything and through everything with admirable justice, with goodness and infinite wisdom, so that there is only entire uprightness or equity in all that He does. Now it is true that here is an article to deduce, namely, how Job recognized that God took away from him what had been carried away by robbers; which seems to us very strange; but what we cannot explain this hour we shall reserve until tomorrow. It is enough to have shown that if we are afflicted we must not think that it happens without reason, but God has just cause to do it. And whenever we are tried and anguished let us run back to Him, let us pray to Him that He will give us grace to acknowledge that nothing happens to us in this world except as He disposes; indeed, and to be certain that He disposes in such manner that everything always comes back to our salvation. And when we shall have this knowledge, it will cause us to bear patiently the afflictions which He will send us. It will also be to make us humble ourselves before Him, and that having tasted for ourselves His fatherly goodness, we shall ask only to glorify Him in everything and through everything, as much in affliction as in prosperity.

Now we shall bow before the face of our God.

---

[6] Fr. *En Dieu.*
[7] Fr. *de quel courage.*
[8] Fr. *se iettent hors des gonds,* throw themselves off their hinges.

BIBLIOGRAPHY ENTRY FOR RESEARCH PAPERS:

Calvin, John. *Sermons from Job,* ed. Leroy Nixon. Grand Rapids: Wm. B. Eerd-mans Publishing Co., 1952. Sermon 2, pp. 18-30. Reprinted in *The Voice out of the Whirlwind: The Book of Job,* ed. Ralph E. Hone. San Francisco, 1960.

FIRST FOOTNOTE:

* John Calvin, *Sermons from Job,* ed. Leroy Nixon (Grand Rapids: Wm. B. Eerdmans Publishing Co., 1952), Sermon 2 reprinted in *The Voice out of the Whirlwind: The Book of Job,* ed. Ralph E. Hone (San Francisco, 1960), pp. 126-136.

SUBSEQUENT FOOTNOTES:

* Calvin, *op. cit., The Voice,* p. ■.
* Calvin, *Sermons, The Voice,* p. ■.
* Calvin, *The Voice,* p. ■.

In place of *"The Voice,"* "ed. Hone" may be used in these subsequent-footnote forms.

SØREN KIERKEGAARD

ON

the Example of Job

||||||||||||||||||||||||||||||||||||||||||||||||||||||||||||||||||||||||||||||||||||||||||||||||||||||||||||||||||||||||||||||||||||||||||||||||||||||||||||||||||||||||||

*Speaking from over a century ago, the voice of Søren Kierke-
gaard (1813-1855) has been one of the most important in theological discussion in our day. His concern was fairly consistently
with the individual and with the inner life of the spirit. Real
manhood to Kierkegaard, as well as to Job, was born unto anguish
as the sparks fly upward. Life presents such absolute disjunctions
that there can be no mediation. In the last analysis, man is shut
up to the leap of faith. The source of the selection is Kierkegaard's Edifying Discourses, from Vol. II, translated from the
Danish by David F. Swenson and Lillian Marvin Swenson (Minneapolis: Augsburg Publishing House, 1944), pp. 7-26.*

THE LORD GAVE, AND THE LORD HATH
TAKEN AWAY, BLESSED BE THE NAME
OF THE LORD

*Then Job arose, and rent his mantle, and shaved his head, and fell upon the ground
and worshipped, and said: Naked came I out of my mother's womb, and naked shall
I return thither: the Lord gave, and the Lord hath taken away; blessed be the name
of the Lord.*—JOB 1:20-21

NOT ONLY do we call that man a teacher of men who through some particularly happy talent discovered, or by unremitting toil and continued
perseverance brought to light one or another truth; left what he had acquired as a principle of knowledge, which the following generations strove

to understand, and through this understanding to appropriate to themselves. Perhaps, in an even stricter sense, we also call that one a teacher of men who had no doctrine to pass on to others, but who merely left himself as a pattern to succeeding generations, his life as a principle of guidance to every man, his name as an assurance to the many, his own deeds as an encouragement to the striving. Such a teacher and guide of men was Job, whose significance is by no means due to what he said but to what he did. He has indeed left a saying which because of its brevity and its beauty has become a proverb, preserved from generation to generation, and no one has been presumptuous enough to add anything to it or to take anything away from it. But the expression itself is not the guidance, and Job's significance does not lie in the fact that he said it, but in the fact that he acted in accordance with it. The expression itself is truly beautiful and worthy of consideration, but if another had used it, or if Job had been different, or if he had uttered it under different circumstances, then the word itself would have become something different—significant, if, as uttered, it would otherwise have been so, but not significant from the fact that he acted in asserting it, so that the expression itself was the action. If Job had devoted his whole life to emphasizing this word, if he had regarded it as the sum and fulfillment of what a man ought to let life teach him, if he had constantly only *taught* it, but had never himself practiced it, had never himself acted in accordance with what he taught, then Job would have been a different kind of man, his significance different. Then would Job's name have been forgotten, or it would have been unimportant whether anyone remembered it or not, the principal thing being the content of the word, the richness of the thought it embodied.

If the race had accepted the saying, then it would have been this which one generation transmitted to the next; while now, on the contrary, it is Job himself who guides the generations. When one generation has served its time, fulfilled its duty, fought its battle, then Job has guided it; when the new generation, wth its innumerable ranks and every individual among them in his place, stands ready to begin the journey, then Job is again present, takes his place, which is the outpost of humanity. If the generation sees only happy days and prosperous times, then Job faithfully goes with them, and if, nevertheless, an individual in his thought experiences the terrible, is apprehensive because of his conception of what life may conceal of horror and distress, of the fact that no one knows when the hour of despair may strike for him, then his troubled thought resorts to Job, dwells upon him, is reassured by him. For Job keeps faithfully by his side and comforts him, not as if he had thus suffered once for all what he would never again have to endure, but he comforts him as one who witnesses that the terror is endured, the horror experienced, the battle of despair waged, to the honor of God, to his own salvation, to the profit and happiness of others. In joyful days, in fortunate times, Job walks by the side of the race and guarantees it its happiness, combats the apprehensive dream that some horror may suddenly befall a man and have power to destroy his soul as its certain prey.

Only the thoughtless man could wish that Job should not accompany him, that his venerable name should not remind him of what he seeks to forget, that terror and anxiety exist in life. Only the selfish man could wish that Job had not existed, so that the idea of his suffering might not disturb with its austere earnestness his own unsubstantial joy, and frighten him out of his intoxicated security in obduracy and perdition. In stormy times, when the foundation of existence is shaken, when the moment trembles in fearful expectation of what may happen, when every explanation is silent at the sight of the wild uproar, when a man's heart groans in despair, and "in bitterness of soul" he cries to heaven, then Job still walks at the side of the race and guarantees that there is a victory, guarantees that even if the individual loses in the strife, there is still a God, who, as with every human temptation, even if a man fails to endure it, will still make its outcome such that we may be able to bear it; yea, more glorious than any human expectation. Only the defiant could wish that Job had not existed, so that he might absolutely free his soul from the last vestiges of love which still remained in the plaintive shriek of despair; so that he might complain, aye, even curse life; so that there might be no consonance of faith and confidence and humility in his speech; so that in his defiance he might stifle the shriek so that it might not even seem as if there were anyone whom it defied. Only the effeminate could wish that Job had not existed, so that he might relinquish every thought, the sooner the better; might renounce every emotion in the most abhorrent impotence and completely efface himself in the most wretched and miserable oblivion.

The expression which, when it is mentioned, at once reminds us of Job, immediately becomes vividly present in everyone's thought, is a plain and simple one; it conceals no secret wisdom that must be unearthed from the depths. If a child learns this word, if it is entrusted to him as an endowment, he does not understand for what purpose he will use it; when he understands the word, he understands essentially the same thing by it as does the wisest. Still, the child does not understand it, or rather he does not understand Job; for what he does not comprehend is all the distress and wretchedness with which Job was tested. About that the child can have only a dark premonition; and yet, happy the child who understood the word and got an impression of what he did not comprehend, that it was the most terrible thing imaginable; who possessed, before sorrow and adversity made its thought cunning, the convincing and childishly vivid conviction that it was in truth the most terrible. When the youth turns his attention to this word, then he understands it, and understands it essentially the same as do the child and the wisest. Still he perhaps does not understand it, or rather, he does not understand Job, does not understand why all the distress and wretchedness should come in which Job was tried; and yet, happy the youth who understood the word and humbly bowed before what he did not understand, before his own distress made his thought wayward, as if he had discovered what no one had known before. When the adult reflects on this word, then he understands essentially the same by it as did the child and the wisest. He understands, too, the wretchedness and distress in which Job was tried; and yet perhaps he does not understand Job, for he cannot understand how Job was able to say it; and yet, happy the man who understood the word, and steadfastly admired what he did not understand, before his own distress and wretchedness made him also distrustful of Job. When the man who has been tried, who fought the good fight through remembering this saying, mentions it, then he understands it, and understands it essentially the same as the child and as the wisest understood it; he understands Job's misery, he understands how Job could say it. He understands the word, he interprets it, even though he never speaks about it, more gloriously than the one who spent a whole life-time in explaining this one word.

Only the one who has been tried, who tested the word through himself being tested, only he interprets the word correctly, and only such a disciple, only such an interpreter, does Job desire. Only such a one learns from Job what there is to learn, the most beautiful and blessed truth, compared with which all other art and all other wisdom is very unessential. Therefore we rightly call Job a teacher of mankind, not of certain individual men, for he offers himself to every man as his pattern, beckons to everyone by his glorious example, summons everyone in his beautiful words. While the more simple-minded man, the one less gifted, or the one less favored by time and circumstances, if not enviously yet in troubled despondency, may sometimes have wished for the talent and the opportunity to be able to understand and absorb himself in those things which scholars from time to time have discovered, may also have felt a desire in his soul to be able to teach others, and not always be the one to receive instruction, Job does not tempt him in this way. How, too, could human wisdom help here? Would it perhaps seek to make that more intelligible which the simplest and the child easily understood, and understood as well as the wisest! How would the art of eloquence and fluency help here? Would it be able to produce in the speaker or in some other man what the simplest is able to do as well as the wisest—action! Would not human wisdom rather tend to make everything more difficult? Would not eloquence, which, despite its pretentiousness, is nevertheless unable to express the differences which always dwell in the heart of man, rather benumb the power of action, and allow it to slumber in extensive reflection! But even if this is true, and even if, as a result of this, the speaker endeavors to avoid intruding disturbingly between the striving individual and the beautiful pattern which is equally near to every man, so that he may not increase sorrow by increasing wisdom; even if he takes care not to ensnare himself in the splendid words of human persuasiveness, which are very unfruitful, still it by no means follows that the reflection and the development might not have their own significance. If the one reflecting had not hitherto known this word, then it would always be an advantage to him that he had learned to know it; if he had known it, but had had no occasion to test it, then it would always be an advantage to him, that he had learned to understand what he perhaps might some time have to use. If he had tested it, but it had deceived him, if he even believed that it was the word which had deceived him, then it would be advantageous to him that he had previously reflected upon it, before he fled from it in the unrest of the strife and the haste of battle! Perhaps the reflection would sometime become significant to him; it might perhaps happen that the reflection would become vividly present in his soul just when he needed it in order to penetrate the confused thoughts of his restless heart; it might perhaps happen that what the reflection had understood only in part, would sometime gather itself regenerated in the moment of decision; that what reflection had sowed in corruption would spring up in the day of need in the incorruptible life of action.

So let us endeavor to understand Job better in his beautiful words: *The Lord gave, the Lord hath taken away; blessed be the name of the Lord!*

In the land toward the east there lived a man whose name was Job. He was blessed with lands, innumerable herds, and rich pastures; "his words had lifted up the fallen, and had strengthened the feeble knees"; his tent was blessed as if it rested in the lap of heaven, and in this tent he lived with his seven sons and three daughters; and "the secret of the Lord" abode there with him. And Job was an old man; his joy in life was his pleasure in his children, over whom he watched that no evil might come upon them. There he sat one day alone by his fireside, while his children were gathered at a festival at the oldest brother's house. There he offered burnt offerings for each one individually, there he also disposed his heart to joy in the thought of his children. As he sat there in the quiet confidence of happiness, there came a messenger, and before he could speak there came another, and while this one was still speaking, there came a third, but the fourth messenger brought news concerning his sons and daughters, that the house had been overthrown and had buried them all. "Then Job stood up and rent his mantle and shaved his head, and fell down upon the ground and worshipped." His sorrow did not express itself in many words, or rather he did not utter a single one; only his appearance bore witness that his heart was broken. Could you wish it otherwise! Is not that one who prides himself on not being able to sorrow in the day of sorrow put to shame by not being able to rejoice in the day of gladness? Is not the sight of such imperturbability unpleasant and distressing, almost revolting, while it is affecting to see an honorable old man, who but now sat in the gladness of the Lord, sitting with his fatherly countenance downcast, his mantle rent and his head shaven! Since he had thus surrendered himself to sorrow, not in despair but stirred by human emotion, he was swift to judge between God and himself, and the words of his judgment are these: "Naked I came forth from my mother's womb, and naked shall I return thither." With these words the struggle was decided, and every claim which would demand something from the Lord, which He did not wish to give, or would desire to retain something, as if it had not been a gift, was brought to silence in his soul. Then follows the confession from the man whom not sorrow alone but worship as well had prostrated on the ground: "The Lord gave, and the Lord hath taken away. Blessed be the name of the Lord!"

The Lord gave, the Lord took. What first arrests the attention is that Job said, "The Lord gave." Is not this word irrelevant to the occasion; does it not contain something different from what lay in the event itself? If a man in a single moment is deprived of everything dear to him, and deprived of the most precious of all, the loss will perhaps at first so overwhelm him that he will not even trust himself to express it, even if in his heart he is conscious before God that he has lost everything. Or he will not permit the loss to rest with its crushing weight upon his soul, but he will put it away from him, and in his heart's agitation he will say, "The Lord took." And thus to humble one's self before the Lord in silence and humility is indeed worthy of praise and emulation, and in the struggle such a man saves his soul though he loses all his gladness. But Job! At the moment when the Lord took everything, he did not say first, "The Lord took," but he said first, "The Lord gave." The word is short, but in its brevity it perfectly expresses what it wishes to indicate, that Job's soul is not crushed down in silent submission to sorrow, but that his heart first expanded in gratitude; that the loss of everything first made him thankful to the Lord that He had given him all the blessings that He now took from him. It did not happen with him, as Joseph predicted, that the abundance of the seven fruitful years would be entirely forgotten in the seven lean years. The nature of his gratitude was not the same as in that long vanished time when he accepted every good and perfect gift from the hand of God with thanksgiving; but still his gratitude was sincere, as was his conception about the goodness of God which now became living in his soul. Now he is reminded of everything which the Lord had given, some individual thing perhaps with even greater thankfulness than when he had received it. It was not become less beautiful to him because it was taken away, nor more beautiful, but still beautiful as before, beautiful because the Lord gave it, and what now might seem more beautiful to him, was not the gift but the goodness of God. He is reminded again of his abundant prosperity, his eyes rest once more upon the rich pastures, and follow the numerous herds; he remembers what joy there was in having seven sons and three daughters, who now needed no offering except that of thankfulness for having had them. He is reminded of those who perhaps still remembered him with gratitude, the many he had instructed, "whose weak hands he had strengthened, whose feeble knees he had upheld." He is reminded of the glorious days when he was powerful and esteemed by the people, "when the young men hid themselves out of reverence for him, and the old men arose and remained standing." He remembers with thankfulness that his step had not turned away from the way of righteousness, that he had rescued the poor who complained, and the fatherless who had no helper; and therefore, even in this moment, the "blessing of the forsaken" was upon him as before.

The Lord gave. It is a short word, but to Job it signified so very much; for Job's memory was not so short, nor was his thankfulness so forgetful. While thankfulness rested in his soul with its quiet sadness, he bade a gentle and friendly farewell to everything at once, and in this farewell everything disappeared like a beautiful memory; moreover, it seemed as if it were not the Lord who took it, but Job who gave it back to Him.

When therefore Job had said, "The Lord gave," then was his mind well prepared to please God also with the next word, "The Lord took."

Perhaps there might be someone who on the day of sorrow was also reminded that he had seen happy days, and his soul would become even more impatient. "Had he never known happiness, then the pain would not have overcome him, for what is pain, after all, other than an idea which he does not have who knows nothing else, but now happiness had so educated and developed him as to make him conscious of the pain." Thus his happiness became pernicious to him; it was never lost but only lacking, and it tempted him more in the lack than ever before. What had been the delight of his eyes, he desired to see again, and his ingratitude punished him by conjuring it up as more beautiful than it had formerly been. What his soul had rejoiced in, it now thirsted for again, and his ingratitude punished him by painting it as more desirable than it had previously been. What he had once been capable of doing, that he now wished to be able to do again, and his ingratitude punished him with visions that had never had reality. Thus he condemned his soul to living famished in the never satisfied craving of want.

Or there awakened a consuming passion in his soul, because he had not even enjoyed the happy days in the right way, had not imbibed all the sweetness from their voluptuous abundance. If there might only be vouchsafed to him one little hour, if he might only regain the glory for a short time so that he might satiate himself with happiness, and thereby learn to disregard the pain! Then he abandoned his soul to a burning unrest; he would not acknowledge to himself whether the enjoyment he desired was worthy of a man; whether he ought not rather to thank God that his soul had not been so extravagant in the time of joy as it had now become in his unhappiness; he was not appalled by the thought that his desires were the cause of his perdition; he refused to be concerned by the fact that more wretched than all his wretchedness was the worm of desire in his soul, which would not die.

Perhaps there might be another man who at the moment of loss also remembered what he had possessed, but who had the audacity to try to prevent the loss from becoming intelligible to him. Even if it were lost, his defiant will would still be able to retain it as if it were not lost. He would not endeavor to bear the loss, but he chose to waste his strength in an impotent defiance, to lose himself in an insane preoccupation with the loss. Or in cowardice he immediately avoided humbly attempting to understand it. Then oblivion opened its abyss, not so much to the loss as to him, and he did not so much escape the loss in forgetfulness as he threw himself away. Or he lyingly sought to belittle the good which he had once enjoyed, as if it never had been beautiful, had never gladdened his heart; he thought to strengthen his soul by a wretched self-deception, as if strength lay in falsehood. Or he irrationally assured himself that life was not so hard as one imagined, that its terror was not as described, was not so hard to bear, if one, as you will remember that he did, began by not finding it terrifying to become such a person.

In fact, who would ever finish, if he wished to speak about what so frequently has happened, and will so frequently be repeated in the world? Would he not tire far sooner than would passion of that ever new ingenuity for transforming the explained and the understood into a new disappointment, wherein it deceives itself!

Let us rather, therefore, turn back to Job. On the day of sorrow when everything was lost, then he first thanked God who gave it, defrauded neither God nor himself, and while everything was being shaken and overthrown, he still remained what he had been from the beginning— "honest and upright before God." He confessed that the blessing of the Lord had been merciful to him, he returned thanks for it; therefore it did not remain in his mind as a torturing memory. He confessed that the Lord had blessed richly and beyond all measure his undertakings; he had been thankful for this, and therefore the memory did not become to him a consuming unrest. He did not conceal from himself that everything had been taken from him; therefore the Lord, who took it, remained in his upright soul. He did not avoid the thought that it was lost; therefore his soul rested quietly until the explanation of the Lord again came to him, and found his heart like the good earth well cultivated in patience.

The Lord took. Did Job say anything except the truth, did he use an indirect expression to indicate what was direct? The word is short, and it signifies the loss of everything; it naturally occurs to us to repeat it after him, since the expression itself has become a sacred proverb; but do we just as naturally link it to Job's thought? For was it not the Sabeans who fell upon his peaceful herds and killed his servants? Did the messenger who brought the news say anything else? Was it not the lightning which destroyed the sheep and their shepherds? Did the messenger who brought the news mean something else, even though he called the lightning the fire from heaven? Was it not a wind-storm from out of the desert which overturned the house and buried his children in the ruins? Did the messenger mention some other perpetrator, or did he name someone who sent the wind? Yet Job said, "The Lord took"; in the very moment of receiving the message, he realized that it was the Lord who had taken everything. Who told Job this? Or was it not a sign of his fear of God that he thus shifted everything over to the Lord, and justified Him in doing it; and are we more devout, we who sometimes hesitate a long time to speak thus?

Perhaps there was a man who had lost everything in the world. Then he set out to consider how it had happened. But everything was inexplicable and obscure to him. His happiness had vanished like a dream, and its memory haunted him like a nightmare, but how he had been cast off from the glory of the one into the wretchedness of the other, he was unable to understand. It was not the Lord who had taken it—it was an accident. Or he assured himself that it was the deceit and cunning of men, or their manifest violence, which had wrested it from him, as the Sabeans had destroyed Job's herds and their keepers. Then his soul became rebellious against men; he believed he did God justice by not reproaching Him. He fully understood how it had happened, and the more immediate explanation was that those men had done it, and furthermore it was because the men were evil and their hearts perverted. He understood that men are his neighbors to his injury; would he perhaps have understood it in the same way if they had benefited him? But that the Lord who dwells far away in heaven might be nearer to him than the man who lived next to him, whether that man did him good or evil, such an idea was remote from his thought. Or he fully understood how it had happened, and knew how to describe it with all the eloquence of horror. For why should he not understand that when the sea rages in its fury, when it flings itself against the heavens, then men and their frail accomplishments are tossed about as in a game; that when the storm rushes forth in its violence, human enterprises are mere child's play; that when the earth trembles in terror of the elements and the mountains groan, then men and their glorious achievements sink as nothing into the abyss. And this explanation was adequate for him, and, above all, sufficient to make his soul indifferent to everything. For it is true that what is built on sand does not even need a storm to overthrow it; but would it not also be true that a man cannot build and dwell elsewhere and be sure his soul is safe! Or he understood that he himself had merited what had befallen him, that he had not been prudent. For had he rightly calculated in time, it would not have happened. And this explanation explained everything by first explaining that he had corrupted himself and made it impossible for him to learn anything from life, and especially impossible for him to learn anything from God.

Still who would ever finish if he tried to explain what has happened and what will frequently be repeated in life? Would he not become tired of talking before the sensual man would weary of deluding himself with plausible and disappointing and deceptive explanations? Let us therefore turn away from that which has nothing to teach us, except in so far as we knew it before, so that we may shun worldly wisdom and turn our attention to him from whom there is a truth to be learned—to Job and to his devout words, "The Lord took." Job referred everything to the Lord; he did not retard his soul and extinguish his spirit in reflections or explanations which only engender and nourish doubt, even if the one who dwells on them does not realize it. In the same instant that everything was taken from him he knew that it was the Lord who had taken it, and therefore in his loss he remained in understanding with the Lord; in his loss, he preserved his confidence in the Lord; he looked upon the Lord and therefore he did not see despair. Or does only that man see God's hand who sees that He gives; does not that one also see God who sees that He takes? Does only that one see God who sees His countenance turned toward him? Does not that one also see God who sees Him turn His back upon him, as Moses always saw only the Lord's back? But he who sees God has overcome the world, and therefore Job in his devout word had overcome the world; was through his devout word greater and stronger and more powerful than the whole world, which here would not so much carry him into temptation but would overcome him with its power, cause him to sink down before its boundless might. And yet how weak, indeed almost childishly so, is not the wild fury of the storm, when it thinks to cause a man to tremble for himself by wresting everything away from him, and he answers, "It is not you who do this, it is the Lord who takes!" How impotent is the arm of every man of violence, how wretched his shrewd cleverness, how all human power becomes almost an object of compassion, when it wishes to plunge the weak into the destruction of despair by wresting everything from him, and he then confidently says, "It is not you, you can do nothing—it is the Lord who takes."

Blessed be the name of the Lord! Hence Job not only overcame the world, but he did what Paul had desired his striving congregation to do: after having overcome everything, he stood. Alas, perhaps there has been someone in the world who overcame everything, but who failed in the moment of victory. The Lord's name be praised! Hence the Lord remained the same, and ought He not to be praised as always? Or had the Lord really changed? Or did not the Lord in truth remain the same, as did Job? The Lord's name be praised! Hence the Lord did not take everything, for He did not take away Job's praise, and his peace of heart, and the sincerity of faith from which it issued; but his confidence in the Lord remained with him as before, perhaps more fervently than before; for now there was nothing at all which could in any way divert his thought from Him. The Lord took it all. Then Job gathered together all his sorrows and "cast them upon the Lord," and then He also took those from him, and only praise remained in the incorruptible joy of his heart. For Job's house was a house of sorrow if ever a house was such, but where this word is spoken, "Blessed be the name of the Lord," there gladness also has its home. And Job indeed stands before us the image of sorrow, expressed in his countenance and in his form; but he who utters this word as Job did still bears witness to the joy, even if his testimony does not direct itself to the joyous but to the concerned, and yet speaks intelligibly to the many who have ears to hear. For the ear of the concerned is fashioned in a special manner, and as the ear of the lover indeed hears many voices but really only one— the voice of the beloved, so the ear of the concerned also hears many voices, but they pass by and do not enter his heart. As faith and hope without love are only sounding brass and tinkling cymbals, so all the gladness in the world in which no sorrow is mingled is only sounding brass and tinkling cymbals, which flatter the ear but are abhorrent to the soul. But this voice of consolation, this voice which trembles in pain and yet proclaims the gladness, this the ear of the concerned hears, his heart treasures it, it strengthens and guides him even to finding joy in the depths of sorrow.

My hearer, is it not true? You have understood Job's eulogy; it has at least seemed beautiful to you in the quiet moment of reflection, so that in thinking of it you had forgotten what you did not wish to be reminded of, that which indeed is sometimes heard in the world in the day of need, instead of praise and blessing. So let it then be forgotten, you will deserve, as little as I, that the memory of it should again be revived.

We have spoken about Job, and have sought to understand him in his devout expression, without the speech wishing to force itself upon anyone. But should it therefore be entirely without significance or application, and concern no one? If you yourself, my hearer, have been tried as Job was, and have stood the testing as he did, then it truly applies to you, if we have spoken rightly about Job. If hitherto you have not been tested in life, then it indeed applies to you. Do you think perhaps that these words apply only under such extraordinary circumstances as those in which Job was placed? Is it perhaps your belief that if such a thing struck you, then the terror itself would give you strength, develop within you that humble courage? Did not Job have a wife, what do we read about her? Perhaps you think that terror cannot get as much power over a man as can the daily thralldom in much smaller adversities. Then look you to it that you, as little as any man, do not become enslaved by some tribulation, and above all learn from Job to be sincere with yourself, so that you may not delude yourself by an imagined strength, through which you experience imaginary victories in an imaginary conflict.

Perhaps you say, if the Lord had taken it from me, but nothing was given to me; perhaps you believe that this is by no means as terrible as was Job's suffering, but that it is far more wearing, and consequently a more difficult struggle. We shall not quarrel with you. For even if this were true, the quarrel would still be unprofitable, and increase the difficulty. But in one thing we are in agreement, that you can learn from Job, and, if you are honest with yourself and love humanity, then you cannot wish to evade Job, in order to venture out into a hitherto unknown difficulty, and keep the rest of us in suspense, until we learn from your testimony that a victory is also possible in this difficulty. So if you then learn from Job to say, "Blessed be the name of the Lord," this applies to you, even if the preceding is less applicable.

Or perhaps you believe that such a thing cannot happen to you? Who taught you this wisdom, or on what do you base your assurance? Are you wise and understanding, and is this your confidence? Job was the teacher of many. Are you young, and your youth your assurance? Job had also been young. Are you old, on the verge of the grave? Job was an old man when sorrow overtook him. Are you powerful, is this your assurance of immunity? Job was reverenced by the people. Are riches your security? Job possessed the blessing of lands. Are your friends your guarantors? Job was loved by everyone. Do you put your confidence in God? Job was the Lord's confidant. Have you reflected on these thoughts, or have you not rather avoided them, so that they might not extort from you a confession, which you now perhaps call a melancholy mood? And yet there is no hiding place in the wide world where troubles may not find you, and there has never lived a man who was able to say more than you can say, that you do not know when sorrow will visit your house. So be sincere with yourself, fix your eyes upon Job; even though he terrifies you, it is not this he wishes, if you yourself do not wish it. You still could not wish, when you survey your life and think of its end, that you should have to confess, "I was fortunate, not like other men; I have never suffered anything in the world, and I have let each day have its own sorrows, or rather bring me new joys." Such a confession, even if it were true, you could still never wish to make, aye, it would involve your own humiliation; for if you had been preserved from sorrow, as no other had, you would still say, "I have indeed not been tested in it, but still my mind has frequently occupied itself seriously with the thought of Job, and with the idea that no man knows the time and the hour when the messengers will come to him, each one more terrifying than the last."

BIBLIOGRAPHY ENTRY FOR RESEARCH PAPERS:

Kierkegaard, Søren. *Edifying Discourses.* Translated from the Danish by David F. Swenson and Lillian Marvin Swenson. Minneapolis: Augsburg Publishing House, 1944. Vol. II, pp. 7-26, reprinted in *The Voice out of the Whirlwind: The Book of Job,* ed. Ralph E. Hone. San Francisco, 1960.

FIRST FOOTNOTE:

* Søren Kierkegaard, *Edifying Discourses,* tr. from the Danish by David F. Swenson and Lillian Marvin Swenson (Minneapolis: Augsburg Publishing House, 1944), Vol. II, pp. 7-26, reprinted in *The Voice out of the Whirlwind: The Book of Job,* ed. Ralph E. Hone (San Francisco, 1960), pp. 138-151.

SUBSEQUENT FOOTNOTES:

* Kierkegaard, *op. cit., The Voice,* p. ■.
* Kierkegaard, *Edifying Discourses, The Voice,* p. ■.
* Kierkegaard, *The Voice,* p. ■.

In place of *"The Voice,"* "ed. Hone" may be used in these subsequent-footnote forms.

JOHN HENRY NEWMAN

ON

the Example of Job

John Henry Newman (1801-1890) was reared a Protestant and in 1845 was received into the Roman Catholic Church. Subsequently he was ordained a priest and in 1879, after a tempestuous and controversial career, was created a cardinal. The sermon which follows was preached while Newman was still an Anglican clergyman. It indicates something of his earnestness and power of concentrating on a single message. It is Sermon VIII from Parochial and Plain Sermons, 8 vols. (London: Rivingtons, 1875).

PEACE AND JOY AMID CHASTISEMENT

Though He slay me, yet will I trust in Him.—JOB xiii.15

THIS IS a sentiment which often occurs in Scripture, whether expressed in words or implied in the conduct of good men. It is founded on the belief that God is our sole strength, our sole refuge; that if good is in any way in store for us, it lies with God; if it is attainable, it is attained by coming to God. Though we be in evil case even after coming to Him, we are sure to be in still worse, if we keep away. If He will but allow sinners such as we are to approach Him, for that is the only question, then it is our wisdom to approach Him at once in such a way as He appoints or appears to approve. At all events, there is no one else we can go to; so that if He refuses to receive us, we are undone. And on the other hand, if He does receive us, then we must be ready to submit to His will, whatever it is towards us, pleasant or painful. Whether He punishes us or not, or how far pardons, or how far restores, or what gifts He bestows, rests with Him; and it is our part to take good or bad, as He gives it.

This is the general feeling which St. Peter seems to express in one way, when he cries out, "Lord, to whom shall we go? Thou hast the words of eternal life." It is the feeling, under different circumstance and in a different tone, of the Prodigal Son, when he said, "I will arise, and go to my Father, and will say unto him, Father, I have sinned against heaven and before thee, and am no more worthy to be called thy son; make me as one of thy hired servants." It shows itself under the form of peace and joy in the words of David: "Yea, though I walk through the valley of the shadow of death, I will fear no evil, for Thou art with me;" and it speaks in the text by the mouth of the heavily afflicted and sorely perplexed Job, "Though He slay me, yet will I trust in Him." Inquirers seeking the truth, prodigals repentant, saints rejoicing in the light, saints walking in darkness, all of them have one word on their lips, one creed in their hearts,— to "trust in the Lord for ever, for with the Lord Jehovah is everlasting strength."

There is another case different from all of these, in which it is equally our duty and wisdom thus to stay ourselves upon God; that of our being actually under punishment for our sins. Job maintained his innocence, which his friends denied, as thinking his afflictions were a judgment upon some secret wickedness now coming to light. He, on the other hand, being conscious of his integrity and sincerity in time past, could but wait in the darkness till God revealed why He chastised as a sinner, one who had been "perfect and upright, one that feared God and eschewed evil."[1] But men may often be conscious that they have incurred God's displeasure, and conscious that they are suffering it; and then their duty is still to trust in God, to acquiesce or rather to concur in His chastisements, as if they were a self-inflicted penance, and not the strokes of His rod. For God is our merciful Father, and when He afflicts His sons, yet it is not willingly; and though in one sense it is in judgment, yet in another and higher, it is in mercy. He provides that what is in itself an evil should become a good; and, while He does not supersede the original law of His just government, that suffering should follow sin, He overrules it to be a healing medicine as well as a punishment. Thus, "in wrath" He "remembers mercy." Thus St. Paul decides, quoting the words of Solomon, "My son, despise not

---

[1] Job i.1.

thou the chastening of the Lord, nor faint when thou art rebuked of Him; for whom the Lord loveth He chasteneth, and scourgeth every son whom He receiveth."[2] You see he calls it a "chastisement" and a "rebuke," but still it is in "love"; and it is our duty to take it as such, and to bless and praise Him under it.

And Scripture affords us some remarkable instances of persons glorifying, or called on to glorify God, when under His hand, some of which it may be well here to mention.

One which deserves especial notice is Joshua's exhortation to Achan, who was about to be put to death for secreting a portion of the spoils of Jericho, and was thus dying apparently under the very rod, and (if any man ever), without encouragement to trust in God, or hope of profit in serving Him. "My son," Joshua says to him, "give, I pray thee, glory to the Lord God of Israel, and make confession unto Him." Thus he began; yet observe, his next words were as severe as if no duty, no consolation, were left to the offender,—despair only. He continues thus sternly, "Why hast thou troubled us? the Lord shall trouble thee this day." "And all Israel stoned him with stones, and burned them with fire," him "and his sons and his daughters," "after they had stoned them with stones."[3]

Another remarkable instance is given us in the history of Jonah; I mean, in his address to Almighty God out of the fish's belly. It illustrates most appositely the case of a true, though erring servant of God, chastised, yet blessing God under the chastisement, and submitting himself even without any clear prospect how he was to escape from it.—"I cried," he says, "by reason of my affliction unto the Lord, and He heard me; out of the belly of hell cried I, and Thou heardest my voice. For Thou hadst cast me into the deep, in the midst of the seas, and the floods compassed me about; all Thy billows and Thy waves passed over me. Then I said, I am cast out of Thy sight; yet I will look again toward Thy Holy Temple. . . . When my soul fainted within me, I remembered the Lord; and my prayer came in unto Thee, into Thine Holy Temple. They that observe lying vanities forsake their own mercy. But I will sacrifice unto Thee with the voice of thanksgiving; I will pay that that I have vowed. Salvation is of the Lord."[4]

Now, one should think, nothing could be more simple to understand than the state of mind described, 'however hard it be to realize; I mean the combined feeling that God loves us yet punishes us, that we are in

---

[2] Hebrews xii.5,6.
[3] Joshua vii.19, 24, 25.
[4] Jonah ii.2-4, 7-9.

His favour, yet are under, or may be brought under His rod; the feeling of mingled hope and fear, of suspense, of not seeing our way, yet having a general conviction that God will bring us on it, if we trust to Him. And this the more so, because very few indeed, or rather none at all, but must be conscious, if they get themselves to think, that they have grievously offended God at various times, in spite of all He has done for them; and that, for what they know, Christ's merits may not be so imputed to them as to exempt them from some punishment, which will demand in them the feelings I have been describing. Yet so it is, at least in this day, men find a difficulty in conceiving how Christians can have hope without certainty, sorrow and pain without gloom, suspense with calmness and confidence; how they can believe that in one sense they are in the light of God's countenance, and that in another sense they have forfeited it. I proceed then to describe a state of mind which it seems to me no one ought to misunderstand; it is so much a matter of common sense.

We will say, a man *is* a serious Christian, for of such I am speaking. He is in the habit of prayer, and he tries to serve God, and he has, through God's mercy, the reward of such a religious course of life. He has a consciousness that God has not given him up; he has a good hope of heaven. I am not speaking of the strength of it, but more or less a good hope. He does not indeed often realize the circumstances of the future, he does not dwell upon what is to become of him; but I mean he does not look forward anxiously, feeling, as he does, around him the proofs, in which he cannot be deceived, of God's present love towards him. His being allowed to attend God's ordinances, his being enabled in a measure to do his duty, his perception of Gospel truth, his being able to accept, admire, and love high and holy views of things, all conspire to prove that at present, without going on to speculate or to calculate how he shall fare at Christ's judgment seat, at present he is in a certain true sense in God's favour. The feeling may vary from a mere trembling guess, a mere dawning and doubtful hope, to a calm though subdued confidence; still, something of this kind is the state of mind of all serious men. They are not in a state of immediate alarm, for the day of judgment is future; and for the present they are conscious somehow they are in God's hands as yet, and are thereby supported.

But now suppose a man (and this is the case of most Christians), who is conscious of some deliberate sin or sins in time past, some course of sin, or in later life has detected himself in some secret and subtle sin. Supposing it breaks on a man that he has been an overindulging father, and his children have suffered from it; or that he has been harsh, and so has alienated those who ought to have confided in him; or that he has been over-fond of worldly goods, and now is suddenly overtaken with some grievous fall in consequence; or that he has on any particular occasions allowed sin in others, when he might have warned them, and they are dead and gone, and the time of retrieving matters is past; or that he has taken some false step in life, formed connexions irreligiously or the like:— what will be his state when the conviction of his sin, whatever it is, breaks upon him? Will he think himself utterly out of God's favour? I think not; he has the consciousness of his present prevailing habits of obedience, in spite of his not being so careful as he ought to be; he knows he has served God on the whole; he knows he has really desired to do God's will, though he has not striven as he ought to have done, or has been negligent in some particulars in ascertaining what that will was. Much as he may be shocked at and condemn and hate himself, much as he will humble himself, yet I do not suppose he will ordinarily *despair*. But on the other hand, will he take up a notion that God has forgiven him? I think not either; I will not believe he has so little humility, and so much presumption. I am not speaking of ordinary men, who have no fixed principle, who take up and lay down religion as it may happen, but of *serious* men; and I will not lightly impute it to any such man that he takes up the notion of his having been absolutely forgiven for the sins of his past life. Who is to forgive him? how is he to know it? No; I see no certainty for him; he will be convinced indeed that God has not cast him out of His sight, whatever his sins have been; for he will argue, "If I were utterly reprobate, I could have no holy wish at all, or could even attempt any good work." His outward privileges, his general frame and habit of mind, assure him of so much as this; but as surely his memory tells him that he has had sins upon his conscience; he has no warrant that they are not there still; and what has come, what is to come of them, what future consequences they imply, is unknown to him. Thus he is under two feelings at once, not at all inconsistent with each other,—one of present enjoyment, another of undefined apprehension; and on looking on to the Day of Judgment, hope and fear both rise within him.

Further, let us suppose such an one actually brought into trouble, and that evidently resulting from the sin in question. For instance: supposing he has been passionate and violent, or unjust, and suppose some serious annoyance in consequence befalls him from the injured party; or supposing he has neglected some obvious duty, and now the consequences of that neglect come upon him; or supposing he has in former years been imprudent in money transactions, and is under the embarrassments which they have occasioned. Now here he certainly experiences, with a clearness which he cannot explain away, a double aspect of God's providence towards him; for he sees His love and fatherly affection plainly enough, in the opportunity he still has of attending God's ordinances, and in the inward evidences of that faith, obedience, and peace, which can come from God only; on the other hand, he sees His displeasure as plainly in the visitation which comes upon him from without. I know it is sometimes said, that such trials are to the true Christian not judgments but corrections; rather they are judgments *and* corrections; surely they are merciful corrections, but they are judgments too. It is impossible but a man must consider (for example) undutiful children a punishment on him for having once neglected them, or penury a judgment on him for past extravagance, whatever may be his present attainments in obedience, greater or less; whatever his hope that God is still gracious to him in spite of past sin; whatever be his duty and his ability to turn it into a blessing. It is against common sense to say otherwise. In spite, then, of the doctrine now popular, that "as to past sin, it is over, God has forgiven it," really I do not think any truly serious lowly Christian of himself will think so, will of himself say so, though many are betrayed into such a way of speaking from want of seriousness, and many because others indulge in it. God has not absolutely forgiven the sin past; here is a proof He has not,—He is punishing it. It will be said, He has forgiven it as to its eternal consequences. Where is the proof of this? all we see is, that He is punishing it. If we argue from what we see, He has not forgiven it at all. Here a man will say, "How can He be gracious to me in other ways, unless He has been gracious so as to forgive? Is not forgiveness the first step in grace?" It *was* when we were baptized; whether it is so since must be decided from Scripture. Certainly, if we go by what our reason tells us (and I insist on what reason would say, not as if I thought Scripture spoke differently, but because persons often seem to have a great difficulty in understanding what is meant by saying that God should both be gracious to us, yet not have absolutely forgiven us), I say nothing is more compatible with reason, judging from our experience of life, than that we should have God's present favour and help without full pardon for the past. Supposing, for instance, a child has disobeyed us, and in disobeying has met with an accident. Do we at once call him to account? and not rather wait a while, till he is in a fit state to be spoken to, and when we can better decide whether or no what has befallen him be a sufficient punishment? We pass the fault over for the present, and act towards him as if we had no cause to be displeased. This is one instance out of a thousand which occur in daily life of our treating kindly, nay loving, persons with whom we are dissatisfied, and mean one day to expostulate. Surely, then, the two ideas are quite separate, of putting aside what is past and of showing kindness at present. Of course, the instance referred to is not an exact parallel to our own state in God's sight; no exact parallel can be found. We do not even know what is meant by saying that God, who sees the end from the beginning, pardons at one time rather than at another. We can but take divine truth as it is given us. We know there is one time at least when He pardons persons, whom He foresees will afterwards fall away and perish; I mean, the time of Baptism. He desires the salvation of those who ultimately come short of it. It does not follow, then, because He is still gracious to us, enables us to serve Him, and makes us love Him, that therefore we have no arrears of obedience, no debt of punishment, to be brought into account against us, when He visits. And so far from its being strange that we are in this double state in His sight, and ought to have these mingled feelings towards Him, rather it is too reasonable for us not to assent to it unless Scripture says the contrary.

But, it may be said, Scripture does say the contrary; it declares that all who repent shall be forgiven. Doubtless; but what is repentance? is repentance the work of a day? is it a mere word? is it enough to say, "I am sorry?" Consider the different frames of mind we are in hour by hour; how much we feel at one time which we do not at another. What degree or kind of feeling is enough? Considering how our hearts deceive us, is even the most passionate feeling to be trusted? Did not the Son in the Parable say, "I go, sir," and went not? Do you suppose that he meant to go, or did not mean when he so promised? did he not think he was in earnest when he was not? If indeed we feel distress at having sinned, let us give God the praise; it shows that He is pleading with our hearts, it shows that He wishes us to repent, that He is bringing us to repentance: but it does not show that we have duly repented, and that He actually has forgiven us.

But it may be said, that Scripture says that faith will apply to us the merits of Christ, and thus become the instrument of washing away sins. I do not know where Scripture so says; but even if it did, I suppose it would not speak of every kind of faith, but of living faith. But how is living faith ascertained? by works;—now, who will maintain that his works can be such as to bring home to him an undoubting assurance, that he has a faith able to do this great thing?

But again, a person may say, "I have a conviction I have this faith; I feel I have; I feel I can appropriate the merits of Christ." Or again, "I have an assurance that I am forgiven." True: but where does Scripture tell us such an assurance, without grounds for it beyond our feeling it, comes from God? where is it promised? till it is found there, we must be content not to be sure, and to fear and hope about ourselves at once.

But it may be said again, that we are told, "Ask, and ye shall receive;" if then we ask for pardon, we are pardoned. It is true; but where is it said that we shall gain it by once asking? on the contrary, are we not expressly told that we must come again and again, that we must "wait on the Lord," that we must "continue in prayer," that we must "pray and not faint," that we must be importunate in our supplications, though God seems as though He hears us not? It is quite true that if we persevere in prayer for pardon through our lives, that in spite of God's not sensibly answering, we shall at length obtain it; but this is the very state of mingled hope and fear, of peace and anxiety, of grace and of insecurity, which I have been describing. Surely, no words can express better such a waiting and persevering temper than the words of the text, "though He slay me, yet will I trust in Him."

Once more, it may be said, and this is a far better answer than any that I have hitherto noticed, that the Sacrament of the Lord's Supper imparts to us forgiveness, and assures us of it. The benefits imparted to our souls by this Holy Sacrament are indeed most high and manifold; but that the absolute forgiveness of our past sins is not one of them, is plain in our Church's judgment from the Confession in the Service, indeed from all our Confessions. We there say, that "the remembrance of our sins is grievous, and the burden intolerable;"—now does our "remembrance" only carry us back to those sins which we have committed since we last came to this blessed ordinance, and not rather those into which we have fallen from our earliest years? and if so, is not this to confess that we are not sure of their pardon? else why are they a "burden?" Again: "for Thy Son our Lord Jesus Christ's sake forgive us all that is past"; our past sins then are not forgiven when we thus pray: does not that "past" extend back through our whole life up to infancy? If so, up to the day of our death, up to the last awful celebration of this Blessed Sacrament in our sick chamber, we confess that our sins all through our life are unforgiven, whatever be the effect, which we know cannot be little, or the grace of that Ordinance and the Absolution therein pronounced over us.

To these considerations I will add one other. We are to be *judged* at the Last Day, and "receive the things done in the body, whether they be good or bad."[5] Our sins will then be had in remembrance; therefore they are not forgiven here.

---

[5] 2 Corinthians v.10.

It seems clear, then, that the sins which we commit here, are not put away here,—are not put away absolutely and once for all, but are in one sense upon us till the Judgment. There is indeed one putting away of sins expressly described in Scripture, which we all received from God's mercy, when though "born in sin and the children of wrath," we were "made the children of grace." This was in Baptism, which accordingly is called in the Creed, the "One Baptism for the remission of sins." And of this great absoluting Scripture speaks in many ways, calling on those who have not received it to "arise, and be baptized, and wash away their sins;" declaring there is "a fountain opened to the house of David, and to the inhabitants of Jerusalem, for sin and for uncleanness;" and promising that "though their sins be as scarlet, they shall be as white as snow; though they be red like crimson, they shall be as wool."[6] This all we have received long since; and none knows but God and His Angels,—nay, I will say, none knows but God Himself and His Only Son, and His Spirit who then is present,—how much Holy Baptism does secretly for our souls, what hidden wounds it heals, and what inbred corruption it allays; but this is past long since. We have sinned in spite of grace then given; many of us grievously; and the question now is, where do we stand, and *how* are we to gain a second pardon?

I answer, we stand in God's presence, we are in His Church, in His favour, in the way of His grace, in the way to be pardoned; and this is our great comfort on the very first view of the matter. We are not in a desperate state, we are not cast out of our Father's house; we have still privileges, aids, powers, from Him; our persons are still acceptable to Him. And this being the case, through God's great mercy, it is quite clear what our duty is, even if Scripture gave us no insight into it. Even if Scripture said nothing of the duty of importunate prayer and patient waiting, in order to obtain that which we need so much, yet our natural sense must suggest it to us. See what our condition is;—at present most happily circumstanced, in the bosom of God's choicest gifts; but with evil behind us, and that through our frailty ever increasing, and a judgment before us. Why, it is plainly our duty to make the most of our time of grace; to be earnest and constant in deprecating God's wrath; to do all we can to please Him; to bring Him of our best, not as if it had any intrinsic merit, but because it is our best; to endeavour so to cherish and bring to fruit the gifts of His grace within us, that "when we fail, they may receive us into everlasting habitations;" and, since He at present condescends to work in us "to will and to do," to aim, as St. Paul directs, at "working

---

6 Acts xxii. 16. Zechariah xiii.1. Isaiah i.18.

out our own salvation with fear and trembling," working while it is day, "before the night cometh," for "now is the accepted time, now is the day of salvation." Though we be at present punished for our sins, though we be uncertain more or less how things will be with us, though the adversary of our souls accuse us before God, though his threatening voice sound in our ears year after year, though we feel the load of our sins and cannot throw them from our memory, nay, though it should be God's will that even to the Day of Judgment, no assurance should be given us, still, wherever we are, and whatever we are, like Jonah "in the belly of hell," with Job among the ashes, with Jeremiah in the dungeon, or like the Holy Children in the flames, let us glorify our Lord God, and trust in Him, and praise Him, and magnify Him for ever. Let us take in good part whatever sorrow He inflicts in His providence, or however long. Let us "glorify the Lord in the fires;"[7] they may circle us, but they cannot really touch us; they may threaten, but they are as yet restrained. "Hitherto hath the Lord helped us." We will sing and praise His Name. When two or three are gathered together, an interior temple, a holy shrine is formed for them, which nothing without can destroy. We will not cease to rejoice in what God has given, because He has not as yet promised us every thing. Nor will we on the other hand forget our past sins, because He allows us peace and joy in spite of them. We will remember them that He may not remember them; we will repent of them again and again, that He may forgive them; we will rejoice in the punishment of them if He punishes, thinking it better to be punished in this life than in the next; and if not yet punished, we will be prepared for the chance of it. He will give us grace according to our day, according to His gracious promise: "Fear not, for I have redeemed thee; I have called thee by thy name; thou art Mine. When thou passest through the waters, I will be with thee; and through the rivers, they shall not overflow thee; when thou walkest through the fire, thou shalt not be burnt, neither shall the flame kindle upon thee."[8]

BIBLIOGRAPHY ENTRY FOR RESEARCH PAPERS:

Newman, John Henry. *Parochial and Plain Sermons.* 8 vols. London: Rivingtons, 1875. Sermon VIII reprinted in *The Voice out of the Whirlwind: The Book of Job,* ed. Ralph E. Hone. San Francisco, 1960.

[7] Isaiah xxiv.15.
[8] Isaiah xliii.1,2.

162   *John Henry Newman*

FIRST FOOTNOTE:

 * John Henry Newman, *Parochial and Plain Sermons,* 8 vols. (London: Rivingtons, 1875), Sermon VIII reprinted in *The Voice out of the Whirlwind: The Book of Job,* ed. Ralph E. Hone (San Francisco, 1960), pp. 152-161.

SUBSEQUENT FOOTNOTES:

 * Newman, *op. cit., The Voice,* p. ■.
 * Newman, Sermon VIII, *The Voice,* p. ■.
 * Newman, *The Voice,* p. ■.

Instead of *"The Voice,"* "ed. Hone" may be used in these subsequent-footnote forms.

PART IV

Essays, Drawings, and Poetry
Referring to the Book of Job

FRANCIS BACON

ON

Adversity

The name of Francis Bacon (1561-1626) is almost synonymous with the earliest essays in English. His essays are famous for their interesting range of topics, their style, and their quotability. Their stature is increased by virtue of the fact that their author was also a British philosopher and statesman. The essay below is from The Works of Francis Bacon, edited by James Spedding, Robert Leslie Ellis, and Douglas Denon Heath, 15 vols. (Boston: Brown and Taggard, 1860-1861), Vol. XII, pp. 93-95.

ESSAY V. OF ADVERSITY.

IT WAS a high speech of Seneca (after the manner of the Stoics), *that the good things which belong to prosperity are to be wished; but the good things that belong to adversity are to be admired. Bona rerum secundarum optabilia; adversarum mirabilia.* Certainly if miracles be the command over nature, they appear most in adversity. It is yet a higher speech of his than the other (much too high for a heathen), *It is true greatness to have in one the frailty of a man, and the security of a God. Vere magnum habere fragilitatem hominis, securitatem Dei.* This would have done better in poesy, where transcendences are more allowed. And the poets indeed have been busy with it; for it is in effect the thing which is figured in that strange fiction of the ancient poets, which seemeth not to be without mystery; nay, and to have some approach to the state of a Christian; that *Hercules, when he went to unbind Prometheus,* (by whom human nature is represented), *sailed the length of the great ocean in an earthen pot or pitcher;* lively describing Christian resolution, that saileth in the frail bark of the flesh through the waves of the world. But to speak in a mean.[1] The virtue of Prosperity is temperance; the virtue of Adversity is fortitude; which in morals is the more heroical virtue. Prosperity is the blessing of the Old Testament; Adversity is the blessing of the New; which carrieth the greater benediction, and the clearer revelation of God's favour. Yet even in the Old Testament, if you listen to David's harp, you shall hear as many hearse-like airs as carols; and the pencil of the Holy Ghost hath laboured more in describing the afflictions of Job than the felicities of Solomon. Prosperity is not without many fears and distastes; and Adversity is not without comforts and hopes. We see in needle-works and em-broideries, it is more pleasing to have a lively work upon a sad and solemn ground, than to have a dark and melancholy work upon a lightsome ground: judge therefore of the pleasure of the heart by the pleasure of the eye. Certainly virtue is like precious odours, most fragrant when they are incensed or crushed: for Prosperity doth best discover vice, but Adversity doth best discover virtue.

BIBLIOGRAPHY ENTRY FOR RESEARCH PAPERS:
   Bacon, Francis. *The Works of Francis Bacon.* Edited by James Spedding *et al.* 15 vols. Boston: Brown and Taggard, 1860-1861. Essay V, "Of Adversity," Vol. XII, pp. 93-95, reprinted in *The Voice out of the Whirlwind: The Book of Job,* ed. Ralph E. Hone. San Francisco, 1960.

FIRST FOOTNOTE:
   * Francis Bacon, *The Works of Francis Bacon,* ed. James Spedding *et al.,* 15 vols. (Boston: Brown and Taggard, 1860-1861), Essay V, "Of Adversity," re-printed in *The Voice out of the Whirlwind: The Book of Job,* ed. Ralph E. Hone (San Francisco, 1960), pp. 164-165.

SUBSEQUENT FOOTNOTES:
   * Bacon, *op. cit., The Voice,* p. ■.
   * Bacon, "Of Adversity," *The Voice,* p. ■.
   * Bacon, *The Voice,* p. ■.

In place of *"The Voice,"* "ed. Hone" may be used in these subsequent-footnote forms.

---

[1] *Ut a granditate verborum ad mediocritatem descendamus.*

BRIEF FORMS:

The full and exact identification furnished by the long bibliography entry and footnotes above may not be needed, since Bacon's *Essays* have been published in many editions that have the same numbering for the essays. The following may be acceptable:

Bacon, Francis. "Of Adversity" (Essay V).
* Francis Bacon, "Of Adversity" (Essay V).
* Bacon, "Of Adversity."

WILLIAM BLAKE

ON

Satan and God

‖‖‖

William Blake (1757-1827) illustrates the principle that genius refuses to be classified easily. Poet, artist, mystic, he produced works which have been perennially inspiring. In The Marriage of Heaven and Hell *(London, 1790) he shows himself something of a prophet, in form and content anticipating Walt Whitman. This short selection is from that work.*

THE VOICE OF THE DEVIL

ALL Bibles or sacred codes have been the causes of the following Errors:

1. That Man has two real existing principles: Viz: a Body & a Soul.

2. That Energy, call'd Evil, is alone from the Body; & that Reason, call'd Good, is alone from the Soul.

3. That God will torment Man in Eternity for following his Energies.

But the following Contraries to these are True:

1. Man has no Body distinct from his Soul; for that call'd Body is a portion of Soul discern'd by the five Senses, the chief inlets of Soul in this age.

2. Energy is the only life, and is from the Body; and Reason is the bound or outward circumference of Energy.

3. Energy is Eternal Delight.

Those who restrain desire, do so because theirs is weak enough to be restrained; and the restrainer or reason usurps its place & governs the unwilling.

And being restrain'd, it by degrees becomes passive, till it is only the shadow of desire.

The history of this is written in Paradise Lost, & the Governor or Reason is call'd Messiah.

And the original Archangel, or possessor of the command of the heavenly host, is call'd the Devil or Satan, and his children are call'd Sin & Death.

But in the Book of Job, Milton's Messiah is call'd Satan.

For this history has been adopted by both parties.

It indeed appear'd to Reason as if Desire was cast out; but the Devil's account is, that the Messiah fell, & formed a heaven of what he stole from the Abyss.

This is shewn in the Gospel, where he prays to the Father to send the comforter, or Desire, that Reason may have Ideas to build on; the Jehovah of the Bible being no other than he who dwells in flaming fire.

Know that after Christ's death, he became Jehovah.

But in Milton, the Father is Destiny, the Son a Ratio of the five senses, & the Holy-ghost Vacuum!

Note: The reason Milton wrote in fetters when he wrote of Angels & God, and at liberty when of Devils & Hell, is because he was a true Poet and of the Devil's party without knowing it.

BIBLIOGRAPHY ENTRY FOR RESEARCH PAPERS:

Blake, William. *The Marriage of Heaven and Hell.* London, 1790. "The Voice of the Devil" reprinted in the *The Voice out of the Whirlwind: The Book of Job,* ed. Ralph E. Hone. San Francisco, 1960.

FIRST FOOTNOTE:

* William Blake, *The Marriage of Heaven and Hell* (London, 1790), "The Voice of the Devil," reprinted in *The Voice out of the Whirlwind: The Book of Job,* ed. Ralph E. Hone (San Francisco, 1960), pp. 167-168.

SUBSEQUENT FOOTNOTES:

* Blake, *op. cit.,* ed. Hone, p. ■.
* Blake, "The Voice of the Devil," ed. Hone, p. ■.
* Blake, ed. Hone, p. ■.

In place of "ed. Hone," these subsequent-footnote forms could have *"The Voice out of The Whirlwind";* but to avoid confusion between two titles beginning with the same words, "ed. Hone" is probably preferable here.

WILLIAM BLAKE

ON

the Book of Job

‖‖‖

Blake's illustrations for the Book of Job, first executed in water color and then duplicated in engravings between 1823 and 1825, are considered his greatest work in creative art. [Illustrations of the Book of Job, in Twenty-One Plates *(London, 1826)*]
Five of these plates are here reproduced from the originals in the Henry E. Huntington Library and Art Gallery, by permission.

‖‖

BIBLIOGRAPHY ENTRY FOR RESEARCH PAPERS:
 Blake, William. *Illustrations of the Book of Job, in Twenty-One Plates.* London, 1826. Reprinted in *The Voice out of the Whirlwind: The Book of Job,* ed. Ralph E. Hone. San Francisco, 1960.

FIRST FOOTNOTE:
 * William Blake, *Illustrations of the Book of Job, in Twenty-One Plates* (London, 1826), reprinted in *The Voice out of the Whirlwind: The Book of Job,* ed. Ralph E. Hone (San Francisco, 1960), pp. 170-174.

SUBSEQUENT FOOTNOTES:
 * Blake, *op. cit.,* ed. Hone, p. ■.
 * Blake, *Illustrations of Job,* ed. Hone, p. ■.
 * Blake, ed. Hone, p. ■.

 In place of "ed. Hone," the title of this collection could have been given—in full, however, if Blake's "The Voice of the Devil" were also in the documentation.

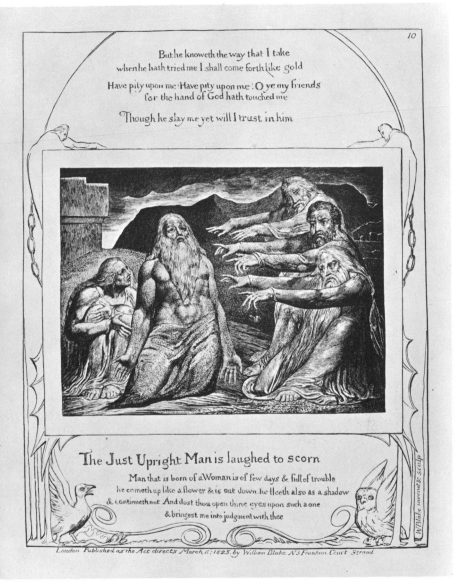

13

14

ROBERT LOWTH

ON

the Provenience of Job

‖‖‖

Bishop Robert Lowth (1710-1787), was appointed professor of poetry at Oxford in 1741, and being well-versed in Hebrew and possessing a keen appreciation of the Old Testament poetry he offered as his praelectiones *a series of lectures in Latin on the sacred poetry of the Hebrews. This was first published in 1753 and helped to gain Lowth a wide reputation in Europe for his knowledge of Hebrew. The first English translation was made by George Gregory in 1793. The selection here reprinted is from* Lectures on the Sacred Poetry of the Hebrews, Translated [from the Latin] by G. Gregory. To Which Are Added the Principal Notes of Professor [John David] Michaelis, and Notes by the Translator and Others, *second edition (Boston, 1815), pp. 445-468.*

The notes of Bishop Lowth are identified as "Author's Note." Those marked M. *are notes by Professor Michaelis; those marked* S.H. *are by Samuel Henley; and those marked* T. *are by the translator himself.*

LECTURE XXXII. OF THE POEM OF JOB.

In order to criticise the book of Job with any degree of satisfaction to his auditors, the critic must explain his own sentiments concerning the work in general—The book of Job a singular composition, and has little or no connection with the affairs of the Hebrews—The seat of the history is Idumæa; and the characters are evidently Idumæan of the family of Abraham; the author appears to be an Idumæan, who spoke the Hebrew as his vernacular tongue—Neither Elihu nor Moses, rather

Job himself, or some contemporary—This appears to be the oldest book extant: founded upon true history, and contains no allegory—Although extremely obscure, still the general subject and design are sufficiently evident—A short and general analysis of the whole work; in which the obscurer passages are brought as little as possible in question—The deductions from this disquisition—1. The subject of the controversy between Job and his friends—2. The subject of the whole poem—3. Its end or purpose—All questions not necessarily appertaining to this point to be avoided.

SUCH A DIVERSITY of opinions has prevailed in the learned world concerning the nature and design of the Poem of Job, that the only point in which commentators seem to agree, is the extreme obscurity of the subject. To engage, therefore, in an undertaking on which so much erudition has been expended, to tread the same paths which so many have already traversed in vain, may seem to require some apology for the temerity, not to say the presumption of the attempt. Though I might alledge, that the authority of the most learned men is lessened in some measure by the discordance of their opinions; and that therefore the failure of others is the more readily to be excused; I will, however, make use of no such defence, but will entrench myself rather in the necessity and in the nature of my present undertaking. I pretend not to any new discoveries; I presume not to determine the subtile controversies of the learned; I scarcely venture to indulge a hope of being able to illustrate any obscurities. My sole intention is to collect, from such passages as appear the least intricate, the most probable conjectures: and what I conceive to have any tolerable foundation in fact, that I mean to propose, not as demonstration, but as opinion only. I proceed in this manner upon the principle, that, considering the great discordance of sentiments upon this subject, it would be impossible for any man to discourse with a sufficient degree of accuracy and perspicuity upon the structure and parts of this poem, unless he previously explained his own ideas concerning the scope and purport of the work in general.

The book of Job appears to me to stand single and unparalleled in the Sacred Volume. It seems to have little connexion with the other writings of the Hebrews, and no relation whatever to the affairs of the Israelites. The scene is laid in Idumæa;[1] the history of an inhabitant of that country

---

[1] The information which the learned have endeavoured to collect from the writings and geography of the Greeks concerning the country and residence of Job and his friends, appears to me so very inconclusive, that I am inclined to take a quite different method for the solution of this question, by applying solely to the Sacred Writings: the hints with which they have furnished me towards the illustration of this subject, I shall explain as briefly as possible.

The land of *Uz*, or *Gnutz*, is evidently *Idumæa*, as appears from LAM. iv. 21.

is the basis of the narrative; the characters who speak are Idumæans, or
at least Arabians of the adjacent country, all originally of the race of

Uz was the grandson of Seir, the Horite: GEN. xxxvi. 20, 21, 28. 1 CHRON. i. 38,
42. Seir inhabited that mountainous tract which was called by his name antecedent
to the time of Abraham, but his posterity being expelled, it was occupied by the
Idumæans: GEN. xiv. 6. DEUT. ii. 12. Two other men are mentioned of the name
Uz; one the grandson of Shem, the other the son of Nachor, the brother of Abraham;
but whether any district was called after their name is not clear. Idumæa is a part
of Arabia Petræa, situated on the southern extremity of the tribe of Judah: NUMB.
xxxiv. 3. JOSH. xv. 1, 21; the land of Uz therefore appears to have been between
Egypt and Philistia. JER. xxv. 20. where the order of the places seems to have been
accurately observed in reviewing the different nations from Egypt to Babylon; and
the same people seem again to be described in exactly the same situations, JER.
xlvi—1.

Children of the East or *Eastern people,* seems to have been the general appellation for that mingled race of people (as they are called, JER. xxv. 20.) who inhabited
between Egypt and the Euphrates, bordering upon Judea from the South to the East;
the Idumæans, the Amalekites, the Midianites, the Moabites, the Ammonites: see
JUD. vi. 3. and ISA. xi. 14. of these the Idumæans and Amalekites certainly possessed
the southern parts; see NUMB. xxxiv. 3. xiii. 29. 1 SAM. xxvii. 8, 10. This appears
to be the true state of the case: the whole region between Egypt and Euphrates was
called the East, at first in respect to Egypt (where the learned Jos. Mede thinks the
Israelites acquired this mode of speaking. MEDE'S *Works,* page 580.) and afterwards
absolutely and without any relation to situation or circumstances. Abraham is said
to have sent the sons of his concubines, Hagar and Keturah, "Eastward, to the
country which is commonly called the East." GEN. xxv. 6. where the name of the
region seems to have been derived from the same situation. Solomon is reported
"to have excelled in wisdom all the Eastern people, and all Egypt:" 1 KINGS iv. 30,
that is, all the neighbouring people on that quarter: for there were people beyond
the boundaries of Egypt, and bordering on the south of Judea, who were famous
for wisdom, namely, the Idumæans, (see JER. xlix. 7. OB. 8.) to whom we may
well believe this passage might have some relation. Thus JEHOVAH addresses the
Babylonians: "Arise, ascend unto Kedar, and lay waste the children of the East,"
JER. xlix. 28. notwithstanding these were really situated to the west of Babylon.
Although Job, therefore, be accounted one of the Orientals, it by no means follows,
that his residence must be in Arabia Deserta.

Eliphaz the *Temanite:* Eliphaz was the son of Esau, and Teman the son of
Eliphaz: GEN. xxxvi. 10, 11. The Eliphaz of Job was without a doubt of this race.
Teman is certainly a city of Idumæa: JER. xlix. 7, 20. EZEK. xxv. 13. AMOS i. 11,
12. OB. 8, 9.

Bildad the *Shuhite:* Shuah was one of the sons of Abraham by Keturah, whose
posterity were numbered among the people of the East, and his situation was probably contiguous to that of his brother, Midian, and of his nephews, Shebah and
Dedan: see GEN. xxv. 2 and 3. Dedan is a city of Idumæa: JER. xlix. 8, and seems
to have been situated on the eastern side, as Teman was on the west, EZEK. xxv. 13.
From Sheba originated the Sabæans in the passage from Arabia Felix to the Red Sea:
Sheba is united to Midian, ISA. lx. 6, it is in the same region however with Midian,
and not far from mount Horeb, EXOD. ii. 15, iii. 1.

Zophar the *Naamathite:* among the cities, which by lot fell to the tribe of
Judah, in the neighbourhood of Idumæa, Naama is enumerated, JOSH. xv. 21, 41.
Nor does this name elsewhere occur: this probably was the country of Zophar.

Elihu the *Buzite:* Buz occurs but once as the name of a place or country, JER.

Abraham. The language is pure Hebrew, although the author appears to be an Idumæan; for it is not improbable that all the posterity of Abraham, Israelites, Idumæans, and Arabians, whether of the family of Keturah or Ishmael, spoke for a considerable length of time one common language. That the Idumæans, however, and the Temanites in particular, were eminent for the reputation of wisdom, appears by the testimony of the prophets, Jeremiah and Obadiah:[2] Baruch also particularly mentions them amongst "the authors (or expounders) of fables, and searchers out of understanding."[3] The learned are very much divided in their sentiments concerning the author of this book. Our Lightfoot conjectures, that it is the production of Elihu; and this conjecture seems at first sight rather countenanced by the exordium to the first speech of Elihu,[4] in which he seems to assume the character of the author, by continuing the narrative in his

---

xxv. 23, where it is mentioned along with Dedan and Thema: Dedan, as was just now demonstrated, is a city of Idumæa, Thema belonged to the children of Ishmael, who are said to have inhabited from Havilah even to Shur, which is in the district of Egypt, GEN. xxv. 15, 18. Saul, however, is said to have smitten the Amalekites from Havilah even to Shur, which is in the district of Egypt, 1 SAM. xv. 7. Havilah cannot, therefore, be very far from the boundaries of the Amalekites; but the Amalekites never exceeded the boundaries of Arabia Petræa. (See RELAND Palæstin. lib. i. c. xiv.) Thema, therefore, lay somewhere between Havilah and the desert of Shur, to the southward of Judea. Thema is also mentioned in connexion with Sheba, JOB vi. 19.

Upon a fair review of these facts I think we may venture to conclude, still with that modesty which such a question demands, that JOB was an inhabitant of Arabia Petræa, as well as his friends, or at least of that neighbourhood. To this solution one objection may be raised: it may be asked, how the Chaldeans, who lived on the borders of the Euphrates, could make depredations on the camels of Job, who lived in Idumæa at so great a distance. This too is thought a sufficient cause for assigning Job a situation in Arabia Deserta, and not far from the Euphrates. But what should prevent the Chaldeans, as well as the Sabæans, a people addicted to rapine, and roving about at immense distances for the sake of plunder, from wandering through these defenceless regions, which were divided into tribes and families rather than into nations, and pervading from Euphrates even to Egypt? Further, I would ask on the other hand, whether it be probable that all the friends of Job, who lived in Idumæa and its neighbourhood, should instantly be informed of all that could happen to Job in the desert of Arabia and on the confines of Chaldea, and immediately repair thither? Or whether it be reasonable to think, that, some of them being inhabitants of Arabia Deserta, it should be concerted among them to meet at the residence of Job; since it is evident, that Eliphaz lived at Theman, in the extreme parts of Idumæa? With respect to the *Aisitas* of Ptolemy (for so it is written, and not *Ausitas*) it has no agreement, not so much as in a single letter with the Hebrew *Gnutz.* The LXX. indeed call that country by the name *Ausitida*, but they describe it as situated in Idumæa; and they account Job himself an Idumæan, and a descendant of Esau. See the Appendix of the LXX. to the book of Job, and HYDE, Not. in *Peritzol.* chap. xi. *Author's Note.*

[2] JER. xlix. 7. OBA. 8.   [3] BARUCH iii. 22, 23.   [4] JOB. xxxii. 15, 16.

own person. That passage, however, which appears to interrupt the speech
of Elihu, and to be a part of the narrative, is, I apprehend, nothing more
than an apostrophe to Job, or possibly to himself; for it manifestly consists
of two distichs, while, on the contrary, it is well known that all the narrative parts, all in which the author himself appears are certainly written
in prose. Another opinion, which has been still more generally received,
attributes the work to Moses. This conjecture, however, for I cannot dignify
it with any higher appellation, will be found to rest altogether upon
another, namely, that this poem was originally a consolatory address to
the Israelites, and an allegorical representation of their situation: and I
must confess, I can scarcely conceive any thing more futile than such an
hypothesis, since it is impossible to trace, throughout the whole book, the
slightest allusion to the manners, customs, ceremonies, or history of the
Israelites. I will add, moreover, that the style of Job appears to me
materially different from the poetical style of Moses; for it is much more
compact, concise, or condensed, more accurate in the poetical conformation
of the sentences: as may be observed also in the prophecies of Balaam, the
Mesopotamian, a foreigner indeed with respect to the Israelites, but neither
unacquainted with their language, nor with the worship of the true God.
I confess myself therefore, on the whole, more inclined to favour the
opinion of those who suppose Job himself, or some contemporary, to be
the author of this poem: for that it is the most ancient of all the sacred
books, is, I think, manifest, from the subject, the language, the general
character, and even from the obscurity of the work.[5] Concerning the time

---

5 In opposition to the antiquity of the poem, and to what I have urged above,
that it appears to have no connection with, or relation to the affairs of the Israelites,
appeals have been made to JOB xxxi. 28. See *A free and candid Examination of
the Bishop of London's Sermon, Anonymous,* p. 165, in which the author enquires,
"In what nation upon earth idolatry was ever accounted a crime but under the
Jewish economy?" His argument is proposed as unanswerable, and is thought to be
sufficiently confirmed by the authority of Mr. LOCKE. I will however appeal to a
higher authority than that of LOCKE, namely, that of reason and the sacred writings;
and will answer the question in a few words: under the Patriarchal Economy, in
every tribe and family under Abraham, Melchizedeck, Job, and the rest. On the
increase of idolatry Abraham was called by the divine command from Chaldea, to
the end, that from him should proceed a nation separate from all others, who should
worship the true God, should afford a perfect example of pure religion, and bear
testimony against the worship of vain gods. Was it not, therefore, the duty of
Abraham, who in his own tribe or family possessed all the attributes of sovereignty,
to punish idolatry as well at homicide, adultery, or other heinous crimes? Was it
not the duty of Melchizedeck, of Job, of all those patriarchal princes, who regarded
the worship of the true God, sedulously to prevent every defection from it; to
restrain those who were disposed to forsake it, and to punish the obstinate and the
rebellious? In fact, in this allusion to the exertion of the judicial authority against

also in which Job lived, although not directly specified, I see no great reason for doubt. The length of his life evinces that he was before Moses, and probably contemporary with the patriarchs. Not however to dwell upon the innumerable hypotheses of the learned on this subject, I will only mention, that there is the utmost probability of his having lived prior to the promulgation of the law, from the nature of the sacrifice which he institutes conformably to the command of God, namely, seven oxen and seven rams: for it is plain from the example of Balaam, that a respect for that number prevailed in those countries, and at that period, from the traditional accounts which were still preserved among them of the seven days of creation.[6] The truth of the narrative would never, I am persuaded, have been called in question, but from the immoderate affection of some allegorizing mystics for their own fictions, which run to such excess, as to prevent them from acceding to any thing but what was visionary and typical. When I speak of the poem as founded in fact, I would be understood no further than concerns the general subject of the narrative, for I apprehend all the dialogue, and most likely some other parts, have par-

---

idolatry, and against the particular species which is mentioned here, namely, the worship of the sun and moon (the earliest species of idolatry) consists the most complete proof of the antiquity of the poem, and the decisive mark of the patriarchal age. But if it should be suspected, that the ingenuity of the poet might lead him to imitate with accuracy the manners of the age which he describes, this indeed would be more to the purpose, and a more plausible argument against the antiquity of the poem: but I cannot possibly attribute such address and refinement to a poet in a barbarous age; and after the Babylonish captivity. Further than this, the style of the poem favours altogether of the antique; insomuch, that whoever could suppose it written after the Babylonish captivity, would fall little short of the error of Hardouin, who ascribed the golden verses of Virgil, Horace, &c. to the *iron age* of monkish pedantry and ignorance.

With regard to the other difficulty, the solution of which appears so embarrassing, namely how any person not acquainted with the Jewish economy could assert, that "God visits the sins of the fathers upon the children," JOB xxi. 19? Let the *candid observer* for the present content himself with this verse of Horace.

"Delicta majorum immeritus lues,
"Romane."———

"Though guiltless of thy father's crimes,
"Roman, 'tis thine, to latest times,
"The vengeance of the gods to bear."—FRANCIS.

Author's Note.

[6] JOB xlii. 8. Compare NUMB. xxiii. 1, &c.

There seems to be but little weight in this reasoning, because Job, as an Idumæan, might have been a worshipper of the true God, like Balaam the Mesopotamian; and therefore, though the law had been given to the Israelites, continued, notwithstanding, to offer sacrifice according to the traditionary mode of his progenitors. S. H.

taken largely of the embellishments of poetry; but I cannot allow that this has by any means extended so far as to convert the whole into an allegory. Indeed I have not been able to trace any vestige of an allegorical meaning throughout the entire poem. And should even the exordium be suspected to be of this nature,[7] we must recollect, that the historical books are not destitute of similar narratives.[8] The exordium and conclusion I agree are

---

[7] Job i. 6, &c. ii. 1, &c. Compare 1 Kings xxii. 19—22.

[8] It has long been a dispute among the learned, whether the poem of Job consists of fable or a true history: this question, if authority alone be applied to, must long since have been decided in favour of those who assert it to be a real history.

With me I confess, on the other hand, it is no longer matter of opinion, but I feel very little doubt that the subject of the Poem is altogether fabulous, and designed to teach us that "the rewards of virtue being in another state, it is "very possible for the good to suffer afflictions in this life: but that when it so "happens, it is permitted by Providence for the wisest reasons, though they may "not be obvious to human eyes." But before I proceed to examine the grounds of this opinion, it may be necessary to premise a few remarks in reply to those who may think the divine authority of the book affected by the supposition of its not being founded in fact. For my own part, I cannot conceive that the sanctity, the dignity, or the utility of that book will be in the least affected, though we should suppose no such person as Job had ever existed.

If moral precepts, conveyed in the garb of fabulous narrations, allure the hearers by the pleasure they afford, if they strike the mind more forcibly, are more easily understood, and better retained than abstract sentiments, I see no reason why this mode of writing should be deemed unworthy of inspiration. Indeed, on the contrary, we find it made use of by Christ himself, nor does it at all derogate from his force as a moral teacher, that the good Samaritan, the rich man and Lazarus, &c. were not real persons.

I shall not however rest here; for I assert further, that the book of Job is more instructive as a fable, than it could possibly be as a true history. Taken as a mere relation of a matter of fact, it is necessary to suppose that the sentiments and conversations are exhibited exactly as they were spoken, and are the sentiments of mere mortals not actuated by the Spirit of God; for we find that God has reproved both Job and his friends as being severally mistaken./It would then be impossible to determine what was true or what false; no doctrine of religion, no precept of morality, could with certainty be deduced from these conversations. In the whole book, the historical part (and how short is that!) and the words attributed to God himself would be alone divine, or of divine authority, the rest would be all human. Considered as a fable, the case is different. The author, composing under the influence of divine inspiration, we may reasonably suppose has attributed to the fictitious characters, such sentiments as were proper and natural to their state and circumstances: we have then, in the first place, a picture of the human mind drawn by the finger of God; and in the next, we may rest satisfied that Job and his friends err only in the principal matter upon which they dispute, and only on the points for which God has reproved them; but that whatever is said exclusive of this is founded on divine truth; such is the mention of the angels by Eliphaz, and the assertion of Job, that there is none pure among mortals. Finally, we are by these means enabled both to determine what are the sentiments which immediately meet with the approbation of God, and what are the errors which are intended to be exposed. An able writer in dialogue never fails to discover his own sentiments: as from the books of Cicero on *the nature of the Gods,* we may collect with ease what the author thought, or rather doubted upon the subject, which would have been

distinct from the poem itself, and stand in the place of an argument or illustration; that they are however coeval with the poetical part, and the

---

impossible, if he had only reported the actual words of the philosophers who are supposed to have conversed on that subject.

I will now proceed freely to explain what at first I undertook to prove concerning the book in question. It is surely more becoming to consider the exordium, in which Satan appears as the accuser of Job, rather in the light of a fable than of a true narrative. It is surely incredible, that such a conversation ever took place between the Almighty and Satan, who is supposed to return with *news* from the terrestrial regions. Indeed, the commentators who have undertaken to vindicate this part of the book, have done it with so much asperity, that they seem conscious of the difficulty under which it labours.

Nor will it suffice to answer as some temperate and rational commentator, like our author, probably will, and indeed as he himself hints: that the great outline of the fact only is true; and that the exordium is set off with some poetical ornaments, among which is to be accounted the conversation between God and Satan. For on this very conversation the whole plot is founded, and the whole story and catastrophe depends. One of the best of men is thrown into so many unexpected and undeserved evils, that neither he nor his adversaries are able to conceive how it can be consistent with a benevolent being, to plunge a good man into so great afflictions: nor has God condescended to explain the motives of it to them, but reproves them all for investigating matters beyond their reach. But the author of the book undoes the knot which is left unresolved in these conversations, and gives the reader to understand how indifferently those reason concerning the Divine Providence, and the happiness or misery of mankind, who are only partially informed of causes and events. The Almighty acts for the honour of Job, of human nature, and of piety itself; he permits Job to be unhappy for a time, and refutes the accusations of Satan even by the very means which he himself pointed out. Suppose, therefore, that what is thus related of Satan be fictitious, and all the rest true, instead of the difficulty being done away, the consequence will be, that the whole plot remains without any solution whatever. What our author has added concerning one of the historical books of Scripture, in which a similar passage occurs, 1 KINGS xxii. 19–22, appears not at all to the purpose. It is not a history related by the author, nor does the author speak in his own person, but a prophet explains a vision which he has had. But those who suppose the book of Job to be founded upon fact, allow that the historian speaks in the first and second chapters, who, if he did invent, would certainly, one would think, take that liberty only in matters which did not affect the great scope of the history, and not in a matter which, if it be supposed fictitious, reduces the whole book to nothing.

Moreover, the style of the whole book being poetical, and so sublime, that I defy any man to imitate it in any extempore effusion, is an irrefragable proof in favour of my opinion. Our author indeed pleads a very specious excuse: he thinks that the conversation and speeches of the different characters have been poetically ornamented. And this argument I do not wish to confute. There are however others who defend the historical truth of the poem in a manner not quite so modest. Among the rest, the famous SCHULTENS alledges it not to be incredible, that these are the actual words of the disputants, if we consider the amazing faculty which the Arabians possess of making extempore verses. In answer to this, I must confess, that all he can urge on this subject will never persuade me, that poetry, which is confessedly superior to all that human genius has been able to produce, is nothing more than an extempore effusion. Indeed nothing can be more ridiculous, than to suppose men in circumstances of so great distress, in the midst of difficulties and afflictions, capable of amusing themselves with making extempore verses.

work of the same author, is evident, since they are indispensably necessary
to the unravelling of the plot, which ·is not developed in the body of the

These objections which I have just stated are well known to the commentators:
but there are others not quite so common, which induce me to suppose the subject
of this poem not historical but fabulous. So many round numbers and multiplications
of them occur in the life of Job, as to be quite incompatible with mere chance. *Ten*
children perish, *seven* sons (which though it be not a round number, is yet held
sacred and mysterious by the Orientals) and three daughters: 7000 sheep, 3000
camels, 1000 oxen, and exactly half the number of asses. In lieu of these there are
restored to him, 14,000 sheep, 6000 camels, 2000 oxen, and 1000 asses, exactly
the duplicate of the former numbers; together with exactly the same number of
children as he had lost, seven sons and three daughters, and these from one wife.
The same principle is found to extend to the years of Job's prosperity, which are
multiplications of the number 70. These circumstances betray art and fiction in the
narrator, who has introduced these round numbers which we know are the first to
present themselves to the mind: it bears no appearance of chance or casualty, which,
when it predominates in a series of events, produces a wonderful variety, but very
little of regularity or equality. The name of JOB too, which in the Arabic means
returning to God, and loving him, and hating whatever is contrary to him, is so
adapted to the character of his latter years, that we can never suppose it a name
given to him by his parents, but invented by the author of the story.

A fourth argument is, that the scene is laid in Arabia, yet the poem abounds
so much in imagery borrowed from Egypt, that it is plain that country must have
been extremely well known to the author, and indeed predominant in his mind, as
I have endeavoured to prove in a Dissertation recited before the R. S. of Gottingen.

But the most powerful of all proofs is, that some things appear in the book of
Job which could not possibly have place in a true history. At a period when the
longevity of the patriarchs was reduced within the limit of two hundred years, Job
is said to have lived 140 years after his malady, and therefore could not be very
ancient when he fell into this malady; nevertheless he upbraids his friends with
their *youth* (who by the way could not be very young, since Elihu in xxxii. 6, 7, 9.
reverences their hoary age) and adds, that "he would have disdained to set their
"fathers with the dogs of his flock," ch. xxx. 1. But what is more extraordinary,
these same men boast of their own age, and seem to exact a degree of reverence
from Job as their junior; thus Eliphaz, chap. xx. 10, "With us are both the grey-
"headed and the very aged men much older than thy father." These passages, therefore, so directly contradict each other, that they cannot be connected with true
history. The opprobrium which he casts upon the birth of his friends seems also
an inconsistency, ch. xxx. 1—6. as it is incredible, that so noble and rich a man
should ever have chosen his friends from the meanest of the people.

It remains only to remove one objection, with which those who contend for
the historical truth of the book of Job may press us. Job is quoted by Ezekiel along
with Noah and Daniel, whom we know to have been real persons, and they are
proposed by James as an example of patience, EZEK. xiv. 14, 20. JAMES v. 11. as if
it were improper or indecent to recommend the virtues of fictitious characters to
our imitation, or as if this were not in fact the end of delineating such characters.
Neither is there the least impropriety in instancing the same virtues in real and
fictitious characters. Suppose a father to recommend to his daughters the examples
of Lucretia and Pamela, as models of chastity and virtue, who would esteem such
a discourse reprehensible, or think that it either took from the truth of the history,
or gave a reality to the fiction?

To return to the point from which we set out: this poem seems to treat of the

poem. There are, it is true, phrases extant in the exordium, in which some
critics have pretended to discover the hand of a later writer; the arguments,

---

affliction which may sometimes happen to good men, at the same time that the
author seems to wish to accommodate the consolation to the people of God, and
to represent their oppression under the character of Job. To this opinion it is ob-
jected by our author, that there appears nothing in the book like an allusion to the
manners, rites, or affairs of the Israelites. Of the latter I shall treat, when we
come to speak of the application of this poem to the history of the Israelites. As to
the manners, they are what I call *Abrahamic,* or such as were at that period common
to all the seed of Abraham at that time, Israelites, Ishmaelites, and Idumæans. But
perhaps it may be thought necessary to instance those customs which were peculiar
to the Israelites, and by which they were distinguished from the Arabians: this,
however, would not display much judgement in the author of a poem, the scene
of which lies in Arabia; besides, that most of the peculiar customs of the Israelites,
those I mean which distinguished them from the other descendants of Abraham,
were either derived from the Egyptians, or were taught them by Moses: and who
would require, that such things as the paschal lamb, and the Mosaic feasts and
priesthood, should be introduced into such a poem? The frequent allusions however
to the country and the productions of Egypt abundantly answer this objection.
Insomuch, that though the scene is laid in Arabia, one would imagine the actors
had been Egyptians. Nor are there wanting allusions to the circumstances of the
Israelites. These like Job lost their children and possessions by the tyranny of
Pharaoh: and, if I am not mistaken, the disease is the same which affected Job, with
that which prevailed among the Egyptians by the command of Moses.
   From these circumstances I am much inclined to the opinion which attributes
this book to Moses. For is it to be imagined, that a native of Idumæa should crowd
his poem with images and figures borrowed from Egypt? Or what native of Arabia
(for it must be allowed that the book of Job has some allusions peculiar to
Arabia) was so likely to intermingle the imagery of both countries as Moses? To
these may be added the allusions to the *isles of the blessed,* which are common to
the book of Job and the Mosaic writings. I am well aware that there is more of the
tragic, more of strong poetic feeling in this book, than in the other relics of Mosaic
poetry, which has induced our author to remark the discrepancy of style. But how
different are the language and sentiments of a man raging in the heights of despair,
from those which are to be sung in the temple of God? We must also remember,
that the poetic style of an author in the flower of his youth is very different from
that of his latter days. If Moses were really the author of this poem, he composed
it about the age of forty years; but the rest of his poems were written between
the 85th and 120th year of his age; at which period I am often surprized to meet
with so much vigour of language and sentiment: and no other difference of style
have I been able to discover.   M.
   If I might flatter myself that the reader would not be wearied with replications
and rejoinders, I would request his attention to a few animadversions on these
remarks of the Gottingen professor. For though I thought it my duty to state his
arguments as fully as I could, consistently with the limits of this work, I must confess that I do not myself feel by any means convinced; nor dare I venture to affirm,
upon any such presumptive proofs, that the book of Job is altogether fabulous. I
think it by no means follows, that because a book contains some things which may
with propriety be termed poetical fictions, it has no foundation whatever in fact.
The poems of Homer contain more fictions of this kind than any commentator has
pretended clearly to discover in the book of Job: and yet no sober critic has denied,

however, of these critics I cannot esteem of any great force or importance. That these points should be accounted of a very ambiguous nature,

---

that there ever was such an event as the Trojan war, on which those poems are founded.

I cannot help thinking with our author, that such a man as Job might very possibly have existed, and that the leading facts concerning his sudden depression and consequent misfortunes might really have happened; and yet that the poet, in relating these facts, may have added such machinery, and other poetical ornaments, as appeared necessary to enliven the story, and illustrate the moral. Though we should not contend with the learned professor for the literal acceptation of the exordium; though we should even admit with him, that it is not probable any such conversation ever took place between the Almighty Governor of the universe and the great enemy of mankind, as is related in the first chapter; yet it by no means follows, that the inspired writer had no grounds whatever for what he describes perhaps poetically. The manner in which the Deity and the other celestial intelligences are spoken of in this poem appears necessary, when the human mind is called upon to contemplate their actions, and may be considered as a kind of personification in accommodation to our limited faculties, and is common in many other parts of Scripture.

With regard to the objection founded on the round numbers, I think it very weak when applied to the children of Job: and as to the cattle, the event being recorded some time after it took place, it is hardly reasonable to expect that the numbers should be specified with the utmost exactness: indeed nothing can be more awkward or ungraceful, in a poetical narration, than to descend to units; and when the numbers are doubled at the conclusion, I look upon it as no more than a periphrasis, expressing, that the Lord gave to Job twice as much as he had before.

As to the name: it is well known, that all the names of the ancients were derived from some distinguishing quality, and not always given at their birth as with us. (See *Essays Historical and Moral,* Ess. vi. p. 119.) Nay, the objection, if admitted, would strike at the authority of a considerable part of holy writ; for not only many of the persons recorded there take their names from circumstances which occurred late in life, but, in some instances, from the very circumstances of their deaths, as *Abel* from *Habal* (vanity or nothingness) because he left no offspring.

There appears at first sight something more formidable in the argument founded on the inconsistencies which he boasts of having detected; nevertheless, I can by no means grant it all the credit which its author seems to claim. Both the expressions of Elihu, and those of the other friends are very general, and I think improperly applied by the professor: for the passage referred to, ch. xv. 10. by no means proves that the friends of Job were older than he: "*with us,* or *among us,*" seems to imply no more than this, "older persons than either you or we, are *with us,* or of our sentiments." Still more general is the complaint of Job, ch. xxx. 1. indeed so general, that to a fair examiner it is impossible it should appear to have any relation at all to the friends of Job, as he is simply complaining of his altered state, and among other evils mentions the loss of that respect which he was accustomed to receive from all ranks of people, insomuch, that now even the *young,* the *children,* presume to hold him in derision. The other argument is by no means conclusive, namely, that which is founded on the supposed opprobrium on the birth of his friends, as really I cannot conceive any part of this speech to have the least reference to them; or if it have, it is easy enough to suppose, that their fathers or themselves might have been raised to opulence from a mean station; and indeed such a supposition is absolutely necessary to give any point to the sarcasm of Job, admitting that it ought to be understood in the light our commentator seems to intend.　　T.

and should cause much embarrassment and controversy in the learned world, is nothing extraordinary; but that the main object and design of the poem should ever have been called in question, may justly excite our astonishment. For though many passages be confessedly obscure, though there be several which I fear no human skill will ever be able to unravel; and though the obscurity consist chiefly in the connection of the incidents and the sentiments, it by no means necessarily follows, that the whole is involved in impenetrable darkness. The case indeed is far otherwise, for one and the same light, though at intervals overcast, shines on through the whole, and, like a conducting star, uniformly leads to the same point. If then any person will follow this guidance without perplexing himself with obscurities which he will occasionally meet, I have very little doubt but that he will clearly discern the end, the subject, the connection, and arrangement of the whole work. It will, perhaps, be worth while to put to trial the efficacy of this maxim: let us, therefore, for the present, pass over those obscurities which might impede our progress; and, making the best use of those lights which are afforded by the more obvious passages, proceed with an attentive eye through the whole of the work, and observe whether something satisfactory is not to be discovered relating to the subject of the narrative, and the design and intent of the poem.

The principal object held forth to our contemplation in this production is the example of a good man, eminent for his piety, and of approved integrity, suddenly precipitated from the very summit of prosperity into the lowest depths of misery and ruin: who having been first bereaved of his wealth, his possessions, and his children, is afterwards afflicted with the most excruciating anguish of a loathsome disease which entirely covers his body. He sustains all however with the mildest submission, and the most complete resignation to the will of Providence: "In all this," says the historian, "Job sinned not, nor charged God foolishly."[9] And after the second trial, "In all this did not Job sin with his lips."[10] The author of the history remarks upon this circumstance a second time, in order to excite the observation of the reader, and to render him more attentive to what follows, which properly constitutes the true subject of the poem: namely, the conduct of Job with respect to his reverence for the Almighty, and the changes which accumulating misery might produce in his temper and behaviour. Accordingly we find that another still more exquisite trial of his patience yet awaits him, and which indeed, as the writer seems to intimate, he scarcely appears to have sustained with equal firmness, namely, the unjust suspicions, the bitter reproaches, and the violent altercations of

---

[9] JOB i. 22.   [10] JOB ii. 10.

his friends, who had visited him on the pretence of affording consolation. Here commences the plot or action of the Poem: for when, after a long silence of all parties, the grief of Job breaks forth into passionate exclamations, and a vehement execration on the day of his birth; the minds of his friends are suddenly exasperated, their intentions are changed, and their consolation, if indeed they originally intended any, is converted into contumely and reproaches. The first of these three singular comforters reproves his impatience; calls in question his integrity, by indirectly insinuating that God does not inflict such punishments upon the righteous; and finally, admonishes him, that the chastisement of God is not to be despised. The next of them, not less intemperate in his reproofs, takes it for granted, that the children of Job had only received the reward due to their offences; and with regard to himself, intimates, that if he be innocent, and will apply with proper humility to the divine mercy, he may be restored. The third upbraids him with arrogance, with vanity, and even with falsehood, because he has presumed to defend himself against the unjust accusations of his companions; and exhorts him to a sounder mode of reasoning and a more holy life. They all, with a manifest, though indirect allusion to Job, discourse very copiously concerning the divine judgements which are always openly displayed against the wicked, and of the certain destruction of hypocritical pretenders to virtue and religion. In reply to this, Job enumerates his sufferings, and complains bitterly of the inhumanity of his friends, and of the severity which he has experienced from the hand of God; he calls to witness both God and man, that he is unjustly oppressed; he intimates, that he is weak in comparison with God, that the contention is consequently unequal, and that be his cause ever so righteous he cannot hope to prevail. He expostulates with God himself still more vehemently, and with greater freedom, affirming, that he does not discriminate characters, but equally afflicts the just and the unjust. The expostulations of Job serve only to irritate still more the resentment of his pretended friends; they reproach him in severer terms with pride, impiety, passion, and madness; they repeat the same arguments respecting the justice of God, the punishment of the wicked, and their certain destruction after a short period of apparent prosperity. This sentiment they confidently pronounce to be confirmed both by their experience and by that of their fathers; and they maliciously exaggerate the ungrateful topic by the most splendid imagery and the most forcible language. On the part of Job, the general scope of the argument is much the same as before, but the expression is considerably heightened; it consists of appeals to the Almighty, asseverations of his own innocence, earnest expostulations, complaints of the cruelty of his friends, melancholy reflections on the vanity of human life, and upon his own severe misfortunes, ending in grief and desperation: he affirms, however, that he places his ultimate hope and confidence in God; and the more vehemently his adversaries urge, that the wicked only are objects of the divine wrath, and obnoxious to punishment, so much the more resolutely does Job assert their perpetual impunity, prosperity, and happiness even to the end of their existence.[11] The first of his opponents, Eliphaz, incensed by this assertion, descends directly to open crimination and contumely; he accuses the most upright of men of the most atrocious crimes, of injustice, rapine, and oppression; inveighs against him as an impious pretender to virtue and religion, and with a kind of sarcastic benevolence exhorts him to penitence. Vehemently affected with this reproof, Job, in a still more animated and confident strain, appeals to the tribunal of All-seeing Justice; and wishes it were only permitted him to plead his cause in the presence of God himself. He complains still more intemperately of the unequal treatment of Providence; exults in his own integrity, and then more tenaciously maintains his former opinion concerning the impunity of the wicked. To this another of the triumvirate, Bildad, replies, by a masterly, though concise dissertation on the majesty and sanctity of the Divine Being, indirectly rebuking the presumption of Job, who has dared to question his decrees. In reply to Bildad, Job demonstrates himself no less expert at wielding the weapons of satire and ridicule, than those of reason and argument; and reverting to a more serious tone, he displays the infinite power and wisdom of God more copiously, and more poetically than the former speaker. The third of the friends making no return, and the others remaining silent, Job at length opens the true sentiments of his heart concerning the fate of the wicked; he allows that their prosperity is unstable, and that they and their descendants shall at last experience on a sudden, that God is the avenger of iniquity. In all this, however, he contends that the divine counsels do not admit of human investigation; but that the chief wisdom of man consists in the fear of God. He beautifully descants upon his former prosperity; and exhibits a striking contrast between it and his present affliction and debasement. Lastly, in answer to the crimination of Eliphaz and the implications of the others, he relates the principal transactions of his past life; he asserts his integrity as displayed in all the duties of life, and in the sight of God and man; and again appeals to the justice and omniscience of God in attestation of his veracity.

---

[11] Chap. xxi. and xxiv. are indeed obscure; the opinion, however, of Schultens on this subject appears to me more than probable.   *Author's Note.*

If these circumstances be fairly collected from the general tenour and series of the work, as far as we are able to trace them through the plainer and more conspicuous passages, it will be no very difficult task to explain and define the subject of this part of the poem, which contains the dispute between Job and his friends. The argument seems chiefly to relate to the piety and integrity of Job, and turns upon this point, whether he, who by the divine providence and visitation is so severely punished and afflicted, ought to be accounted pious and innocent. This leads into a more extensive field of controversy, into a dispute indeed, which less admits of any definition or limit, concerning the nature of the divine counsels, in the dispensations of happiness and misery in this life. The antagonists of Job in this dispute observing him exposed to such severe visitations, conceiving that this affliction has not fallen upon him unmeritedly, accuse him of hypocrisy, and falsely ascribe to him the guilt of some atrocious but concealed offence. Job, on the contrary, conscious of no crime, and wounded by their unjust suspicions, defends his own innocence before God with rather more confidence and ardour than is commendable; and so strenuously contends for his own integrity, that he seems virtually to charge God himself with some degree of injustice.

This state of the controversy is clearly explained by what follows: for when the three friends have ceased to dispute with Job, "because he seemeth just in his own eyes,"[12] that is, because he has uniformly contended, that there was no wickedness in himself which could call down the heavy vengeance of God; Elihu comes forward justly offended with both parties; with Job, because "he justified himself in preference to God,"[13] that is, because he defended so vehemently the justice of his own cause, that he seemed in some measure to arraign the justice of God; against the three friends, because, "though they were unable to answer Job, they ceased not to condemn him:"[14] that is, they concluded in their own minds, that Job was impious and wicked, while, nevertheless, they had nothing specific to object against his assertions of his own innocence, or upon which they might safely ground their accusation.

The conduct of Elihu evidently corresponds with this state of the controversy: he professes, after a slight prefatory mention of himself, to reason with Job, unbiassed equally by favour or resentment. He therefore reproves Job from his own mouth, because he had attributed too much to himself; because he had affirmed himself to be altogether free from guilt and depravity; because he had presumed to contend with God, and had

---

[12] Chap. xxxii. 1.   [13] Chap. xxxii. 2. Compare xxxv. 2. xl. 8.
[14] Chap. xxxiii. 3.

not scrupled to insinuate, that the Deity was hostile to him. He asserts, that it is not necessary for God to explain and develop his counsels to men; that he nevertheless takes many occasions of admonishing them, not only by visions and revelations, but even by the visitations of his providence, by sending calamities and diseases upon them, to repress their arrogance and reform their obduracy. He next rebukes Job, because he had pronounced himself upright, and affirmed that God had acted inimically, if not unjustly towards him, which he proves to be no less improper than indecent. In the third place, he objects to Job, that from the miseries of the good, and the prosperity of the wicked, he has falsely and perversely concluded, that there was no advantage to be derived from the practice of virtue. On the contrary he affirms, that when the afflictions of the just continue, it is because they do not place a proper confidence in God, ask relief at his hands, patiently expect it, nor demean themselves before him with becoming humility and submission. This observation alone, he adds very properly, is at once a sufficient reproof of the contumacy of Job, and a full refutation of the unjust suspicions of his friends.[15] Lastly, he explains the purposes of the Deity in chastening men, which are in general to prove and to amend them, to repress their arrogance, to afford him an opportunity of exemplifying his justice upon the obstinate and rebellious, and of shewing favour to the humble and obedient. He supposes God to have acted in this manner towards Job; on that account he exhorts him to humble himself before his righteous Judge, to beware of appearing obstinate or contumacious in his sight, and of relapsing into a repetition of his sin. He intreats him, from the contemplation of the divine power and majesty, to endeavour to retain a proper reverence for the Almighty. To these frequently intermitted and often repeated admonitions of Elihu, Job makes no return.

The oration of God himself follows that of Elihu, in which disdaining to descend to any particular explication of his divine counsels, but instancing some of the stupendous effects of his infinite power, he insists upon the same topics which Elihu had before touched upon. In the first place, having reproved the temerity of Job, he convicts him of ignorance, in being unable to comprehend the works of his creation, which were obvious to every eye; the nature and structure of the earth, the sea, the light, and the animal kingdom. He then demonstrates his weakness, by challenging him to prove his own power by emulating any single exertion of the divine energy, and then referring him to one or two of

---

[15] Chap. xxxv. 4.

the brute creation, with which he is unable to contend—how much less therefore with the omnipotent Creator and Lord of all things, who is or can be accountable to no being whatever?[16] On this Job humbly submits to the will of Providence, acknowledges his own ignorance and imbecility, and "repents in dust and ashes."

On a due consideration of all these circumstances, the principal object of the poem seems to be this third and last trial of Job, from the injustice and unkindness of his accusing friends. The consequence of which is, in the first place, the anger, indignation, and contumacy of Job, and afterwards his composure, submission, and penitence. The design of the poem is, therefore, to teach men, that having a due respect to the corruption, infirmity, and ignorance of human nature, as well as to the infinite wisdom and majesty of God, they are to reject all confidence in their own strength, in their own righteousness, and to preserve on all occasions an unwavering and unsullied faith, and to submit with becoming reverence to his decrees.

I would wish it, however, to be carefully observed, that the subject of the dispute between Job and his friends differs from the subject of the poem in general: that the end of the poetical part is different from the design of the narrative at large. For although the design and subject of the poem be exactly as I have defined them, it may nevertheless be granted, that the whole history, taken together, contains an example of patience, together with its reward. This point not having been treated with sufficient distinctness by the learned, I cannot help esteeming it the principal cause of the perplexity in which the subject has been involved.

I am not ignorant, that to those who enter upon this inquiry, some questions will occur, which appear to require a separate examination; since many of them, however, are chiefly connected with those passages which are acknowledged to be obscure, which have not yet been clearly explained, and which, whatever they may hereafter be found to import, are not likely to affect the truth of our conclusion, I have thought proper to omit them. Nor will I allow, that because many things yet remain ambiguous and perplexed, we are therefore to doubt of those which are more open and evident. In regard to certain more important doctrines, which some persons of distinguished learning have thought to be established by this extraordinary monument of ancient wisdom, as they either depend in a great degree on the obscure passages above-mentioned, or do not seem to contribute in the least to the main design of the poem, nor to be consistent

---

[16] See Chap. xli. 2. 3.

with the object of it, which I just now pointed out, I thought it still more unnecessary to introduce them in this disquisition. What I have advanced, I conceived fully adequate to the purpose of this undertaking, and a sufficient introduction to a critical examination of the composition and beauties of the poem.

[*Space is lacking for Lecture XXXIII: "The Poem of Job Not a Perfect Drama," and for Lecture XXXIV: "Of the Manners, Sentiments, and Style of the Poem of Job."*]

BIBLIOGRAPHY ENTRY FOR RESEARCH PAPERS:
  Lowth, Robert. *Lectures on the Sacred Poetry of the Hebrews.* Tr. and ed. G. Gregory, with notes by the translator and others. 2nd ed. Boston, 1815. Lecture XXXII, "Of the Poem of Job," reprinted in *The Voice out of the Whirlwind: The Book of Job,* ed. Ralph E. Hone. San Francisco, 1960.

FIRST FOOTNOTE:
  * Robert Lowth, *Lectures on the Sacred Poetry of the Hebrews,* tr. and ed. G. Gregory, with notes by the translator and others, 2nd ed. (Boston, 1815), Lecture XXXII, "Of the Poem of Job," reprinted in *The Voice out of the Whirlwind: The Book of Job,* ed. Ralph E. Hone (San Francisco, 1960), pp. 175-192.

SUBSEQUENT FOOTNOTES:
  * Lowth, *op. cit., The Voice,* p. ■.
  * Lowth, "Of Job," *The Voice,* p. ■.
  * Lowth, *The Voice,* p. ■.

In place of *"The Voice,"* "ed. Hone" may be used in these subsequent-footnote forms.

JOHANN WOLFGANG VON GOETHE

ON

a Job Situation

‖‖‖

*Poet, dramatist, novelist, and scientist, Johann Wolfgang von
Goethe (1749-1832) is an important voice not only for
eighteenth- and nineteenth-century Germany but for all time and
all men. It should be obvious why the following selection has
been included in this volume. [From* Faust, *Part* I, *translated by
Bayard Taylor (New York, 1870-1871).]*

FAUST—PROLOGUE IN HEAVEN

THE LORD.   THE HEAVENLY HOSTS.   *Afterwards* MEPHISTOPHELES.

(The THREE ARCHANGELS *come forward.)*

RAPHAEL   The sun-orb sings, in emulation,
'Mid brother-spheres, his ancient round:
His path predestined through Creation
He ends with step of thunder-sound.
The angels from his visage splendid
Draw power, whose measure none can say;
The lofty works, uncomprehended,
Are bright as on the earliest day.

GABRIEL   And swift, and swift beyond conceiving,
The splendor of the world goes round,
Day's Edenbrightness still relieving

The awful Night's intense profound:
The ocean-tides in foam are breaking,
Against the rocks' deep bases hurled,
And both, the spheric race partaking,
Eternal, swift, are onward whirled!

MICHAEL   And rival storms abroad are surging
From sea to land, from land to sea.
A chain of deepest action forging
Round all, in wrathful energy.
There flames a desolation, blazing
Before the Thunder's crashing way:
Yet, Lord, Thy messengers are praising
The gentle movement of Thy Day.

THE THREE   Though still by them uncomprehended,
From these the angels draw their power,
And all Thy works, sublime and splendid,
Are bright as in Creation's hour.

MEPHISTOPHELES   Since Thou, O Lord, deign'st to approach again
And ask us how we do, in manner kindest,
And heretofore to meet myself were fain,
Among Thy menials, now, my face Thou findest.
Pardon, this troop I cannot follow after
With lofty speech, though by them scorned and spurned,
My pathos certainly would move Thy laughter,
If Thou hadst not all merriment unlearned.
Of suns and worlds I've nothing to be quoted;
How men torment themselves, is all I've noted.
The little god o' the world sticks to the same old way,
And is as whimsical as on Creation's day.
Life somewhat better might content him,
But for the gleam of heavenly light which Thou hast lent him:
He calls it Reason—thence his power's increased,
To be far beastlier than any beast.
Saving Thy Gracious Presence, he to me
A long-legged grasshopper appears to be,
That springing flies, and flying springs,
And in the grass the same old ditty sings.
Would he still lay among the grass he grows in!
Each bit of dung he seeks, to stick his nose in.

THE LORD Hast thou, then, nothing more to mention?
Com'st ever, thus, with ill intention?
Find'st nothing right on earth, eternally?

MEPHISTOPHELES No, Lord! I find things, there, still bad as they can be.
Man's misery even to pity moves my nature;
I've scarce the heart to plague the wretched creature.

THE LORD Know'st Faust?

MEPHISTOPHELES   The Doctor Faust?

THE LORD   My servant, he!

MEPHISTOPHELES Forsooth! He serves you after strange devices:
No earthly meat or drink the fool suffices:
His spirit's ferment far aspireth;
Half conscious of his frenzied, crazed unrest,
The fairest stars from Heaven he requireth,
From Earth the highest raptures and the best,
And all the Near and Far that he desireth
Fails to subdue the tumult of his breast.

THE LORD Though still confused his service unto Me,
I soon shall lead him to a clearer morning.
Sees not the gardener, even while buds his tree,
Both flower and fruit the future years adorning?

MEPHISTOPHELES What will you bet? There's still a chance to gain him,
If unto me full leave you give,
Gently upon *my* road to train him!

THE LORD As long as he on earth shall live,
So long I make no prohibition.
While Man's desires and aspirations stir,
He cannot choose but err.

MEPHISTOPHELES My thanks! I find the dead no acquisition,
And never cared to have them in my keeping.
I much prefer the cheeks where ruddy blood is leaping,
And when a corpse approaches, close my house:
It goes with me, as with the cat the mouse.

THE LORD Enough! What thou hast asked is granted.
Turn off this spirit from his fountain-head;
To trap him, let thy snares be planted,

And him, with thee, be downward led;
Then stand abashed, when thou art forced to say:
A good man, through obscurest aspiration,
Has still an instinct of the one true way.

MEPHISTOPHELES   Agreed! But 't is a short probation.
About my bet I feel no trepidation.
If I fulfil my expectation,
You'll let me triumph with a swelling breast:
Dust shall he eat, and with a zest,
As did a certain snake, my near relation.

THE LORD   Therein thou 'rt free, according to thy merits;
The like of thee have never moved My hate.
Of all the bold, denying Spirits,
The waggish knave least trouble doth create.
Man's active nature, flagging, seeks too soon the level;
Unqualified repose he learns to crave;
Whence, willingly, the comrade him I gave,
Who works, excites, and must create, as Devil.
But ye, God's sons in love and duty,
Enjoy the rich, the ever-living Beauty!
Creative Power, that works eternal schemes,
Clasp you in bonds of love, relaxing never,
And what in wavering apparition gleams
Fix in its place with thoughts that stand forever!

(Heaven closes: the ARCHANGELS *separate.)*

MEPHISTOPHELES *(solus)*   I like, at times, to hear The Ancient's word,
And have a care to be most civil:
It's really kind of such a noble Lord
So humanly to gossip with the Devil!

―――

BIBLIOGRAPHY ENTRY FOR RESEARCH PAPERS:
Goethe, Johann Wolfgang von. *Faust, Part I.* Tr. Bayard Taylor. "The Prologue in Heaven."

It is needless to give further bibliographical information for a work that has been published in so many editions as this one.

FIRST FOOTNOTE:

   * Johann Wolfgang von Goethe, *Faust, Part I*, tr. Bayard Taylor, "The Prologue in Heaven."

SUBSEQUENT FOOTNOTES:

   * Goethe, *op. cit.*
   * Goethe, Faust, Part I, Prologue.

THOMAS CARLYLE

ON

the Poetry of Job

<hr/>

Thomas Carlyle (1795-1881) was one of the great stylists of nine-teenth-century British literature. Typical of many thinkers in the period was his unflagging attempt to seek out and to express the truth about the nature and destiny of man during a time when rationalism was denuding the world of many of its simple old beliefs. He was greatly influenced by German thought, especially by that of Kant, Goethe, and Fichte. The selection which follows is taken from the book which is commonly accepted as the maturest statement of his beliefs. [On Heroes, Hero-Worship, and the Heroic in History, *ed. Archibald MacMechan (Boston: Ginn and Co., 1901), "The Hero as a Prophet," pp. 55-56.*]

From *THE HERO AS A PROPHET*

THEY HAD many Prophets, these Arabs; Teachers each to his tribe, each according to the light he had. But indeed, have we not from of old the noblest of proofs, still palpable to every one of us, of what devoutness and noble-mindedness had dwelt in these rustic thoughtful peoples? Biblical critics seem agreed that our own *Book of Job* was written in that region of the world. I call that, apart from all the theories about it, one of the grandest things ever written with pen. One feels, indeed, as if it were not Hebrew; such a noble universality, different from noble patriotism or sectarianism, reigns in it. A noble Book; all men's Book! It is our first, oldest statement of the never-ending Problem,—man's destiny, and God's ways with him here in this earth. And all in such free flowing outlines; grand in its sincerity, in its simplicity; in its epic melody, and repose of reconcilement. There is the seeing eye, the mildly understanding heart. So *true* everyway; true eyesight and vision for all things; material things no less than spiritual: the Horse,—"hast thou clothed his neck with *thunder?*"—he *"laughs* at the shaking of the spear!" Such living likenesses were never since drawn. Sublime sorrow, sublime reconciliation; oldest choral melody as of the heart of mankind;—so soft, and great; as the summer midnight, as the world with its seas and stars! There is nothing written, I think, in the Bible or out of it, of equal literary merit.—

BIBLIOGRAPHY ENTRY FOR RESEARCH PAPERS:

Carlyle, Thomas. *On Heroes, Hero-Worship, and the Heroic in History*. Ed. Archibald MacMechan. Boston: Ginn and Co., 1901. "The Hero as Prophet" reprinted in part in *The Voice out of the Whirlwind: The Book of Job*, ed. Ralph E. Hone. San Francisco, 1950.

FIRST FOOTNOTE:

* Thomas Carlyle, *On Heroes, Hero-Worship, and the Heroic in History*, ed. Archibald MacMechan (Boston: Ginn and Co., 1901), "The Hero as Prophet" reprinted in part in *The Voice out of the Whirlwind: The Book of Job*, ed. Ralph. E. Hone (San Francisco, 1960), pp. 198-199.

SUBSEQUENT FOOTNOTES:

* Carlyle, *op. cit., The Voice*, p. ■.
* Carlyle, "The Hero as Prophet," *The Voice*, p. ■.
* Carlyle, *The Voice*, p. ■.

In place of *"The Voice,"* "ed. Hone" may be used in these subsequent-footnote forms.

JAMES ANTHONY FROUDE

ON

the Meaning of Job

||||||||||||||||||||||||||||||||||||||||||||||||||||||||||||||||||||||||||||||||||||||||||||||||||||||||||||||||||||||||||||||||||||||||||||||||||||||||||||||

A student at Oxford, James Anthony Froude (1818-1894) came under the same influence that led Newman to break with Anglicanism and to turn to Roman Catholicism, but Froude resisted the Oxford Movement and became a skeptic. His tirelessness and consuming curiosity about the past led him to produce a vast number of works on a wide array of subjects, ancient history, social problems, his friendship with Carlyle, and, not the least, the following essay, which is reprinted from Short Studies on Great Subjects *(New York: Charles Scribner and Co., 1908), 5 vols., vol. 1, pp. 244-293.*

THE BOOK OF JOB.[1]

IT WILL BE matter some day of curious inquiry to ascertain why, notwithstanding the high reverence with which the English people regard the Bible, they have done so little in comparison with their continental contemporaries towards arriving at a proper understanding of it. The books named below[2] form but a section of a long list which has appeared during

---

[1] *Westminster Review,* 1853.

[2] 1. *Die poetischen Bücher des Alten Bundes.* Erklart von Heinrich Ewald. Göttingen: bei Vanderhoeck und Ruprecht. 1836.

2. *Kurz gefasstes exegetisches Handbuch zum Alten Testament.* Zweite Lieferung. *Hiob.* Von Ludwig Hirzel. Zweite Auflage, durchgesehen von Dr Justus Olshausen. Leipzig. 1852.

3. *Quæstionum in Jobeidos locos vexatos Specimen.* Von D. Hermannus Hupfeld. Halis Saxonum. 1853.

the last few years in Germany on the Book of Job alone; and this book has not received any larger share of attention than the others, either of the Old or the New Testament. Whatever be the nature or the origin of these books (and on this point there is much difference of opinion among the Germans as among ourselves) they are all agreed, orthodox and unorthodox, that at least we should endeavour to understand them; and that no efforts can be too great, either of research or criticism, to discover their history, or elucidate their meaning.

We shall assent, doubtless, eagerly, perhaps noisily and indignantly, to so obvious a truism; but our own efforts in the same direction will not bear us out. Able men in England employ themselves in matters of a more practical character; and while we refuse to avail ourselves of what has been done elsewhere, no book, or books, which we produce on the interpretation of Scripture acquire more than a partial or an ephemeral reputation. The most important contribution to our knowledge on this subject which has been made in these recent years is the translation of the 'Library of the Fathers,' by which it is about as rational to suppose that the analytical criticism of modern times can be superseded, as that the place of Herman and Dindorf could be supplied by an edition of the old scholiasts.

It is, indeed, reasonable that as long as we are persuaded that our English theory of the Bible, as a whole, is the right one, we should shrink from contact with investigations which, however ingenious in themselves, are based on what we know to be a false foundation. But there are some learned Germans whose orthodoxy would pass examination at Exeter Hall; and there are many subjects, such, for instance, as the present, on which all their able men are agreed in conclusions that cannot rationally give offence to any one. With the Book of Job, analytical criticism has only served to clear up the uncertainties which have hitherto always hung about it. It is now considered to be, beyond all doubt, a genuine Hebrew original, completed by its writer almost in the form in which it now remains to us. The questions on the authenticity of the Prologue and Epilogue, which once were thought important, have given way before a more sound conception of the dramatic unity of the entire poem; and the volumes before us contain merely an inquiry into its meaning, bringing, at the same time, all the resources of modern scholarship and historical and mythological research to bear upon the obscurity of separate passages. It is the most difficult of all the Hebrew compositions—many words occurring in it, and many thoughts, not to be found elsewhere in the Bible. How difficult our translators found it may be seen by the number of words which they were obliged to insert in italics, and the doubtful renderings which they have suggested in the margin. One instance of this, in passing, we will notice in this place—it will be familiar to every one as the passage quoted at the opening of the English burial service, and adduced as one of the doctrinal proofs of the resurrection of the body:—'I know that my Redeemer liveth, and that He shall stand at the latter *day* upon the earth; and *though,* after my skin *worms* destroy this *body,* yet in my flesh I shall see God.' So this passage stands in the ordinary version. But the words in italics have nothing answering to them in the original—they were all added by the translators[1] to fill out their interpretation; and for *in my flesh,* they tell us themselves in the margin that we may read (and, in fact, we ought to read, and must read) *'out of,'* or *'without' my flesh.* It is but to write out the verses, omitting the conjectural additions, and making that one small but vital correction, to see how frail a support is there for so large a conclusion: 'I know that my Redeemer liveth, and shall stand at the latter upon the earth; and after my skin destroy this ; yet without my flesh I shall see God.' If there is any doctrine of a resurrection here, it is a resurrection precisely *not* of the body, but of the spirit. And now let us only add, that the word translated Redeemer is the technical expression for the 'avenger of blood;' and that the second paragraph ought to be rendered—'and one to come after me (my next of kin, to whom the avenging my injuries belongs) shall stand upon my dust,' and we shall see how much was to be done towards the mere exegesis of the text. This is an extreme instance, and no one will question the general beauty and majesty of our translation; but there are many mythical and physical allusions scattered over the poem, which, in the sixteenth century, there were positively no means of understanding; and perhaps, too, there were mental tendencies in the translators themselves which prevented them from adequately apprehending even the drift and spirit of the composition. The form of the story was too stringent to allow such tendencies any latitude; but they appear, from time to time, sufficiently to produce serious confusion. With these recent assistances, therefore, we propose to say something of the nature of this extraordinary book—a book of which it is to say little to call unequalled of its kind, and which will one day, perhaps, when it is allowed to stand on its own merits, be seen towering up alone, far away above all the poetry of the world. How it found its way into the canon, smiting as it does through and through the most deeply-seated Jewish prejudices, is the chief difficulty about it now; to be explained only by a traditional acceptance among the sacred books, dating back from the old times of the national greatness, when the minds of the people were

---

[1] Or rather by St Jerome, whom our translators have followed.

hewn in a larger type than was to be found among the Pharisees of the great synagogue. But its authorship, its date, and its history, are alike a mystery to us: it existed at the time when the canon was composed; and this is all that we know beyond what we can gather out of the language and contents of the poem itself.

Before going further, however, we must make room for a few remarks of a very general kind. Let it have been written when it would, it marks a period in which the religious convictions of thinking men were passing through a vast crisis; and we shall not understand it without having before us clearly something of the conditions which periods of such a kind always and necessarily exhibit.

The history of religious speculation appears in extreme outline to have been of the following character. We may conceive mankind to have been originally launched into the universe with no knowledge either of themselves or of the scene in which they were placed; with no actual knowledge, but distinguished from the rest of the creation by a faculty of gaining knowledge; and first unconsciously, and afterwards consciously and laboriously, to have commenced that long series of experience and observation which has accumulated in thousands of years to what we now see around us. Limited on all sides by conditions which they must have felt to be none of their own imposing, and finding everywhere forces working, over which they had no control, the fear which they would naturally entertain of these invisible and mighty agents assumed, under the direction of an idea which we may perhaps call inborn and inherent in human nature, a more generous character of reverence and awe. The laws of the outer world, as they discovered them, they regarded as the decrees, or as the immediate energies of personal beings; and as knowledge grew up among them, they looked upon it, not as knowledge of nature, but of God, or the gods. All early paganism appears, on careful examination, to have arisen out of a consecration of the first rudiments of physical or speculative science. The twelve labours of Hercules are the labours of the sun, of which Hercules is an old name, through the twelve signs. Chronos, or *time,* being measured by the apparent motion of the heavens, is figured as their child; Time, the universal parent, devours its own offspring, yet is again itself, in the high faith of a human soul conscious of its power and its endurance, supposed to be baffled and dethroned by Zeus, or *life;* and so on through all the elaborate theogonies of Greece and Egypt. They are no more than real insight into real phenomena, allegorized as time went on, elaborated by fancy, or idealized by imagination, but never losing their original character.

Thus paganism, in its very nature, was expansive, self-developing, and, as Mr Hume observed, tolerant; a new god was welcomed to the Pantheon as a new scientific discovery is welcomed by the Royal Society; and the various nations found no difficulty in interchanging their divinities —a new god either representing a new power not hitherto discovered, or one with which they were already familiar under a new name. With such a power of adaptation and enlargement, if there had been nothing more in it than this, such a system might have gone on accommodating itself to the change of times, and keeping pace with the growth of human character. Already in its later forms, as the unity of nature was more clearly observed, and the identity of nature throughout the known world, the separate powers were subordinating themselves to a single supreme king; and, as the poets had originally personified the elemental forces, the thinkers were reversing the earlier process, and discovering the law under the person. Happily or unhappily, however, what they could do for themselves they could not do for the multitude. Phœbus and Aphrodite had been made too human to be allegorized. Humanized, and yet, we may say, only half-humanized, retaining their purely physical nature, and without any proper moral attribute at all, these gods and goddesses remained to the many examples of sensuality made beautiful; and, as soon as right and wrong came to have a meaning, it was impossible to worship any more these idealized despisers of it. The human caprices and passions which served at first to deepen the illusion, justly revenged themselves; paganism became a lie, and perished.

In the meantime, the Jews (and perhaps some other nations, but the Jews chiefly and principally) had been moving forward along a road wholly different. Breaking early away from the gods of nature, they advanced along the line of their moral consciousness; and leaving the nations to study physics, philosophy, and art, they confined themselves to man and to human life. Their theology grew up round the knowledge of good and evil, and God, with them, was the supreme Lord of the world, who stood towards man in the relation of a ruler and a judge. Holding such a faith, to them the toleration of paganism was an impossibility; the laws of nature might be many, but the law of conduct was one; there was one law and one king; and the conditions under which He governed the world, as embodied in the Decalogue or other similar code, were looked upon as iron and inflexible certainties, unalterable revelations of the will of an unalterable Being. So far there was little in common between this process and the other; but it was identical with it in this one important feature, that moral knowledge, like physical, admitted of degrees; and the successive steps of it were only purchasable by experience. The dispensation of the law, in the language of modern theology, was not the dispensation of grace, and the nature of good and evil disclosed itself slowly as men were able to comprehend it. Thus, no system of law or articles of belief were or could be complete and exhaustive for all time. Experience accumulates; new facts are observed, new forces display themselves, and all such formulæ must necessarily be from period to period broken up and moulded afresh. And yet the steps already gained are a treasure so sacred, so liable are they at all times to be attacked by those lower and baser elements in our nature which it is their business to hold in check, that the better part of mankind have at all times practically regarded their creed as a sacred total to which nothing may be added, and from which nothing may be taken away; the suggestion of a new idea is resented as an encroachment, punished as an insidious piece of treason, and resisted by the combined forces of all common practical understandings, which know too well the value of what they have, to risk the venture upon untried change. Periods of religious transition, therefore, when the advance has been a real one, always have been violent, and probably will always continue to be so. They to whom the precious gift of fresh light has been given are called upon to exhibit their credentials as teachers in suffering for it. They, and those who oppose them, have alike a sacred cause; and the fearful spectacle arises of earnest, vehement men contending against each other as for their own souls, in fiery struggle. Persecutions come, and martyrdoms and religious wars; and, at last,.the old faith, like the phœnix, expires upon its altar, and the new rises out of the ashes.

Such, in briefest outline, has been the history of religions, natural and moral; the first, indeed, being in no proper sense a religion at all, as we understand religion; and only assuming the character of it in the minds of great men whose moral sense had raised them beyond their time and country, and who, feeling the necessity of a real creed, with an effort and with indifferent success, endeavoured to express, under the systems which they found, emotions which had no proper place in them.

Of the transition periods which we have described as taking place under the religion which we call moral, the first known to us is marked at its opening by the appearance of the Book of Job, the first fierce collision of the new fact with the formula which will not stretch to cover it.

The earliest phenomenon likely to be observed connected with the moral government of the world is the general one, that on the whole, as things are constituted, good men prosper and are happy, bad men fail and are miserable. The cause of such a condition is no mystery, and lies very near the surface. As soon as men combine in society, they are forced to obey certain laws under which alone society is possible, and these laws, even in their rudest form, approach the laws of conscience. To a certain extent, every one is obliged to sacrifice his private inclinations; and those who refuse to do so are punished, or are crushed. If society were perfect, the imperfect tendency would carry itself out till the two sets of laws were identical; but perfection so far has been only in Utopia, and, as far as we can judge by experience hitherto, they have approximated most nearly in the simplest and most rudimentary forms of life. Under the systems which we call patriarchal, the modern distinction between sins and crimes had no existence. All gross sins were offences against society, as it then was constituted, and, wherever it was possible, were punished as being so; chicanery and those subtle advantages which the acute and unscrupulous can take over the simple, without open breach of enacted statutes, became only possible under the complications of more artificial polities; and the oppression or injury of man by man was open, violent, obvious, and therefore easily understood. Doubtless, therefore, in such a state of things it would, on the whole, be true to experience that, judging merely by outward prosperity or the reverse, good and bad men would be rewarded and punished as such in this actual world; so far, that is, as the administration of such rewards and punishments was left in the power of mankind. But theology could not content itself with general tendencies. Theological propositions then, as much as now, were held to be absolute, universal, admitting of no exceptions, and explaining every phenomenon. Superficial generalizations were construed into immutable decrees; the God of this world was just and righteous, and temporal prosperity or wretchedness were dealt out by Him immediately by His own will to His subjects according to their behaviour. Thus the same disposition towards completeness which was the ruin of paganism, here, too, was found generating the same evils; the half truth rounding itself out with falsehoods. Not only the consequences of ill actions which followed through themselves, but the accidents, as we call them, of nature—earthquakes, storms, and pestilences—were the ministers of God's justice, and struck sinners only with discriminating accuracy. That the sun should shine alike on the evil and the good was a creed too high for the early divines, or that the victims of a fallen tower were no greater offenders than their neighbors. The conceptions of such men could not pass beyond the outward temporal consequence; and if God's hand was not there it was nowhere. We might have expected that such a theory of things could not long resist the accumulated contradictions of experience; but the same experience shows also what a marvellous power is in us of thrusting aside phenomena which interfere with our cherished convictions; and when such convictions are consecrated into a creed which it is a sacred duty to believe, experience is but like water dropping upon a rock, which wears it away, indeed, at last, but only in thousands of years. This theory was and is the central idea of the Jewish polity, the obstinate toughness of which has been the perplexity of Gentiles and Christians from the first dawn of its existence; it lingers among ourselves in our Liturgy and in the popular belief; and in spite of the emphatic censure of Him after whose name we call ourselves, is still the instant interpreter for us of any unusual calamity, a potato blight, a famine, or an epidemic; such vitality is there in a moral faith, though now, at any rate, contradicted by the experience of all mankind, and at issue even with Christianity itself.

At what period in the world's history misgivings about it began to show themselves it is now impossible to say; it was at the close, probably, of the patriarchal period, when men who really *thought* must have found the ground palpably shaking under them. Indications of such misgivings are to be found in the Psalms, those especially passing under the name of Asaph; and all through Ecclesiastes there breathes a spirit of deepest and saddest scepticism. But Asaph thrusts his doubts aside, and forces himself back into his old position; and the scepticism of Ecclesiastes is confessedly that of a man who had gone wandering after enjoyment; searching after pleasures—pleasures of sense and pleasures of intellect—and who, at last, bears reluctant testimony that, by such methods, no pleasures can be found which will endure; that he had squandered the power which might have been used for better things, and had only strength remaining to tell his own sad tale as a warning to mankind. There is nothing in Ecclesiastes like the misgivings of a noble nature. The writer's own personal happiness had been all for which he had cared; he had failed, as all men gifted as he was gifted are sure to fail, and the lights of heaven were extinguished by the disappointment with which his own spirit had been clouded.

Utterly different from these, both in character and in the lesson which it teaches, is the Book of Job. Of unknown date, as we said, and unknown authorship, the language impregnated with strange idioms and strange allusions, un-Jewish in form, and in fiercest hostility with Judaism, it hovers like a meteor over the old Hebrew literature, in it, but not of it, compelling the acknowledgment of itself by its own internal majesty, yet exerting no influence over the minds of the people, never alluded to, and scarcely ever quoted, till at last the light which it had heralded rose up full over the world in Christianity.

The conjectures which have been formed upon the date of this book are so various, that they show of themselves on how slight a foundation the best of them must rest. The language is no guide, for although un-questionably of Hebrew origin, the poem bears no analogy to any of the other books in the Bible; while of its external history nothing is known at all, except that it was received into the canon at the time of the great synagogue. Ewald decides, with some confidence, that it belongs to the great prophetic period, and that the writer was a contemporary of Jeremiah. Ewald is a high authority in these matters, and this opinion is the one which we believe is now commonly received among biblical scholars. In the absence of proof, however (and the reasons which he brings forward are really no more than conjectures), these opposite considerations may be of moment. It is only natural that at first thought we should ascribe the grandest poem in a literature to the time at which the poetry of the nation to which it belongs was generally at its best; but, on reflection, the time when the poetry of prophecy is the richest, is not likely to be favourable to compositions of another kind. The prophets wrote in an era of decrepi-tude, dissolution, sin, and shame, when the glory of Israel was falling round them into ruin, and their mission, glowing as they were with the ancient spirit, was to rebuke, to warn, to threaten, and to promise. Finding themselves too late to save, and only, like Cassandra, despised and dis-regarded, their voices rise up singing the swan song of a dying people, now falling away in the wild wailing of despondency over the shameful and desperate present, now swelling in triumphant hope that God will not leave them for ever, and in His own time will take His chosen to Himself again. But such a period is an ill occasion for searching into the broad problems of human destiny; the present is all-important and all-absorbing; and such a book as that of Job could have arisen only out of an isolation of mind, and life, and interest, which we cannot conceive of as possible under such conditions.

The more it is studied, the more the conclusion forces itself upon us that, let the writer have lived when he would, in his struggle with the central falsehood of his own people's creed, he must have divorced him-self from them outwardly as well as inwardly; that he travelled away into the world, and lived long, perhaps all his matured life, in exile. Every-thing about the book speaks of a person who had broken free from the narrow littleness of 'the peculiar people.' The language, as we said, is full of strange words. The hero of the poem is of strange land and parentage—a Gentile certainly, not a Jew. The life, the manners, the customs are of all varieties and places—Egypt, with its river and its pyramids, is there; the description of mining points to Phœnicia; the settled life in cities, the nomad Arabs, the wandering caravans, the heat of the tropics, and the ice of the north, all are foreign to Canaan, speaking of foreign things and foreign people. No mention, or hint of mention, is there throughout the poem of Jewish traditions or Jewish certainties. We look to find the three friends vindicate themselves, as they so well might have done, by appeals to the fertile annals of Israel, to the Flood, to the cities of the plain, to the plagues of Egypt, or the thunders of Sinai. But of all this there is not a word; they are passed by as if they had no existence; and instead of them, when witnesses are required for the power of God, we have strange un-Hebrew stories of the eastern astronomic mythology, the old wars of the giants, the imprisoned Orion, the wounded dragon, 'the sweet influences of the seven stars,' and the glittering fragments of the sea-snake Rahab[1] trailing across the northern sky. Again, God is not the God of Israel, but the father of mankind; we hear nothing of a chosen people, nothing of a special revelation, nothing of peculiar privileges; and in the court of heaven there is a Satan, not the prince of this world and the enemy of God, but the angel of judgment, the accusing spirit whose mission was to walk to and fro over the earth, and carry up to heaven an account of the sins of mankind. We cannot believe that thoughts of this kind arose out of Jerusalem in the days of Josiah. In this book, if anywhere, we have the record of some ἀνὴρ πολύτροπος who, like the old hero of Ithaca,

> πολλῶν ἀνθρώπων ἴδεν ἄστεα καί νόον ἔγνω,
> πολλὰ δ᾿ ὅγ ἐν πόντῳ πάθεν ἄλγεα ὃν κατὰ θυμόν,
> ἀρνύμενος ψυχήν . . . . . .

but the scenes, the names, and the incidents, are all contrived as if to baffle curiosity—as if, in the very form of the poem, to teach us that it is no story of a single thing which happened once, but that it belongs to humanity itself, and is the drama of the trial of man, with Almighty God and the angels as the spectators of it.

No reader can have failed to have been struck with the simplicity of the opening. Still, calm, and most majestic, it tells us everything which is necessary to be known in the fewest possible words. The history of Job was probably a tradition in the East; his name, like that of Priam in Greece, the symbol of fallen greatness, and his misfortunes the problem of philosophers. In keeping with the current belief, he is described as a model of excellence, the most perfect and upright man upon the earth, 'and the same was the greatest man in all the east.' So far, greatness and goodness had gone hand in hand together, as the popular theory required. The details of his character are brought out in the progress of the poem. He was 'the

---

[1] See Ewald on Job ix. 13, and xxvi. 14.

father of the oppressed, and of those who had none to help them.' When he sat as a judge in the market-places, 'righteousness clothed him' there, and 'his justice was a robe and a diadem.' He 'broke the jaws of the wicked, and plucked the spoil out of his teeth;' and, humble in the midst of his power, he 'did not despise the cause of his manservant, or his maidservant, when they contended with him,' knowing (and amidst those old people where the multitude of mankind were regarded as the born slaves of the powerful, to be carved into eunuchs or polluted into concubines at their master's pleasure, it was no easy matter to know it)—knowing that 'He who had made him had made them,' and *one* 'had fashioned them both in the womb.' Above all, he was the friend of the poor; 'the blessing of him that was ready to perish came upon him,' and he 'made the widow's heart to sing for joy.'

Setting these characteristics of his daily life by the side of his un-affected piety, as it is described in the first chapter, we have a picture of the best man who could then be conceived; not a hard ascetic, living in haughty or cowardly isolation, but a warm figure of flesh and blood, a man full of all human loveliness, and to whom, that no room might be left for any possible Calvinistic falsehood, God Himself bears the emphatic testi-mony, that 'there was none like him upon the earth, a perfect and upright man, who feared God and eschewed evil.' If such a person as this, there-fore, could be made miserable, necessarily the current belief of the Jews was false to the root; and tradition furnished the fact that he had been visited by every worst calamity. How was it then to be accounted for? Out of a thousand possible explanations, the poet introduces a single one. He admits us behind the veil which covers the ways of Providence, and we hear the accusing angel charging Job with an interested piety, and of being obedient because it was his policy. 'Job does not serve God for nought,' he says; 'strip him of his splendour, and see if he will care for God then. Humble him into poverty and wretchedness, so only we shall know what is in his heart.' The cause thus introduced is itself a rebuke to the belief which, with its 'rewards and punishments,' immediately fostered selfish-ness; and the poem opens with a double action, on one side to try the question whether it is possible for man to love God disinterestedly—the issue of which trial is not foreseen or even foretold, and we watch the progress of it with an anxious and fearful interest; on the other side, to bring out, in contrast to the truth which we already know, the cruel false-hood of the popular faith—to show how, instead of leading men to mercy and affection, it hardens their heart, narrows their sympathies, and en-hances the trials of the sufferer, by refinements which even Satan had not anticipated. The combination of evils, as blow falls on blow, suddenly, swiftly, and terribly, has all the appearance of a purposed visitation (as indeed it was), if ever outward incidents might with justice be interpreted as the immediate action of Providence, those which fell on Job might be so interpreted. The world turns disdainfully from the fallen in the world's way; but far worse than this, his chosen friends, wise, good, pious men, as wisdom and piety were then, without one glimpse of the true cause of his sufferings, see in them a judgment upon his secret sins. He becomes to them an illustration, and even (such are the paralogisms of men of this description) a proof of their theory that 'the prosperity of the wicked is but for a while;' and instead of the comfort and help which they might have brought him, and which in the end they were made to bring him, he is to them no more than a text for the enunciation of solemn falsehood. And even worse again, the sufferer himself had been educated in the same creed; he, too, had been taught to see the hand of God in the outward dispensation; and feeling from the bottom of his heart, that he, in his own case, was a sure contradiction of what he had learnt to believe, he himself finds his very faith in God shaken from its foundation. The worst evils which Satan had devised were distanced far by those which had been created by human folly.

The creed in which Job had believed was tried and found wanting, and, as it ever will be when the facts of experience come in contact with the inadequate formula, the true is found so mingled with the false, that they can hardly be disentangled, and are in danger of being swept away together.

A studied respect is shown, however, to orthodoxy, even while it is arraigned for judgment. It may be doubtful whether the writer purposely intended it. He probably cared only to tell the real truth; to say for the old theory the best which could be said, and to produce as its defenders the best and wisest men whom in his experience he had known to believe and defend it. At any rate, he represents the three friends, not as a weaker person would have represented them, as foolish, obstinate bigots, but as wise, humane, and almost great men, who, at the outset, at least, are animated only by the kindest feelings, and speak what they have to say with the most earnest conviction that it is true. Job is vehement, desperate, reckless. His language is the wild, natural outpouring of suffering. The friends, true to the eternal nature of man, are grave, solemn, and indignant, preaching their half truth, and mistaken only in supposing that it is the whole; speaking, as all such persons would speak and still do speak, in defending what they consider sacred truth against the assaults of folly and scepticism. How beautiful is their first introduction:—

'Now when Job's three friends heard of all this evil which was come upon him, they came every one from his own place; Eliphaz the Temanite, and Bildad the Shuhite, and Zophar the Naamathite: for they had made an appointment together to come to mourn with him and to comfort him. And when they lifted up their eyes afar off, and knew him not, they lifted up their voice and wept, and they rent every one his mantle, and sprinkled dust upon their heads towards heaven. So they sat down with him upon the ground seven days and seven nights, and none spake a word unto him, for they saw that his grief was very great.'

What a picture is there! What majestic tenderness! His wife had scoffed at his faith, bidding him 'leave God and die.' His 'acquaintance had turned from him.' He 'had called his servant, and he had given him no answer.' Even the children, in their unconscious cruelty, had gathered round and mocked him as he lay among the ashes. But 'his friends sprinkle dust towards heaven, and sit silently by him, and weep for him seven days and seven nights upon the ground.' That is, they were true-hearted, truly loving, devout, religious men; and yet they, with their religion, were to become the instruments of the most poignant sufferings, the sharpest temptations, which he had to endure. So it was, and is, and will be—of such materials is this human life of ours composed.

And now, remembering the double action of the drama—the actual trial of Job, the result of which is uncertain; and the delusion of these men, which is, at the outset, certain—let us go rapidly through the dialogue. Satan's share in the temptation had already been overcome. Lying sick in the loathsome disease which had been sent upon him, his wife, in Satan's own words, had tempted Job to say, 'Farewell to God,'—think no more of God or goodness, since this was all which came of it; and Job had told her that she spoke as one of the foolish women. He 'had received good at the hand of the Lord, and should he not receive evil?' But now, when real love and real affection appear, his heart melts in him; he loses his forced self-composure, and bursts into a passionate regret that he had ever been born. In the agony of his sufferings, hope of better things had died away. He does not complain of injustice; as yet, and before his friends have stung and wounded him, he makes no questioning of Providence,—but why was life given to him at all, if only for this? Sick in mind, and sick in body, but one wish remains to him, that death will come quickly and end all. It is a cry from the very depth of a single and simple heart. But for such simplicity and singleness his friends could not give him credit; possessed beforehand with their idea, they see in his misery only a fatal witness against him; such calamities could not have befallen a man, the justice of God would not have permitted it, unless they had been deserved. Job had sinned and he had suffered, and this wild passion was but impenitence and rebellion.

Being as certain that they were right in this opinion as they were that God Himself existed, that they should speak what they felt was only natural and necessary; and their language at the outset is all which would be dictated by the tenderest sympathy. Eliphaz opens, the oldest and most important of the three, in a soft, subdued, suggestive strain, contriving in every way to spare the feelings of the sufferer, to the extreme to which his love will allow him. All is general, impersonal, indirect,—the rule of the world, the order of Providence. He does not accuse Job, but he describes his calamities, and leaves him to gather for himself the occasion which had produced them; and then passes off, as if further to soften the blow, to the mysterious vision in which the infirmity of mortal nature had been revealed to him, the universal weakness which involved both the certainty that Job had shared in it, and the excuse for him, if he would confess and humble himself: the blessed virtue of repentance follows, and the promise that all shall be well.

This is the note on which each of the friends strikes successively, in the first of the three divisions into which the dialogue divides itself, but each with increasing peremptoriness and confidence, as Job, so far from accepting their interpretation of what had befallen him, hurls it from him in anger and disdain. Let us observe (and the Calvinists should consider this), he will hear as little of the charges against mankind as of charges against himself. He will not listen to the 'corruption of humanity,' because in the consciousness of his own innocency, he knows that it is not corrupt: he knows that he is himself just and good, and we know it, the Divine sentence upon him having been already passed. He will not acknowledge his sin, for he knows not of what to repent. If he could have reflected calmly, he might have foreseen what they would say. He knew all that as well as they: it was the old story which he had learnt, and could repeat, if necessary, as well as any one: and if it had been no more than a philosophical discussion, touching himself no more nearly than it touched his friends, he might have allowed for the tenacity of opinion in such matters, and listened to it and replied to it with equanimity. But as the proverb says, 'It is ill talking between a full man and a fasting:' and in Job such equanimity would have been but Stoicism, or the affectation of it, and unreal as the others' theories. Possessed with the certainty that he had not deserved what had befallen him, harassed with doubt, and worn out with pain and unkindness, he had assumed (and how natural that he should assume it!)

that those who loved him should not have been hasty to believe evil of him; he had spoken to them as he really felt, and he thought that he might have looked to them for something warmer and more sympathizing than such dreary eloquence. So when the revelation comes upon him of what was passing in them, he attributes it (and now he is unjust to them) to a falsehood of heart, and not to a blindness of understanding. Their sermons, so kindly intended, roll past him as a dismal mockery. They had been shocked (and how true again is this to nature!) at his passionate cry for death. 'Do ye reprove words?' he says, 'and the speeches of one that is desperate, which are as wind?' It was but poor friendship and narrow wisdom. He had looked to them for pity, for comfort, and love. He had longed for it as the parched caravans in the desert for the water-streams, and 'his brethren had dealt deceitfully with him.' The brooks, in the cool winter, roll in a full turbid torrent; 'what time it waxes warm they vanish, when it is hot they are consumed out of their place; the caravans of Tema looked for them, the companies of Sheba waited for them; they were confounded because they had hoped; they came hither, and there was nothing.' If for once these poor men could have trusted their hearts, if for once they could have believed that there might be 'more things in heaven and earth' than were dreamt of in their philosophy—but this is the one thing which they could not do, which the theologian proper never has done or will do. And thus whatever of calmness or endurance Job alone, on his ash-heap, might have conquered for himself, is all scattered away; and as the strong gusts of passion sweep to and fro across his heart, he pours himself out in wild fitful music, so beautiful because so true, not answering them or their speeches, but now flinging them from him in scorn, now appealing to their mercy, or turning indignantly to God; now praying for death; now in perplexity doubting whether, in some mystic way which he cannot understand, he may not, perhaps, after all, really have sinned, and praying to be shown his fault; and then staggering further into the darkness, and breaking out into upbraidings of the Power which has become so dreadful an enigma to him. 'Thou inquirest after my iniquity, thou searchest after my sin, and thou knowest that I am not wicked. Why didst thou bring me forth out of the womb? Oh, that I had given up the ghost, and no eye had seen me. Cease, let me alone. It is but a little while that I have to live. Let me alone, that I may take comfort a little before I go, whence I shall not return, to the land of darkness and the shadow of death.' In what other poem in the world is there pathos deep as this? With experience so stern as his, it was not for Job to be calm, and self-possessed, and delicate in his words. He speaks not what he knows, but what he feels; and without fear the writer allows him to throw out his passion all genuine as it rises, not overmuch caring how nice ears might be offended, but contented to be true to the real emotion of a genuine human heart. So the poem runs on to the end of the first answer to Zophar.

But now, with admirable fitness, as the contest goes forward, the relative position of the speakers begins to change. Hitherto, Job only had been passionate; and his friends temperate and collected. Now, becoming shocked at his obstinacy, and disappointed in the result of their homilies, they stray still further from the truth in an endeavour to strengthen their position, and, as a natural consequence, visibly grow angry. To them, Job's vehement and desperate speeches are damning evidence of the truth of their suspicion. Impiety is added to his first sin, and they begin to see in him a rebel against God. At first they had been contented to speak generally, and much which they had urged was partially true; now they step forward to a direct application, and formally and personally accuse himself. Here their ground is positively false; and with delicate art it is they who are now growing violent, and wounded self-love begins to show behind their zeal for God; while in contrast to them, as there is less and less truth in what they say, Job grows more and more collected. For a time it had seemed doubtful how he would endure his trial. The light of his faith was burning feebly and unsteadily; a little more, and it seemed as if it might have utterly gone out. But at last the storm was lulling; as the charges are brought personally home to him, the confidence in his own real innocence rises against them. He had before known that he was innocent; now he feels the strength which lies in innocence, as if God were beginning to reveal Himself within him, to prepare the way for the after outward manifestation of Himself.

The friends, as before, repeat one another with but little difference; the sameness being of course intentional, as showing that they were not speaking for themselves, but as representatives of a prevailing opinion. Eliphaz, again, gives the note which the others follow. Hear this Calvinist of the old world: 'Thy own mouth condemneth thee, and thine own lips testify against thee. What is man that he should be clean, and he that is born of woman that he should be righteous? Behold, he putteth no trust in his saints; yea, the heavens are not clean in his sight; how much more abominable and filthy is man, which drinketh iniquity like water?' Strange, that after all these thousands of years we should still persist in this degrading confession, as a thing which it is impious to deny and impious to attempt to render otherwise, when Scripture itself, in language so emphatic, declares that it is a lie. Job *is* innocent, perfect, righteous. God Himself bears witness to it. It is Job who is found at last to have spoken truth, and the friends to have sinned in denying it. And he holds fast by his innocency, and with a generous confidence thrusts away the misgivings which had begun to cling to him. Among his complainings he had exclaimed, that God was remembering upon him the sins of his youth—not denying them; knowing well that he, like others, had gone astray before he had learnt to control himself, but feeling that at least in an earthly father it is unjust to visit the faults of childhood on the matured man; feeling that he had long, long shaken them off from him, and they did not even impair the probity of his after-life. But now these doubts, too, pass away in the brave certainty that God is not less just than man. As the denouncings grow louder and darker, he appeals from his narrow judges to the Supreme Tribunal—calls on God to hear him and to try his cause—and then, in the strength of this appeal the mist rises from before his eyes. His sickness is mortal; he has no hope in life, and death is near; but the intense feeling that justice must and will be done, holds to him closer and closer. God may appear on earth for him; or if that be too bold a hope, and death finds him as he is—what is death then? God will clear his memory in the place where he lived; his injuries will be righted over his grave; while for himself, like a sudden gleam of sunlight between clouds, a clear, bright hope beams up, that he too, then, in another life, if not in this, when his skin is wasted off his bones, and the worms have done their work on the prison of his spirit, he too, at last, may then see God; may see Him, and have his pleadings heard.

With such a hope, or even the shadow of one, he turns back to the world again to look at it. Facts against which he had before closed his eyes he allows and confronts, and he sees that his own little experience is but the reflection of a law. You tell me, he seems to say, that the good are rewarded, and that the wicked are punished; that God is just, and that this is always so. Perhaps it is, or will be, but not in the way which you imagine. You have known me, you have known what my life has been; you see what I am, and it is no difficulty to you. You prefer believing that I, whom you call your friend, am a deceiver or a pretender, to admitting the possibility of the falsehood of your hypothesis. You will not listen to my assurance, and you are angry with me because I will not lie against my own soul, and acknowledge sins which I have not committed. You appeal to the course of the world in proof of your faith, and challenge me to answer you. Well, then, I accept your challenge. The world is not what you say. You have told me what you have seen of it: I will tell you what I have seen.

'Even while I remember I am afraid, and trembling taketh hold upon my flesh. Wherefore do the wicked become old, yea, and are mighty in power? Their seed is established in their sight with them, and their off-spring before their eyes. Their houses are safe from fear, neither is the rod of God upon them. Their bull gendereth and faileth not; their cow calveth, and casteth not her calf. They send forth their little ones like a flock, and their children dance. They take the timbrel and harp, and re-joice at the sound of the organ. They spend their days in wealth, and in a moment go down into the grave. Therefore they say unto God, Depart from us, for we desire not the knowledge of Thy ways. What is the Al-mighty that we should serve Him? and what profit should we have if we pray to Him?'

Will you quote the weary proverb? Will you say that 'God layeth up his iniquity for his children'? (Our translators have wholly lost the sense of this passage, and endeavour to make Job acknowledge what he is stead-fastly denying.) Well, and what then? What will he care? 'Will his own eye see his own fall? Will he drink the wrath of the Almighty? What are the fortunes of his house to him if the number of his own months is ful-filled?' One man is good and another wicked, one is happy and another is miserable: In the great indifference of nature they share alike in the common lot. 'They lie down alike in the dust, and the worms cover them.'

Ewald, and many other critics, suppose that Job was hurried away by his feelings to say all this; and that in his calmer moments he must have felt that it was untrue. It is a point on which we must decline accepting even Ewald's high authority. Even then, in those old times, it was begin-ning to be terribly true. Even then the current theory was obliged to bend to large exceptions; and what Job saw as exceptions we see round us every-where. It was true then, it is infinitely more true now, that what is called virtue in the common sense of the word, still more that nobleness, godli-ness, or heroism of character in any form whatsoever, have nothing to do with this or that man's prosperity, or even happiness. The thoroughly vi-cious man is no doubt wretched enough; but the worldly, prudent, self-restraining man, with his five senses, which he understands how to gratify with tempered indulgence, with a conscience satisfied with the hack routine of what is called respectability,—such a man feels no wretchedness; no inward uneasiness disturbs him, no desires which he cannot gratify; and this though he be the basest and most contemptible slave of his own selfish-ness. Providence will not interfere to punish him. Let him obey the laws under which prosperity is obtainable, and he will obtain it, let him never fear. He will obtain it, be he base or noble. Nature is indifferent; the famine and the earthquake, and the blight or the accident, will not discriminate to strike him. He may insure himself against casualties in these days of ours, with the money perhaps which a better man would have given away, and he will have his reward. He need not doubt it.

And, again, it is not true, as optimists would persuade us, that such prosperity brings no real pleasure. A man with no high aspirations, who thrives, and makes money, and envelops himself in comforts, is as happy as such a nature can be. If unbroken satisfaction be the most blessed state for a man (and this certainly is the practical notion of happiness), he is the happiest of men. Nor are those idle phrases any truer, that the good man's goodness is a never-ceasing sunshine; that virtue is its own reward, &c. &c. If men truly virtuous care to be rewarded for it, their virtue is but a poor investment of their moral capital. Was Job so happy then on that ash-heap of his, the mark of the world's scorn, and the butt for the spiritual archery of the theologian, alone in his forlorn nakedness, like some old dreary stump which the lightning has scathed, rotting away in the wind and rain? If happiness be indeed what we men are sent into this world to seek for, those hitherto thought the noblest among us were the pitifullest and wretchedest. Surely it was no error in Job. It was that real insight which once was given to all the world in Christianity, however we have forgotten it now. Job was learning to see that it was not in the possession of enjoyment, no, nor of happiness itself, that the difference lies between the good and the bad. True, it might be that God sometimes, even generally, gives such happiness—gives it in what Aristotle calls an ἐπιγιγνόμενον τέλος, but it is no part of the terms on which He admits us to His service, still less is it the end which we may propose to ourselves on entering His service. Happiness He gives to whom He will, or leaves to the angel of nature to distribute among those who fulfil the laws upon which *it* depends. But to serve God and to love Him is higher and better than happiness, though it be with wounded feet, and bleeding brows, and hearts loaded with sorrow.

Into this high faith Job is rising, treading his temptations under his feet, and finding in them a ladder on which his spirit rises. Thus he is passing further and even further from his friends, soaring where their imaginations cannot follow him. To them he is a blasphemer whom they gaze at with awe and terror. They had charged him with sinning on the strength of their hypothesis, and he has answered with a deliberate denial of it. Losing now all mastery over themselves, they pour out a torrent of mere extravagant invective and baseless falsehood, which in the calmer outset they would have blushed to think of. They *know* no evil of Job, but they do not hesitate to convert conjecture into certainty, and specify in detail the particular crimes which he must have committed. He *ought* to have committed them, and so he had; the old argument then as now.—'Is not thy wickedness great?' says Eliphaz. 'Thou hast taken a pledge from thy brother for nought, and stripped the naked of their clothing; thou hast not given water to the weary, and thou hast withholden bread from the hungry;' and so on through a series of mere distracted lies. But the time was past when words like these could make Job angry. Bildad follows them up with an attempt to frighten him by a picture of the power of that God whom he was blaspheming; but Job cuts short his harangue, and ends it for him in a spirit of loftiness which Bildad could not have approached; and then proudly and calmly rebukes them all, no longer in scorn and irony, but in high, tranquil self-possession. 'God forbid that I should justify you,' he says; 'till I die I will not remove my integrity from me. My righteousness I hold fast, and will not let it go. My heart shall not reproach me so long as I live.'

So far all has been clear, each party, with increasing confidence, having insisted on their own position, and denounced their adversaries. A difficulty now arises which, at first sight, appears insurmountable. As the chapters are at present printed, the entire of the twenty-seventh is assigned to Job, and the paragraph from the eleventh to the twenty-third verses is in direct contradiction to all which he has maintained before—is, in fact, a concession of having been wrong from the beginning. Ewald, who, as we said above, himself refuses to allow the truth of Job's last and highest position, supposes that he is here receding from it, and confessing that an over-precipitate passion had betrayed him into denying. For many reasons, principally because we are satisfied that Job said then no more than the real fact, we cannot think Ewald right; and the concessions are too large and too inconsistent to be reconciled even with his own general theory of the poem. Another solution of the difficulty is very simple, although it is to be admitted that it rather cuts the knot than unties it. Eliphaz and Bildad have each spoken a third time; the symmetry of the general form requires that now Zophar should speak; and the suggestion, we believe, was first made by Dr Kennicott, that he did speak, and that the verses in question belong to him. Any one who is accustomed to MSS. will understand easily how such a mistake, if it be one, might have arisen. Even in Shakespeare, the speeches in the early editions are in many instances wrongly divided, and assigned to the wrong persons. It might have arisen from inadvertence; it might have arisen from the foolishness of some Jewish transcriber, who resolved, at all costs, to drag the book into harmony with Judaism, and make Job unsay his heresy. This view has the merit of fully clearing up the obscurity. Another, however, has been suggested by Eichorn, who originally followed Kennicott, but discovered, as he supposed, a less violent hypothesis, which was equally satisfactory. Eichorn imagines the verses to be a summary by Job of his adversaries' opinions, as if he said—'Listen now; you know what the facts are as well as I, and yet you maintain this;' and then passed on with his indirect reply to it. It is possible that Eichorn may be right—at any rate, either he is right, or else Dr Kennicott is. Certainly, Ewald is not. Taken as an account of Job's own conviction, the passage contradicts the burden of the whole poem. Passing it by, therefore, and going to what immediately follows, we arrive at what, in a human sense, is the final climax—Job's victory and triumph. He had appealed to God, and God had not appeared; he had doubted and fought against his doubts, and at last had crushed them down. He, too, had been taught to look for God in outward judgments; and when his own experience had shown him his mistake, he knew not where to turn. He had been leaning on a bruised reed, and it had run into his hand and pierced him. But as soon as in the speeches of his friend he saw it all laid down in its weakness and its false conclusions—when he saw the defenders of it wandering further and further from what he knew to be true, growing every moment, as if from a consciousness of the unsoundness of their standing ground, more violent, obstinate, and unreasonable, the scales fell more and more from his eyes—he had seen the fact that the wicked might prosper, and in learning to depend upon his innocency he had felt that the good man's support was there, if it was anywhere; and at last, with all his heart, was reconciled to the truth. The mystery of the outer world becomes deeper to him, but he does not any more try to understand it. The wisdom which can compass that mystery, he knows, is not in man, though man search for it deeper and harder than the miner searches for the hidden treasures of the earth; the wisdom which alone is attainable is resignation to God.

'Where,' he cries, 'shall wisdom be found, and where is the place of understanding? Man knoweth not the price thereof, neither is it found in the land of the living. The depth said it is not with me; and the sea said it is not in me. It is hid from the eyes of all living, and kept close from the fowls of the air.[1] God understandeth the way thereof, and He knoweth the place thereof [He, not man, understands the mysteries of the world which He has made]. And unto man He said, Behold! the fear of the Lord, that is wisdom; and to depart from evil, that is understanding.'

Here, therefore, it might seem as if all was over. There is no clearer

---

[1] An allusion, perhaps, to the old bird auguries. The birds, as the inhabitants of the air, were supposed to be the messengers between heaven and earth.

or purer faith possible for man; and Job had achieved it. His evil had turned to good; and sorrow had severed for him the last links which bound him to lower things. He had felt that he could do without happiness, that it was no longer essential, and that he could live on, and still love God, and cling to Him. But he is not described as of preternatural, or at all Titanic nature, but as very man, full of all human tenderness and suscepti-bility. His old life was still beautiful to him. He does not hate it because he can renounce it; and now that the struggle is over, the battle fought and won, and his heart has flowed over in that magnificent song of victory, the note once more changes: he turns back to earth to linger over those old departed days, with which the present is so hard a contrast; and his parable dies away in a strain of plaintive, but resigned melancholy. Once more he throws himself on God, no longer in passionate expostulation, but in pleading humility.[1] And then comes (perhaps, as Ewald says, it *could not* have come before) the answer out of the whirlwind. Job had called on God, and prayed that He might appear, that he might plead his cause with Him; and now He comes, and what will Job do? He comes not as the healing spirit in the heart of man; but, as Job had at first de-manded, the outward God, the Almighty Creator of the universe, and clad in the terrors and the glory of it. Job, in his first precipitancy, had desired to reason with Him on His government. The poet, in gleaming lines, describes for an answer the universe as it then was known, the majesty and awfulness of it; and then asks whether it is this which he requires to have explained to him, or which he believes himself capable of conducting. The revelation acts on Job as the sign of the Macrocosmos on the modern Faust; but when he sinks, crushed, it is not as the rebellious upstart, struck

---

[1] The speech of Elihu, which lies between Job's last words and God's appear-ance, is now decisively pronounced by Hebrew scholars not to be genuine. The most superficial reader will have been perplexed by the introduction of a speaker to whom no allusion is made, either in the prologue or the epilogue; by a long dissertation, which adds nothing to the progress of the argument, proceeding evidently on the false hypothesis of the three friends, and betraying not the faintest conception of the real cause of Job's sufferings. And the suspicions which such an anomaly would naturally suggest, are now made certainties by a fuller knowledge of the language, and the detection of a different hand. The interpolator has unconsciously confessed the feeling which allowed him to take so great a liberty. He, too, possessed with the old Jew theory, was unable to accept in its fulness so great a contradiction to it: and, missing the spirit of the poem, he believed that God's honour could still be vindicated in the old way. 'His wrath was kindled' against the friends, because they could not answer Job; and against Job, because he would not be answered; and con-ceiving himself 'full of matter,' and 'ready to burst like new bottles,' he could not contain himself, and delivered into the text a sermon on the *Theodice,* such, we suppose, as formed the current doctrine of the time in which he lived.

down in his pride—for he had himself, partially at least, subdued his own presumption—but as a humble penitent, struggling to overcome his weakness. He abhors himself for his murmurs, and 'repents in dust and ashes.' It will have occurred to every one that the secret which has been revealed to the reader is not, after all, revealed to Job or to his friends, and for this plain reason: the burden of the drama is, not that we do, but that we do not, and cannot, know the mystery of the government of the world— that it is not for man to seek it, or for God to reveal it. We, the readers, are, in this one instance, admitted behind the scenes—for once, in this single case—because it was necessary to meet the received theory by a positive fact which contradicted it. But the explanation of one case need not be the explanation of another; our business is to do what we know to be right and ask no questions. The veil which in the Ægyptian legend lay before the face of Isis is not to be raised; and we are not to seek to penetrate secrets which are not ours.

While, however, God does not condescend to justify His ways to man, He gives judgment on the past controversy. The self-constituted pleaders for Him, the acceptors of His person, were all wrong; and Job —the passionate, vehement, scornful, misbelieving Job—he had spoken the truth; he at least had spoken facts, and they had been defending a transient theory as an everlasting truth.

'And it was so, that after the Lord had spoken these words to Job, the Lord said to Eliphaz the Temanite, My wrath is kindled against thee and against thy two friends; for ye have not spoken of me the thing that is right, as my servant Job hath. Therefore take unto you now seven bullocks and seven rams, and go to my servant Job; and offer for yourselves a burnt-offering. And my servant Job shall pray for you, and him will I accept. Lest I deal with you after your folly, for that ye have not spoken of me the thing which is right, like my servant Job.'

One act of justice remains. Knowing as we do the cause of Job's misfortunes, and that as soon as his trial was over it was no longer operative, our sense of fitness could not be satisfied unless he were indemnified outwardly for his outward sufferings. Satan is defeated, and Job's integrity proved; and there is no reason why the general law should be interfered with, which, however large the exceptions, tends to connect goodness and prosperity; or why obvious calamities, obviously undeserved, should remain any more unremoved. Perhaps, too, a deeper lesson still lies below his restoration—something perhaps of this kind. Prosperity, enjoyment, happiness, comfort, peace, whatever be the name by which we designate that state in which life is to our own selves pleasant and delightful, as long as they are sought or prized as things essential, so far have a tendency to disennoble our nature, and are a sign that we are still in servitude to selfishness. Only when they lie outside us, as ornaments merely to be worn or laid aside as God pleases—only then may such things be possessed with impunity. Job's heart in early times had clung to them more than he knew, but now he was purged clean, and they were restored because he had ceased to need them.

Such in outline is this wonderful poem. With the material of which it is woven we have not here been concerned, although it is so rich and pregnant that we might with little difficulty construct out of it a complete picture of the world as then it was: its life, knowledge, arts, habits, superstitions, hopes, and fears. The subject is the problem of all mankind, and the composition embraces no less wide a range. But what we are here most interested upon is the epoch which it marks in the progress of mankind, as the first recorded struggle of a new experience with an established orthodox belief. True, for hundreds of years, perhaps for a thousand, the superstition against which it was directed continued. When Christ came it was still in its vitality. Nay, as we saw, it is alive, or in a sort of mock life, among us at this very day. But even those who retained their imperfect belief had received into their canon a book which treated it with contumely and scorn, so irresistible was the majesty of truth.

In days like these, when we hear so much of progress, it is worth while to ask ourselves what advances we have made further in the same direction? and once more, at the risk of some repetition, let us look at the position in which this book leaves us. It had been assumed that man, if he lived a just and upright life, had a right to expect to be happy. Happiness, 'his being's end and aim,' was his legitimate and covenanted reward. If God therefore was just, such a man would be happy; and inasmuch as God was just, the man who was not happy had not deserved to be. There is no flaw in this argument; and if it is unsound, the fallacy can only lie in the supposed right to happiness. It is idle to talk of inward consolations. Job felt them, but they were not everything. They did not relieve the anguish of his wounds; they did not make the loss of his children, or his friends' unkindness, any the less painful to him.

The poet, indeed, restores him in the book; but in life it need not have been so. He might have died upon his ash-heap, as thousands of good men have died, and will die again, in misery. Happiness, therefore, is *not* what we are to look for. Our place is to be true to the best which we know, to seek that and do that; and if by 'virtue its own reward' be meant that the good man cares only to continue good, desiring nothing more, then it is

a true and noble saying. But if virtue be valued because it is politic, because in pursuit of it will be found most enjoyment and fewest sufferings,
then it is not noble any more, and it is turning the truth of God into a lie.
Let us do right, and whether happiness come or unhappiness it is no very
mighty matter. If it come, life will be sweet; if it do not come, life will be
bitter—bitter, not sweet, and yet to be borne. On such a theory alone is
the government of this world intelligibly just. The well-being of our souls
depends only on what we *are;* and nobleness of character is nothing else
but steady love of good and steady scorn of evil. The government of the
world is a problem while the desire of selfish enjoyment survives; and when
justice is not done according to such standard (which will not be till the
day after doomsday, and not then), self-loving men will still ask, why? and
find no answer. Only to those who have the heart to say, 'We can do without that; it is not what we ask or desire,' is there no secret. Man will have
what he deserves, and will find what is really best for him, exactly as he
honestly seeks for it. Happiness may fly away, pleasure pall or cease to
be obtainable, wealth decay, friends fail or prove unkind, and fame turn
to infamy; but the power to serve God never fails, and the love of Him
is never rejected.

Most of us, at one time or other of our lives, have known something
of love—of that only pure love in which no *self* is left remaining. We have
loved as children, we have loved as lovers; some of us have learnt to love
a cause, a faith, a country; and what love would that be which existed
only with a prudent view to after-interests. Surely there is a love which
exults in the power of self-abandonment, and can glory in the privilege
of suffering for what is good. *Que mon nom soit flétri, pourvu que la
France soit libre,* said Danton; and those wild patriots who had trampled
into scorn the faith in an immortal life in which they would be rewarded
for what they were suffering, went to their graves as beds, for the dream
of a people's liberty; Justice is done; the balance is not deranged. It only
seems deranged, as long as we have not learnt to serve without looking
to be paid for it.

Such is the theory of life which is to be found in the Book of Job;
a faith which has flashed up in all times and all lands, wherever high-
minded men were to be found, and which passed in Christianity into
the acknowledged creed of half the world. The cross was the new symbol,
the Divine sufferer the great example; and mankind answered to the
call, because the appeal was not to what was poor and selfish in them,
but to whatever of best and bravest was in their nature. The law of
reward and punishment was superseded by the law of love. Thou shalt
love God and thou shalt love man; and that was not love—man knew it

once—which was bought by the prospect of reward. Times are changed with us now. Thou shalt love God and thou shalt love man, in the hands of a Paley, are found to mean no more than, Thou shalt love thyself after an enlightened manner. And the same base tone has saturated not only our common feelings, but our Christian theologies and our Antichristian philosophies. A prudent regard to our future interests; an abstinence from present unlawful pleasures, because they will entail the loss of greater pleasure by-and-by or perhaps be paid for with pain,—this is called virtue now; and the belief that such beings as men can be influenced by any more elevated feelings, is smiled at as the dream of enthusiasts whose hearts have outrun their understandings. Indeed, he were but a poor lover whose devotion to his mistress lay resting on the feeling that a marriage with her would conduce to his own comforts. That were a poor patriot who served his country for the hire which his country would give to him. And we should think but poorly of a son who thus addressed his earthly father: 'Father, on whom my fortunes depend, teach me to do what pleases thee, that I, pleasing thee in all things, may obtain those good things which thou hast promised to give to thy obedient children.' If any of us who have lived in so meagre a faith venture, by-and-by, to put in our claims, Satan will be likely to say of us (with better reason than he did of Job), 'Did they serve God for nought, then? Take their reward from them, and they will curse Him to His face.' If Christianity had never borne itself more loftily than this, do we suppose that those fierce Norsemen who had learnt, in the fiery war-songs of the Edda, of what stuff the hearts of heroes are composed, would have fashioned their sword-hilts into crosses, and themselves into a crusading chivalry? Let us not dishonour our great fathers with the dream of it. The Christians, like the Stoics and the Epicureans, would have lived their little day among the ignoble sects of an effete civilization, and would have passed off and been heard of no more. It was in another spirit that those first preachers of righteousness went out upon their warfare with evil. They preached, not enlightened prudence, but purity, justice, goodness; holding out no promises in this world except of suffering as their great Master had suffered, and rejoicing that they were counted worthy to suffer for his sake. And that crown of glory which they did believe to await them in a life beyond the grave, was no enjoyment of what they had surrendered in life, was not enjoyment at all in any sense which human thought or language can attach to the words; as little like it as the crown of love is like it, which the true lover looks for when at last he obtains his mistress. It was to be with Christ—to lose themselves in Him.

How these high feelings ebbed away, and Christianity became what we know it, we are partially beginning to see. The living spirit organized for itself a body of perishable flesh: not only the real gains of real experience, but mere conjectural hypotheses, current at the day for the solution of unexplained phenomena, became formulæ and articles of faith. Again, as before, the living and the dead were bound together, and the seeds of decay were already planted on the birth of a constructed polity.

But there was another cause allied to this, and yet different from it, which, though a law of human nature itself, seems now-a-days altogether forgotten. In the rapid and steady advance of our knowledge of material things, we are apt to believe that all our knowledge follows the same law; that it is merely generalized experience; that experience accumulates daily, and, therefore, that 'progress of the species,' *in all senses,* is an obvious and necessary fact. There is something which is true in this view, mixed with a great deal which is false. Material knowledge, the physical and mechanical sciences, make their way from step to step, from experiment to experiment, and each advance is secured and made good, and cannot again be lost. One generation takes up the general sum of experience where the last laid it down, adds to it what it has the opportunity of adding, and leaves it with interest to the next. The successive positions, as they are gained, require nothing for the apprehension of them but an understanding ordinarily cultivated. Prejudices have to be encountered, but prejudices of opinion merely, not prejudices of conscience or prejudices of self-love, like those which beset our progress in the science of morality. But in morals we enter upon conditions wholly different—conditions in which age differs from age, man differs from man, and even from himself, at different moments. We all have experienced times when, as we say, we should not know ourselves; some, when we fall below our average level; some, when we are lifted above, and put on, as it were, a higher nature. At such intervals as these last (unfortunately, with most of us, of rare occurrence), many things become clear to us which before were hard sayings; propositions become alive which, usually, are but dry words; our hearts seem purer, our motives loftier; our purposes, what we are proud to acknowledge to ourselves.

And, as man is unequal to himself, so is man to his neighbour, and period to period. The entire method of action, the theories of human life which in one era prevail universally, to the next are unpractical and insane, as those of this next would have seemed mere baseness to the first, if the first could have anticipated them. One epoch, we may suppose, holds some 'greatest nobleness principle,' the other some 'greatest happiness principle;' and then their very systems of axioms will contradict one another; their general conceptions and their detailed interpretations, their rules, judgments, opinions, practices will be in perpetual and endless collision. Our minds take shape from our hearts, and the facts of moral experience do not teach their own meaning, but submit to many readings according to the power of the eye which we bring with us.

The want of a clear perception of so important a feature about us leads to many singular contradictions. A believer in popular Protestantism, who is also a believer in progress, ought, if he were consistent, to regard mankind as growing every day towards a more and more advantageous position with respect to the trials of life; and yet if he were asked whether it was easier for him to 'save his soul' in the nineteenth century than it would have been in the first or second, or whether the said soul was necessarily better worth saving, he would be perplexed for an answer. There is hardly one of us who, in childhood, has not felt like the Jews to whom Christ spoke, that if he had 'lived in the days of the Fathers,' if he had had their advantages, he would have found duty a much easier matter; and some of us in mature life have felt that in old Athens, or old republican Rome, in the first ages of Christianity, in the Crusades, or at the Reformation, there was a contagious atmosphere of heroism, in which we should have been less troubled with the little feelings which cling about us now. At any rate, it is at these rare epochs only that real additions are made to our moral knowledge. At such times, new truths are, indeed, sent down among us, and, for periods longer or shorter, may be seen to exercise an elevating influence on mankind. Perhaps what is gained on these occasions is never entirely lost. The historical monuments of their effects are at least indestructible; and when the spirit which gave them birth reappears, their dormant energy awakens again.

But it seems from our present experience of what, in some at least of its modern forms, Christianity has been capable of becoming, that there is no doctrine in itself so pure, but what the meaner nature which is in us can disarm and distort it, and adapt it to its own littleness. The once living spirit dries up into formulæ, and formulæ, whether of mass-sacrifice or vicarious righteousness, or 'reward and punishment,' are contrived ever so as to escape making over-high demands upon the conscience. Some aim at dispensing with obedience altogether, and those which insist on obedience rest the obligations of it on the poorest of motives. So things go on till there is no life left at all; till, from all higher aspirations, we are lowered down to the love of self after an enlightened manner; and then nothing remains but to fight the battle over again. The once beneficial truth has become, as in Job's case, a cruel and mischievous deception, and the whole question of life and its obligations must again be opened.

It is now some three centuries since the last of such re-openings. If we ask ourselves how much during this time has been actually added to the sum of our knowledge in these matters; what, in all the thousands upon thousands of sermons, and theologies, and philosophies with which Europe has been deluged, has been gained for mankind beyond what we have found in this Book of Job, how far all this has advanced us in the 'progress of humanity,' it were hard, or rather it is easy, to answer. How far we have fallen below, let Paley and the rest bear witness. But what moral question can be asked which admits now of a grander solution than was offered two, perhaps three, thousand years ago? The world has not been standing still; experience of man and life has increased; questions have multiplied on questions, while the answers of the established teachers to them have been growing every day more and more incredible. What other answers have there been? Of all the countless books which have appeared, there has been only one of enduring importance, in which an attempt is made to carry on the solution of the great problem. Job is given over into Satan's hand to be tempted; and though he shakes, he does not fall. Taking the temptation of Job for his model, Goethe has similarly exposed his Faust to trial, and with him the tempter succeeds. His hero falls from sin to sin, from crime to crime; he becomes a seducer, a murderer, a betrayer, following recklessly his evil angel wherever he chooses to lead him; and yet, with all this, he never wholly forfeits our sympathy. In spite of his weakness, his heart is still true to his higher nature; sick and restless, even in the delirium of enjoyment he always longs for something better, and he never can be brought to say of evil that it is good. And therefore, after all, the devil is baulked of his prey; in virtue of this one fact, that the evil in which he steeped himself remained to the last hateful to him, Faust is saved by the angels. . . It will be eagerly answered for the established belief, that such cases are its especial province. All men are sinners, and *it* possesses the blessed remedy for sin. But, among the countless numbers of those characters so strangely mixed among us, in which the dark and the bright fibres cross like a meshwork; characters at one moment capable of acts of heroic greatness, at another hurried by temptation into actions which even common men may deplore, how many are there who have never availed themselves of the conditions of reconciliation as orthodoxy proffers them, and of such men what is to be said? It was said once of a sinner that to her 'much was forgiven, for she loved much.' But this is language which theology has as little appropriated as the Jews could appropriate the language of Job. It cannot recognize the power of the human heart. It has no balance in which to weigh the good against the evil; and when a great Burns or a Mirabeau comes before it, can but tremblingly count up the offences committed, and then, looking to the end, and finding its own terms not to have been complied with, it faintly mutters its anathema. Sin only it can apprehend and judge; and for the poor acts of struggling heroism, 'Forasmuch as they were not done,' &c., &c., it doubts not but they have the nature of sin.[1]

Something of the difficulty has been met by Goethe, but it cannot be said that he has resolved it; or at least that he has furnished others with a solution which may guide their judgment. In the writer of the Book of Job there is an awful moral earnestness before which we bend as in the presence of a superior being. The orthodoxy against which he contended is not set aside or denied; he sees what truth is in it; only he sees more than it, and over it, and through it. But in Goethe, who needed it more, inasmuch as his problem was more delicate and difficult, the moral earnestness is not awful, is not even high. We cannot feel that in dealing with sin he entertains any great horror of it; he looks on it as a mistake, as undesirable, but scarcely as more. Goethe's great powers are of another kind; and this particular question, though in appearance the primary subject of the poem, is really only secondary. In substance, Faust is more like Ecclesiastes than it is like Job, and describes rather the restlessness of a largely-gifted nature which, missing the guidance of the heart, plays experiments with life, trying knowledge, pleasure, dissipation, one after another, and hating them all; and then hating life itself as a weary, stale, flat, unprofitable mockery. The temper exhibited here will probably be perennial in the world. But the remedy for it will scarcely be more clear under other circumstances than it is at present, and lies in the disposition of the emotions, and not in any propositions which can be addressed to the understanding.

For that other question—how rightly to estimate a human being; what constitutes a real vitiation of character, and how to distinguish, without either denying the good or making light of the evil; how to be just to the popular theories, and yet not to blind ourselves to their shallowness and injustice—that is a problem for us, for the solution of which we are at present left to our ordinary instinct, without any recognized guidance whatsoever.

Nor is this the only problem which is in the same situation. There can scarely be a more startling contrast between fact and theory than the conditions under which, practically, positions of power and influence are distributed among us—between the theory of human worth which the necessities of life oblige us to act upon, and the theory which we believe that we believe. As we look around among our leading men, our statesmen,

---

[1] See the Thirteenth Article.

our legislators, the judges on our bench, the commanders of our armies, the men to whom this English nation commits the conduct of its best interests, profane and sacred, what do we see to be the principles which guide our selection? How entirely do they lie beside and beyond the negative tests! and how little respect do we pay to the breach of this or that commandment in comparison with ability! So wholly impossible is it to apply the received opinions on such matters to practice—to treat men known to be guilty of what theology calls deadly sins, as really guilty of them, that it would almost seem we had fallen into a moral anarchy; that ability *alone* is what we regard, without any reference at all, except in glaring and outrageous cases, to moral disqualifications. It is invidious to mention names of living men; it is worse than invidious to drag out of their graves men who have gone down into them with honour, to make a point for an argument. But we know, all of us, that among the best servants of our country there have been, and there are, many whose lives will not stand scrutiny by the negative tests, and who do not appear very greatly to repent, or to have repented, of their sins according to recognized methods.

Once more: among our daily or weekly confessions, which we are supposed to repeat as if we were all of us at all times in precisely the same moral condition, we are made to say that we have done those things which we ought not to have done, and to have left undone those things which we ought to have done. An earthly father to whom his children were day after day to make this acknowledgment would be apt to inquire whether they were trying to do better—whether, at any rate, they were endeavouring to learn; and if he were told that although they had made some faint attempts to understand the negative part of their duty, yet that of the positive part, of those things which they ought to do, they had no notions at all, and had no idea that they were under obligation to form any, he would come to rather strange conclusions about them. But, really and truly, what practical notions of duty have we beyond that of abstaining from committing sins? Not to commit sin, we suppose, covers but a small part of what is expected of us. Through the entire tissue of our employments there runs a good and a bad. Bishop Butler tells us, for instance, that even of our time there is a portion which is ours, and a portion which is our neighbour's; and if we spend more of it on personal interests than our own share, we are stealing. This sounds strange doctrine; we prefer making vague acknowledgments, and shrink from pursuing them into detail. We say vaguely, that in all we do we should consecrate ourselves to God, and our own lips condemn us; for which among us cares to learn the way to do it? The *devoir* of a knight was understood in the courts of chivalry; the lives of heroic men, Pagan and Christian, were once held up before the world as patterns of detailed imitation; and now, when such ideals are wanted more than ever, Protestantism stands with a drawn sword on the threshold of the inquiry, and tells us that it is impious. The law, we are told, has been fulfilled for us in condescension to our inherent worthlessness, and our business is to appropriate another's righteousness, and not, like Titans, to be scaling heaven by profane efforts of our own. Protestants, we know very well, will cry out in tones loud enough at such a representation of their doctrines. But we know also that unless men may feel a cheerful conviction that they can do right if they try,—that they can purify themselves, can live noble and worthy lives,—unless this is set before them as *the* thing which they are to do, and *can* succeed in doing, they will not waste their energies on what they know beforehand will end in failure; and if they may not live for God, they will live for themselves.

And all this while the whole complex frame of society is a meshwork of duty woven of living fibre, and the condition of its remaining sound is, that every thread of it, of its own free energy, shall do what it ought. The penalties of duties neglected are to the full as terrible as those of sins committed; more terrible, perhaps, because more palpable and sure. A lord of the land, or an employer of labour, supposes that he has no duty except to keep what he calls the commandments in his own person, to go to church, and to do what he will with his own,—and Irish famines follow, and trade strikes, and chartisms, and Paris revolutions. We look for a remedy in impossible legislative enactments, and there is but one remedy which will avail—that the thing which we call public opinion learn something of the meaning of human obligation, and demand some approximation to it. As things are, we have no idea of what a human being ought to be. After the first rudimental conditions we pass at once into meaningless generalities; and with no knowledge to guide our judgment, we allow it to be guided by meaner principles; we respect money, we respect rank, we respect ability—character is as if it had no existence.

In the midst of this loud talk of progress, therefore, in which so many of us at present are agreed to believe, which is, indeed, the common meeting point of all the thousand sects into which we are split, it is with saddened feelings that we see so little of it in so large a matter. Progress there is in knowledge; and science has enabled the number of human beings capable of existing upon this earth to be indefinitely multiplied. But this is but a small triumph if the ratio of the good and bad, the wise and the foolish, the full and the hungry, remains unaffected. And we cheat ourselves with words when we conclude out of our material splendour an advance of the race.

In two things there is progress—progress in knowledge of the outward world, and progress in material wealth. This last, for the present, creates, perhaps, more evils than it relieves; but suppose this difficulty solved—suppose the wealth distributed, and every peasant living like a peer—what then? If this is all, one noble soul outweighs the whole of it. Let us follow knowledge to the outer circle of the universe—the eye will not be satisfied with seeing, nor the ear with hearing. Let us build our streets of gold and they will hide as many aching hearts as hovels of straw. The well-being of mankind is not advanced a single step. Knowledge is power, and wealth is power; and harnessed, as in Plato's fable, to the chariot of the soul, and guided by wisdom, they may bear it through the circle of the stars; but left to their own guidance, or reined by a fool's hand, the wild horses may bring the poor fool to Phaeton's end, and set a world on fire.

BIBLIOGRAPHY ENTRY FOR RESEARCH PAPERS:

  Froude, James Anthony. *Short Studies on Great Subjects.* New York: Charles Scribner and Co., 1908. "The Book of Job," pp. 244-293, reprinted in *The Voice out of the Whirlwind: The Book of Job,* ed. Ralph E. Hone. San Francisco, 1960.

FIRST FOOTNOTE:

  * James Anthony Froude, *Short Studies on Great Subjects* (New York: Charles Scribner and Co., 1908), "The Book of Job," pp. 244-293, reprinted in *The Voice out of the Whirlwind: The Book of Job,* ed. Ralph E. Hone (San Francisco, 1960), pp. 200-232.

SUBSEQUENT FOOTNOTES:

  * Froude, *op. cit., The Voice,* p. ■.
  * Froude, "Job," *The Voice,* p. ■.
  * Froude, *The Voice,* p. ■.

In place of *"The Voice,"* "ed. Hone" may be used in these subsequent-footnote forms.

JOSIAH ROYCE

ON

the Problem of Evil

||||||||||||||||||||||||||||||||||||||||||||||||||||||||||||||||||||||||||||||||||||||||||||||||||||||||||||||||||||||||||||||||||||||||||||||||||||||||||

Josiah Royce (1855-1916) called himself a philosophical idealist. In the essay which follows he says he has dealt "with the metaphysical and religious 'Problem of Evil.'" The essay "presupposes, and does not endeavour either to justify or with any elaboration to explain, the idealistic theory of the nature of reality." Also, "special attention is given to the psychological basis upon which every metaphysical generalization concerning the nature and glorification of evil may be . . . properly said to be founded" (pp. vi, vii).

Born in California and educated at the University of California, he studied in Germany and at Johns Hopkins, returning to teach in California from 1878 to 1882. From 1882 until his death he taught at Harvard.

The selection is from Royce's Studies of Good and Evil. A Series of Essays upon Problems of Philosophy and of Life *(New York: D. Appleton and Co., 1898), pp. 1-28.*

THE PROBLEM OF JOB

IN SPEAKING of the problem of Job, the present writer comes to the subject as a layman in theology, and as one ignorant of Hebrew scholarship. In referring to the original core of the Book of Job he follows, in a general way, the advice of Professor C. H. Toy; and concerning the text of the poem he is guided by the translation of Dr. Gilbert. What this paper has to attempt is neither criticism of the book, nor philological exposition of its obscurities, but a brief study of the central problem of the poem from the point of view of a student of philosophy.

The problem of our book is the personal problem of its hero, Job himself. Discarding, for the first, as of possibly separate authorship, the Prologue, the Epilogue and the addresses of Elihu and of the Lord, one may as well come at once to the point of view of Job, as expressed in his speeches to his friends. Here is stated the problem of which none of the later additions in our poem offer any intelligible solution. In the exposition of this problem the original author develops all his poetical skill, and records thoughts that can never grow old. This is the portion of our book which is most frequently quoted and which best expresses the genuine experience of suffering humanity. Here, then, the philosophical as well as the human interest of our poem centres.

I.

Job's world, as he sees it, is organized in a fashion extremely familiar to us all. The main ideas of this cosmology are easy to be reviewed. The very simplicity of the scheme of the universe here involved serves to bring into clearer view the mystery and horror of the problem that besets Job himself. The world, for Job, is the work of a being who, in the very nature of the case, ought to be intelligible (since he is wise), and friendly to the righteous, since, according to tradition, and by virtue of his divine wisdom itself, this God must know the value of a righteous man. But—here is the mystery—this God, as his works get known through our human experiences of evil, appears to us not friendly, but hopelessly foreign and hostile in his plans and his doings. The more, too, we study his ways with man, the less intelligible seems his nature. Tradition has dwelt upon his righteousness, has called him merciful, has magnified his love towards his servants, has described his justice in bringing to naught the wicked. One has learned to trust all these things, to conceive God in these terms, and to expect all this righteous government from him. Moreover, tradition joins with the pious observation of nature in assuring us of the omnipotence of God. Job himself pathetically insists that he never doubts, for an instant, God's power to do whatever in heaven or earth he may please to do. Nothing hinders God. No blind faith thwarts him. Sheol is naked before him. The abyss has no covering. The earth hangs over chaos because he orders it to do so. His power shatters the monsters and pierces the dragons. He can, then, do with evil precisely what he does with Rahab or with the shades, with the clouds or with the light or with the sea, namely, exactly what he chooses. Moreover, since he knows everything, and since the actual value of a righteous man is, for Job, an unquestionable and objective fact, God cannot fail to know this real worth of righteousness in his servants, as well as the real hatefulness and mischief of the wicked. God knows worth, and cannot be blind to it, since it is as real a fact as heaven and earth themselves.

Yet despite all these unquestioned facts, this God, who can do just what he chooses, "deprives of right" the righteous man, in Job's own case, and "vexes his soul," becomes towards him as a "tyrant," "persecutes" him "with strong hand," "dissolves" him "into storm," makes him a "byword" for outcasts, "casts" him "into the mire," renders him "a brother to jackals," deprives him of the poor joy of his "one day as a hireling," of the little delight that might come to him as a man before he descends hopelessly to the dark world of the shades, "watches over" him by day to oppress, by night to "terrify" him "with dreams and with visions"—in brief, acts as his enemy, "tears" him "in anger," "gnashes upon" him "with his teeth." All these are the expressions of Job himself. On the other hand, as, with equal wonder and horror the righteous Job reports, God on occasion does just the reverse of all this to the notoriously and deliberately wicked, who "grow old," "wax mighty in power," "see their offspring established," and their homes "secure from fear." If one turns from this view of God's especially unjust dealings with righteous and with wicked individuals to a general survey of his providential government of the world, one sees vast processes going on, as ingenious as they are merciless, as full of hints of a majestic wisdom as they are of indifference to every individual right.

> A mountain that falleth is shattered,
> And a rock is removed from its place;
> The waters do wear away stones,
> Its floods sweep the earth's dust away;
> And the hope of frail man thou destroyest.
> Thou subdu'st him for aye, and he goes,
> Marring his face thou rejectest him.

Here is a mere outline of the divine government as Job sees it. To express himself thus is for Job no momentary outburst of passion. Long days and nights he has brooded over these bitter facts of experience, before he has spoken at all. Unweariedly, in presence of his friends' objections, he reiterates his charges. He has the right of the sufferer to speak, and he uses it. He reports the facts that he sees. Of the paradox involved in all this he can make nothing. What is clear to him, however, is that this paradox is a matter for reasoning, not for blind authority. God ought to meet him face to face, and have the matter out in plain words. Job fears not to face his judge, or to demand his answer from God. God knows that Job has done nothing to deserve this fury. The question at issue between maker and creature is therefore one that demands a direct statement and a clear decision. "Why, since you can do precisely as you choose, and since you know, as all-knower, the value of a righteous servant, do you choose, as enemy, to persecute the righteous with this fury and persistence of hate?" Here is the problem.

The human interest of the issue thus so clearly stated by Job lies, of course, in the universality of just such experiences of undeserved ill here upon earth. What Job saw of evil we can see ourselves to-day whenever we choose. Witness Armenia. Witness the tornadoes and the earthquakes. Less interesting to us is the thesis mentioned by Job's friends, in the antiquated form in which they state it, although to be sure, a similar thesis, in altered forms, is prevalent among us still. And of dramatic significance only is the earnestness with which Job defends his own personal righteousness. So naïve a self-assurance as is his is not in accordance with our modern conscience, and it is seldom indeed that our day would see any man sincerely using this phraseology of Job regarding his own consciousness of rectitude. But what is to-day as fresh and real to us as it was to our poet is the fact that all about us, say in every child born with an unearned heredity of misery, or in every pang of the oppressed, or in every arbitrary coming of ill fortune, some form of innocence is beset with an evil that the sufferer has not deserved. Job wins dramatic sympathy as an extreme, but for the purpose all the more typical, case of this universal experience of unearned ill fortune. In every such case we therefore still have the interest that Job had in demanding the solution of this central problem of evil. Herein, I need not say, lies the permanent significance of the problem of Job,—a problem that wholly outlasts any ancient Jewish controversy as to the question whether the divine justice always does or does not act as Job's friends, in their devotion to tradition, declare that it acts. Here, then, is the point where our poem touches a question, not merely of an older religion, but of philosophy, and of all time.

II.

The general problem of evil has received, as is well known, a great deal of attention from the philosophers. Few of them, at least in European thought, have been as fearless in stating the issue as was the original author of Job. The solutions offered have, however, been very numerous. For our purposes they may be reduced to a few.

First, then, one may escape Job's paradox by declining altogether to view the world in teleological terms. Evils, such as death, disease, tempests, enemies, fires, are not, so one may declare, the works of God or of Satan, but are natural phenomena. Natural, too, are the phenomena of our desires, of our pains, sorrows and failures. No divine purpose rules or overrules any of these things. That happens to us, at any time, which must happen, in view of our natural limitations and of our ignorance. The way to better things is to understand nature better than we now do. For this view—a view often maintained in our day—there is no problem of evil, in Job's sense, at all. Evil there indeed is, but the only rational problems are those of natural laws. I need not here further consider this method, not of solving but of abolishing the problem before us, since my intent is, in this paper, to suggest the possibility of some genuinely teleological answer to Job's question. I mention this first view only to recognize, historically, its existence.

In the second place, one may deal with our problem by attempting any one, or a number, of those familiar and popular compromises between the belief in a world of natural law and the belief in a teleological order, which are all, as compromises, reducible to the assertion that the presence of evil in the creation is a relatively insignificant, and an inevitable, incident of a plan that produces sentient creatures subject to law. Writers who expound such compromises have to point out that, since a burnt child dreads the fire, pain is, on the whole, useful as a warning. Evil is a transient discipline, whereby finite creatures learn their place in the system of things. Again, a sentient world cannot get on without some experience of suffering, since sentience means tenderness. Take away pain (so one still again often insists), take away pain, and we should not learn our share of natural truth. Pain is the pedagogue to teach us natural science. The contagious diseases, for instance, are useful in so far as they lead us in the end to study Bacteriology, and thus to get an insight into the life of certain beautiful creatures of God whose presence in the world we should otherwise blindly overlook! Moreover (to pass to still another variation of this sort of explanation), created beings obviously grow from less to more. First the lower, then the higher. Otherwise there could be no Evolution. And were there no evolution, how much of edifying natural science we should miss! But if one is evolved, if one grows from less to more, there must be something to mark the stages of growth. Now evil is useful to mark the lower stages of evolution. If you are to be, first an infant, then a man, or first a savage, then a civilized being, there must be evils attendant upon the earlier stages of your life—evils that make growth welcome and conscious. Thus, were there no colic and croup, were there no tumbles and crying-spells in infancy, there would be no sufficient incentives to loving parents to hasten the growing robustness of their children, and no motives to impel the children to long to grow big! Just so, cannibalism is valuable as a mark of a lower grade of evolution. Had there been no cannibalism we should realize less joyously than we do what a respectable thing it is to have become civilized! In brief, evil is, as it were, the dirt of the natural order, whose value is that, when you wash it off, you thereby learn the charm of the bath of evolution.

The foregoing are mere hints of familiar methods of playing about the edges of our problem, as children play barefoot in the shallowest reaches of the foam of the sea. In our poem, as Professor Toy expounds it, the speeches ascribed to Elihu contain the most hints of some such way of defining evil, as a merely transient incident of the discipline of the individual. With many writers explanations of this sort fill much space. They are even not without their proper place in popular discussion. But they have no interest for whoever has once come into the presence of Job's problem as it is in itself. A moment's thought reminds us of their superficiality. Pain is useful as a warning of danger. If we did not suffer, we should burn our hands off. Yes, but this explanation of one evil presupposes another, and a still unexplained and greater evil, namely, the existence of the danger of which we need to be thus warned. No doubt it is well that the past sufferings of the Armenians should teach the survivors, say the defenseless women and children, to have a wholesome fear in future of Turks. Does that explain, however, the need for the existence, or for the murderous doings of the Turks? If I can only reach a given goal by passing over a given road, say of evolution, it may be well for me to consent to the toilsome journey. Does that explain why I was created so far from my goal? Discipline, toil, penalty, surgery, are all explicable as means to ends, if only it be presupposed that there exists, and that there is quite otherwise explicable, the necessity for the situations which involve such fearful expenses. One justifies the surgery, but not the disease; the toil, but not the existence of the need for the toil; the penalty, but not the situation which has made the penalty necessary, when one points out that evil is in so many cases medicinal or disciplinary or prophylactic—an incident of imperfect stages of evolution, or the price of a distant good attained through misery. All such explanations, I insist, trade upon borrowed capital. But God, by hypothesis, is no borrower. He produces his own capital of ends and means. Every evil is explained on the foregoing plan only by presupposing at least an equal, and often a greater and a preëxistent evil, namely, the very state of things which renders the first evil the only physically possible way of reaching a given goal. But what Job wants his judge to explain is not that evil *A* is a physical means of warding off some other greater evil *B*, in this cruel world where the waters wear away even the stones, and where hopes of man are so much frailer than the stones; but why a God who can do whatever he wishes chooses situations where such a heaped-up mass of evil means become what we should call physical necessities to the ends now physically possible.

No real explanation of the presence of evil can succeed which declares evil to be a merely physical necessity for one who desires, in this present world, to reach a given goal. Job's business is not with physical accidents, but with the God who chose to make this present nature; and an answer to Job must show that evil is not a physical but a logical necessity—something whose non-existence would simply contradict the very essence, the very perfection of God's own nature and power. This talk of medicinal and disciplinary evil, perfectly fair when applied to our poor fate-bound human surgeons, judges, jailors, or teachers, becomes cruelly, even cynically trivial when applied to explain the ways of a God who is to choose, not only the physical means to an end, but the very *Physis* itself in which path and goal are to exist together. I confess, as a layman, that whenever, at a funeral, in the company of mourners who are immediately facing Job's own personal problem, and who are sometimes, to say the least, wide enough awake to desire not to be stayed with relative comforts, but to ask that terrible and uttermost question of God himself, and to require the direct answer—that whenever, I say, in such company I have to listen to these half-way answers, to these superficial plashes in the wavelets at the water's edge of sorrow, while the black, unfathomed ocean of finite evil spreads out before our wide-opened eyes—well, at such times this trivial speech about useful burns and salutary medicines makes me, and I fancy others, simply and wearily heartsick. Some words are due to children at school, to peevish patients in the sickroom who need a little temporary quieting. But quite other speech is due to men and women when they are wakened to the higher reason of Job by the fierce anguish of our mortal life's ultimate facts. They deserve either our simple silence, or, if we are ready to speak, the speech of people who ourselves inquire as Job inquired.

III.

A third method of dealing with our problem is in essence identical with the course which, in a very antiquated form, the friends of Job adopt.

This method takes its best known expression in the doctrine that the presence of evil in the world is explained by the fact that the value of free will in moral agents logically involves, and so explains and justifies, the divine permission of the evil deeds of those finite beings who freely choose to sin, as well as the inevitable fruits of the sins. God creates agents with free will. He does so because the existence of such agents has of itself an infinite worth. Were there no free agents, the highest good could not be. But such agents, because they are free, can offend. The divine justice of necessity pursues such offenses with attendant evils. These evils, the result of sin, must, logically speaking, be permitted to exist, if God once creates the agents who have free will, and himself remains, as he must logically do, a just God. How much ill thus results depends upon the choice of the free agents, not upon God, who wills to have only good chosen, but of necessity must leave his free creatures to their own devices, so far as concerns their power to sin.

This view has the advantage of undertaking to regard evil as a logically necessary part of a perfect moral order, and not as a mere incident of an imperfectly adjusted physical mechanism. So dignified a doctrine, by virtue of its long history and its high theological reputation, needs here no extended exposition. I assume it as familiar, and pass at once to its difficulties. It has its share of truth. There is, I doubt not, moral free will in the universe. But the presence of evil in the world simply cannot be explained by free will alone. This is easy to show. One who maintains this view asserts, in substance, "All real evils are the results of the acts of free and finite moral agents." These agents may be angels or men. If there is evil in the city, the Lord has *not* done it, except in so far as his justice has acted in readjusting wrongs already done. Such ill is due to the deeds of his creatures. But hereupon one asks at once, in presence of any ill, "Who did this?" Job's friends answer: "The sufferer himself; his deed wrought his own undoing. God punishes only the sinner. Every one suffers for his own wrongdoing. Your ill is the result of your crime."

But Job, and all his defenders of innocence, must at once reply: "Empirically speaking, this is obviously, in our visible world, simply not true. The sufferer may suffer innocently. The ill is often undeserved. The fathers sin; the child, diseased from birth, degraded, or a born wretch, may pay the penalty. The Turk or the active rebel sins. Armenia's helpless women and babes cry in vain unto God for help."

Hereupon the reply comes, although not indeed from Job's friends: "Alas! it is so. Sin means suffering; but the innocent may suffer *for* the guilty. This, to be sure, is God's way. One cannot help it. It is so." But therewith the whole effort to explain evil as a logically necessary result of free will and of divine justice alone is simply abandoned. The unearned ills are not justly due to the free will that indeed partly caused them, but to God who declines to protect the innocent. God owes the Turk and the rebel their due. He also owes to his innocent creatures, the babes and the women, his shelter. He owes to the sinning father his penalty, but to the son, born in our visible world a lost soul from the womb, God owes the shelter of his almighty wing, and no penalty. Thus Job's cry is once more in place. The ways of God are not thus justified.

But the partisan of free will as the true explanation of ill may reiterate his view in a new form. He may insist that we see but a fragment. Perhaps the soul born here as if lost, or the wretch doomed to pangs now unearned, sinned of old, in some previous state of existence. Perhaps Karma is to blame. You expiate to-day the sins of your own former existences. Thus the Hindoos varied the theme of our familiar doctrine. This is what Hindoo friends might have said to Job. Well, admit even that, if you like; and what then follows? Admit that here or in former ages the free deed of every present sufferer earned as its penalty every ill, physical or moral, that appears as besetting just this sufferer to-day. Admit that, and what logically follows? It follows, so I must insist, that the moral world itself, which this free-will theory of the source of evil, thus abstractly stated, was to save, is destroyed in its very heart and centre.

For consider. A suffers ill. B sees A suffering. Can B, the onlooker, help his suffering neighbor, A? Can he comfort him in any true way? No, a miserable comforter must B prove, like Job's friends, so long as B, believing in our present hypothesis, clings strictly to the logic of this abstract free-will explanation of the origin of evil. To A he says: "Well, you suffer for your own ill-doing. I therefore simply cannot relieve you. This is God's world of justice. If I tried to hinder God's justice from working in your case, I should at best only postpone your evil day. It would come, for God is just. You are hungry, thirsty, naked, sick, in prison. What can I do about it? All this is your own deed come back to you. God himself, although justly punishing, is not the author of this evil. You are the sole originator of the ill." "Ah!" so A may cry out, "but can you not give me light, insight, instruction, sympathy? Can you not at least teach me to become good?" "No," B must reply, if he is a logical believer in the sole efficacy of the private free will of each finite agent as the one source, under the divine justice, of that agent's ill: "No, if you deserved light or any other comfort, God, being just, would enlighten you himself, even if I absolutely refused. But if you do not deserve light, I should preach to you in vain, for God's justice would harden your heart against any such good fortune as I could offer you from without, even if I spoke with the tongues of men and of angels. Your free will is yours. No deed of mine could give you a good free will, for what I gave you from without would not be *your* free will at all. Nor can any one but you cause your free will to be this or that. A great gulf is fixed between us. You and I, as sovereign free agents, live in God's holy world in sin-tight compartments and in evil-tight compartments too. I cannot hurt you, nor you me. You are damned for your own sins, while all that I can do is to look out for my own salvation." This, I say, is the logically inevitable result of asserting that every ill, physical or moral, that can happen to any agent, is solely the result of that agent's own free will acting under the government of the divine justice. The only possible consequence would indeed be that we live, every soul of us, in separate, as it were absolutely fire-proof, free-will compartments, so that real coöperation as to good and ill is excluded. What more cynical denial of the reality of any sort of moral world could be imagined than is involved in this horrible thesis, which no sane partisan of the abstract and traditional free-will explanation of the source of evil will to-day maintain, precisely because no such partisan really knows or can know what his doctrine logically means, while still continuing to maintain it. Yet whenever one asserts with pious obscurity, that "No harm can come to the righteous," one in fact implies, with logical necessity, just this cynical consequence.

IV.

There remains a fourth doctrine as to our problem. This doctrine is in essence the thesis of philosophical idealism, a thesis which I myself feel bound to maintain, and, so far as space here permits, to explain. The theoretical basis of this view, the philosophical reasons for the notion of the divine nature which it implies, I cannot here explain. That is another argument. But I desire to indicate how the view in question deals with Job's problem.

This view first frankly admits that Job's problem is, upon Job's presuppositions, simply and absolutely insoluble. Grant Job's own presupposition that God is a being other than this world, that he is its external creator and ruler, and then all solutions fail. God is then either cruel or helpless, as regards all real finite ill of the sort that Job endures. Job, moreover, is right in demanding a reasonable answer to his question. The only possible answer is, however, one that undertakes to develop what I hold to be the immortal soul of the doctrine of the divine atonement. The answer to Job is: God is not in ultimate essence another being than yourself. He is the Absolute Being. You truly are one with God, part of his life. He is the very soul of your soul. And so, here is the first truth: When you suffer, *your sufferings are God's sufferings,* not his external work, not his external penalty, not the fruit of his neglect, but identically his own personal woe. In you God himself suffers, precisely as you do, and has all your concern in overcoming this grief.

The true question then is: Why does God thus suffer? The sole possible, necessary, and sufficient answer is, Because without suffering, without ill, without woe, evil, tragedy, God's life could not be perfected. This grief is not a physical means to an external end. It is a logically necessary and eternal constituent of the divine life. It is logically necessary that the Captain of your salvation should be perfect through suffering. No outer nature compels him. He chooses this because he chooses his own perfect selfhood. He is perfect. His world is the best possible world. Yet all its finite regions know not only of joy but of defeat and sorrow, for thus alone, in the completeness of his eternity, can God in his wholeness be triumphantly perfect.

This, I say, is my thesis. In the absolute oneness of God with the sufferer, in the concept of the suffering and therefore triumphant God, lies the logical solution of the problem of evil. The doctrine of philosophical idealism is, as regards its purely theoretical aspects, a fairly familiar metaphysical theory at the present time. One may, then, presuppose here as known the fact that, for reasons which I have not now to expound, the idealist maintains that there is in the universe but one perfectly real being, namely, the Absolute, that the Absolute is self-conscious, and that his world is essentially in its wholeness the fulfillment *in actu* of an all-perfect ideal. We ourselves exist as fragments of the absolute life, or better, as partial functions in the unity of the absolute and conscious process of the world. On the other hand, our existence and our individuality are not illusory, but are what they are in an organic unity with the whole life of the Absolute Being. This doctrine once presupposed, our present task is to inquire what case idealism can make for the thesis just indicated as its answer to Job's problem.

In endeavoring to grapple with the theoretical problem of the place of evil in a world that, on the whole, is to be conceived, not only as good, but as perfect, there is happily one essentially decisive consideration concerning good and evil which falls directly within the scope of our own human experience, and which concerns matters at once familiar and momentous as well as too much neglected in philosophy. When we use such words as good, evil, perfect, we easily deceive ourselves by the merely abstract meanings which we associate with each of the terms taken apart from the other. We forget the experiences from which the words have been abstracted. To these experiences we must return whenever we want really to comprehend the words. If we take the mere words, in their abstraction, it is easy to say, for instance, that if life has any evil in it at all, it must needs not be so perfect as life would be were there no evil in it whatever. Just so, speaking abstractly, it is easy to say that, in estimating life, one has to set the good over against the evil, and to compare their respective sums. It is easy to declare that, since we hate evil, wherever and just so far as we recognize it, our sole human interest in the world must be furthered by the removal of evil from the world. And thus viewing the case, one readily comes to say that if God views as not only good but perfect a world in which we find so much evil, the divine point of view must be very foreign to ours, so that Job's rebellious pessimism seems well in order, and Prometheus appears to defy the world-ruler in a genuinely humane spirit. Shocked, however, by the apparent impiety of this result, some teachers, considering divine matters, still misled by the same one-sided use of words, have opposed one falsely abstract view by another, and have strangely asserted that the solution must be in proclaiming that since God's world, the real world, in order to be perfect, must be without evil, what we men call evil must be a mere illusion—a mirage of the human point of view—a dark vision which God, who sees all truth, sees not at all. To God, so this view asserts, the eternal world in its wholeness is not only perfect, but has merely the perfection of an utterly transparent crystal, unstained by any color of ill. Only mortal error imagines that there is any evil. There is no evil but only good in the real world, and that is why God finds the world perfect, whatever mortals dream.

Now neither of these abstract views is my view. I consider them both the result of a thoughtless trust in abstract words. I regard evil as a distinctly real fact, a fact just as real as the most helpless and hopeless sufferer finds it to be when he is in pain. Furthermore, I hold that God's point of view is not foreign to ours. I hold that God willingly, freely, and consciously suffers in us when we suffer, and that our grief is his. And despite all this I maintain that the world from God's point of view fulfills the divine ideal and is perfect. And I hold that when we abandon the one-sided abstract ideas which the words good, evil, and perfect suggest, and when we go back to the concrete experiences upon which these very words are founded, we can see, even within the limits of our own experience, facts which make these very paradoxes perfectly intelligible, and even commonplace.

As for that essentially pernicious view, nowadays somewhat current amongst a certain class of gentle but inconsequent people—the view that all evil is *merely* an illusion and that there is no such thing in God's world —I can say of it only in passing that it is often advanced as an idealistic view, but that, in my opinion, it is false idealism. Good idealism it is to regard all finite experience as an appearance, a hint, often a very poor hint, of deeper truth. Good idealism it is to admit that man can err about truth that lies beyond his finite range of experience. And very good idealism it is to assert that all truth, and so all finite experience, exists in and for the mind of God, and nowhere outside of or apart from God. But it is not good idealism to assert that any facts which fall within the range of finite experience are, even while they are experienced, mere illusions. God's truth is inclusive, not exclusive. What you experience God experiences. The difference lies only in this, that God sees in unity what you see in fragments. For the rest, if one said, "The source and seat of evil is only the error of mortal mind," one would but have changed the name of one's problem. If the evil were but the error, the error would still be the evil, and altering the name would not have diminished the horror of the evil of this finite world.

V.

But I hasten from the false idealism to the true; from the abstractions to the enlightening insights of our life. As a fact, idealism does not say: The finite world is, as such, a mere illusion. A sound idealism says, whatever we experience is a fragment, and, as far as it goes, a genuine fragment of the truth of the divine mind. With this principle before us, let us consider directly our own experiences of good and of evil, to see whether they are as abstractly opposed to each other as the mere words often suggest. We must begin with the elementary and even trivial facts. We shall soon come to something deeper.

By good, as we mortals experience it, we mean something that, when it comes or is expected, we actively welcome, try to attain or keep, and regard with content. By evil in general, as it is in our experience, we mean whatever we find in any sense repugnant and intolerable. I use the words repugnant and intolerable because I wish to indicate that words for evil frequently, like the words for good, directly refer to our actions as such. Commonly and rightly, when we speak of evil, we make reference to acts of resistance, of struggle, of shrinking, of flight, of removal of ourselves from a source of mischief—acts which not only follow upon the experience of evil, but which serve to define in a useful fashion what we mean by evil. The opposing acts of pursuit and of welcome define what we mean by good. By the evil which we experience we mean precisely whatever we regard as something to be gotten rid of, shrunken from, put out of sight, of hearing, or of memory, eschewed, expelled, assailed, or otherwise directly or indirectly resisted. By good we mean whatever we regard as something to be welcomed, pursued, won, grasped, held, persisted in, preserved. And we show all this in our acts in presence of any grade of good or evil, sensuous, æsthetic, ideal, moral. To shun, to flee, to resist, to destroy, these are our primary attitudes towards ill; the opposing acts are our primary attitudes towards the good; and whether you regard us as animals or as moralists, whether it is a sweet taste, a poem, a virtue, or God that we look to as good, and whether it is a burn or a temptation, an outward physical foe, or a stealthy, inward, ideal enemy, that we regard as evil. In all our organs of voluntary movement, in all our deeds, in a turn of the eye, in a sigh, a groan, in a hostile gesture, in an act of silent contempt, we can show in endlessly varied ways the same general attitude of repugnance.

But man is a very complex creature. He has many organs. He performs many acts at once, and he experiences his performance of these acts in one highly complex life of consciousness. As the next feature of his life we all observe that he can at the same time shun one object and grasp at another. In this way he can have at once present to him a consciousness of good and a consciousness of ill. But so far in our account these sorts of experience appear merely as facts side by side. Man loves, and he *also* hates, loves this, and hates that, assumes an attitude of repugnance towards one object, while he welcomes another. So far the usual theory follows man's life, and calls it an experience of good and ill as mingled but exclusively and abstractly opposed facts. For such a view the final question as to the worth of a man's life is merely the question whether there are more intense acts of satisfaction and of welcome than of repugnance and disdain in his conscious life.

But this is by no means an adequate notion of the complexity of man's life, even as an animal. If every conscious act of hindrance, of thwarting, of repugnance, means just in so far an awareness of some evil, it is noteworthy that men can have and can show just such tendencies, not only towards external experiences, but towards their own acts. That is, men can be seen trying to thwart and to hinder even their own acts themselves, at the very moment when they note the occurrence of these acts. One can consciously have an impulse to do something, and at that very moment a conscious disposition to hinder or to thwart as an evil that very impulse. If, on the other hand, every conscious act of attainment, of pursuit, of reinforcement, involves the awareness of some good, it is equally obvious that one can show by one's acts a disposition to reinforce or to emphasize or to increase, not only the externally present gifts of fortune, but also one's own deeds, in so far as one observes them. And in our complex lives it is common enough to find ourselves actually trying to reinforce and to insist upon a situation which involves for us, even at the moment of its occurrence, a great deal of repugnance. In such cases we often act as if we felt the very thwarting of our own primary impulses to be so much of a conscious good that we persist in pursuing and reinforcing the very situation in which this thwarting and hindering of our own impulses is sure to arise.

In brief, as phenomena of this kind show, man is a being who can to a very great extent find a sort of secondary satisfaction in the very act of thwarting his own desires, and thus of assuring for the time his own dissatisfactions. On the other hand, man can to an indefinite degree find himself dissatisfied with his satisfactions and disposed to thwart, not merely his external enemies, but his own inmost impulses themselves. But I now affirm that in all such cases you cannot simply say that man is preferring the less of two evils, or the greater of two goods, as if the good and the evil stood merely side by side in his experience. On the contrary, in such cases, man is not merely setting his acts or his estimates of good and evil side by side and taking the sum of each; but he is making his own relatively primary acts, impulses, desires, the objects of all sorts of secondary impulses, desires, and reflective observations. His whole inner state is one of tension; and he is either making a secondary experience of evil out of his estimate of a primary experience of good, as is the case when he at once finds himself disposed to pursue a given good and to thwart this pursuit as being an evil pursuit; or else he is making a secondary experience of good out of his primary experience of evil, as when he is primarily dissatisfied with his situation, but yet secondarily regards this very dissatisfaction as itself a desirable state. In this way man comes not only to love some things and also to hate other things, he comes to love his own hates and to hate his own loves in an endlessly complex hierarchy of superposed interests in his own interests.

Now it is easy to say that such states of inner tension, where our conscious lives are full of a warfare of the self with itself, are contradictory or absurd states. But it is easy to say this only when you dwell on the words and fail to observe the facts of experience. As a fact, not only our lowest but our highest states of activity are the ones which are fullest of this crossing, conflict, and complex interrelation of loves and hates, of attractions and repugnances. As a merely physiological fact, we begin no muscular act without at the same time initiating acts which involve the innervation of opposing sets of muscles, and these opposing sets of muscles hinder each other's freedom. Every sort of control of movement means the conflicting play of opposed muscular impulses. We do nothing simple, and we will no complex act without willing what involves a certain measure of opposition between the impulses or partial acts which go to make up the whole act. If one passes from single acts to long series of acts, one finds only the more obviously this interweaving of repugnance and of acceptance, of pursuit and of flight, upon which every complex type of conduct depends.

One could easily at this point spend time by dwelling upon numerous and relatively trivial instances of this interweaving of conflicting motives as it appears in all our life. I prefer to pass such instances over with a mere mention. There is, for instance, the whole marvelous consciousness of play, in its benign and in its evil forms. In any game that fascinates, one loves victory and shuns defeat, and yet as a loyal supporter of the game scorns anything that makes victory certain in advance; thus as a lover of fair play preferring to risk the defeat that he all the while shuns, and partly thwarting the very love of victory that from moment to moment fires his hopes. There are, again, the numerous cases in which we prefer to go to places where we are sure to be in a considerable measure dissatisfied; to engage, for instance, in social functions that absorbingly fascinate us despite or even in view of the very fact that, as long as they continue, they keep us in a state of tension which makes us, amongst other things, long to have the whole occasion over. Taking a wider view, one may observe that the greater part of the freest products of the activity of civilization, in ceremonies, in formalities, in the long social drama of flight, of pursuit, of repartee, of contest and of courtesy, involve an elaborate and systematic delaying and hindering of elemental human desires, which we continually outwit, postpone and thwart, even while we nourish them. When students of human nature assert that hunger and love rule the social world, they recognize that the elemental in human nature is trained by civilization into the service of the highest demands of the Spirit. But such students have to recognize that the elemental rules the higher world only in so far as the elemental is not only cultivated, but endlessly thwarted, delayed, outwitted, like a constitutional monarch, who is said to be a sovereign, but who, while he rules, must not govern.

But I pass from such instances, which in all their universality are still, I admit, philosophically speaking, trivial, because they depend upon the accidents of human nature. I pass from these instances to point out what must be the law, not only of human nature, but of every broader form of life as well. I maintain that this organization of life by virtue of the tension of manifold impulses and interests is not a mere accident of our imperfect human nature, but must be a type of the organization of every rational life. There are good and bad states of tension, there are conflicts that can only be justified when resolved into some higher form of harmony. But I insist that, in general, the only harmony that can exist in the realm of the spirit is the harmony that we possess when we thwart the present but more elemental impulse for the sake of the higher unity of experience; as when we rejoice in the endurance of the tragedies of life, because they show us the depth of life, or when we know that it is better to have loved and lost than never to have loved at all, or when we possess a virtue in the moment of victory over the tempter. And the reason why this is true lies in the fact that the more one's experience fulfills ideals, the more that experience presents to one, not of ignorance, but of triumphantly wealthy acquaintance with the facts of manifold, varied and tragic life, full of tension and thereby of unity. Now this is an universal and not merely human law. It is not those innocent of evil who are fullest of the life of God, but those who in their own case have experienced the triumph over evil. It is not those naturally ignorant of fear, or those who, like Siegfried, have never shivered, who possess the genuine experience of courage; but the brave are those who have fears, but control their fears. Such know the genuine virtues of the hero. Were it otherwise, only the stupid could be perfect heroes.

To be sure it is quite false to say, as the foolish do, that the object of life is merely that we may "know life" as an irrational chaos of experiences of good and of evil. But knowing the good in life is a matter which concerns the form, rather than the mere content of life. One who knows life wisely knows indeed much of the content of life; but he knows the good of life in so far as, in the unity of his experience, he finds the evil of his experience not abolished, but subordinated, and in so far relatively thwarted by a control which annuls its triumph even while experiencing its existence.

VI.

Generalizing the lesson of experience we may then say: It is logically impossible that a complete knower of truth should fail to know, to experience, to have present to his insight, the fact of actually existing evil. On the other hand, it is equally impossible for one to know a higher good than comes from the subordination of evil to good in a total experience. When one first loving, in an elemental way, whatever you please, himself hinders, delays, thwarts his elemental interest in the interest of some larger whole of experience, he not only knows more fact, but he possesses a higher good than would or could be present to one who was aware neither of the elemental impulse, nor of the thwarting of it in the tension of a richer life. The knowing of the good, in the higher sense, depends upon contemplating the overcoming and subordination of a less significant impulse, which survives even in order that it should be subordinated. Now this law, this form of the knowledge of the good, applies as well to the existence of moral as to that of sensuous ill. If moral evil were simply destroyed and wiped away from the external world, the knowledge of moral goodness would also be destroyed. For the love of moral good is the thwarting of lower loves for the sake of the higher organization. What is needed, then, for the definition of the divine knowledge of a world that in its wholeness is perfect, is not a divine knowledge that shall ignore, wipe out and utterly make naught the existence of any ill, whether physical or moral, but a divine knowledge to which shall be present that love of the world as a whole which is fulfilled in the endurance of physical ill, in the subordination of moral ill, in the thwarting of impulses which survive even when subordinated, in the acceptance of repugnances which are still eternal, in the triumph over an enemy that endures even through its eternal defeat, and in the discovery that the endless tension of the finite world is included in the contemplative consciousness of the repose and harmony of eternity. To view God's nature thus is to view his nature as the whole idealistic theory views him, not as the Infinite One beyond the finite imperfections, but as the being whose unity determines the very constitution, the lack, the tension, and relative disharmony of the finite world.

The existence of evil, then, is not only consistent with the perfection of the universe, but is necessary for the very existence of that perfection. This is what we see when we no longer permit ourselves to be deceived by the abstract meanings of the words good and evil into thinking that these two opponents exist merely as mutually exclusive facts side by side in experience, but when we go back to the facts of life and perceive that all relatively higher good, in the trivial as in the more truly spiritual realm, is known only in so far as, from some higher reflective point of view, we accept as good the thwarting of an existent interest that is even thereby declared to be a relative ill, and love a tension of various impulses which even thereby involves, as the object of our love, the existence of what gives us aversion or grief. Now if the love of God is more inclusive than the love of man, even as the divine world of experience is richer than the human world, we can simply set no human limit to the intensity of conflict, to the tragedies of existence, to the pangs of finitude, to the degree of moral ill, which in the end is included in the life that God not only loves, but finds the fulfillment of the perfect ideal. If peace means satisfaction, acceptance of the whole of an experience as good, and if even we, in our weakness, can frequently find rest in the very presence of conflict and of tension, in the very endurance of ill in a good cause, in the hero's triumph over temptation, or in the mourner's tearless refusal to accept the lower comforts of forgetfulness, or to wish that the lost one's preciousness had been less painfully revealed by death—well, if even we know our little share of this harmony in the midst of the wrecks and disorders of life, what limit shall we set to the divine power to face this world of his own sorrows, and to find peace in the victory over all its ills.

But in this last expression I have pronounced the word that serves to link this theory as to the place of evil in a good world with the practical problem of every sufferer. Job's rebellion came from the thought that God, as a sovereign, is far off, and that, for his pleasure, his creature suffers. Our own theory comes to the mourner with the assurance: "Your suffering, just as it is in you, is God's suffering. No chasm divides you from God. He is not remote from you even in his eternity. He is here. His eternity means merely the completeness of his experience. But that completeness is inclusive. Your sorrow is one of the included facts." I do not say: "God sympathizes with you from without, would spare you if he could, pities you with helpless external pity merely as a father pities his children." I say: "God here sorrows, not *with* but *in* your sorrow. Your grief is identically his grief, and what you know as your loss, God knows as his loss, just in and through the very moment when you grieve."

But hereupon the sufferer perchance responds: "If this is God's loss, could he not have prevented it? To him are present in unity all the worlds; and yet he must lack just this for which I grieve." I respond: "He suffers here that he may triumph. For the triumph of the wise is no easy thing. Their lives are not light, but sorrowful. Yet they rejoice in their sorrow, not, to be sure, because it is mere experience, but because, for them, it becomes part of a strenuous whole of life. They wander and find their home even in wandering. They long, and attain through their very love of longing. Peace they find in triumphant warfare. Contentment they have most of all in endurance. Sovereignty they win in endless service. The eternal world contains Gethsemane."

Yet the mourner may still insist: "If my sorrow is God's, his triumph is not mine. Mine is the woe. His is the peace." But my theory is a philosophy. It proposes to be coherent. I must persist: "It is your fault that you are thus sundered from God's triumph. His experience in its wholeness cannot now be yours, for you just as you—this individual—are now but a fragment, and see his truth as through a glass darkly. But if you see his truth at all, through even the dimmest light of a glimmering reason, remember, that truth is in fact your own truth, your own fulfillment, the whole from which your life cannot be divorced, the reality that you mean even when you most doubt, the desire of your heart even when you are most blind, the perfection that you unconsciously strove for even when you were an infant, the complete Self apart from whom you mean nothing, the very life that gives your life the only value which it can have. In thought, if not in the fulfillment of thought, in aim if not in attainment of aim, in aspiration if not in the presence of the revealed fact, you can view God's triumph and peace as your triumph and peace. Your defeat will be no less real than it is, nor will you falsely call your evil a mere illusion. But you will see not only the grief but the truth, your truth, your rescue, your triumph."

Well, to what ill-fortune does not just such reasoning apply? I insist: our conclusion is essentially universal. It discounts any evil that experience may contain. All the horrors of the natural order, all the concealments of the divine plan by our natural ignorance, find their general relation to the unity of the divine experience indicated in advance by this account of the problem of evil.

"Yes," one may continue, "ill-fortune you have discovered, but how about moral evil? What if the sinner now triumphantly retorts: 'Aha! So my will is God's will. All then is well with me.'" I reply: What I have said disposes of moral ill precisely as definitely as of physical ill. What the evil will is to the good man, whose goodness depends upon its existence, but also upon the thwarting and the condemnation of its aim, just such is the sinner's will to the divine plan. God's will, we say to the sinner, is your will. Yes, but it is your will thwarted, scorned, overcome, defeated. In the eternal world you are seen, possessed, present, but your damnation is also seen including and thwarting you. Your apparent victory in this world stands simply for the vigor of your impulses. God wills you not to triumph. And that is the use of you in the world—the use of evil generally—to be hated but endured, to be triumphed over through the very fact of your presence, to be willed down even in the very life of which you are a part.

But to the serious moral agent we say: What you mean when you say that evil in this temporal world ought not to exist, and ought to be suppressed, is simply what God means by seeing that evil ought to be and is endlessly thwarted, endured, but subordinated. In the natural world you are the minister of God's triumph. Your deed is his. You can never clean the world of evil; but you can subordinate evil. The justification of the presence in the world of the morally evil becomes apparent to us mortals only in so far as this evil is overcome and condemned. It exists only that it may be cast down. Courage, then, for God works in you. In the order of time you embody in outer acts what is for him the truth of his eternity.

BIBLIOGRAPHY ENTRY FOR RESEARCH PAPERS:

Royce, Josiah. *Studies of Good and Evil. A Series of Essays upon the Problems of Philosophy and of Life.* New York: D. Appleton and Co., 1898. "The Problem of Job," pp. 1-28, reprinted in *The Voice out of the Whirlwind: The Book of Job,* ed. Ralph E. Hone. San Francisco, 1960.

FIRST FOOTNOTE:

* Josiah Royce, *Studies of Good and Evil. A Series of Essays upon the Problems of Philosophy and of Life* (New York: D. Appleton and Co., 1898), "The Problem of Job," pp. 1-28, reprinted in *The Voice out of the Whirlwind: The Book of Job,* ed. Ralph E. Hone (San Francisco, 1960), pp. 233-253.

SUBSEQUENT FOOTNOTES:

* Royce, *op. cit., The Voice,* p. ■.
* Royce, "The Problem," *The Voice,* p. ■.
* Royce, *The Voice,* p. ■.

In place of *"The Voice,"* "ed. Hone" may be used in these subsequent-footnote forms.

PART V

Modern Dramatic Adaptations
of the Book of Job

THORNTON WILDER

ON

a Job Situation

‖‖

*Thornton Wilder is one of the eminent men of American letters.
He has won the Pulitzer Prize in fiction (*The Bridge of San Luis
Rey *in 1928) and in drama (*Our Town *in 1938 and* The Skin
of Our Teeth *in 1943). The selection which follows is from* The
Angel That Troubled the Waters and Other Plays *(New York:
Coward-McCann, Inc., 1928), pp. 129-133.*

"HAST THOU CONSIDERED MY SERVANT JOB?"

*Now it came to pass on the day when the sons of God came to present
themselves before* SATAN *that* CHRIST *also came among them. And*
SATAN [*Said unto* CHRIST] Whence comest Thou?

CHRIST [*Answered* SATAN *and said*] From going to and fro in the earth,
and from walking up and down in it.

[*And*] SATAN [*Said unto Christ*] Hast Thou considered my servant
Judas? For there is none like him in the earth, an evil and a faithless
man, one that feareth me and turneth away from God.

[*Then*] CHRIST [*Answered* SATAN *and said*] Doth Judas fear thee for
naught? Hast thou not made a hedge about him, and about his house,
and about all that he hath on every side? But draw back thy hand
now and he will renounce thee to thy face.

[*And*] SATAN [*Said unto* CHRIST] Behold, all that he hath is in thy
power.

[*So* CHRIST *went forth from the presence of* SATAN.]

*　　*　　*　　*　　*

[*He descended to the earth. Thirty-three years are but a moment before* SATAN *and before* GOD, *and at the end of this moment* CHRIST *ascends again to His own place. He passes on this journey before the presence of the adversary.*]

SATAN You are alone! Where is my son Judas whom I gave into your hands?

CHRIST He follows me.

SATAN I know what you have done. And the earth rejected you? The earth rejected you! All Hell murmurs in astonishment. But where is Judas, my son and my joy?

CHRIST Even now he is coming.

SATAN Even Heaven, when I reigned there, was not so tedious as this waiting. Know, Prince, that I am too proud to show all my astonishment at your defeat. But now that you are swallowing your last humiliation, now that your failure has shut the mouths of the angels, I may confess that for a while I feared you. There is a fretfulness in the hearts of men. Many are inconstant, even to me. Alas, every man is not a Judas. I knew even from the beginning that you would be able, for a season, to win their hearts with your mild eloquence. I feared that you would turn to your own uses this fretfulness that visits them. But my fears were useless. Even Judas, even when my power was withdrawn from him, even Judas betrayed you. Am I not right in this?

CHRIST You are.

SATAN You admitted him into your chosen company. Is it permitted to me to ask for how much he betrayed you?

CHRIST For thirty pieces of silver.

SATAN [*After a pause*] Am I permitted to ask to what rôle he was assigned in your company?

CHRIST He held its money-bags.

SATAN [*Dazed*] Does Heaven understand human nature as little as that? Surely the greater part of your closest companions stayed beside you to the end?

CHRIST One stayed beside me.

SATAN I have overestimated my enemy. Learn again, Prince, that if I were permitted to return to the earth in my own person, not for thirty years, but for thirty hours, I would seal all men to me and all the temptations in Heaven's gift could not persuade one to betray me. For I build not on intermittent dreams and timid aspirations, but on the unshakable passions of greed and lust and self-love. At last this is made clear: Judas, Judas, all the triumphs of Hell await you. Already above the eternal pavements of black marble the banquet is laid. Listen, how my nations are stirring in new hope and in new joy. Such music has not been lifted above my lakes and my mountains since the day I placed the apple of knowledge between the teeth of Adam.

[*Suddenly the thirty pieces of silver are cast upward from the revolted hand of* JUDAS. *They hurtle through the skies, flinging their enormous shadows across the stars and continue falling forever through the vast funnel of space.*

[*Presently* JUDAS *rises, the black stains about his throat and the rope of suicide.*]

SATAN   What have they done to you, my beloved son? What last poor revenge have they attempted upon you? Come to me. Here there is comfort. Here all this violence can be repaired. The futile spite of Heaven cannot reach you here. But why do you not speak to me? My son, my treasure!

[JUDAS *remains with lowered eyes.*]

CHRIST   Speak to him then, my beloved son.

JUDAS [*Still with lowered eyes, softly, to* SATAN]   Accursed be thou, from eternity to eternity.

[*These two mount upward to their due place and* SATAN *remains to this day, uncomprehending, upon the pavement of Hell.*]

BIBLIOGRAPHY ENTRY FOR RESEARCH PAPERS:

Wilder, Thornton. *The Angel That Troubled the Waters and Other Plays.* New York: Coward-McCann, Inc., 1928. "Hast Thou Considered My Servant Job?" pp. 129-133, reprinted in *The Voice out of the Whirlwind: The Book of Job,* ed. Ralph E. Hone. San Francisco, 1960.

FIRST FOOTNOTE:

   * Thornton Wilder, *The Angel That Troubled the Waters and Other Plays* (New York: Coward-McCann, Inc., 1928), "Hast Thou Considered My Servant

Job?" pp. 129-133, reprinted in *The Voice out of the Whirlwind: The Book of Job,* ed. Ralph E. Hone (San Francisco, 1960), pp. 256-259.

SUBSEQUENT FOOTNOTES:

    * Wilder, *op. cit., The Voice,* p. ■.
    * Wilder, "Hast Thou Considered," *The Voice,* p. ■.
    * Wilder, *The Voice,* p. ■.

In place of *"The Voice,"* "ed. Hone" may be used in these subsequent-footnote forms.

ROBERT FROST

WRITES

a Sequel to Job

The sly, wise humor of Robert Frost (1875-) is clearly apparent in the selection which follows. At the close of the poem he says: "Here endeth chapter forty-three of Job." *But this work is more than sly, wise humor. It is a poem of our time which anticipated Archibald MacLeish's J. B. by a decade. It serves to indicate, also, the perennial significance of the Book of Job itself. The selection is the entire text of* A Masque of Reason *(New York: Henry Holt and Company, 1945).*

A MASQUE OF REASON

A FAIR *oasis in the purest desert.*
A man sits leaning back against a palm.
His wife lies by him looking at the sky.

MAN   You're not asleep?

WIFE   No, I can hear you. Why?

MAN   I said the incense tree's on fire again.

WIFE   You mean the Burning Bush?

MAN   The Christmas Tree.

WIFE   I shouldn't be surprised.

MAN   The strangest light!

WIFE   There's a strange light on everything today.

MAN   The myrrh tree gives it. Smell the rosin burning?
The ornaments the Greek artificers
Made for the Emperor Alexius,
The Star of Bethlehem, the pomegranates,
The birds, seem all on fire with Paradise.
And hark, the gold enameled nightingales
Are singing. Yes, and look, the Tree is troubled.
Someone's caught in the branches.

WIFE   So there is.
He can't get out.

MAN   He's loose! He's out!

WIFE   It's God.
I'd know Him by Blake's picture anywhere.
Now what's He doing?

MAN   Pitching throne, I guess,
Here by our atoll.

WIFE   Something Byzantine.
(The throne's a plywood flat, prefabricated,
That God pulls lightly upright on its hinges
And stands beside, supporting it in place.)
Perhaps for an Olympic Tournament,
Or Court of Love.

MAN   More likely Royal Court—
Or Court of Law, and this is Judgment Day.
I trust it is. Here's where I lay aside
My varying opinion of myself
And come to rest in an official verdict.
Suffer yourself to be admired, my love,
As Waller says.

WIFE   Or not admired. Go over
And speak to Him before the others come.
Tell Him He may remember you: you're Job.

GOD   Oh, I remember well: you're Job, my Patient.
How are you now? I trust you're quite recovered,
And feel no ill effects from what I gave you.

JOB   Gave me in truth: I like the frank admission.
I am a name for being put upon.

But, yes, I'm fine, except for now and then
A reminiscent twinge of rheumatism.
The let-up's heavenly. You perhaps will tell us
If that is all there is to be of Heaven,
Escape from so great pains of life on earth
It gives a sense of let-up calculated
To last a fellow to Eternity.

GOD   Yes, by and by. But first a larger matter.
I've had you on my mind a thousand years
To thank you someday for the way you helped me
Establish once for all the principle
There's no connection man can reason out
Between his just deserts and what he gets.
Virtue may fail and wickedness succeed.
'Twas a great demonstration we put on.
I should have spoken sooner had I found
The word I wanted. You would have supposed
One who in the beginning *was* the Word
Would be in a position to command it.
I have to wait for words like anyone.
Too long I've owed you this apology
For the apparently unmeaning sorrow
You were afflicted with in those old days.
But it was of the essence of the trial
You shouldn't understand it at the time.
It had to seem unmeaning to have meaning.
And it came out all right. I have no doubt
You realize by now the part you played
To stultify the Deuteronomist
And change the tenor of religious thought.
My thanks are to you for releasing me
From moral bondage to the human race.
The only free will there at first was man's,
Who could do good or evil as he chose.
I had no choice but I must follow him
With forfeits and rewards he understood—
Unless I liked to suffer loss of worship.
I had to prosper good and punish evil.
You changed all that. You set me free to reign.

You are the Emancipator of your God,
And as such I promote you to a saint.

JOB You hear him, Thyatira: we're a saint.
Salvation in our case is retroactive.
We're saved, we're saved, whatever else it means.

JOB'S WIFE Well, after all these years!

JOB   This is my wife.

JOB'S WIFE If You're the deity I assume You are—
(I'd know You by Blake's picture anywhere)—

GOD The best, I'm told, I ever have had taken.

JOB'S WIFE —I have a protest I would lodge with You.
I want to ask You if it stands to reason
That women prophets should be burned as witches
Whereas men prophets are received with honor.

JOB Except in their own country, Thyatira.

GOD You're not a witch?

JOB'S WIFE   No.

GOD   Have you ever been one?

JOB Sometimes she thinks she has and gets herself
Worked up about it. But she really hasn't—
Not in the sense of having to my knowledge
Predicted anything that came to pass.

·JOB'S WIFE The witch of Endor was a friend of mine.

GOD You wouldn't say she fared so very badly.
I noticed when she called up Samuel
His spirit had to come. Apparently
A witch was stronger than a prophet there.

JOB'S WIFE But she was burned for witchcraft.

GOD   That is not
Of record in my Note Book.

JOB'S WIFE   Well, she was.
And I should like to know the reason why.

GOD There you go asking for the very thing
We've just agreed I didn't have to give.

(*The throne collapses. But He picks it up*
And this time locks it up and leaves it.)
Where has she been the last half hour or so?
She wants to know why there is still injustice.
I answer flatly: That's the way it is,
And bid my will avouch it like Macbeth.
We may as well go back to the beginning
And look for justice in the case of Segub.

JOB   Oh, Lord, let's not go *back* to anything.

GOD   Because your wife's past won't bear looking into?
In our great moment what did you do, Madam?
What did you try to make your husband say?

JOB'S WIFE   No, let's not live things over. I don't care.
I stood by Job. I may have turned on You.
Job scratched his boils and tried to think what he
Had done or not done to or for the poor.
The test is always how we treat the poor.
It's time the poor were treated by the state
In some way not so penal as the poorhouse.
That's one thing more to put on Your agenda.
Job hadn't done a thing, poor innocent.
I told him not to scratch: it made it worse.
If I said once I said a thousand times,
Don't scratch! And when, as rotten as his skin,
His tents blew all to pieces, I picked up
Enough to build him every night a pup tent
Around him so it wouldn't touch and hurt him.
I did my wifely duty. I should tremble!
All You can seem to do is lose Your temper
When reason-hungry mortals ask for reasons.
Of course, in the abstract high singular
There isn't any universal reason;
And no one but a man would think there was.
You don't catch women trying to be Plato.
Still there must be lots of unsystematic
Stray scraps of palliative reason
It wouldn't hurt You to vouchsafe the faithful.
You thought it was agreed You needn't give them.
You thought to suit Yourself. I've not agreed
To anything with anyone.

JOB   There, there,
   You go to sleep. God must await events
   As well as words.

JOB'S WIFE   I'm serious. God's had
   Aeons of time and still it's mostly women
   Get burned for prophecy, men almost never.

JOB   God needs time just as much as you or I
   To get things done. Reformers fail to see that.
   She'll go to sleep. Nothing keeps her awake
   But physical activity, I find.
   Try to read to her and she drops right off.

GOD   She's beautiful.

JOB   Yes, she was just remarking
   She now felt younger by a thousand years
   Than the day she was born.

GOD   That's about right,
   I should have said. You got your age reversed
   When time was found to be a space dimension
   That could, like any space, be turned around in?

JOB   Yes, both of us: we saw to that at once.
   But, God, I have a question too to raise.
   (My wife gets in ahead of me with hers.)
   I need some help about this reason problem
   Before I am too late to be got right
   As to what reasons I agree to waive.
   I'm apt to string along with Thyatira.
   God knows—or rather, You know (God forgive me)
   I waived the reason for my ordeal—but—
   I have a question even there to ask—
   In confidence. There's no one here but her,
   And she's a woman: she's not interested
   In general ideas and principles.

GOD   What are her interests, Job?

JOB   Witch-women's rights.
   Humor her there or she will be confirmed
   In her suspicion You're no feminist.
   You have it in for women, she believes.
   Kipling invokes You as Lord God of Hosts.

She'd like to know how You would take a prayer
That started off Lord God of Hostesses.

GOD   I'm charmed with her.

JOB   Yes, I could see You were.
But to my question. I am much impressed
With what You say we have established.
Between us, You and I.

GOD   I make you see?
It would be too bad if Columbus-like
You failed to see the worth of your achievement.

JOB   You call it mine.

GOD   We groped it out together.
Any originality it showed
I give you credit for. My forte is truth,
Or metaphysics, long the world's reproach
For standing still in one place true forever;
While science goes self-superseding on.
Look at how far we've left the current science
Of Genesis behind. The wisdom there though,
Is just as good as when I uttered it.
Still, novelty has doubtless an attraction.

JOB   So it's important who first thinks of things?

GOD   I'm a great stickler for the author's name.
By proper names I find I do my thinking.

JOB'S WIFE   God, who invented earth?

JOB   What, still awake?

GOD   Any originality it showed
Was of the Devil. He invented Hell,
False premises that are the original
Of all originality, the sin
That felled the angels, Wolsey should have said.
As for the earth, we groped that out together,
Much as your husband Job and I together
Found out the discipline man needed most
Was to learn his submission to unreason;
And that for man's own sake as well as mine,
So he won't find it hard to take his orders

From his inferiors in intelligence
In peace and war—especially in war.

JOB   So he won't find it hard to take his war.

GOD   You have the idea. There's not much I can tell you.

JOB   All very splendid. I am flattered proud
To have been in on anything with You.
'Twas a great demonstration if You say so.
Though incidentally I sometimes wonder
Why it had to be at my expense.

GOD   It had to be at somebody's expense.
Society can never think things out:
It has to see them acted out by actors,
Devoted actors at a sacrifice—
The ablest actors I can lay my hands on.
Is that your answer?

JOB   No, for I have yet
To ask my question. We disparage reason.
But all the time it's what we're most concerned with.
There's will as motor and there's will as brakes.
Reason is, I suppose, the steering gear.
The will as brakes can't stop the will as motor
For very long. We're plainly made to go.
We're going anyway and may as well
Have some say as to where we're headed for;
Just as we will be talking anyway
And may as well throw in a little sense.
Let's do so now. Because I let You off
From telling me Your reason, don't assume
I thought You had none. Somewhere back
I knew You had one. But this isn't it
You're giving me. You say we groped this out.
But if You will forgive me the irreverence,
It sounds to me as if You thought it out,
And took Your time to it. It seems to me
An afterthought, a long long afterthought.
I'd give more for one least beforehand reason
Than all the justifying ex-post-facto
Excuses trumped up by You for theologists.

The front of being answerable to no one
I'm with You in maintaining to the public.
But Lord, we showed them that. The audience
Has all gone home to bed. The play's played out.
Come, after all these years—to satisfy me.
I'm curious. And I'm a grown-up man:
I'm not a child for You to put me off
And tantalize me with another "Oh, because."
You'd be the last to want me to believe
All Your effects were merely lucky blunders.
That would be unbelief and atheism.
The artist in me cries out for design.
Such devilish ingenuity of torture
Did seem unlike You, and I tried to think
The reason might have been some other person's.
But there is nothing You are not behind.
I did not ask then, but it seems as if
Now after all these years You might indulge me.
Why did You hurt me so? I am reduced
To asking flatly for a reason—outright.

GOD   I'd tell you, Job—

JOB   All right, don't tell me then
If you don't want to. I don't want to know.
But what is all this secrecy about?
I fail to see what fun, what satisfaction
A God can find in laughing at how badly
Men fumble at the possibilities
When left to guess forever for themselves.
The chances are when there's so much pretense
Of metaphysical profundity
The obscurity's a fraud to cover nothing.
I've come to think no so-called hidden value's
Worth going after. Get down into things
It will be found there's no more given there
Than on the surface. If there ever was,
The crypt was long since rifled by the Greeks.
We don't know where we are, or who we are.
We don't know one another; don't know You;
Don't know what time it is. We don't know, don't we?

Who says we don't? Who got up these misgivings?
Oh, we know well enough to go ahead with.
I mean we seem to know enough to act on.
It comes down to a doubt about the wisdom
Of having children—after having had them,
So there is nothing we can do about it
But warn the children they perhaps should have none.
You could end this by simply coming out
And saying plainly and unequivocally
Whether there's any part of man immortal.
Yet You don't speak. Let fools bemuse themselves
By being baffled for the sake of being.
I'm sick of the whole artificial puzzle.

JOB'S WIFE   You won't get any answers out of God.

GOD   My kingdom, what an outbreak!

JOB'S WIFE   Job is right.
Your kingdom, yes, Your kingdom come on earth.
Pray tell me what does that mean. Anything?
Perhaps that earth is going to crack someday
Like a big egg and hatch a heaven out
Of all the dead and buried from their graves.
One simple little statement from the throne
Would put an end to such fantastic nonsense;
And, too, take care of twenty of the four
And twenty freedoms on the party docket.
Or is it only four? My extra twenty
Are freedoms from the need of asking questions.
(I hope You know the game called twenty questions.)
For instance, is there such a thing as Progress?
Job says there's no such thing as Earth's becoming
An easier place for man to save his soul in.
Except as a hard place to save his soul in,
A trial ground where he can try himself
And find out whether he is any good,
It would be meaningless. It might as well
Be Heaven at once and have it over with.

GOD   Two pitching on like this tend to confuse me.
One at a time, please. I will answer Job first.
I'm going to tell Job why I tortured him

And trust it won't be adding to the torture.
I was just showing off to the Devil, Job,
As is set forth in chapters One and Two.
(*Job takes a few steps pacing.*) Do you mind?
(*God eyes him anxiously.*)

JOB   No. No, I mustn't.
'Twas human of You. I expected more
Than I could understand and what I get
Is almost less than I can understand.
But I don't mind. Let's leave it as it stood.
The point was it was none of my concern.
I stick to that. But talk about confusion!
How is that for a mix-up, Thyatira?
Yet I suppose what seems to us confusion
Is not confusion, but the form of forms,
The serpent's tail stuck down the serpent's throat,
Which is the symbol of eternity
And also of the way all things come round,
Or of how rays return upon themselves,
To quote the greatest Western poem yet.
Though I hold rays deteriorate to nothing,
First white, then red, then ultra red, then out.

GOD   Job, you must understand my provocation.
The tempter comes to me and I am tempted.
I'd had about enough of his derision
Of what I valued most in human nature.
He thinks he's smart. He thinks he can convince me
It is no different with my followers
From what it is with his. Both serve for pay.
Disinterestedness never did exist
And if it did, it wouldn't be a virtue.
Neither would fairness. You have heard the doctrine.
It's on the increase. He could count on no one:
That was his look out. I could count on you.
I wanted him forced to acknowledge so much.
I gave you over to him, but with safeguards.
I took care of you. And before you died
I trust I made it clear I took your side
Against your comforters in their contention

You must be wicked to deserve such pain.
That's Browning and sheer Chapel Non-conformism.

JOB   God, please, enough for now. I'm in no mood
      For more excuses.

GOD   What I mean to say:
      Your comforters were wrong.

JOB   Oh, that committee!

GOD   I saw you had no fondness for committees.
      Next time you find yourself pressed on to one
      For the revision of the Book of Prayer
      Put that in if it isn't in already:
      Deliver us from committees. 'Twill remind me.
      I would do anything for you in reason.

JOB   Yes, yes.

GOD   You don't seem satisfied.

JOB   I am.

GOD   You're pensive.

JOB   Oh, I'm thinking of the Devil.
      You must remember he was in on this.
      We can't leave him out.

GOD   No. No, we don't need to.
      We're too well off.

JOB   Someday we three should have
      A good old get-together celebration.

GOD   Why not right now?

JOB   We can't without the Devil.

GOD   The Devil's never very far away.
      He too is pretty circumambient.
      He has but to appear. He'll come for me,
      Precipitated from the desert air.
      Show yourself, son. I'll get back on my throne
      For this I think. I find it always best
      To be upon my dignity with him.

      *(The Devil enters like a sapphire wasp
      That flickers mica wings. He lifts a hand*

To brush away a disrespectful smile.
Job's wife sits up.)

JOB'S WIFE   Well, if we aren't all here,
Including me, the only Dramatis
Personae needed to enact the problem.

JOB   We've waked her up.

JOB'S WIFE   I haven't been asleep.
I've heard what you were saying—every word.

JOB   What did we say?

JOB'S WIFE   You said the Devil's in it.

JOB   She always claims she hasn't been asleep.
And what else did we say?

JOB'S WIFE   Well, what led up—
Something about— (*The three men laugh.*)
—The Devil's being God's best inspiration.

JOB   Good, pretty good.

JOB'S WIFE   Wait till I get my Kodak.
Would you two please draw in a little closer?
No—no, that's not a smile there. That's a grin.
Satan, what ails you? Where's the famous tongue,
Thou onetime Prince of Conversationists?
This is polite society you're in
Where good and bad are mingled everywhichway,
And ears are lent to any sophistry
Just as if nothing mattered but our manners.
You look as if you either hoped or feared
You were more guilty of mischief than you are.
Nothing has been brought out that for my part
I'm not prepared for or that Job himself
Won't find a formula for taking care of.

SATAN   Like the one Milton founded to fool himself
About his blindness.

JOB'S WIFE   Oh, he speaks! He *can* speak!
That strain again! Give me excess of it!
As dulcet as a pagan temple gong!
He's twitting us. Oh, by the way, you haven't

By any chance a Lady Apple on you?
I saw a boxful in the Christmas market.
How I should prize one personally from you.

GOD   Don't *you* twit. He's unhappy. Church neglect
And figurative use have pretty well
Reduced him to a shadow of himself.

JOB'S WIFE   *That* explains why he's so diaphanous
And easy to see through. But where's he off to?
I thought there were to be festivities
Of some kind. We could have charades.

GOD   He has his business he must be about.
Job mentioned him and so I brought him in
More to give his reality its due
Than anything.

JOB'S WIFE   He's very real to me
And always will be. Please don't go. Stay, stay
But to the evensong and having played
Together we will go with you along.
There are who won't have had enough of you
If you go now. Look how he takes no steps!
He isn't really going, yet he's leaving.

JOB   *(Who has been standing dazed with new ideas)*
He's on that tendency that like the Gulf Stream,
Only of sand not water, runs through here.
It has a rate distinctly different
From the surrounding desert; just today
I stumbled over it and got tripped up.

JOB'S WIFE   Oh, yes, that tendency! Oh, do come off it.
Don't let it carry you away. I hate
A tendency. The minute you get on one
It seems to start right off accelerating.
Here, take my hand.

> *(He takes it and alights*
> *In three quick steps as off an escalator.*
> *The tendency, a long, long narrow strip*
> *Of middle-aisle church carpet, sisal hemp,*
> *Is worked by hands invisible off stage.)*

I want you in my group beside the throne—
Must have you. There, that's just the right arrangement.
Now someone can light up the Burning Bush
And turn the gold enameled artificial birds on.
I recognize them. Greek artificers
Devised them for Alexius Comnenus.
They won't show in the picture. That's too bad.
Neither will I show. That's too bad moreover.
Now if you three have settled anything
You'd as well smile as frown on the occasion.

(Here endeth chapter forty-three of Job.)

BIBLIOGRAPHY ENTRY FOR RESEARCH PAPERS:

Frost, Robert. *A Masque of Reason.* New York: Henry Holt and Company, 1945. Reprinted in *The Voice out of the Whirlwind: The Book of Job,* ed. Ralph E. Hone. San Francisco, 1960.

FIRST FOOTNOTE:

  * Robert Frost, *A Masque of Reason* (New York: Henry Holt and Company, 1945), reprinted in *The Voice out of the Whirlwind: The Book of Job,* ed. Ralph E. Hone (San Francisco, 1960), pages 260-274.

SUBSEQUENT FOOTNOTES:

  * Frost, *op. cit., The Voice,* p. ■.
  * Frost, *Masque, The Voice,* p. ■.
  * Frost, *The Voice,* p. ■.

In place of *"The Voice,"* "ed. Hone" may be used in these subsequent-footnote forms.

ARCHIBALD MacLEISH

AND

J. B. and Job

||||||||||||||||||||||||||||||||||||||||||||||||||||||||||||||||||||||||||||||||||||||||||||||||||||||||||||||||||||||||||||||||||||||||||||||||||||||||||||||||||||||||||||||||||||||||||||||

In 1956 Archibald MacLeish, distinguished American poet, published J. B., a play with prologue and eleven scenes developing a modern adaptation of the Job theme. In 1958 this play opened in New Haven and by the following year reached Broadway. We regret that the publishers of the play have decided not to release it to anthologists at the present time, but some notice of it must be taken in a collection of materials devoted to the Book of Job.

Accordingly, there follow in this section reviews and observations on the play. From this material the student may observe variant critical appraisals of the relationship between MacLeish's work and the Book of Job.

JOHN CIARDI

ON

J. B. and Job

———

John Ciardi, teacher and poet, is poetry editor for The Saturday Review, *in which the following essay appeared: March 8, 1958, at pages 11-12 and 48.*

THE BIRTH OF A CLASSIC

ARCHIBALD MACLEISH'S "J. B." is great poetry, great drama, and—as far as my limitations permit me to sense it—great stagecraft. The distinction between drama and stagecraft is a necessary one. By drama one must intend a gathering of intellectual, spiritual, and physical forces about the lives of characters who move those forces and who move within them to a conclusion that echoes within us to the root of our values. By stagecraft one must intend the manipulation of the illusions of the stage for momentary effect.

It is a simple fact of English and American literature that there has been no great poetic drama since Shakespeare. Nor need one imply that MacLeish is the equal of Shakespeare in pointing out that, until now, no one since Shakespeare has found a sufficient answer to the problems that arise from the combination of poetry and the stage. MacLeish's earlier radio plays showed him to be working valuably toward a solution of these problems. By the time his "Trojan Horse" and "This Music Crept by Me on the Water"—both one-act plays—were published, it was clear that MacLeish had solved the problems within a limited framework. He had shown anyone who cared to be shown, how to write poetic drama in the twentieth century. "J. B." now makes it clear that he had above all shown himself how to apply his own discoveries to a full-length treatment of a great theme.

MacLeish's great technical achievement is in his forging of a true poetic stage line for our times. Such a line must answer to four basic requirements.

It must have range. It must be able to speak, with equal assurance, passion, sublimity, chitchat, and every way-station of the emotions. MacLeish's range is magnificent and unstrained. He is capable of the resonance and agony of Job's cry: "God is unthinkable if we are innocent." And he can chill the flesh about us with the response of the child, Jolly Adams, who, told to look away from Job's sores for fear she will remember them, speaks the thrilled depravity in all of us, answering proudly: "Every sore I seen I remember!"

Such a line must be recognizably a line of poetry. It is difficult to say what makes a line of poetry something more than a quantity of words. It must respond to measure—metrical or not—but measure is not enough, and if the measure is mechanical, all is lost. Perhaps it may best be said that it *plays against the measure,* observing measure not as does a metronome but in a constant play of variations and compensations. It is a unit somehow as organic as a good phrase in music: stopped anywhere short of its conclusion it becomes obviously a fragment of a thing rather than the thing itself. A good poetic line, moreover, is an *irreducible statement* in the way a proverb is irreducible: it is clearly the shortest distance to itself and nothing can be spared from it. Partly because it is irreducible, it is *memorable:* something about it hooks naturally onto the mind and clings there. And it is *nervous*—as a battle cry or a cheer is nervous: it addresses itself not to detached contemplation alone (whatever that is) but suggests sensation to the whole body.

Such a line must be truly a unit of the spoken language. The means by which a line responds to the living speech of a people seem to defy definition, yet their effect is unmistakable. What is obvious is that languages have a tune to them. One can sit at a café table in Paris, just at the edge of hearing the talk at another table and be certain, without making out a single word, that what is being spoken is German or Italian or English or American. Such speech rhythms change not only from language to language but from time to time within the same language, and good poetry is forever renewing its rhythms by responding to the rhythms of prose. The basic mark of mature achievement in American poetry of the twentieth century is the success of our poets in capturing the rhythms of the American voice box.

Such a line, finally, must have a pace that works in the theatre. Pace is the rate at which the writing (here, the saying) reveals itself to the reader. Some young poets, for example, have tried to use Dylan Thomas's tight lyric line for the stage, and the results have been disastrous. When the speaking voice offers a tightly knotted phrase or metaphor, one naturally fastens onto it. He stops to examine it, caught by its complexities. But the speaking voice goes on. By the time the listener solves or gives up his puzzle, the voice may have covered fifteen or twenty unheard lines, and by that time who has any notion of what is being said? The stage line must manage to offer the richness of true poetry at a pace which the ear can absorb.

MacLeish's great technical achievement is that he has forged a line that answers superbly to all four of these requirements. No one else has managed such a line in our time. Auden seems to do it occasionally, but only momentarily. To my reading at least, Eliot's stage line usually sounds like an Anglican bishop's translation from the Latin, and of late even Mr. Eliot, though perhaps a bit artfully, confesses himself bored by his own plays. Christopher Fry has made the fundamental mistake of trying to use the Shakespearean line in the twentieth century. And who else is there? Maxwell Anderson? Norman Corwin? Both have tried poetic plays but their line goes stagey and windy and lacks integrity as poetry. Only Mac-Leish has found the line that teaches the American language how to go greatly on stage.

But such technical achievement is nothing unless it leads to human consequence. What is forever consequential is not only that "J. B." is a great dramatization of the human position, but that the poetry and the drama are organically one. The poetry is not an enrichment of the prose sense: it is itself the way of knowing. Which is to say that great themes can be truly engaged only by great art. MacLeish's triumph is that he has been equal to his great theme.

Job's descent through his sufferings acquires an enormous momentum. Carried along with it, our fear seems to be that Job's suffering is indeed a descent, meaningless and irreparable: his children gone one by one in a series of indecent deaths, his prosperity gone in what would have been an anticlimax had not the Waste of Power blasted a whole city to rubble in order to destroy Job's substance, his health gone in one nauseating affliction after another, even his wife's love gone in the end. All gone. All down.

Except that Job emerges triumphant. Not Job-the-servant, but Job the world-offended and God-offended man. Job cries for Justice in his misery and God answers, the Biblical phrases ringing hugely:

> Where wast thou
> When I laid the foundations of the earth . . .
>
> Hast Thou an arm like God? Or canst thou
> Thunder with a voice like Him?

And so on. But Job already knew that God was big. He had asked for Justice and he had been answered with Size. And Job triumphs in understanding at last that he needs no forgiveness. Instead he bows his head in its insignificance *and forgives God.* His triumph is that he need feel guilty no longer: what is monstrous is not of his doing and can therefore be borne. He does not think again of his own great line, "God is unthinkable if we are innocent," but it is there to be thought, and its implications are clear. The final position is humanism, and humanism is man-centered.

And Job the humanist triumphs once again by reclaiming himself from his losses in the name of human love. So at the end when Sarah, his wife, returns:

> SARAH: You wanted justice and there was none—Only love.
> J. B.: He does not love. He Is.
> SARAH: But we do. That's the wonder.
> J. B.: Yet you left me.
> SARAH: Yes, I left you. I thought there was a way away . . .

But in the Universe of the humanist all ways lead us either to one another or to the void. What Job learns from the accident-strewn orbits is that we are one another's only hope. And, by implication, that we are somehow hope enough for one another if we can learn our loves to live to.

Massive as these themes are, the basic action of Job is the simplest sort of dramatic sequence. The man of all blessings becomes the man of all sufferings: only that. The sequence is as clear as an alphabet and the end foreknown. Only by placing that simple sequence within the framework of great concept can the Job theme rise to greatness. As a local drama of events Job is nothing: its stage must be no less than the spaces of the Universe held in the arch of Man's mind.

What gives unique dimension and penetration to MacLeish's treatment of the theme is his handling of the two commentators who bring the drama to pass. It is they who most immediately summon the Universe and the Human Position into the drama. For his Universe MacLeish returns to the image of the Big Top, which he made so memorable in his early lyric "The End of the World." His commentators are two broken-down actors, now reduced to selling popcorn and balloons at the Circus. They are named Mr. Zuss and Nickles, and they obviously represent a kind of human-size Zeus and Old Nick principle, two views of Good and Evil. They enter and identify the scene with great economy. They are looking at a raised platform on which some sort of sideshow is acted as part of the Circus program. The platform is now deserted but still strewn with the props of the play, above all with a God-mask and a Satan-mask:

> MR. ZUSS: This is it.
> NICKLES: This is what?
> MR. ZUSS: Where they play the play, Horatio!
> NICKLES: Bare stage?
> MR. ZUSS: Not in the least. Heaven and earth. The platform's
> Heaven.
> *They step onto the stage together.*
> NICKLES: Looks like Heaven!
> MR. ZUSS: As you remember it?
> NICKLES: Somebody's got to. You weren't there. They never sold
> balloons in Heaven—Not in my time.

Zuss and Nickles, we soon discover, are multiple commentators. When they view the actions of Job (on the lower stage) they discuss them primarily as human beings. When they take part in the action, they are carried away as artists. When they comment on the performance—both their own and that of the other players—they are critics of dramatic values. When, moreover, they find the masks of God and Satan, they cannot resist putting them on (the act of the imagination), and at once they find themselves looking through the inhuman eyes of Ultimate Good and Evil. Nickles, appalled at first, struggles painfully out of his mask and stares at it. "Those eyes see," he declares. It is primarily through the subtly multiple means of perception that Zuss and Nickles bring to bear upon the events of the drama that the events soar to such consequence.

"J. B.," it must be added, is strong stuff. Too strong, one knows, for Broadway success this season or next. And yet Broadway will come to it in time, because it must, because great imagination and great talent cannot be denied forever. Meanwhile, Yale is preparing it for production, and certainly the summer theatres and the college groups throughout the country will have found a new star feature forever. For "J. B." adds a dimension to the accomplishment of American literature. We now have a great American poetic drama.

BIBLIOGRAPHY ENTRY FOR RESEARCH PAPERS:

Ciardi, John. "The Birth of a Classic." *The Saturday Review,* March 8, 1958, pp. 11-12, 48. Reprinted in *The Voice out of the Whirlwind: The Book of Job,* ed. Ralph E. Hone. San Francisco, 1960.

FIRST FOOTNOTE:

* John Ciardi, "The Birth of a Classic," *The Saturday Review,* March 8, 1958, pp. 11-12, 48. Reprinted in *The Voice out of the Whirlwind: The Book of Job,* ed. Ralph E. Hone (San Francisco, 1960), pp. 276-280.

SUBSEQUENT FOOTNOTES:

* Ciardi, *op. cit., The Voice.* p. ■.
* Ciardi, "The Birth," *The Voice,* p. ■.
* Ciardi, *The Voice,* p. ■.

In place of *"The Voice,"* "ed. Hone" may be used in these subsequent-footnote forms.

TOM F. DRIVER

ON

J. B. and Job

Tom F. Driver is the drama critic for The Christian Century *and also teaches on the faculty of the Union Theological Seminary in New York City. His review of* J. B. *appeared in* The Christian Century *of January 7, 1959, at pages 21-22.*

NOTABLE, REGRETTABLE

ELIA KAZAN's production of *J. B.*, by Archibald MacLeish, is as noteworthy and regrettable an event as Broadway will offer this season. One of America's most famed poets has joined forces with the theater's most celebrated director and three distinguished actors to present a highly theatrical study of the human predicament based on the book of Job. The result is something that neither the religious nor the secular community can afford to ignore. I noticed at intermission that the theatergoers were actually discussing the play, not their friends' clothes, Manhattan scandals or the high cost of baby-sitters. It is a phenomenon rare in our theaters.

In my review of the Yale University production of *J. B.* (The Christian Century, June 11, 1958) I noted the objections which may fairly be brought against Mr. MacLeish's script: that it begins by raising the most difficult of religious questions, the justification of the ways of God to man; and that before it is through it jumps down from that high religious plane to a purely humanistic one, with the result that the play seems to be divided against itself.

The present production does nothing to alter one's opinion on those matters. A few changes in the script have been made. Notably, a speech has been added for the character who plays God (Mr. Zuss), in which near the play's conclusion he addresses J. B. directly, urging him to forsake the temptation of suicide, which Satan (Nickles) has just put before him. Zuss urges J. B. to receive the gift of the good life from the hand of God and thus say yes to the inscrutable divine will. As it turns out, J. B. rebuffs both God and Satan. He does start all over again, but it is because he discovers within himself the courage and confidence to do so. He is made to assert that he will never bow to God again.

The effect of these and a few other changes in the closing scene of the play is to make things even clearer than they were before. There is no doubt that the poet wishes us to realize that J. B.'s inner strength is alone the source of his recovery. But there is also no doubt that this makes nonsense of the earlier climax, in which J. B. heard the voice of God out of the whirlwind and repented "in dust and ashes." I cannot help feeling that the play suffers from a sort of theological schizophrenia, and that this becomes a dramatic as well as a theological fault. For after all this is not a play of character but of ideas. As a play of ideas, it is a welcome refreshment in our theater. But to the extent that its ideas are in confusion, it must be adjudged unsuccessful. If MacLeish would not write his secular play as if it were a religious one, and if Graham Greene would stop writing religious plays as if they were secular ones, we might all get somewhere. Greene introduces a thoroughly unbelievable God (usually through a miracle), while MacLeish (by a kind of miracle in reverse) banishes from the stage a God who has been thoroughly visible and thoroughly believable all evening. In the one case you say "Where did He come from?" and in the other you say "Where did He go?" The poor theatergoer begins to feel like a stranded passenger missing trains going in both directions.

As for the production of *J. B.*, it is thoroughly exciting. MacLeish's original idea—to set the action in a circus tent and to have God and Satan played by two run-down actors—was brilliant. If the play is weak dramatically it is strong theatrically. This theatricality Elia Kazan has seized upon and played for all it is worth. By proper restraint he has not played it for more than it is worth. He shows here his ability to handle the stage as a free, plastic playing area—an ability he most notably demonstrated before in Williams' *Camino Real*. From Boris Aronson he has got a setting which combines the sordidness, excitement and mystery of a circus. The central ring is almost in the audience's lap. The trapeze platform on which Zuss (God) stands most of the time is as lofty as heaven. When the giant canvas is lowered the sky backdrop seems to reach to infinity. There being no front curtain, the set is fully visible to the assembling audience.

When the play begins, the house lights do not dim. A circus hand wanders on and begins to fool around with the tent ropes. Another begins to tighten guy wires. A fat lady, whose job it is to help set up the table for Job's family, waddles in about her work. Only gradually, as one is drawn into the stage business, do the house lights fade. Then Zuss and Nickles, balloon and popcorn salesmen, enter down the aisle. We are skillfully drawn from the ANTA theater on 52nd street to the circus tent, then to the play being prepared there, then to the contrasting personalities of the two actors, then to the roles of God and Satan, and finally to heaven and to Satan's wanderings "to and fro upon the earth." It is a masterpiece of theatrical invention, and Kazan has handled it masterfully. As a director, he will probably always be most at home in the semipsychological world of Tennessee Williams; but his essentially symbolic understanding of the stage has never been more advantageously manifest than it is here.

The actors have not let their director nor the audience down. Pat Hingle is surely no one's ideal for the role of Job; his voice has a bit too much southern drawl in it for the character's universality. But if he lacks the heroism the script asks for in the last scenes, he nevertheless has the pathos which the earlier ones require. Raymond Massey is excellent in the role of Zuss. And as the diabolic, cynical Nickles, Christopher Plummer again scores solidly. Agile, arch, both likable and irritating, he carries much of the action on his rascally shoulders. Mr. Plummer should be given a medal for meritorious service, with ribbon for graceful accomplishment.

The Kazan production has changed my mind about one aspect of the play. At Yale, I found the verse hard to listen to. That was not the case here. I am still not certain how good the writing is as poetry. Some dimension of depth and vitality of image is missing. But it is certainly right for the ear in the theater, when properly spoken.

As I left the theater I heard a customer complain: "There was a lot of religion but not much drama." Sorry, sir, but you are mistaken. There is, in final tally, not much religion and not much drama. But there is theater all over the place. And it will hold your interest all evening, and longer. Your discussions of it will probably make more sense than *it* does.

BIBLIOGRAPHY ENTRY FOR RESEARCH PAPERS:

Driver, Tom F. "Notable, Regrettable." *The Christian Century,* January 7, 1959, pp. 21-22. Reprinted in *The Voice out of the Whirlwind: The Book of Job,* ed. Ralph E. Hone. San Francisco, 1960.

FIRST FOOTNOTE:

* Tom F. Driver, "Notable, Regrettable," *The Christian Century,* January 7, 1959, pp. 21-22. Reprinted in *The Voice out of the Whirlwind: The Book of Job,* ed. Ralph E. Hone (San Francisco, 1960), pp. 282-284.

SUBSEQUENT FOOTNOTES:

* Driver, *op. cit., The Voice,* p. ■.
* Driver, "Notable, Regrettable," *The Voice,* p. ■.
* Driver, *The Voice,* p. ■.

In place of *"The Voice,"* "ed. Hone" may be used in these subsequent-footnote forms.

SAMUEL TERRIEN

ON

J. B. and Job

Samuel Terrien, born in France, is a member of the faculty of the Union Theological Seminary. He contributed the introduction and the exegesis for the Book of Job in The Interpreter's Bible. *His review of* J. B. *appeared in the same issue of* The Christian Century *with Dr. Driver's (the one preceding this), on January 7, 1959, at pages 9-11.*

J. B. AND JOB

WHILE Archibald MacLeish's verse drama brilliantly re-creates the tale of Job, the character of J. B. is completely foreign to that of the biblical hero.

[*Headnote to the review*]

HIGH TRIBUTE should be paid to Archibald MacLeish for his audacity in bringing to the stage a subject of biblical magnitude. The verse drama *J. B.,* which opened on Broadway December 11, was first performed last spring at the Yale University school of drama, and was presented during the summer at the Brussels Exposition. Critics have hailed it as "great poetry," "an epic of mankind," "the model from which great poetic drama may hope to follow in our time." Undoubtedly we are witnessing an artistic event, one bound to arouse much discussion in the coming months.

Even when inspired by a classic, any modern play deserves to be judged for itself, standing as an autonomous monument. Nevertheless, since Mr. MacLeish has chosen to present in J. B. the biblical Job in modern dress, a comparison between the two figures is inevitable. Such comparison reveals, at least to this observer, a sharp contrast below the superficial similarity of dramatic situations. While Mr. MacLeish's verse drama is a brilliant re-creation of the *story* of Job, the character of J. B. is completely foreign to that of the hero who speaks in the biblical *poem*.

With a talent that at times is close to genius, the playwright has dramatized the folk tale of the "pious" Job as told in the prose chapters (1 and 2) of the Old Testament book, but he has deliberately ignored or distorted the figure of the "impious" Job which is the focus of the ancient Hebrew poem (3:1-42:6). Of course Mr. MacLeish has a perfect right to do this, but let us not accept this verse drama of his as a faithful interpretation of the scriptural masterpiece.

Psychologically and theologically J. B. stands at the antipodes of Job, and the question is not whether one is more satisfactory to the contemporary mood or mind than the other. The matter at hand is merely the need to recognize the differences. The Joban poet deals with the problem of faith in an evil world, while the author of *J. B.* presents modern man's reaction to the problem of evil without the category of faith in a loving God.

I.

It is easy to agree with MacLeish that the biblical hero is the type of suffering humanity. In the Prologue to the play, Mr. Zuss and Nickles, two aged actors who are now employed in a circus to peddle balloons and popcorn and who play respectively the masks of God and of Satan, soon reveal the poet's concern for the relevance of the Joban story to the contemporary situation.

> MR. ZUSS: Oh, there's always
> Someone playing Job.
> NICKLES: There must be
> Thousands! What's that got to do with it?
> Thousands—not with camels either:
> Millions and millions of mankind
> Burned, crushed, broken, mutilated,
> Slaughtered, and for what? For thinking!
> For walking round the world in the wrong
> Skin, the wrong-shaped noses, eyelids:
> Sleeping the wrong night the wrong city—
> There never could have been so many
> Suffered more for less.

Mr. MacLeish's dramatic inventiveness is such that, as soon as the spotlights are turned on, the circus tent of the set becomes at once the whole world, the world of unexpurgated horror, which is also the world of the 20th century. The most sophisticated theatergoer cannot help entering fully into the tortures of J. B. and of Sarah, his wife, while the news of their son's death, just after the war, is told them by two drunken G.I.'s. As in the biblical story, messengers of woe swiftly come and go. We learn that an automobile accident has killed two more of J. B.'s children, a daughter has been raped and murdered by a psychopath, J. B.'s bank has been destroyed by a bombing in which his last child met death. Finally we witness the breaking down of J. B.'s health, the physical gnawing of his disease, and the desertion of his wife, who cannot endure the sight of his suffering or the burden of her own. All this makes for compelling theater, and the most blasé audience submits to the spell in an almost unbearable experience of empathy.

II.

It would, however, be an error to think that the play presents the poem of Job in contemporary language. For if MacLeish has used the biblical plot with a superlative gift of creativity, showing convincingly that Job is the victim of all the incongruities of existence, he has radically transformed the character of his hero. He has chosen to forget the answer which the Joban poet gave and has substituted for it his own resolution.

In the Hebrew poem Job, unlike the legendary model of resignation, shouts his pride, shrieks his blasphemy and fights with a God who eludes his attacks. He knows much more than physical and moral pain or intellectual bewilderment. He also tastes—and this is his real torture—the cup of bitterest solitude: estrangement not only from men but also from Deity. At times he almost succumbs to the fascination of the void. He penetrates alive into the lower circles of the hell of being and nonbeing. At other times he rises to the stature of a titan, trying to outreach the limits of humanity, believing himself to be more than a man, the incarnation of an anti-God. He accuses God, his enemy, of caprice, sadism, infra-human cruelty. He compares the Deity to a wild beast, a drunken brute, a monster of irresponsibility. He asks,

> Why dost thou take me for a practice target?
> Leave me alone, that I may swallow my spittle!

The Job of the biblical poem is no longer the exemplar of resignation and faith who blesses the name of the Lord (1:21); he demands justice, with a bloody forehead but unbowed knees. He hurls his accusations at his Creator, forgetting that he is a creature, and his last word, at the end of the discussion with his comforters, shows an attitude of unmitigated defiance: "My defense act is signed. Let the Almighty answer me! I shall approach him as a prince [welcomes an equal]!"

By comparison, the J. B. of the modern play is a Job emasculated. Throughout his ordeal J. B. appears as the type of pious convention. His character remains as dormant as the water of a pond, with green scum on its surface. J. B. is merely the diseased victim of fate, who hardly, if ever at all, rises above the level of intellectual stupor and spiritual impassibility.

III.

Of course, any dramatization of the poem of Job must depart from the biblical text, especially from the pattern of discussion between the hero and his three friends. The Oriental didacticism of their lengthy discourses would produce on the stage an effect of unendurable monotony. MacLeish has rightly transformed the biblical "dialogue" by introducing the three friends as spokesmen for three major forces of our culture, psychiatry, political science (strongly tinged by Marxist philosophy) and religion, but he has not succeeded in creating an authentic exchange between the sufferer and his "comforters," with give-and-take and resulting growth for the central character. Unlike their biblical prototypes who subtly blend truth with error, J. B.'s interlocutors are exaggerated caricatures. Unlike Job, J. B. never comes to grips with the insinuations of his adversaries. Consequently he never rises, as Job does, to the stature of a champion, in the manner of the heroes of Sophocles or Shakespeare. He remains a static character, an unconvincing figure of legend, exactly as in the folk tale of chapters 1 and 2.

Incidentally, the passage which in the King James Version reads, "Though he slay me, yet will I trust in him" (13:15), represents a marginal correction by the scribes. The Hebrew manuscripts make Job say, "Behold he will slay me; I have no hope" (R. S. V.)—a statement which is confirmed by the context, "Yet I will defend my ways to his face." MacLeish's J. B. suffers from the taming process which orthodox traditionalism imposed upon the original poem.

Toward the end of his verse drama MacLeish returns unexpectedly to the biblical text by having the Lord's distant voice boom through a public address system:

> Who is this that darkeneth counsel
> By words without knowledge?

While the modern poet thus pays lip service to the words of the Bible, the effect is theologically misleading and psychologically incoherent. Because

J. B. is not a rebel, the intervention of the Lord speaking from the whirlwind appears no longer as the irony of love which creates faith but as a
manifestation of impersonal and senseless power which produces in man
only abject resignation. The repentance of J. B. loses its *raison d'être*
since it does not follow a display of Promethean arrogance.

IV.

For the mystery of divine love which is at the root of human faith,
the dramatist substitutes the motif of human love. He brings J. B.'s wife,
Sarah, back to her husband before she suspects his eventual healing, and
her move represents an act of pure devotion. Obviously, however, she does
not believe that life has any ultimate significance, for her selfless act of
love is not rooted in hope.

In the present Broadway production the playwright has considerably
altered the original ending of the drama. J. B. no longer denies the love of
God, as he did in the printed text. And he is willing to live again, to
accept life with a stoic sort of courage. Nevertheless, the impression remains that the wonder of human love is unrelated to faith in a loving and
suffering God. Man remains on his own. The play becomes in effect a song
of praise for man's unconquerable will.

As the curtain falls one readily admits that the final scene is exquisite.
But a further question must be asked: What is the spring of human love
and what kind of knowledge does it provide? What is it, this force, this
mystery, which prompts a woman like this one to return to the ruins of
her home, from which her children, the fruits of her womb, will be forever absent? What drives her back to her husband, a helpless victim of
a fate which defies human explanation? To be sure, Sarah does not come
back out of self-interest, for J. B. has nothing to offer. He cannot give her
security, material ease, aesthetic thrill, physical passion, romantic fulfillment, intellectual companionship, spiritual comfort. No, not the J. B. of
the play, who is an empty shell, a broken man. Therefore, there is intrinsic
beauty and heroism in Sarah's return. She comes back to him not for herself but for his sake. She comes back to him because she will offer love
to a dying man. She comes back to him because she loves him. Again, what
is this love that expects nothing in return, not even a word or a smile of
gratitude? What is this love that is not related to any frame of eternal
meaning?

In this respect, Mr. MacLeish is not different from other significant
artists of our time. In *Baby Doll, Cat on a Hot Tin Roof, Blue Denim,
Heloise, By Love Possessed*—almost everywhere in novel and drama, we
discover the same wistfulness in the call for human sympathy above and

beyond the mere offering of a cup of tea, the acceptance of self and others, the understanding of those who are different, the overcoming with sweetness of our neighbor's hostility, the melting of our fellow man's aloofness. Our generation has come to sense the need for this simple and sublime reality of existence: *compassion.* But compassion must be positive and a life-giving force, else it means merely sharing another's grief without the strength to overcome misery, heal despondency, transmute despair—to people the cosmic solitude.

V.

There can be a negative communion in sorrow which only generates further hopelessness. In MacLeish's play the hero's wife indeed loves, but her self-giving is still bound by despair. Because in her estimation "The lights have gone out in the sky," there is no principle of duration beyond the present moment. Old age and death, if not tomorrow's weakness, will put an end to her aspirations, in a world that remains empty and a life that is deprived of purpose. The love that MacLeish proposes appears to be noble, but it is noble only on the surface. For it cannot engender victory over the enigma of man's lonely last breath, the ultimate shudder before the open grave. It is a love that dies with the human flesh, for it knows nothing of eternity. It is a sentiment born of man, not of God, and man remains a speck lost in the infinity of space and time. The only God is man's feeling deified, which is a caricature of divinity.

In the playbill of the Yale production, the poet inserted a note which read in part, "It is in man's love that God exists and triumphs." He might have said that we create God when we love. Jean-Paul Sartre, the French existentialist, perhaps on account of his atheism or in spite of it, pinpointed the situation of unfaith when he wrote: "Started from nothing, man finds himself thereby in the obligation, in order to fulfill any kind of human type, to create himself—as a ridiculous divinity, deprived of all the attributes of God."

Many are reluctant to make the affirmation of God's love, and this reluctance perhaps implies a condemnation of those who profess biblical faith without living the love they believe in. In this respect *J. B.* might be considered an indictment of the conventional religionists for their failures. It is not God who needs to be forgiven, as Nickles, the Satanic character, suggests; but rather the avowed admirer of the Bible who miscarries when he attempts to mediate divine love to men.

Let us look again at the Job of the biblical poem. From active participation in universal creativity, he becomes alive in the presence of the Mover of the worlds,

When the morning stars sing together,
and the sons of God shout for joy.

The man left destitute is granted in dynamic contemplation an image of the faithful Creator. A God who cares for man sufficiently to disclose part of his own way of life is a God who is infinitely concerned for the suffering of humanity. There is no love without sharing, and a God who shares his burden with man is a God who suffers. The pathetic concept of Deity is at the center of biblical faith, in the Old Testament as well as in the New. Under the high notes of cosmic transcendence, a De Profundis of God's own agony may be heard. In vain man attempts to penetrate through the scandal of his own existence into the heart of the mystery of being. Yet because the Lord speaks to Job from the whirlwind, and while darkness still shrouds his sight, Job is lifted out of his regard for self and discovers a world of harmony where God himself is at work. As Martin Buber said of Job: "The Absolute Power is, for human personality's sake, become personality. . . . He offers Himself to him as an answer."

This is Israel's vision, inherited by Christianity. Such language may shock 20th century man unless he comes to see that human compassion is a fragile sentiment when it is not rooted in a faith that overcomes the limitations of human nature by reflecting in intelligent, eternal and gracious Power.

BIBLIOGRAPHY ENTRY FOR RESEARCH PAPERS:

Terrien, Samuel. "J. B. and Job." *The Christian Century,* January 7, 1959, pp. 9-11. Reprinted in *The Voice out of the Whirlwind: The Book of Job,* ed. Ralph E. Hone. San Francisco, 1960.

FIRST FOOTNOTE:

* Samuel Terrien, "J. B. and Job," *The Christian Century,* January 7, 1959, pp. 9-11. Reprinted in *The Voice out of the Whirlwind: The Book of Job* (San Francisco, 1960), pp. 286-292.

SUBSEQUENT FOOTNOTES:

* Terrien, *op. cit., The Voice,* p. ■.
* Terrien, "J. B. and Job," *The Voice,* p. ■.
* Terrien, *The Voice,* p. ■.

In place of *"The Voice,"* "ed. Hone" may be used in these subsequent-footnote forms.

HENRY P. VAN DUSEN

ON

J. B. and Job

Henry Pitney Van Dusen, president of the Union Theological Seminary, started his own teaching career in the school he now directs. His views on J. B. were published in The Christian Century *of January 28, 1959, at pages 106-107.*

THIRD THOUGHTS ON J. B.

UNION THEOLOGICAL SEMINARY's president takes issue with the criticisms leveled by two of his faculty members at Archibald MacLeish's drama.

[Headnote to the essay]

IN THE January 7 issue of The Christian Century judgment is passed on Archibald MacLeish's *J.B.* by two of my eminent colleagues on the faculty of Union Seminary: Samuel Terrien, one of the foremost authorities on the biblical book of Job, the author of an admirable study volume on it as well as of the exegesis of Job in *The Interpreter's Bible;* and Tom Driver, certainly one of our ablest and probably the most influential critic of drama in a Christian perspective. Who am I, a mere academic administrator with hardly more competence in the Old Testament than a B.D. graduate and no expertness whatever in drama, to pass judgment on my colleagues' strictures?

It happens that, like Dr. Terrien and Dr. Driver, I saw *J.B.* in both its New Haven and Broadway productions—indeed in the case of Dr. Terrien the same performances. I must confess that I was led to very different conclusions, that both my colleagues' critiques strike me as strangely one-sided, perverse and unconvincing. It would be an exaggeration to say that their evaluations are wholly wrong-headed; each contains sound and valuable comment. But it seems to me that on balance, in the Terrien and Driver *vs.* MacLeish dispute, the latter comes off victor. And since Dr. MacLeish is not available to plead his cause against his accusers, perhaps I may be permitted to venture a few remarks in his defense.

I

Let us begin with the recognition that Mr. MacLeish, or any author who essayed to transpose Job into contemporary terms, confronted not one but two problems. The first is the problem of Job the man, the hapless victim of undeserved and well-nigh insupportable injustices, cruelties, sufferings. But the second and by far the more difficult is the problem posed by the *book* of Job, by the biblical text.

That problem is imposed on the transposer by the guardians of the Bible, the scholars and interpreters who have foisted on generations of devout and credulous readers the belief that the book of Job is *a* book. Had it not been for this orthodox dogma, the ordinary reader would have recognized, centuries before the advent and illumination of higher criticism, that what is set before him in the Bible is not *a* book but *two* books, or rather a magnificent poem encased in and encrusted by a prose introduction and conclusion which not only are obviously from a different hand and a different period and patently on an immeasurably lower spiritual as well as intellectual and literary level, but which also contradict in the most flagrant terms the very meaning and purpose and faith of the poem and go far to negate its message.

No wonder any modern rendering of Job is threatened with inner confusion and self-contradiction; how could it be otherwise if it adheres to its model, since those are precisely the characteristics of the "book" of Job? The enlightened Old Testament scholar of today may disclaim responsibility for the old, misleading interpretation; but there is a sound doctrine of "vicarious penitence," and he would do well to confess at the outset that the most baffling problems posed for wrestlers with Job have been created by his own predecessors.

Dr. MacLeish, following the devout of the ages, has elected to take the book of Job exactly as it stands on the pages of Scripture (not only in the King James Version but also in the Revised Standard Version), without benefit of a footnote or hint as to the true dual character of the "book." Terrien may take MacLeish to task for not portraying the character of the man Job as it is presented in Scripture. But at least MacLeish has been scrupulously faithful to the final resolution of the scriptural Job's problem —restoration twofold, sheep and camels and oxen and she-asses, yes, even sons and daughters. In the judgment of many, this is the greatest weakness in *J.B.*, qualifying much of the play's power. But that weakness—if such it is—results from fidelity to the Bible.

The problem posed by the biblical Job, however, is more difficult than that. Not only do the prose introduction and conclusion stand in direct contradiction to the central poem; the poem itself is not free of ambiguities, inconsistencies and contradictions. Dr. Terrien writes as though there were a single accepted understanding of the poem. As a matter of fact, there is hardly a story in the Bible which has been and is more disputed by equally learned scholars. Terrien has given us one interpretation, his own; but it is by no means universally accepted.

Dr. Terrien's principal charge against Dr. MacLeish is that the playwright's portrait of the man Job is not faithful to the biblical prototype. Why should it be? MacLeish sought to transpose into a contemporary setting the problem of Job—his sufferings and their injustice. This he has accomplished not only with imaginative fidelity but also with nearly insupportable power and poignancy. As Terrien himself testifies, "the most blasé audience submits to the spell in an almost unbearable experience of empathy." The calamities that befall Job, which test credence as the Bible chronicles them, become credible and convincing in *J.B.* But why should J.B. be expected to react to these calamities in slavish imitation of his biblical model? If I understand him, Mr. MacLeish authentically sets forth the response of a very modern man to substantially parallel adversities. And again, his J.B. is far more convincing, as he is certainly vastly more moving, than the incredible Job.

In the same fashion, MacLeish recasts the three "comforters," reversing their roles vis-à-vis the abject sufferer. Whereas Job's "friends" insist upon his guilt against his protestations of innocence, J.B.'s counselors attempt to establish his slavery to circumstance against his insistence on assuming responsibility for his own misfortunes—again, a brilliant and sound translation of the biblical confrontation into the realities of today.

For Mr. Terrien, the real protagonist of Mr. MacLeish's play is Sarah, J.B.'s wife, who rejoins her destitute husband "not for herself but for his sake . . . because she loves him." But I think that is a partial misreading of the text. What Sarah actually says is:

> Yes, I left you.
> I thought there was a way away . . .

But she has discovered that there is none. She returns because she has come to realize that she cannot get along without her husband; she returns for her own sake. No, the play is rightly titled; its hero is J.B. himself.

Lastly, Terrien discovers the solution of Job's problem in "God's love," "an intelligent, eternal and gracious Power." But where is love *gracious* power in a deity whose final word is: "Who is this that darkeneth counsel by words without knowledge? Gird up thy loins like a man: I will demand of thee, and declare thou unto me"? If MacLeish has recourse to human integrity and human love for the answer to J.B.'s need, it is, again, because the biblical Job offers him nothing beyond obeisance before an arbitrary and heartless Cosmic Power.

II

Dr. Driver, expectedly, is especially interested in *J.B.* as drama. In the light of the New York production he has withdrawn some of his severest strictures against the play as he first saw it in New Haven. As he points out, the play has undergone some changes on the way from Yale to Broadway.

The changes are of two kinds. The text has been altered at a few places, mainly by a thorough rewriting of the final scene. In the opinion of most of those who witnessed the two productions, this rewriting has greatly strengthened the conclusion.

The other changes have been wrought by a new director, Elia Kazan. Mr. Driver finds these changes altogether for the good; he becomes almost rhapsodic over Mr. Kazan's "theatricality." My reaction is precisely the reverse. I agree with a correspondent in the *New York Times*: "Elia Kazan has accomplished a directorial tour de force at the expense of *J.B.* . . . . Whatever values he may have added to the acted play are negated by his distortion of Archibald MacLeish's theme."

It would be wearisome to detail this indictment: the gratuitous introduction of scene-setters and prostitutes which are not in the text, the spectacular collapse of the scenery, half a hundred obvious theatrical tricks. The Yale director allowed the play, speaking through MacLeish's inspired text, to make its own way and effect its own impact. Broadway insists on dressing it up with all manner of unnecessary theatrical gadgets and devices, and these go far toward nullifying the play's inherent effectiveness. Driver holds that the play is "weak dramatically" but "strong theatrically." But can there be strong theater except in the portrayal of good drama? Mark up one more count against Broadway's cheap best.

III

From this discussion, three conclusions may perhaps be adduced: First, Archibald MacLeish has given us a drama of heroic proportions and immense suggestiveness, of chastening poignancy and inescapable power. Second, this drama may evoke the most diverse and even opposite responses from people of like presuppositions dwelling within an intimate spiritual community. Third, don't trust any of the interpreters. Don't allow anything to stop you from first reading *J.B.* and then seeing it for yourself.

BIBLIOGRAPHY ENTRY FOR RESEARCH PAPERS:

Van Dusen, Henry Pitney. "Third Thoughts on *J. B.*" *The Christian Century,* January 28, 1959, pp. 106-107. Reprinted in *The Voice out of the Whirlwind: The Book of Job,* ed. Ralph E. Hone. San Francisco, 1960.

FIRST FOOTNOTE:

* Henry Pitney Van Dusen, "Third Thoughts on *J. B.*," *The Christian Century,* January 28, 1959, pp. 106-107, reprinted in *The Voice out of the Whirlwind: The Book of Job,* ed. Ralph E. Hone (San Francisco, 1960), pp. 293-297.

SUBSEQUENT FOOTNOTES:

* Van Dusen, *op. cit., The Voice,* p. ■.
* Van Dusen, "Third Thoughts," *The Voice,* p. ■.
* Van Dusen, *The Voice,* p. ■.

In place of *"The Voice,"* "ed. Hone" may be used in these subsequent-footnote forms.

THE EDITORS OF *LIFE*

ON

J. B. and Job

This unsigned editorial appeared in the magazine Life, *May 18, 1959, at p. 42. In the same issue appeared the opinions of three clergymen which are also printed in this collection as the three selections following this one.*

A FINE PLAY REVEALS A NEED

CONCERNING MacLeish's *J.B.*, we have a question not touched on by our commentators. Does its success indicate any change in America's famous incapacity for great tragic drama?

That incapacity was explored on this page some years ago (*Life*, Dec. 2, 1946). We there defined dramatic tragedy (the art of the greatest Greeks, Shakespeare and few others) as the ennobling spectacle of a great man confronting his own finiteness and being punished for letting his reach exceed his grasp. "Is significant dramatic tragedy possible in a democratic (*i.e.* egalitarian) society?" This question, raised in that editorial, was also the subject of a panel discussion last February at the University of Detroit, before a four-state conference of the intercollegiate literary society Lambda Iota Tau. For texts the students took writings of Playwrights Arthur Miller and the late Maxwell Anderson as well as the *Life* editorial, which had argued that America's faith in human progress, plus our democratic reluctance to heroize human nobility of any kind, were obstacles to the tragic sense.

The Detroit panelists concluded, in general, that the modern American theater has *not* produced significant tragedy, that, although ours is a tragic age, we take ourselves seriously in nontragic ways; but that this is less an American than a 20th Century failing, related to the agnosticism of the age. Thus while the playwrights fared poorly, the *Life* editorial was also declared outdated—particularly since this alert and serious group of undergraduates was so obviously ready to appreciate high tragedy if anyone would write it for them. In fact the executive secretary of Lambda Iota Tau has suggested a new *Life* editorial to be called "Tragic Young America."

This isn't that. Instead we re-examine our earlier theme. Even if the audience is ready, don't American efforts to write serious tragedy still somehow fall short of the classical standards? Why? Two recent efforts bear on the point.

One is *The Ballad of Baby Doe,* the Moore-Latouche opera whose real-life heroine, Baby Doe Tabor, graced *Life's* cover last week. Less than three years old, this opera is established in many critical minds as a real contribution to the classical tradition. The story is a great love triangle and the setting is Colorado silver mining in the '80s and '90s.

Haw Tabor has the attributes of a tragic hero. He was the richest and most powerful man of his time and place and Baby, his bride, was the loveliest filly. There is a great wedding scene in Washington (Tabor was briefly a senator) attended by President Chester A. Arthur, and a wonderful campaign speech of William Jennings Bryan delivered as an aria. The opera ends when Tabor's silver luck runs out and he dies, old and broke, in 1899. But as no Coloradan needs to be reminded, Baby Doe did not die until 1935, older and broker than Tabor and more truly tragic.

She died still guarding the dead Matchless Mine, faithful to his last words: "Hang on to the Matchless!" It took a three-day blizzard to end her 36-year vigil and freeze her on the floor. But the opera scarcely hints at this fabulous fixation, this heroic dedication to an illusion of perpetual riches. Instead its last words are Baby Doe's farewell song to Tabor, declaring that their love has conquered all. The true story was better art than the opera. Good as it is, *Baby Doe* gets off stage too soon as a mere love story, and is therefore a case of American evasiveness when confronted with a genuinely tragic theme.

Now about *J.B.* This exciting play deals audaciously with those eternal problems of life, death, the meaning of suffering and the existence of God, which this generation of Americans has become most eager to take seriously. If only for that reason (and there are others) *J.B.* is a welcome enlargement of the dimensions of the American theater.

J.B. can be considered either as a human drama or as a "theodicy" (an explanation of God). As a theodicy, the play requires the fuller explanation, which MacLeish has elsewhere given, of how he sees God's conflict with Satan and man's role therein. "In the struggle between good and evil," says MacLeish, "God stakes his supremacy as God upon man's fortitude and love. . . . Man depends on God for all things; God depends on man for one," that one being man's love freely and unreasoningly given. This might be called a proto-Christian theodicy.

Now consider *J.B.* as a human drama. The hero is denied the one thing he thinks he needs most: a clear explanation of his sufferings from God. The play is therefore a formal tragedy. But it is not a complete tragedy, for the catharsis is blurred by an ambiguous, humanistic ending. Instead of answers, J.B. gets his wife back and a chance at a fresh start. The love they "blow on" is not divine love; it is pathetic, not transcendent. Thus the ending is too biological for good theodicy; and also a little too cozy for good tragedy. Is there a touch of that same escapism that spoils the end of *Baby Doe?*

Ever since Matthew Arnold marked the ebb of faith in *Dover Beach,* artists have used romantic love as a handy solvent for man's philosophical dilemmas. But it is not so much a solvent as a way of changing the subject. Our dramatists seem incapable either of sticking to the stark tragic line that withholds this balm, or of transmuting the balm into the genuine solvent of divine love. The undergraduates at Detroit may well have put their finger on the reason for this incapacity: the agnosticism of the age, an age interested in God but still remote from him. The ambiguity of *J.B.* reflects this ambiguity of the age. But by opening the question it may somewhat lessen our remoteness from God, and bring us closer to the day when Americans can confront the tragic aspects of their existence with ennobling humility instead of evasion.

||||||||||||||||||||||||||||||||||||||||||||||||||||||||||||||||||||||||||||||||||||||||||||||||||||||||||||||||||||||||||||||||||||||||||||||||||||||||||||||||||||||||||||

BIBLIOGRAPHY ENTRY FOR RESEARCH PAPERS:

"A Fine Play Reveals a Need." Editorial, *Life,* May 18, 1959, p. 42. Reprinted in *The Voice out of the Whirlwind: The Book of Job,* ed. Ralph E. Hone. San Francisco, 1960.

This entry might be worded, "Fine Play Reveals a Need, A." In either wording, the alphabetical position is at "Fine."

FIRST FOOTNOTE:

* "A Fine Play Reveals a Need," editorial, *Life,* May 18, 1959, p. 42, reprinted in *The Voice out of the Whirlwind: The Book of Job,* ed. Ralph E. Hone (San Francisco, 1960), pp. 298-300.

SUBSEQUENT FOOTNOTES:

   * "A Fine Play," *The Voice,* p. ■.

In place of *"The Voice,"* "ed. Hone" may be used in this subsequent-footnote form.

REINHOLD NIEBUHR

ON

J. B. and Job

||||||||||||||||||||||||||||||||||||||||||||||||||||||||||||||||||||||||||||||||||||||||||||||||||||||||||||||||||||||||||||||||||||||||||||||

Reinhold Niebuhr, often considered America's leading Protestant theologian, contributed this article on J.B. *to the magazine* Life, *May 18, 1959, pages 135, 137.*

MODERN ANSWERS TO AN ENIGMA

IN *J.B.*, Archibald MacLeish has undertaken a difficult task. He attempts to answer searching questions about the meaninglessness of extreme human suffering. He concentrates on whether this suffering accords with the idea that God is "just," and expresses the ancient enigma of God's power and goodness in these words: "If God is God He is not good. If God is good He is not God." It is a perennial moral and religious problem.

MacLeish owes his dramatic success both to the honesty with which he states the problem and to the artistic ingenuity with which he fits his modern play into the old framework. Much of the original story as told in the Bible is devoted to long dialogues between Job and his "comforters," all of whom give conventional answers to Job's rather unconventional, and searching, faith and doubt. MacLeish has artfully transformed these comforters into a determinist (perhaps a Communist) who thinks the triumph of "humanity" makes an individual's suffering sufferable, a sophisticated man (perhaps a psychiatrist) who tries to reduce Job's sense of guilt to a neurosis, and a religious stereotype (perhaps a clergyman) who thinks that the idea that all men are guilty is enough to explain the unique sufferings of a particular human being. The last "comforter" represents only one aspect of religion. Modern believers may find his answer grotesque, but he does resemble one of the original comforters.

The Book of Job itself is apparently based on an even older folk tale, a tale in which the devil suggests that Job's piety is due to his prosperity. So God allows the devil to "try" Job by harassing him with every kind of disaster. In the popular concept of Job, that is the heart of the matter—and MacLeish cannot be blamed if he bases most of his drama on it. But by his emphasis on the question of meaningless suffering, the modern poet neglects the ancient book's even more searching question about the meaning of life and thus its even more important "message" to modern man.

This is the puzzle of human existence raised by the sharp contrast between man's greatness and his insignificance. As Job 7:17, 18 puts it: "What is man, that Thou dost make so much of him, and that Thou dost set Thy mind upon him, dost visit him every morning, and test him every moment?" This is not only an even deeper problem than that of meaningless suffering but one more poignantly relevant to an atomic age which has the greatness to discover nuclear energy but lacks the wisdom to avoid the risk of nuclear war. MacLeish neglects this vital dimension of the original.

Like the Book of Job itself, the modern play does provide two answers to the problem of life. Though MacLeish himself evidently does not believe in a personal God, he faithfully echoes the first answer given in the original. God appears to Job in a "whirlwind" and confronts him with all the mysteries of creation to prove that there is a meaning to life beyond that which any mere man can provide from his own limited perspective. The biblical Job admits (42:3-6): "Therefore I have uttered what I did not understand, things too wonderful for me, which I did not know. . . . Therefore I despise myself, and I repent in dust and ashes." Some modern critics of religion say that the whirlwind was simply an immoral display of power on God's part instead of a specific reply to Job's anguished query. Such a criticism assumes there *is* a rational answer to all the many tragic contradictions of human life. While apparently not a theist or believer in God, MacLeish clearly does not agree with this form of agnosticism. He lets the ancient answer stand in full force and majesty.

MacLeish's second answer combines a courageous acceptance and affirmation of life with a modern romantic emphasis on love, shown by Job's reconciliation with his wife. Thus an "island of love" is created as an island of meaning in an existence threatened by no meaning. Some find MacLeish's second answer a sentimental anticlimax. In a sense it is. But it can be said that MacLeish is more adequate than the parallel second answer in the Bible—taken from the original folk story—where Job is promised the return of his wife, many new children and all the camels and she-asses his heart desires. For this materialistic conclusion, from the ancient folk tale, rather begs the question. The Bible ending is a distinct letdown from the lofty poetic treatment of eternal mysteries which has made the bulk of the Book of Job so fascinating to its readers for more than 2,000 years.

BIBLIOGRAPHY ENTRY FOR RESEARCH PAPERS:

Niebuhr, Reinhold. "Modern Answers to an Enigma." *Life,* May 18, 1959, pp. 135, 137. Reprinted in *The Voice out of the Whirlwind: The Book of Job,* ed. Ralph E. Hone. San Francisco, 1960.

FIRST FOOTNOTE:

* Reinhold Niebuhr, "Modern Answers to an Enigma," *Life,* May 18, 1959, pp. 135, 137, reprinted in *The Voice out of the Whirlwind: The Book of Job,* ed. Ralph E. Hone (San Francisco, 1960), pp. 302-304.

SUBSEQUENT FOOTNOTES:

* Niebuhr, *op. cit., The Voice,* p. ■.
* Niebuhr, "Modern Answers," *The Voice,* p. ■.
* Niebuhr, *The Voice,* p. ■.

In place of *"The Voice,"* "ed. Hone" may be used in these subsequent-footnote forms.

LOUIS FINKELSTEIN

ON

J. B. and Job

Louis Finkelstein, of the faculty of the Jewish Theological Seminary in New York, contributed this article to the magazine Life, *May 18, 1959, at pages 135, 137, 138.*

INSIGHT INTO OUR DEEP NEED

WHAT IS most startling about MacLeish's distinguished play is its success as a Broadway production. A moralistic fable, based on the most difficult and perplexing book in Scriptures, attracts crowds in numbers usually expected only at musical comedies. Obviously *J.B.* answers a deep need. What is it?

The play conveys, of course, the unspoken agony of a generation which, having witnessed the most horrible war in history, fears even more horrible catastrophes. No doubt, too, it conveys the private agony of the American in our times, who seems to have everything but really finds himself having nothing.

But the special appeal and effectiveness of *J.B.*, it seems to me, stems from the fact that ours is a Job-minded and Job-hearted generation. This is the unique discovery of MacLeish, the poet. In the character of J.B. he has created a symbol in which we see ourselves and our society, troubled and guilt-ridden.

In MacLeish's view one of our greatest problems is our failure to find any purpose in the sufferings of our time. Neither as individuals nor as a community can we rise to the heights of prophecy, envisioning a future different from our own in quality of life rather than in quantity of comforts. We have no Isaiahs portraying a true Kingdom of God which could justify our suffering. We do not see ourselves in childbirth, almost delighting in pain as part of creation. We are not even a praying generation which, although deaf to the divine word, might yet seek the inspiration and vision needed for prophecy.

Instead we are rather like Job, who never prays to God in his distress, who never contemplates the future except hopelessly in adversity and, says MacLeish, smugly in prosperity.

We are not, of course, dumb beasts. We try to explain our torment. But being neither prophets nor men of prayer, we rivet its explanation to the past, blaming it on either our folly or our guilt. And because the last thing in the world we can admit of ourselves is folly, we are led to confess our guilt.

MacLeish, speaking through J.B., dismisses the three comforters familiar to us—the historian, the psychoanalyst and the theologian. Yet he does not leave man comfortless. One comforter, unseen but felt throughout the play, is MacLeish himself. The comfort he offers is obviously the theme of the play. As poet, scholar and teacher, MacLeish is singularly equipped for this role. He knows the pangs of creation, the torment of seeking a vision, of trying to instruct. Like J.B.'s wife he does not complain at the pain of creation. He sympathizes with and understands the woman who, anesthetized just before childbirth, regrets her unconsciousness during the great miracle.

The character in the Book of Job with whom MacLeish apparently identifies himself is Elihu. Elihu does not appear in the play, but his point of view is always in evidence. In the Bible, Elihu is young, whereas the three comforters are old. Elihu recognizes that age, for all its maturity and experience, may miss the whole point of life, which is concern with the future. He is convinced that whether or not Job has transgressed before he suffered, he certainly transgressed *during* his suffering: he did not welcome the pain, as would a dedicated servant of God, a soldier in the armies of the Creator, one who is indeed part of the Creator. If Job could see life as a school and experience as instruction, he might be glad for the opportunity to study in this supremely demanding way under the guidance of a supremely demanding teacher. The conquests of the Mt. Everests of the spirit may be arduous, but the reward like the effort is of supreme worth.

In the biblical story Elihu therefore calls upon Job to do the one thing that has not occurred to him: pray. He demands that Job transform his pain into a means of obtaining a new vision of God, one not possible except in adversity. He wants Job to emerge a greater man because he has had the experience needed to make him creative as well as blessed.

Both Elihu and the MacLeish play, for all their apparent concern with a specific human drama, are preoccupied with the *universal* agony of man. They leave out of account such awful sufferings as the death of babes, such horrors as the death of millions in the gas chambers of Dachau and Auschwitz. To be sure, God asserts that such sufferings also have meaning, but it is a meaning that transcends the mind of man. To probe them completely man would have to be part of God while still mortal. He would have to recognize, clearly, his own soul and its relation to God. In the end Job apparently discovers the nature of this mystery, a first step to transcending it. "I had heard of Thee by hearing," he finally says, "and now mine eye seeth Thee."

Yet the vision remains blurred, as it might be through a murky glass. Job knows what has happened to him but not why it could not happen without pain. He is grateful for his new children but cannot explain the death of the first ones.

For all the beauty and depth of his insight, MacLeish accepts this blurred vision as all that is available to mortal man. The vision of the Kingdom of God, awaiting a purified, ennobled and exalted humanity, remains outside *J.B.* as it remains beyond Job. One feels that it does not remain outside MacLeish, and one hopes that he will return to it.

BIBLIOGRAPHY ENTRY FOR RESEARCH PAPERS:

Finkelstein, Louis. "Insight into Our Deep Need." *Life,* May 18, 1959, pp. 135, 137, 138. Reprinted in *The Voice out of the Whirlwind: The Book of Job,* ed. Ralph E. Hone. San Francisco, 1960.

FIRST FOOTNOTE:

* Louis Finkelstein, "Insight into Our Deep Need," *Life,* May 18, 1959, pp. 135, 137, 138, reprinted in *The Voice out of the Whirlwind: The Book of Job,* ed. Ralph E. Hone (San Francisco, 1960), pp. 305-307.

SUBSEQUENT FOOTNOTES:

* Finkelstein, *op. cit., The Voice,* p. ■.
* Finkelstein, "Insight," *The Voice,* p. ■.
* Finkelstein, *The Voice,* p. ■.

In place of *"The Voice,"* "ed. Hone" may be used in these subsequent-footnote forms.

THURSTON N. DAVIS

ON

J. B. and Job

Thurston N. Davis, S.J., editor of the Catholic publication America, *contributed this article to the magazine* Life, *May 18, 1959, at pages 135, 138.*

ARID REPUDIATION OF RELIGION

MOST OF the people who see *J.B.* make the quite natural mistake of judging Archibald MacLeish's play to be about God. As a matter of fact, it isn't at all. *J.B.* is about Man—Man liberated from old theologies, Man obsessed with the notion that, as the final lines of the play have it,

> The candles in churches are out.
> The lights have gone out in the sky.

Despite the fact that these and many other clues to its real meaning are scattered through the final five minutes of the MacLeish drama, night after night many members of the *J.B.* audience pick up their coats and rubbers at closing time and move in solemn and reverent procession out of the theater, acting for all the world as though they have been attending a revival or making a mission. But what they have just witnessed is not a religious drama or a morality play. If *J.B.* means anything, it is an urbane but shallow repudiation of religious faith. On the positive side *J.B.* tries hard in its closing moments to become a secular affirmation of human life and human love as the sole props and rationale of bewildered humanity.

Long ago Professor MacLeish wrote in *Ars Poetica:* "A poem should not mean/But be." Doubtless he would in some sense claim the same prerogative for his play. But a play must ultimately mean something, and *J.B.,* if it delivers any message at all, certainly does so in the brief muted exchange just before the curtain. J.B.'s wife Sarah says to him at the end: "Then blow on the coal of the heart, my darling." And when our modern, suburban Job echoes: "The coal of the heart . . ." Sarah says: "It's all the light now."

Years ago, as a college student, I read and have since remembered Mr. MacLeish's sonnet called *The End of the World,* which was published in 1926. The sonnet tells how the top of an immense and crowded circus tent [the lid of the world in the poet's image] blew off quite unexpectedly in the middle of a three-ring performance [the poet's figure for the turmoil of human life]. The sonnet's sestet tells what happened then:

And there, there overhead, there, there, hung over
Those thousands of white faces, those dazed eyes,
There in the starless dark the poise, the hover,
There with vast wings across the canceled skies,
There in the sudden blackness the black pall
Of nothing, nothing, nothing—nothing at all.

Having read the *J.B.* script and seen the play itself on two occasions, I am sure that Mr. MacLeish's controversial drama about God, Man, sin, guilt and the meaning of human life and suffering is being acted under the same old canvas top that blew off in his sonnet 33 years ago. Moreover, the play comes to approximately the same conclusion as the sonnet.

The scene of *J.B.* is laid in "a corner inside an enormous circus tent where a side show of some kind has been set up." And when, in a sense, the top goes blowing off in the last five minutes of the play, it is quite obvious that the God who has been "bull-whipping" our contemporary Job with his thundering, amplified pronouncements suddenly becomes, in Mr. MacLeish's hands, about as meaningless as the mask worn by Mr. Zuss, the old balloon vendor who plays the role and speaks the lines of God. If *J.B.* "means" anything, it means that the God of the Job story—He who commands the morning, enters into the springs of the sea and binds the sweet influences of the Pleiades—gets told off and sent ingloriously to the wings by Man, the eternal J.B. of history.

Are there divine "reasons" for human pain? Is there at last a Justice that will set things right? Is there a Mind and a Providence at work in human affairs? Is Man enveloped by God's Love? If I read and hear him aright, MacLeish is saying No. The play ends with the firm avowal that—apart from our sempiternal human urge to "blow on the coal of the heart" —there is really "nothing, nothing, nothing—nothing at all." The old image of the traveling circus apparently still haunts Mr. MacLeish. But the circus hasn't been traveling anywhere in all the intervening years. It still stands on the same arid ground in which he pegged down his tents some 30 years ago.

BIBLIOGRAPHY ENTRY FOR RESEARCH PAPERS:

Davis, Thurston N. "Arid Repudiation of Religion." *Life,* May 18, 1959, pp. 135, 138. Reprinted in *The Voice out of the Whirlwind: The Book of Job,* ed. Ralph E. Hone. San Francisco, 1960.

FIRST FOOTNOTE:

* Thurston N. Davis, "Arid Repudiation of Religion," *Life,* May 18, 1959, pp. 135, 138, reprinted in *The Voice out of the Whirlwind: The Book of Job,* ed. Ralph E. Hone (San Francisco, 1960), pp. 308-310.

SUBSEQUENT FOOTNOTES:

* Davis, *op. cit., The Voice,* p. ■.
* Davis, "Arid Repudiation," *The Voice,* p. ■.
* Davis, *The Voice,* p. ■.

In place of *"The Voice,"* "ed. Hone" may be used in these subsequent-footnote forms.

A SELECTED BIBLIOGRAPHY

THE LITERATURE on the Book of Job is so extensive that the compiler of a selected bibliography must be merely one voice out of the whirlwind. The principle governing the following selection complies with the primary focus of the readings collected in this volume, namely, the Book of Job as a *literary* work. There are, therefore, two assumptions made by the compiler: the first is that every student will want to consult for himself standard general reference works, including *The Catholic Encyclopedia, The Jewish Encyclopedia, The Universal Jewish Encyclopedia, A Dictionary of the Bible,* and the Schaff-Herzog *Encyclopedia of Religious Knowledge* (all of which contain good bibliographies); the second assumption is that the student will wish to consult some of the voluminous commentaries, critical, homiletical, and exegetical, on the Book of Job which frequently address themselves to the literary aspects of the work. Supported by these assumptions, I have not included the standard reference works in religion or many general commentaries. My experience of reading sermonic literature related to the Book of Job has been so unrewarding that I have decided to include no sermons in the bibliography.

Charles F. Aked. *The Divine Drama of Job.* Edinburgh: T. & T. Clark, 1913.

Edward Chauncey Baldwin. "The Drama." *Types of Literature in the Old Testament.* New York: Thomas Nelson and Sons, 1929.

C. J. Ball. *The Book of Job: A Revised Text and Version.* Oxford: Clarendon Press, 1922.

Julius A. Bewer. "The Wisdom Literature." *The Literature of the Old Testament.* New York: Columbia University Press, 1947.

The Book of Job, from the Translation Prepared at Cambridge in 1611 for King James I, with a Preface by Mary Ellen Chase and Illustrations by Arthur Szyk. New York: Limited Editions Club, 1946.

Charles Reynolds Brown. *The Strange Ways of God. A Study in the Book of Job.* Boston: The Pilgrim Press, 1908.

Moses Buttenwieser. *The Book of Job.* New York: Macmillan, 1922.

Mary Ellen Chase. "The Book of Job." *The Bible and the Common Reader.* Rev. ed. New York: The Macmillan Company, 1952.

G. K. Chesterton. "The Book of Job." *G. K. C. as M. C.* London: Methuen & Co., Ltd., 1929.

Margaret Crook. *The Cruel God.* Boston: Beacon Press, 1959.

Charles Allen Dinsmore. "Biblical Poetry." *The English Bible as Literature.* Boston: Houghton Mifflin Co., 1931.

Samuel Rolles Driver and George Buchanan Gray, *A Critical and Exegetical Commentary on the Book of Job together with a New Translation.* 2 vols. New York: Charles Scribner's Sons, 1921. [The International Critical Commentary]

H. L. Ellison. *From Tragedy to Triumph: The Message of the Book of Job.* Grand Rapids, Mich.: Wm. B. Eerdmans, 1958.

Henry Thatcher Fowler. "The Great Masterpiece, Job." *A History of the Literature of Ancient Israel.* New York: Macmillan, 1912. [Reprinted in Mary Esson Reid, ed. *The Bible Read as Literature.* Cleveland: Howard Allen, Inc., 1959.]

John F. Genung. *The Epic of the Inner Life.* Boston: Houghton Mifflin Co., 1891.

R. Gordis. "The Conflict of Tradition and Experience: The Book of Job." R. M. MacIver, ed. *Great Moral Dilemmas in Literature, Past and Present.* New York: Institute for Religious and Social Studies, 1956.

R. Gordis. "The Temptation of Job—Tradition versus Experience in Religion." *Judaism,* IV (1955), 195-208.

Alex R. Gordon. *The Poets of the Old Testament.* New York: Hodder and Stoughton, 1912.

Emily S. Hamblen. *The Book of Job Interpreted; Illustrated with the Designs of William Blake.* New York: Delphic Studios, 1939.

Anthony and Miriam Hanson. *The Book of Job: Introduction and Commentary.* London: SCM Press, Ltd., 1953.

James Hastings, ed. *The Great Texts of the Bible, Job to Psalm XXIII.* New York: Charles Scribner's Sons, 1913.

C. G. Jung. *Answer to Job.* Trans., R. F. C. Hull. London: Routledge & Kegan Paul, 1954.

H. M. Kallen. *The Book of Job as a Greek Tragedy.* New York: Moffat, Yard & Co., 1918.

Emil G. Kraeling. *The Book of the Ways of God.* New York: Charles Scribner's Sons, 1939.

Abraham L. Lassen, trans. *The Commentary of Levi Ben Gersom (Gersonides) on the Book of Job.* New York: Block Publishing Co., 1946.

Archibald MacLeish. *J. B. A Play in Verse.* Boston: Houghton Mifflin Co., 1956.

John Milton. "The Reason of Church Government." F. A. Patterson *et al.,* ed. *The Works of John Milton* [Columbia Edition]. New York: Columbia University Press, 1931.

John Milton. *Paradise Regained.* London, 1671. Book I, 130-136, 140-149, 357-382, 402-426; Book III, 43, 60-70, 95.

John Milton. *Paradise Lost.* London, 1674. Book I.

Richard G. Moulton, ed. "The Book of Job, a Dramatic Poem Framed in Epic Story." *The Modern Reader's Bible.* New York: Macmillan, 1952.

Richard G. Moulton. "The Book of Job: and the Various Kinds of Literary Interest Illustrated by It." *The Literary Study of the Bible.* London: Isbister and Co., 1900.

L. S. Portor. "Book of Job." *Greatest Books in the World.* Boston: Houghton Mifflin Co., 1913.

James B. Pritchard, ed. *Ancient Near Eastern Texts Relating to the Old Testament.* Princeton: Princeton University Press, 1950. "The Protest of the Eloquent Peasant," tr. John A. Wilson, pp. 407-410; an Egyptian text dating from the Middle Kingdom. "I Will Praise the Lord of Wisdom," tr. Robert H. Pfeiffer, pp. 434-437; the so-called Babylonian Job. "A Dialogue about Human Misery," tr. Robert H. Pfeiffer, pp. 438-440; Samuel Terrien in *The Interpreter's Bible* expresses a belief that this Babylonian text allows "the hypothesis of an influence upon Job."

Francis Quarles. "On Iobs Temptations." *Divine Fancies,* pp. 84-85. London, 1632.

Francis Quarles. *Emblemes.* London, 1635. pp. 140-151, 168-175.

Rossiter W. Raymond. *The Book of Job: Essays and a Metrical Paraphrase.* New York: D. Appleton and Co., 1878.

Sister M. Genevieve. "Job; a Drama: The Battle of the Soul." *Catholic Educational Review,* XXIX (1931), 345-348.

Richard B. Sewall, "The Book of Job," *The Vision of Tragedy* (New Haven: Yale University Press, 1959).

William Barron Stevenson. *The Poem of Job, a Literary Study with a New Translation.* London: Oxford University Press, 1947. [The Schweich Lectures of the British Academy, 1943]

Samuel Terrien. *Job: Poet of Existence.* Indianapolis: Bobbs-Merrill, 1957.

Alfred Walls. *The Oldest Drama in the World: The Book of Job Arranged in Dramatic Form with Elucidations.* New York: Hunt & Eaton, 1891.

SELECTED TOPICS FOR
RESEARCH PAPERS

Brief Annotated Papers (500 words)
The Authorship of Job
The Date of Composition of Job
The Character of Job (or Job's Wife; One of Job's Friends; Satan;
God)
The Theme of One of the Interpretations of Job

Larger Papers (1000 words)
The Biblical Portrayal of the Character of Job Compared to the Job
Figure in One of the Interpretations
A Comparison of Two Sermons on Job: Their Themes, Style, and
Tone
An Artist's Interpretation of the Story of Job
The Character of Satan in the Book of Job and in an Adaptation of
the Book of Job
Comparison of the Views of a Historian and a Philosopher on the
Book of Job
"Sources" of Job
Was Job Patient?

Full-Length Papers (2500-4000 words)
The Literary Form of the Book of Job
The Idea of Justice Posed by the Book of Job
The Uses of Adversity
A Comparison of Job in the Bible with Job in Adaptations
Job and *Prometheus Bound* (or *Oedipus at Colonus,* or *King Lear*)

DOCUMENTING YOUR RESEARCH PAPER

*Footnotes and Bibliography***

THE READER of your research paper expects to find in it both your work and an accounting of the sources from which you have drawn your information. This accounting is your documentation. It is also your thanks, or at least your acknowledgment, to any people whose writings or other works have furnished you the information that you have organized into your paper.

Whether as thanks or as report of sources, your documentation must be explicit and specific. It must tell your reader where you found your information so that he can, if he wishes, appraise your sources, perhaps go to them himself and see whether you have conveyed their facts faithfully or reasoned soundly from them.

All of your sources are listed together in a bibliography at the end of your paper; this is *general* documentation. Any source you cite is named at the point where you cite it, usually in a footnote; this is *specific* documentation.

Most of your sources will be books or magazine articles, aside from the selections in this book.

DOCUMENTATION REFERRING TO A BOOK

A bibliography entry for a book will be organized thus:

May, Rollo. *Man's Search for Himself*. New York, 1953.

Period	Period	Comma Period
Name of the author, surname first for alphabetizing.	Title of book, in italic type or underscored to indicate that it is a publication.	City and year of publication. The name of the publisher may appear between the city and the date.

First line begins at margin; if there is a second line, indent it 5 spaces.

---

* Prepared for the series by the general editor of Howard Chandler, Publisher.

The footnote for a citation from this book would be organized thus:

[1] Rollo May, *Man's Search for Himself* (New York, 1953), pp. 223-224.

Comma	Paren- thesis	Paren- thesis Comma Comma
Index (num- ber or aster- isk). Period	Name of author, in normal order, as footnotes are not alphabetized.	Title of book, in italic type or under- scored to indicate that it is a publication.	City and year of publication.

Numbers of pages that contain the information documented. Some people prefer to omit the abbreviation "pp."

First line of footnote indented as paragraph; second line at margin.

The order of the items in this information, the use of the index mark (raised number or asterisk), the punctuation, the parentheses, and the use of italic or underscores are customs that spare a writer the labor of writing many words and his reader some quantity of reading. The footnote would otherwise have to be something like:

This information comes from pages 223-224 of a book by Rollo May, entitled *Man's Search for Himself,* published in New York in 1953.

If you name the publisher of a book, the forms for bibliography and footnote are:

May, Rollo. *Man's Search for Himself.* New York, W. W. Norton & Company, 1953.

[1] Rollo May, *Man's Search for Himself* (New York: W. W. Norton & Company, 1953), pp. 223-224.

DOCUMENTATION REFERRING TO A PLAY

Any citation of a play almost necessarily refers to it as published in a book. Accordingly you cite a play as you would a book. To specify the location of a passage, the page number may be sufficient. But it may be more useful to give act, scene, and if possible line numbers. Hence:

Shakespeare, William. *The Tragedy of Coriolanus,* ed. William Allan Neilson. New York, 1906.

[1] William Shakespeare. *The Tragedy of Coriolanus,* ed. William Allan Neilson (New York, 1906), Act IV, Sc. vii, lines 2-3.

DOCUMENTATION REFERRING TO A MAGAZINE ARTICLE

If your source is a magazine article, your bibliography entry might read:

Kirstein, Lincoln. "The Future of American Opera," *Atlantic* 199:3 (March, 1957), pp. 50-55.

Comma	Period		Comma	
Name of author, surname first.	Title of article, in quotation marks to indicate that it is not a separate publication.		Name of magazine, in italic type or underscored to indicate that it is a publication.	Volume and number.

	Comma	Period
Issue, in parentheses.	Page numbers of the entire article.	

First line begins at margin; second and subsequent lines indented 5 spaces.

Your footnote to this magazine article as your source might read:

[1] Lincoln Kirstein, "The Future of American Opera," *Atlantic* 199:3 (March, 1957), p. 54.

	Comma		Comma	
Index (number or asterisk).	Name of author, in normal order.	Title of article in quotation marks.	Name of magazine, italic or underscored.	Volume and number.

	Comma	Period
Issue, in parentheses.	Page number to which the footnote refers.	

First line of footnote indented as paragraph; second line at margin.

As is documentation from books, documentation from magazines is made briefer and less laborious by the customs of word order and punctuation.

DOCUMENTATION REFERRING TO A NEWSPAPER ARTICLE

Citations from newspapers cannot be so precise as citations from books or magazines, since many newspapers have several editions in a day and the same article may appear on different pages in different editions; even more troublesome, it may be rewritten, reheaded, or dropped in later editions, and it may not appear in the early editions of a given date.

A bibliography entry concerning a newspaper might therefore appear thus:

"State to Up Vet Home Loan Rate," *San Francisco Chronicle,* Sept. 17, 1959. Dated Sacramento, Sept. 16.

The corresponding footnote might be:

[1] "State to Up Vet Home Loan Rate," *San Francisco Chronicle,* Sept. 17, 1959; dated Sacramento, Sept. 16.

If the writer of this newspaper article were named, his name would precede the title of the article in both the bibliography entry and the footnote. If the story were sent to the *Chronicle* by a news service, such as United Press International or Associated Press, this fact should appear in parentheses at the end of both bibliography and footnote, in full or abbreviated:

. . . Sept. 16 (United Press International).
. . . Sept. 16 (UPI).

THE ESSENTIAL IN DOCUMENTATION

Information comes to the writer from so many sources that specimen bibliography entries and footnotes for all possible needs would overflow any book. So it is necessary to keep in mind the basic reason for documenting: namely, to give the source of a statement so it can be appraised, and located, by the reader. These are basic, though some other details may be put into the documentation.

If your bibliography entries and footnotes answer the following questions, they will be satisfactory:

1. *Who?* Who is the author who made the statement? What individual, collaborating group, or institution is the author? Or is the statement published in a work that does not identify the author?
2. *In what publication?* What book, magazine article, newspaper story, speech, broadcast program, or other? At exactly what point in this work? (Can a reader find your citation, from what the documentation tells him?)
3. *When and whence?* In what city and in what year was the book published? On what date was the periodical published?

The next sections contain numerous models for footnotes and bibliography entries, but all are guided by these three principles. Since almost every research project will require documentation referring to some source not covered by a model, you need to perceive the principles as they are demonstrated in the models.

EXAMPLES OF BIBLIOGRAPHY ENTRIES

The entries in a bibliography are ordinarily arranged in alphabetical order, as these examples are. To help in comparing them with corresponding footnotes, the footnote examples (pages 253-256) are numbered in series and the explanatory remark that follows each bibliography entry gives the number of the footnote.

Baker, Charles T. "Patients' Perceptions of Psychologists." Unpublished master's thesis, Ohio State University, 1953. [An unpublished doctor's dissertation or other research paper would be treated in this same way. See footnote 18.]

Boddy, Francis M., *et al. Applied Economic Analysis.* New York, 1948. [This book has six authors. If only one author card is carried in a library catalogue for it, the card will be in the name of the senior author, here given. See footnote 3 and pages 329-330 of this book.]

Bowman, Isaiah. *The New World.* 4th ed., Yonkers and Chicago, 1928. [An often revised book in political geography; marked differences between editions make it important to specify the edition used, as here. See footnote 6.]

Brahms, Johannes. *Concerto No. 2 in B Flat Major for Piano.* Alexander Uninsky, piano; Willem van Oterloo conducting The Hague Philharmonic Orchestra. Epic LC-3303, 1958. [For some purposes it might be unnecessary to identify the musicians presented on a phonograph record, but the information usually is significant. The record number and the "publisher" appear on the record label. See footnote 23.]

Doe, John. "Indexing of Dissertations." Paper read at methodology seminar, —— University, October 19, 1962. In —— University Library. [If this paper were not in a library and you were citing from your notes, you would write instead, "Notes of reading," or something of the sort. See footnote 19.]

Dumas, Alexandre, fils. Letter to Joseph Méry, Oct. 18, 1844. Unpublished. Collection of Simone André-Maurois. [Letters of famous men often are microfilmed for study, even if not published. If you use a microfilm letter, mention it; as, "Microfilm in —— Library." See footnote 20.]

"The Good ex-President." *Time,* 74:14 (Oct. 5, 1959), p. 34. [A magazine article published without the author's name. It is therefore alphabetized according to its title, ignoring "The." See footnote 14.]

Gunther, John. "Inside Space." *John Gunther's High Road,* American Broadcasting Company (WABC-TV), Oct. 17, 1959. [A broadcast program in a series. The same form could be used for either radio or television. The station call letters and date might be enough in addition to the program name and the name of its "author." If no author, alphabetize on the program name. See footnote 26.]

Joyce, James. *Finnegan's Wake.* Folkways Records, FDF934, 1956. Tape. [It might be unnecessary to write "Tape," but may be useful. See footnote 25.]

Keats, John. *The Complete Poetical Works and Letters of John Keats,* [ed. Horace E. Scudder]. Cambridge, Mass., 1899. [Scudder's name does not appear in this book, but he is known to be the editor, hence the information is supplied but enclosed in brackets; if the fact appeared on the title page no brackets would be needed. Note that "Mass." is specified to avoid giving the impression that the book was published in Cambridge, England. See footnote 5.]

Kelly, Alfred H., and Winfred A. Harbison. *The American Constitution.* New York, 1948. [A book by two authors; observe that the second author's name is in normal order. Incidentally, this is the first edition of a book that was later published in a second edition; unless another edition is specified, the edition of a book is assumed to be the first. See footnote 2. See also the entry for Isaiah Bowman's book above.]

Kelly, George A. *The Psychology of Personal Constructs.* 2 vols. New York, 1955. [If your references were to only one of these volumes, you would write "2 vols., vol 1. New York, 1955." See footnote 7.]

Kirstein, Lincoln. "The Future of American Opera." *Atlantic* 199:3 (March, 1957), pp. 50-55. [Discussed earlier in detail. See footnote 13 and page 317 in this book.]

"Kite." *Encyclopedia Americana,* 1955 ed. [Encyclopedia article by an unnamed author. The names of editors and the like for a well-known reference book are not ordinarily needed. Neither is the page number in a book whose contents are alphabetically arranged. See footnote 12.]

Learned, Philip. Lecture given in English 346, Edwardian Criticism, ——— University, May 17, 1962. Tape recording. [If there were no tape recording, an equivalent statement should appear: "Notes taken by John Doe, student," or the like. Observe that the course title is not italicized or enclosed in quotation marks. See footnote 21.]

Macaulay, Thomas Babington. "Bunyan, John." *Encyclopaedia Britannica,* 11th ed. [Macaulay signed this article simply "M"; the full name was gotten from the list at the end of the last volume. Observe the order of Bunyan's names; he is listed under Bunyan, not John. Observe that there are no page numbers or volume number, since neither is needed for locating an article in an alphabetically organized reference book. See also "Kite," above in this list. See footnote 11.]

May, Rollo. *Man's Search for Himself.* New York, 1953. [Discussed earlier in detail. See footnote 1 and page 315 of this book.]

Ohneschatten, Dermann, Director, ——— State Hospital. Interview, May

27, 1964. Tape recorded. [The subject of the interview could be mentioned, if important. See footnote 22.]

Poore, Charles. Review of Henry B. Kranz, ed., *Abraham Lincoln: A New Portrait. New York Times,* Oct. 17, 1959. [See footnote 16, footnote 17, and "Review . . ." below.]

Quintanilla, Luis. "Basic Tenets of Latin American International Policy." In Philip W. Buck and Martin B. Travis, Jr., eds., *Control of Foreign Relations in Modern Nations.* New York, 1957. [See footnote 8.]

Review, unsigned, of Henry B. Kranz, ed., *Abraham Lincoln: A New Portrait. Reviews of the Quarter,* vol. 21, no. 4 (Nov., 1959), p. 37. [To alphabetize the entry for this review at K for Kranz would suggest that Kranz wrote the review or that the entry was for the book rather than for the review. There is much variety of opinion about how to handle this kind of entry. If your reader-instructor has a strong opinion, follow his preference. See footnote 17.]

Shakespeare, William. *The Tragedy of Coriolanus,* ed. William Allan Neilson. New York, 1906. [See page 248 of this book, and see footnote 9.]

"State to Up Vet Home Loan Rate." *San Francisco Chronicle,* Sept. 17, 1959. Dated Sacramento, Sept. 18. [Discussed on page 318 of this book. See footnote 15.]

Swedish Modern Jazz. Arne Domnerus and his group. RCA Camden, CAL-417, 1958. Record. ["Record" is unnecessary unless needed to distinguish the described item from a tape recording or other work of similar name. The record is a collection of works performed by one orchestra. If the name of one work or its composer were the important item, this information would be given first, followed by "In *Swedish Modern Jazz.* . . ." See footnote 24.]

Sypher, Wiley, ed. *Enlightened England.* New York, 1947. [An anthology. Any book identified by the name of its editor rather than an author would be presented similarly. See footnote 4.]

Two Thousand Years of Season's Greetings. New York: Photogravure and Color Company, 1951. [This is the kind of irregular publication sometimes called a "bulletin." Since it may be hard to locate, you help the reader by giving the name of the publisher. Since no author name is given, alphabetize it by the title. See footnote 10.]

We Discover the Dictionary. Coronet Films, 16V4906, 1949. Film. [The author's name, if one were given, would precede the title in this entry, and would govern the alphabetical position of the entry. "Film" may be unnecessary. See footnote 27.]

EXAMPLES OF FOOTNOTES

These specimen footnotes are numbered to help in referring to them for comparison with the corresponding specimen bibliography entries in the section preceding this.

[1] Rollo May, *Man's Search for Himself* (New York, 1953), pp. 223-224. [Book, single author. Discussed on page 316 of this book.]

[2] Alfred H. Kelly and Winfred A. Harbison, *The American Constitution* (New York, 1948), p. 64. [Book, two authors.]

[3] Francis H. Boddy *et al., Applied Economic Analysis* (New York, 1948), p. 346. [Book with many authors, in this instance six. Unless courtesy or other special reason calls for them, the names of the junior authors are replaced by *et al.* See pages 329-330 of this book.]

[4] Wiley Sypher, ed., *Enlightened England* (New York, 1947), p. 451. [Book, single editor. This is an anthology, containing works of numerous writers, who need not be named in this kind of entry. To cite the work of one author included in such a collection, follow the model of footnote 8 below.]

[5] John Keats, *The Complete Poetical Works and Letters of John Keats,* [ed. Horace E. Scudder] (Cambridge, Mass., 1899), p. 232. [Book by a single author in a version edited by another person. Observe the brackets enclosing the editor's name; these are present because Scudder is not named on the title page of the book but is known to be the editor; if the title page bore his name there would be no brackets; compare footnote 9, below. Note the "Mass." to prevent confusion with Cambridge, England, another publishing center.]

[6] Isaiah Bowman, *The New World,* 4th ed. (Yonkers and Chicago, 1928), p. 704. [Book, edition specified. Unless an edition is specified, it is assumed that the first edition is being cited.]

[7] George A. Kelly, *The Psychology of Personal Constructs* (New York, 1955), vol. 1, p. 133. [Book, more than one volume. The citation here is to a page in one volume, and the number of volumes need not be stated; that information is in the bibliography entry. If your paper were to have no bibliography, this kind of footnote should read: ". . . 1955), 2 vols., vol. 1, p. 133."]

[8] Luis Quintanilla, "Basic Tenets of Latin American International Policy," in Philip W. Buck and Martin B. Travis, Jr., eds., *Control of Foreign Relations in Modern Nations* (New York, 1957), p. 188. [Work of one author in an edited collection of works by several authors.]

[9] William Shakespeare, *The Tragedy of Coriolanus,* ed. William Allan Neilson (New York, 1906), Act IV, Sc. vii, lines 2-3. [Play, in book form. Unless the printed version has line numbers, a page number would be given rather than the line numbers. Discussed in the text of this book, page 316.]

[10] *Two Thousand Years of Season's Greetings* (New York: Photogravure and Color Company), p. 5. [Irregular publication, that is, something not published in the usual course of any publishing enterprise—the named publisher is an engraver-printer and this cited work is an advertising piece. The name of the publisher is therefore given even in a footnote plan which does not include names of publishers of standard books. If it had a named author, his name would be at the beginning, as usual.]

[11] Thomas Babington Macaulay in *Encylopaedia Britannica,* 11th ed., *s.v.* "Bunyan, John." [Signed article in a reference book alphabetically

organized. The abbreviation *"s.v."* means *"sub verbo"* or *"sub voce,"* English "under the word" or "under the heading." The word "Bunyan" is as accurate a guide as a page number could be, and may be better since encyclopedias are sometimes repaged to make room for new entries inserted late in the life of a numbered edition. Macaulay's article on Bunyan fills two pages; if it were a very long article, and the citation to a single sentence or other brief passage, the reader might be helped by being given a volume and page number: ". . . 'Bunyan, John,' vol. 4, p. 805." Observe the spelling *Encyclopaedia.*]

[12] "Kite," *Encyclopedia Americana,* 1955 ed. [Unsigned article in a reference book alphabetically organized. See footnote 11 concerning the omission of page number. Observe the spelling *Encyclopedia* in the title of this work.]

[13] Lincoln Kirstein, "The Future of American Opera," *Atlantic* 199:3 (March, 1957), p. 54. [Magazine article. Discussed at length in this book, page 317.]

[14] "The Good ex-President," *Time* 74:14 (Oct. 5, 1959), p. 34. [Magazine article, unsigned.]

[15] "State to Up Vet Home Loan Rate," *San Francisco Chronicle,* Sept. 17, 1959; dated Sacramento, Sept. 16. [News article in a newspaper. Discussed in this book, page 318.]

[16] Charles Poore, review of Henry B. Kranz, ed., *Abraham Lincoln: A New Portrait, New York Times,* Oct. 17, 1959. [Signed book review. Such reviews often have titles, either individual or departmental; it is usually unnecessary and confusing to give such titles.]

[17] Unsigned review of Henry B. Kranz, ed., *Abraham Lincoln: A New Portrait, Reviews of the Quarter* 21:4 (Nov. 1959), p. 37. [Unsigned review of a book, in a periodical—here an imaginary periodical. The bibliography entry corresponding to this footnote is alphabetized at Review.]

[18] Charles T. Baker, "Patients' Perceptions of Psychologists" (unpublished master's thesis, Ohio State University, 1953), p. 31. [Unpublished work, such as thesis or dissertation.]

[19] John Doe, "Indexing of Dissertations" (paper read at methodology seminar, —— University, October 16, 1962; in —— University Library). [Paper read but not published. See the specimen bibliography entry at Doe.]

[20] Alexandre Dumas fils, letter to Joseph Méry, Oct. 18, 1844, unpublished, in the collection of Simone André-Maurois. [Unpublished letter.]

[21] Philip Learned, lecture given in English 346, Edwardian Criticism, —— University, May 17, 1962, from a tape recording. [Unpublished lecture. If the lecture were cited from memory, or from the writer's notes, or from notes of another listener, that fact should be given instead of the reference to a tape recording.]

[22] Dermann Ohneschatten, Director, —— State Hospital, interview, May 27, 1964, from a tape recording. [Unpublished interview. No interviewer being named, the assumption is that the interview was with the writer. If the citation were not from a recording, that fact should be given instead.]

[23] Johannes Brahms, *Concerto No. 2 in B Flat Major for Piano,* Alexander Uninsky, piano; Willem van Oterloo conducting The Hague Philharmonic Orchestra (Epic LC-3303, 1958), record. [Phonograph record. The word "record" may be unnecessary, or may distinguish between a disk and a tape recording of the same work and performance.]

[24] *Swedish Modern Jazz,* Arne Domnerus and his group (RCA Camden CAL-417, 1958), record. [Phonograph record, title without composer's name. This record has several works by various composers and is thus comparable to a book of the type cited in footnote 8 above.]

[25] James Joyce, *Finnegan's Wake* (Folkways Records, FDF 934, 1956), tape recording. [Recorded book. To locate a cited passage more exactly, one might add "at 22 min." or the like. The tape does not contain the entire book. When a recorded work has several tapes, the one concerned may be specified, as "tape 3 at 17 min."]

[26] John Gunther, "Inside Space," *John Gunther's High Road,* American Broadcasting Company (WABC-TV, New York), October 17, 1959. [Television or radio broadcast; this footnote is for a television program. The network being named, the station call letters and city are extra information; but the latter would suffice if there were no network or the network were not known.]

[27] *We Discover the Dictionary* (Coronet Films, 16V4906, 1949), film. [Film. If the text at the citation does not make it clear that a film is meant, the word "film" is needed in the footnote, since many companies that distribute films also distribute sound tapes, disk records, and books having the same titles. Films usually are the work of writing-producing teams and are published without any "author" name; if an author is named, his name belongs first in the footnote.]

HOW TO FIND DOCUMENTATION DATA

Where do you get information for documentation?

Most books published in the United States and many published in other countries carry this information in the preliminary pages of the book itself. The title page normally has the name of the author (or authors), the title of the book, the name of the editor instead of or in addition to the name of the author, the name of the publisher, the volume number and number of volumes if the book has more than one, the edition number if later than the first, the city of publication, and sometimes the date. But the date may appear only in the copyright notice on the back of the title page, and there may be several copyright dates owing to renewals and revisions (if there are, use the latest). If the title-page date is other than the copyright date, give both dates (as "New York, 1938; title page dated 1949"). You and your reader, seeing this discrepancy, may reasonably wonder whether the title-page date is an effort to suggest that the book is more recent than it really is.

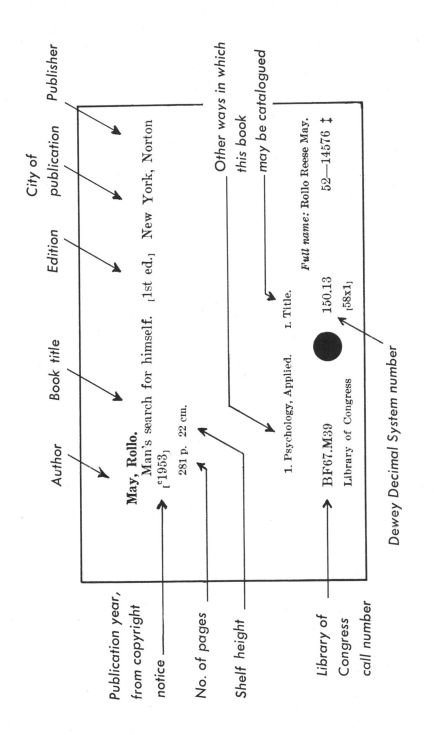

Author　　　Book title

Publication year,
from copyright
notice

No. of pages

Shelf height

Library of
Congress
call number

City of
publication　Publisher

Edition

Other ways in which
this book
may be catalogued

Dewey Decimal System number

May, Rollo.
　Man's search for himself. [1st ed.]　New York, Norton
[ᶜ1953]
　281 p.　22 cm.

　　1. Psychology, Applied.　ɪ. Title.

BF67.M39　　150.13
[58x1]

Library of Congress

Full name: Rollo Reese May.

52—14576 ‡

Often you have documentation information on a book even before you see the book itself, for library cards usually contain all of it, and more, especially those cards prepared by the Library of Congress and distributed to libraries throughout the country. (See page 257.)

Magazines usually provide the bibliographical information in a note somewhere in the early pages, less often on the cover or on a page near the end of the issue. Finding it may take some hunting, since practice is not uniform. In most magazines it will be on the page with the table of contents. Also, as with books, a researcher often gets the information from a library card for the article before he has to search it out from the publication itself. He may also get it from the entry for the article in *The Readers' Guide to Periodical Literature.*

The title page of an unpublished dissertation or thesis will give you all the information you need for documentation, as will the file copy of a paper read at a scholarly meeting but not published. For letters, personal communications, lectures, interviews, and the like, you must formulate the documenting statement from information you get at first hand.

The label of a phonograph record gives you the name of the song, speech, collection, or other work recorded, the names of the composer and of the performing musician or his analogue, the name of the maker, distributor, or publisher of the record, his identifying number or code letters, the date of issue, and sometimes other information. You may have to get some facts from the album cover or record envelope, or from the distributor's list.

Documentation data for tape recordings and films will almost necessarily come from the label. Films usually carry it on the title frames at the beginning.

Radio and television programs contain almost too frequent mention of the program name, its principal personality, the call letters of the broadcasting station, and the name of the broadcasting system. You may thus get this information from the program itself. You may also be able to get it from the program listing in a newspaper or periodical. Sometimes you may get the script of a program from the sponsor or the broadcasting company; if so, the first page or two of the script will contain many of the documentation data.

RECORDING DOCUMENTATION DATA

You begin documenting your research paper before you begin writing it, even before you begin taking your research notes. If you were to collect material, write your paper, then try to work back to find where you got your material in order to document it, you would find the effort hopeless. When you decide to investigate a book or magazine article or other source, therefore, you should prepare a bibliography card immediately, recording all the documenting information you will need if you refer to the source—this before you take your first note! Then, when you write a note card, it should have a record of its source. The record need not be complete to identify it with your bibliography card—a short "slug" something like "May *Man's Search*" is enough. Thus your bibliography card would read:

> May *Man's Search*   M 150.13
>
> · May, Rollo. *Man's Search for Himself*. New York, 1953.

Then a note card might look like this:

> May *Man's Search*   224
>
> "... Courage is the capacity to meet the anxiety which arises as one achieves freedom. ..."

With the note card and the bibliography card, you are prepared to put accurate documentation into your finished research paper.

CITATIONS AFTER THE FIRST—BOOKS

When a writer must cite numerous statements from the same source at intervals throughout his paper, repeating long footnotes would become tedious for him and for his reader. When the first footnote has given full information, later footnotes may be shortened in many ways, providing the shortening does not make them confusing.

A second citation from the May book might come immediately after the first one, with no other footnote intervening. For such immediately succeeding footnotes, scholars have long used this style of shortening:

> ² *Ibid.,* p. 231.

This means "From page 231 of the same source given in the immediately preceding footnote." The abbreviation *Ibid.* for *ibidem* (literally, "in the same") is typical of the many abbreviations and Latin expressions that we have inherited and continued to use since early scholars established them. Because they are in some sense part of an omnilingual scholarly vocabulary, many instructors require their students to learn them and use them. But some people think of them as Latin and, if they or their readers do not know Latin, feel that the use of Latin expressions is pretentious or even dishonest. Such people would prefer to use some equivalent English-language form like

> ² May, p. 231.

—or even, if May's name is mentioned in the text, nothing more than

> ² P. 231.

The writer of a research paper does well to learn what preference his instructor has in matters of this sort, and to follow it.

If some citation from other source material were to intervene between the first and second citations from the May work, then the *ibid.* would be wrong, for "in the same" would point to the most recently cited work. The old scholarly usage would be

> ³ May, *op. cit.,* p. 231.

This means, "From page 231 of the work by May which has already been cited." "*Opere citato*" is the unabbreviated Latin. Those who misgive Latin expressions might prefer to write any of four other forms:

> ³ May, p. 231.
> ³ May, *Man's Search,* p. 231.
> ³ *Man's Search,* p. 231.
> ³ P. 231.

The first-given form would serve if only one of May's books were being used as a source. If two or more were being used, it would be necessary to mention the title and to mention the author's name also, as in the second-given form, unless May's name were mentioned in the text. If the text mentioned May, but not the book title, the third-given form would be sufficient documentation. The last-given and briefest form would be correct and sufficient if the text language made clear what book and author were being considered.

When these English shortened forms are to be used, it is a frequent and helpful practice to tell the reader so in the first full footnote. Thus, after citing the source in full, you would add, perhaps: "This will here(in)- after be cited as May," or ". . . as May, *Man's Search.*"

CITATIONS AFTER THE FIRST—
MAGAZINE ARTICLES

The short expression *op. cit.* is not used when the source cited is a magazine article or other work not independent and complete in itself, such as an article in a symposium, an encyclopedia entry, or a newspaper story. For such sources, instead of *op. cit.* the footnote Latin is *loc. cit.* for *locus citatus,* Englished as "the place cited" or "the passage cited." Thus several alternative entries for the later footnote to a magazine article:

[3] Kirstein, *loc. cit.*
[3] Kirstein, p. 55.
[3] Kirstein, "Future," p. 55.
[3] "Future," p. 55.
[3] P. 55.

These five forms of short documentation correspond in function to the similar five forms for books. But note that *loc. cit.* cannot be followed by a page number; such is the convention. The other forms may therefore be preferable as more specific.

CITING WORKS BY NUMEROUS AUTHORS

A Latin expression that often appears in documentation is the abbreviation combination *et al.* for *et alii,* which means "and others." Writers who are not alert in their Latin often punctuate this expression improperly; those who choose to use it need to remember that *et* is a word and that *al.* is an abbreviation.

The proper use of this expression is to save writing or repeating the names of two or more co-authors of a cited source. Thus a first and later footnote might be:

[1] Francis M. Boddy, Frank E. Childs, Wendell R. Smith, O. H. Brownlee, Alvin E. Coons, and Virgil Salera, *Applied Economic Analysis,* New York, 1948, p. 363.

[3] Boddy *et al., op. cit.,* p. 370.

Instead of *et al.,* those who object to Latin would use "and others":

[3] Boddy and others, p. 370.

If the names of the junior authors are not important for the citation, even the first footnote may have them packaged into *et al.* or "and others":

[1] Francis M. Boddy *et al., Applied Economic Analysis,* New York, 1948.

It is not courteous to use *et al.* in substitution for the name of a single author.

DOCUMENTATION WITHOUT FOOTNOTES

In some people's view the footnote is the most useful and explicit form of specific documentation, the least likely to be misconstrued, and the minimum civil acknowledgment that a writer can make to his source. With all these merits, footnotes are disliked by other people as obtrusive, overformal, distracting, and an extreme nuisance for the typist. Their preference is to put some or all of the specific documentation into the text itself.

In-text documentation for books, magazine articles, and other sources requires the same information that is given in footnotes. A writer citing a statement from a book might therefore write:

> . . . A definition of Rollo May (*Man's Search for Himself,* New York, 1953, p. 224) describes courage as ". . . the capacity to meet the anxiety which arises as one achieves freedom." Seen as such, courage is demanded . . .

The parenthetical documentation would be worded to accord with the text language. If it were to follow the quoted passage rather than precede it:

> "The capacity to meet the anxiety which arises as one achieves freedom" (Rollo May, *Man's Search for Himself,* New York, 1953, p. 224) is a definition of courage as it is demanded from all of us. . . .

A writer uses footnote or in-text documentation as he and his readers prefer. If his readers are instructors who grade his research papers, their preference may well overrule the writer's. The general documentation is needed, in the usual bibliography form, to support either style of specific documentation.

Some writers attempt to have the best features of both kinds of documentation by using a footnote for the first mention of a source, then using brief parenthetical notes for later references. This practice might give:

> . . . May found that "the greatest block to a person's development of courage is his having to take on a way of life which is not rooted in his own powers" (*Man's Search,* p. 231). . . .

Or it might give:

> . . . May (p. 231) found that . . .

Either of these two parenthetical documentations might be replaced by the more traditional *"op. cit.,* p. 231" or if proper by *"Ibid.,* p. 231."

BRIEF DOCUMENTATION

It is often unnecessary to give a complete footnote for every citation from a source, yet necessary to document the citation. It seems redundant, when a text has mentioned an author's name or his book's title, or both, to repeat them in a footnote. The footnote then need contain only those facts not given in the text; but all the documenting facts must be given in one place or the other. For examples:

> . . . Rollo May, in his *Man's Search for Himself,*[1] defincs courage . . .
> [1] New York, 1953, p. 224.

> . . . Rollo May[1] defines courage as . . .
> [1] *Man's Search for Himself* (New York, 1953), p. 224.

Specific documentation can be kept brief by using the general documentation, the bibliography, after notifying the reader that footnotes or in-text references identify the names of sources given in full in the bibliography. Thus a writer might refer to Rollo May's book thus, even on first mention:

> . . . Courage is "the capacity to meet the anxiety which arises as one achieves freedom" (May, p. 224). Seen as such, . . .

The reader is then expected to understand that he will find the source given in full in the bibliography, thus:

> May, Rollo. *Man's Search for Himself.* New York, 1953.

If several books by May were in the bibliography, the brief documentation would have to be explicit enough to prevent confusion. To this end, "May, *Man's Search*" would be used rather than "May" alone. Sometimes the entries in the bibliography are numbered. If in such a bibliography the May book were to be numbered 221, then the citing note might read "221, p. 224."

DIVERSE PRACTICE IN DOCUMENTATION

Custom and agreement have not established uniform practice as to correct documentation. Readers' needs differ; scholars in different fields have different kinds of source material to identify and describe; and editors, teachers, and research directors have strong preferences which they can enforce on their contributors, students, and staff. The student writer who goes beyond this discussion in exploring documentation can find some additional and different recommendations in any of four books especially:

ELINOR YAGGY, *How to Write Your Term Paper*. Chandler Publishing Company, 124 Spear Street, San Francisco, California 94105. Contains a thorough discussion of documentation forms, with numerous examples. Primarily for undergraduate writers.

BLANCHE ELLSWORTH, *English Simplified*. Chandler Publishing Company, 124 Spear Street, San Francisco, California 94105. An appendix on Writing the Research Paper contains directions for preparing a bibliography and for using footnotes, with a chart of model footnotes and corresponding bibliography entries in parallel columns. Primarily for undergraduate writers.

KATE L. TURABIAN, *A Manual for Writers of Term Papers, Theses, and Dissertations*. The University of Chicago Press, Chicago 37, Illinois. Has chapters on footnotes and bibliography, with numerous examples. Primarily for graduates and advanced undergraduate writers.

WILLIAM RILEY PARKER, compiler, *The MLA Style Sheet*. The Modern Language Association of America, 6 Washington Square North, New York 3, New York. Primarily for writers of material to be published in Modern Language Association periodicals. This has a supplement dealing with the preparation of masters' theses and doctors' dissertations. Widely accepted and authoritative, especially for papers on literary subjects.

THE DOCUMENTATION OF MATERIAL IN THIS COLLECTION

This collection, being a book of special character compiled for the convenience of students writing research papers, differs from general books and periodicals that might be found in a library. Footnotes and bibliographical entries describing sources in this collection must identify both the source and the collection. Acceptable forms for these are given at the end of each selection. These name the original source and its author (if known), giving facts of publication, and also name this collection and its editor.

There would be some question of propriety, or even of honesty, if a writer were to name an original source in a documentary citation without making it clear that he examined the material in a collection—whether this collection or another. A reader has the right to know whether a writer is working from original or secondary sources: whether for instance he has seen George Washington's actual diary or has seen only an edited version of the diary in print. For edited versions, even carefully and scrupulously edited versions, may depart from originals.